THE TIME OF JACOB'S TROUBLE

CHRIS HAMBLETON

Outskirts Press, Inc.
Denver, Colorado

The Time of Jacob's Trouble
All Rights Reserved.
Copyright © 2009 Chris Hambleton
V4.0 R1.1

Outskirts Press, Inc.
http://www.outskirtspress.com

ISBN: 978-1-4327-2469-6

Outskirts Press and the "OP" logo are trademarks belonging to Outskirts Press, Inc.

PRINTED IN THE UNITED STATES OF AMERICA

CONTENTS

FOREWORD

What will happen in the days ahead? Will the coming years be better or worse than those we have left behind? What does the future hold for our families, our nations, and our planet?

These are questions that every person on earth asks at one time or another. Horoscopes, soothsayers, palm-readers, and fortune-tellers are those the secular world turns to in order to have their questions of the future answered. But to whom should Christians and Jews look for answers?

Amos 3:7 provides the answer: "Surely the Lord GOD does nothing, unless He reveals His secret to His servants the prophets." What a comfort this verse is to those who look to the Lord and His Word to provide insight and answers to the uncertain times ahead. The Bible is nearly one-third prophecy, with many of those prophetic passages yet to be fulfilled. For those who earnestly desire to know what the future holds for the world and humanity, the Bible is available today on an unprecedented scale.

Bible prophecy has been an interest of mine since a few years after I was saved in the early 1990s. In fact, I first became serious about Christianity after reading "Evidence that Demands a Verdict" by Josh McDowell. When I began asking questions about the current state of the world (with Israel in particular) and reading what the Bible had to say, I soon found the answers to many of my questions.

Both of my parents were born less than a year before Israel became a nation. The changes that the United States and the rest of the world have undergone in that short amount of time are staggering. There is more political, economic, and global unrest than ever before, yet one would expect that it should be growing more stable as we advance in knowledge and technology. Nevertheless, the opposite seems to be true: the more advanced humanity becomes, the more unstable the world grows.

Stop and consider Israel for a moment. Why is Israel such a problem to the world at large today? Why does the world, especially the Middle East, feel so threatened by a tiny democracy that for the most part, simply wants to be left alone? Why do even the universities consistently disparage this secular, democratic state that holds to many of the same values as they do?

Why does most of the world continually turn against Israel? Could there be a spiritual element to this irrational, unexplainable hatred?

There are other indicators to monitor in our time, such as the dramatic advancements in technology, genetic engineering, and increased UFO sightings. If Satan is the master deceiver, will he not do everything in his power to deceive the world as his time draws short?

The Bible mentions in the Book of Luke that "as it was in the days of Noah, so shall it be in the days of the Son of Man (the Messiah)." Was this simply a passing reference to the evil of Noah's day or will the last days be characterized with a high degree of technology, extraterrestrial-human hybrids, and unspeakable evil and violence? And as in the time of the Flood, will only a few survive in the end?

These are questions to continually keep in mind and search the Scriptures for as time marches on. This work of fiction seeks to paint a portrait of what the last days – possibly only years ahead – could look like. Many of the prophetic passages of the Bible have been fictionalized in the book, but also cited for reference. Every Bible student has a different picture of what the End Times may look like, and this is the portrait I have drawn from my own study of the Scriptures.

I hope this book helps you examine and further refine your own views of the days ahead and stimulates you to have a greater respect for the Bible and its exhortations to be watchful during the times in which we live.

"Watch therefore, and pray always that you may be counted worthy to escape all these things that will come to pass and to stand before the Son of Man." Luke 21:36 (NKJV)

PROLOGUE

"Go! Go!" Jacob yelled, pushing his teenage daughter ahead of him into the bomb shelter. "Hurry! Don't look back!"

Others were pressing in behind him, and he scowled back at them angrily, even though some of them were his own neighbors. He could hear the crying of babies and children in the dim light.

A few moments later, everyone was safely inside. When the doors closed, everyone suddenly became quiet, listening carefully for any sounds outside. Like many others in the bomb shelter, Jacob was afraid, but he was also angry.

His country of Israel had shown herself to be weak for too many years, and this was where it had gotten them. Her people were sick of the rocket and mortar attacks that continued to go unanswered. They were sick of trying to make peace with those who wanted no peace.

He looked over at his wife, who was holding their daughter Ruth, and both had tears in their eyes. He tried to reassure them that everything would be okay and apologized to Ruth for his rudeness earlier. They had only been forced to go into the shelter once before during a long series of terrorist attacks, but this time was much different – much more frightening. Much more deadly. He closed his eyes and thought about how his nation had gotten into this mess.

Even in the first fragile days of her second birth in 1948, Israel had not been in such a dire situation. Her people were frustrated and tired, and her leaders cowered behind the treaties that they had been forced into by nations who proclaimed to be Israel's allies. The war against Hezbollah in Lebanon had left the nation shaken as to the state of her defenses.

Israel had not been attacked by her neighbors in a long time, and the constant suicide bombings during the Intifada had caused her military to steadily shift its focus away from external threats to internal ones. But with the death of Yasser Arafat, even her civilian defenses had also gradually relaxed and let down their guard.

The recent war between Israel and Hezbollah had surprised many on both sides of the lasting conflict. Israel and her intelligence agencies were dismayed at the sheer number and sophistication of the missiles and the anti-tank weaponry. The bulk of Hezbollah's missiles and weapons were no longer the inaccurate, homegrown kind that Israel expected, but sophisticated weaponry from Iran. The intelligence community knew that Hezbollah was heavily supported by the mullahs, but no one had the courage to do anything other than verbally condemn Iran for her support of terrorists.

Hezbollah had been equally caught off-guard at Israel's reaction, especially when Israel had launched a broad military attack in response to the kidnapping of a handful of her soldiers. Israel quickly wiped out many of Hezbollah's missile launchers and a significant portion of their infrastructure in Lebanon, and all the while defended her citizens against the thousands of missiles and rockets that rained down upon them.

But in the end, Israel ceased fighting to stave off world pressure. All the weaponry they had destroyed was quickly replaced by Hezbollah's sponsors: Syria and Iran. Within six months, Hezbollah was fully re-armed, and with better weapons than they'd had before. Very little had been accomplished by the month-long war, and Israel had not even been able to retrieve the hostages.

In the weeks and months that followed the cease-fire, the citizens of Israel and large sections of her military expressed their outrage at not being allowed to destroy Hezbollah. Her leaders and officials ceaselessly blamed each other, in the hopes of shifting the blame and keeping their political careers alive. The Israeli military faulted the Prime Minister and his cabinet, who in turn complained of faulty intelligence from the Mossad and also the IDF for its lack of preparedness. The nation was becoming more and more fractured, and her defenses continued to deteriorate.

Israel's enemies smelled blood and salivated at the prospects of the Jews' final demise. Hezbollah, Hamas, Al Qaeda, and dozens of other terrorist organizations plotted her downfall. Both Hezbollah and Hamas were firmly entrenched in Lebanon and the Gaza Strip, and their henchmen executed minor attacks upon Israel while at the same time disavowing the very attackers they supported. For the Western media, they condemned the attacks in speech after speech and then silently re-armed the very terrorists who carried them out.

Suddenly, Jacob heard the roar of fighter jets overhead and opened his eyes. The roof of the bomb shelter shook and the metal beams above them rattled. He could hear tremendous explosions that he hoped were much further away than they felt.

Jacob closed his eyes, and found himself praying for the first time in many years.

* * *

In the months that followed the Israel-Hezbollah War, the sponsors of Hezbollah and Hamas concluded that Israel would not be overcome by a regional war or terrorist attacks alone. Her citizen military was still somewhat prepared for both. Perhaps a combination of both would overwhelm Israel. Perhaps launching attacks from within and without would bring about her final defeat.

Hezbollah and some of the other terrorist groups had recently been at odds with Bashir Assad in Syria, since he was steadily caving under the tremendous pressure placed on his government by the United States, Europe, Iraq, and Israel. Russia was still his staunch ally, but remained silent and uncommitted as the pressure increased. Assad was weak and wanted to remain in power above all else.

The mullahs in Iran and Hezbollah in Lebanon had deemed Assad a traitor to their renewed Islamic Revolution, and had even instigated a number of minor terrorist attacks in Syria in an attempt to get him back in line. Hezbollah decided that Assad must suffer, and Damascus would bear the brunt of any Israeli retaliation. And the despicable nation of Egypt would also pay for her unprecedented thirty-plus years of peace towards Israel.

The plan was put into action and in the week after Ramadan, the terrorist groups quietly entered Israel. On Hanukah, while most of the Israelis were at home or on vacation, the terrorists from within Israel quickly launched fifteen tactical nuclear weapons towards the population centers of Beirut, Damascus, Cairo, Riyadh, and even one that would try to reach Istanbul. The nuclear missiles launched from within Israel would surely rally all the Islamic faithful, and finally put an end to the infidel nation in their midst.

The Mossad was shocked when they discovered that missiles were being launched from within Israel's own borders. They immediately alerted the other governments in the Middle East and disavowed that the missiles had come from their weapons systems. The first barrage struck Beirut just before dawn, killing tens of thousands of people, and Lebanon promptly responded with desperate missile attacks of their own. Most of the missiles against Egypt failed and exploded harmlessly in the deserts south of Cairo. Egypt decided not to retaliate immediately, but ranted and raged against the Jewish state and tore up the treaty that Sadat had made with Israel decades before.

However, one of the missiles did strike near the Aswan Dam, and while the dam itself was not destroyed, it incurred enough damage such that the billions of tons of water pressure succeeded where the bomb had failed. Within a matter of hours, the huge dam could no longer hold back the waters of the Nile, and the entire delta flooded with water as the Nile rejoined the Mediterranean Sea.

Syria refused to listen to Israel's pleas and warnings, and threatened with nuclear weapons of their own against Tel Aviv.

Israel continued to deny launching any missiles, and countered that if Syria launched missiles against them, Israel would in turn destroy Damascus. But Assad had been threatened with that before, and Israel had never yet launched a strike against them. Also, this time Assad knew he could not back hold back his generals any longer; if he did, he would incur Tehran's wrath.

Assad was certain the Israelis were bluffing, and decided that the day had now come that he had more to fear from Iran than Israel. Also, he knew something about the Iranians that the Israelis did not, and that made him all the more afraid. He made his decision, and ordered some of his own secret nuclear arsenal to be launched at Tel Aviv and Haifa.

But to Assad's dismay, he discovered that Israel was not uttering another empty threat. As soon as the Syrian missiles were in the air, the off-shore Israeli missile shield was activated and the missiles were quickly shot down just outside the northern border of Israel. And then came Israel's response – the destruction of whatever nation attacked them.

As the reports came in from his defense ministry, Bashir Assad realized that he would not likely survive the day. With the nuclear attack on Tel Aviv, he had sealed his fate. Moments after he realized what he had unleashed, he heard the scream of the missiles and felt a terrible flash of intense heat as he met his doom.

Unlike Tel Aviv, Damascus was far from the sea and the East winds would blow the radiation across the entire countryside, and millions would die from radiation poisoning in the months and years to come. The city of Damascus, one of the few continuously inhabited cities since people began migrating westward from Mesopotamia, was little more than a pile of rubble.[1]

When most of the world heard the news the next morning, they learned that the unthinkable had finally happened: a nuclear exchange had occurred in the Middle East. Millions had been

---

[1]   The city of Damascus has been continually inhabited for over 4000 years. But it is foretold that it will someday be completely destroyed. (Isaiah 17:1)

killed and more would die in the days that followed. Though it had long been predicted, everyone in the civilized world was still shocked.

For years, everyone had known that it was simply a matter of time until the caldron of the Middle East boiled over. But they never imagined how awful it would be when it finally happened.

And that terrible day had finally come.

CHAPTER 1
THE COALITION FOR PEACE

The immediate reaction of the civilized world was to de-escalate the crisis in the Middle East and prevent the war from spreading. Israel immediately complied and reduced her alert levels. A significant part of Egypt was now under the muddy waters of the Nile, and relief organizations were scrambling to move their resources into Egypt. Food, water, and antibiotics would need to be immediately distributed if the survivors were to endure the coming diseases.

In Israel, the hazardous materials teams moved their supplies into the northern areas near the Lebanon border. Though the defense shield had successfully shot down all the Syrian missiles, there would be some amount of radioactive residue and contamination. The missile debris was scattered in small pieces in several distinct locations, and was cleaned up in a matter of hours. Remarkably, the contamination was much less within Israel than just across the border in Lebanon. For the most part, Israel had not been touched by the nuclear attack.

In Damascus and Beirut, however, the scene was much different. The sophistication of the weapons used by Israel left few survivors within the blast radius. The radiation levels were enormously high, and very little relief could make its way through. Due to the radiation, the relief organizations were helpless to provide aid, and thousands of people who survived the destruction died of radiation poisoning, hunger, and thirst in the days that followed. In less than a day, Syria had been turned into a wasteland, and would be good for little else than a vapid desert.

After the initial shock of the nuclear exchange had worn off, the media and many prominent politicians clamored for an immediate nuclear disarmament of the entire region. The accusations that flew back and forth between the Arab nations and Israel were swift and harsh. They contended that Israel had launched a nuclear strike upon her neighbors without warning and without reason, and as they had repeated time and time again, Israel was the biggest threat to peace in the world.

With her response, Israel had been the first nation to unleash nuclear weapons against another nation since the United States' bombing of Japan in 1945. Europe, Russia, China, and most of the other nations of the world took the Arab side against Israel, decrying that the exchange was completely their fault. The United States soundly condemned Israel's retaliatory actions, but also denounced those of the neighboring nations. America did not turn against Israel completely, and wanted a thorough investigation of what had occurred.

Israel countered that they had not launched any missiles at Egypt, Syria, and Lebanon – at least not at first. In fact, they had immediately warned them about the missiles as soon as they had been detected. Israel had been extremely fast in apprehending the terrorists within her borders and provided conclusive evidence that the IDF had indeed not launched the initial attack. The United States believed Israel's account and helped them analyze and verify the evidence. For over sixty years, Israel had simply wanted to peacefully co-exist with her neighbors, and it made no sense for them to start any war for no reason.

In the end, the evidence was clear that the nuclear weapons that had started the entire incident had come from Iran and used by Hezbollah. The weapons had been set up and had been launched from within Israel with the goal of starting a final, regional war that would have ended in the complete annihilation of the Jewish state.

The deaths of thousands upon thousands of innocent Muslims from their own countries mattered little to the Islamic terrorists – all that was important was the destruction of Israel. The terrorists had been thoroughly interrogated by Israel and paper trails back to Iran were firmly established within a matter of weeks.

The second great shock to the world was the discovery that the nuclear missiles used by Hezbollah had been manufactured and supplied by Iran. All the intelligence agencies had estimated that Iran would not have nuclear arms for at least another two to four years. Even the Mossad of Israel had been taken aback by the source of the weapons.

Iran brazenly claimed it was their right to build and maintain nuclear weapons of their own, especially now that the Zionists had used them against her own neighbors. But Iran denied that they had given nuclear weapons to Hezbollah; they claimed that they had discovered that nuclear materials had been stolen from one of their factories less than a month before. Few believed their claims though; one did not simply steal nuclear materials out from under Iran's nose.

While Saudi Arabia, Egypt, and Iraq had often feared reprisals from Israel, they did acknowledge that Israel had been a good neighbor to them and had never been aggressive unless they were (or were going to soon be) attacked, as in 1948, 1967, and 1973. This admission alone was a huge step forward in Israel-Islamic relations.

But the nation that made the Middle East and the rest of the world tremble was not Israel, but Iran, and few other than Israel and the United States had the courage to say so. They had long feared that Iran would acquire their own nuclear arsenal, and now that it was a reality, there was little anyone could do but appease them.

Iran was stilled ruled by the mullahs, and the Iranian people despised their tyrannical rule. But the people of Iran had no means of removing them from power, regardless of how much they hated them. The United States, Israel, and even Iraq to some extent had been trying to assist them in overthrowing the mullahs but could not do so. They were simply too well-armed, too brutal, and too unpredictable. And for those reasons, no one wanted Iran to have nuclear weapons, but now it was pointless.

The mullahs would not hesitate to use their nuclear weapons

at even the hint of an overthrow or invasion. If the mullahs were to suddenly fall, the entire region and much of the world's immediate oil supply could be destroyed along with them.

* * *

Jacob Rosenberg was still in shock over the nuclear exchange, along with most of his fellow Israelis. It was good to be back in his own home – they had only been in the bomb shelter a few hours before it was announced that the threat had been stopped. He had long feared that Israel's enemies would launch a "final jihad" against them, but he had never imagined it would happen so soon.

Fortunately, Israel had put a working missile defense shield into place years before, and though it had been expensive and fraught with trials and problems, everyone was now thankful that it had been put in place before it had been too late. In the north where the majority of the population of Israel lived, the missiles had come a little too close for comfort. But then again, given the tiny size of Israel, any missile strike was too close for comfort.

Jacob considered himself very fortunate – although he had served numerous months in the IDF as a reserve, he had never seen active duty in any of the wars. During Arafat's brutal Intifada, none of his family or immediate friends had been maimed or killed by the suicide bombings. Some of his neighbors and friends of his friends had lost loved ones, but he had not personally been affected. For a long time, whenever his wife or children had gone to work or school, he had feared for their lives. To be that fortunate in such a time of constant strife and tumult was more than he could have asked for.

His business, Rosenberg Construction, had been consistently growing for years. He had started the business by himself over twenty years before, and it had provided well for his family. His oldest son Ahban had finished his studies at the University of Tel Aviv four years ago and was working for an architecture firm there. Jacob hoped that he would one day take over the family business and keep it going. He was a bright, young, clear-thinking engineer who already had much of the technical information he needed. But he was very green on the business side, and that would have to be learned with time and patience.

Jacob and Naomi had been married nearly thirty years, and while they still loved one another, they were not as close as they once had been. Part of it was due to being married for so long, but more distance was from being too busy with their businesses and their own personal interests. She had been born and raised in the United States in Queens of New York City, and had immigrated to Israel in 1981.

They had met in Israel while she was visiting, and they had married soon after she immigrated. Ahban had come along just over a year later, and several years after that Saul and then Ruth had been born. Saul was a third-year student at Haifa University studying software engineering, and already had several excellent job prospects available to him once he finished school. And Ruth only had another year of school after this one was finished.

Both Ahban and Saul had seen some military action over the last few years, already more than he had, as a matter of fact. Ahban had been called up for active duty during the recent Hezbollah War. Saul had served on some of the patrols during the last Passover and previously during Purim. And now with the recent nuclear exchange with Syria, all of the reserves had been put on standby.

He would probably see no action because he was just under the age-cutoff by a few years, but also because he was a successful business owner. Not only that, but his business was a valuable commodity in Israel: construction. If something wasn't being rebuilt from a recent bombing, it was being built for the first time.

But the nuclear exchange had shattered any hopes for peaceful times ahead, at least for the immediate future. Like most of his people over the last two thousand years, he wanted his children and grandchildren to live in peace. But now that too seemed increasingly unlikely.

* * *

For the first time in twenty years, Naomi Rosenberg was entertaining thoughts about leaving Israel and going back to New York. She was not really that serious about them though – after all, her life, friends, and family were all there in Israel. She had known fear before; she had almost grown accustomed to the daily threat of the suicide bombings years ago.

But the nuclear attacks had badly shaken her – they had been too close, too quick, and too final. What if just one missile slipped through their defenses? She wanted her children to live their lives, raise their families, and grow old. No parent should have to worry about their children being blown up when they get on a school bus or when they go to the mall with their friends. Back in the United States – even in New York City – she had never known those fears.

She had closed her floral business for the week following the attack, and generously offered to pay her two employees for that time. She enjoyed her small business, but it was more of a hobby than anything else. She figured she would sell it when she became too old to run it any longer, but that was a long time away. Over the last thirty years, Israel had become renowned for their lush flowers, fruits, and vegetables. The flowers in Israel were among the best in the world.

No other nation in recent times had such barbaric enemies as they did. Nearly thirty years living there had convinced her of that. Just when it seemed the terrorists could not further shock the world with their brutality, they invented new ways to kill and maim. Before the nuclear exchange, the latest outrage had been to pack their children's backpacks with explosives and then detonate them once they reached their classrooms.

Like every mother, she worried most about her children – especially Ruth. She was so carefree and happy. She was her only daughter, and they had always been close. Ahban was like his father in so many ways, while Ruth was like her. Saul was somewhere in between, having the compassion and practicalness of his mother and the mischievousness of his father in his younger days. After raising three lively children, she had begun wondering what she would do with the rest of her life.

THE TIME OF JACOB'S TROUBLE

But now Israel was once again in the midst of a firestorm, and it would be months before things would be getting back to normal.

* * *

Nearly a month had passed since the War of the Middle East and the United States, Great Britain, and Australia put forth a United Nations resolution to permanently disarm Iran and outlaw her nuclear weapons development program. Both the United States and Great Britain offered to help secure Iran's nuclear facilities, but Iran immediately refused. The UN Security Council knew Iran had probably orchestrated the entire incident with Hezbollah, but no one had the courage to say so.

With the conclusive findings of the investigatory teams, the nuclear arsenal of Iran was now the world's greatest threat. The United States and Great Britain increased the pressure for Iran to live up to the terms of the Nuclear Non-Proliferation Treaty and ensure that no more of their nuclear weapons would ever leave her borders. Though Hezbollah had been wiped out from Israel's nuclear response in Lebanon and Syria, there were still plenty of other terrorist groups that Iran could use as proxies.

Most of the industrialized nations were still attempting to recover from the economic shockwaves that had ripped through the markets. The New York Stock Exchange had dropped 20% on the day after the attack, and had finally settled down later that week. Investors had lost billions and the price of oil, gold, and the prices of other vital commodities had skyrocketed. The other world markets had fared much worse. Oil had jumped from $130 a barrel to $180 within the first week, and then slowly inched to $200. It would take months for the prices to drop back to their previous levels.

Israel's economy had also suffered from the nuclear attack, but they had an economic insurance policy of sorts. Previously unknown to the world, Israeli oil companies had finally discovered a huge oil and natural gas deposit in her northern region two years earlier. The analysts rated it as the fourth largest deposit in the world, and the Israeli government had immediately set it aside for emergency use in the event that her suppliers refused to continue distributing to her.[2]

Incredibly, the Israeli government had been able to keep the discovery quiet, all the while developing the means to begin extracting the oil and natural gas.[3] If they announced their discovery upon an unsuspecting market, it could cause global instability, making the prices drop and further angering her oil-rich enemies. But since the war, her foreign suppliers were refusing petroleum deliveries, and Israel had little choice but to fast-track their oil program and made their discovery public.

For the past ten years, Russia, Saudi Arabia, and other OPEC nations were enjoying the huge profits from the instability in the Middle East. The never-ending terrorism and bombings had been their greatest ally in making record profits. Their distribution lines had not been affected in the least from the war, and the demand for oil was at its highest levels ever with all the industrialized nations rushing to fill their reserves in the event of any further disruptions.

But the latest announcement by the Israelis now threatened those extravagant profits.

* * *

Soon after the world's oil prices began to stabilize and then steadily drop, Russia began seeing the proverbial writing on the wall. The Israeli reserves would have a disastrous effect on their economy if they did not take counteractive steps immediately. Though Russia's economy had greatly improved over the last

---

[2] Several companies are actively exploring for oil in Israel. At least one of these companies has used several Scripture passages to help them in their search for oil in both the north-western and Dead Sea areas of Israel. (Genesis 14:10, 49:25-26; Deuteronomy 33:24-25)

[3] Greed and jealousy are the primary reasons Israel will be invaded by Magog and his allies. A significant oil discovery in Israel would likely threaten the world oil markets controlled by Russia and OPEC. (Ezekiel 38:11-12)

two decades since the fall of the Soviet Union, it was still largely dependent upon oil, natural gas, and other energy commodities. Their experts estimated the new petroleum discovery in Israel would have disastrous effects on their economy in less than three years.

In the two decades before the fall of the Soviet Empire, Russia had quietly but methodically set herself up for dominance in the world's energy markets. The United States and the West had been largely energy independent until the 1960s, and their petroleum consumption had grown enormous. Realizing this weakness, the Russian planners came up with a framework to achieve the world-dominance that they had sought since World War II. But instead of using only their military might to force the West into submission, they would use capitalism and energy dependence to achieve the same ends at a far less cost.

The Russian planners quietly planted numerous groups that instigated a slew of environmental studies, lawsuits, and energy policy changes first in Western Europe and then in the United States. These groups contended that the existing energy policies of the West were a grave threat to the environment, and these nations should thereby restrict their own energy production. After all, what civilized nation would want to damage the environment? And so in the name of "saving the earth", the West themselves restricted their own supplies and became dependent upon the less stable, more erratic countries of the Middle East, and then later on even Russia.

The long-term plan of the Russians was brilliant – the industrialized nations must become dependent upon others for their energy supplies, and thereby more easily manipulated. One did not have to personally enslave a nation's citizens when their own laws and government could do it for them. Oil was cheap and plentiful in the Middle East, and it would be easy to have those capitalist nations shift their dependence over to the Middle East. Russia did not care whom the West was dependent upon for oil, as long as they were not independent.

The environmental policies that had been put into law in Europe and especially the United States had been the key to Russia's stability in the transition from the Soviet Empire to a loose coalition of semi-democratic, Western-style nations. The fall of the Soviet Empire had been masterfully orchestrated, disguising both their massive governmental and economic restructuring. The naïve West had even supplied them with billions of dollars in loans and grants during the upheaval. In the end, Russia's greatest threat – the United States of America – now viewed them as an ally, even though their weapons production and sales had never really changed.

The second half of the Russian plan was to bring all the OPEC nations into their sphere of influence, in which Russia would provide the military protection over the entire energy-rich coalition. China and the United States were also economically dependent upon one another, and where America went, China would soon follow. The Russians feared China even more than the United States. Once most of the world was dependent upon Russia for their energy needs, there would be little they could do to break free. Russia would not need a huge military to dominate them, just control the oil spigots.

In less than twenty years, nearly all the industrialized nations had become dependent upon either the Middle East or Russia for their energy needs, even though their own domestic supplies were often plentiful. Their own laws and environmental policies had made them virtual hostages, and the useful idiots in the press ensured no great energy policy shifts would take place. But because of the after-effects of the War of the Middle East, these long-laid plans were being threatened.

Germany was once-again exploring the means to convert her large coal supplies into gasoline, and the United States had begun doing likewise. Not only that, but the United States had recently announced that they would immediately begin extracting millions of barrels of oil a year from their deposits in Alaska and the Gulf of Mexico. These developments would hamper Russia's plans for the next phase, but they were confident that the environmental groups they had planted and financed long ago would slow or even stop the new developments. They had been tremendously effective in preventing the United States from building new refineries and nuclear power plants, and they would likely prevent any future drilling also.

But it was the sudden announcement of Israel's massive oil deposits that had pushed Russia into action ahead of their carefully-planned timetables. The United States had been seeking a way out of her dependence upon OPEC for decades, and they were the first to approach Israel to offer a comprehensive "oil for defense" treaty, and Israel had readily accepted. The United States and Israel were now joined at the hip, and the Russian planners' schemes were beginning to unravel. In the end, Israel would have a well-armed, well-supplied military once again, a robust economy from the oil profits, and the United States would benefit from the stable, cheaper supply of non-OPEC oil.

The Russian planners saw a critical window of opportunity to both halt the new energy developments and retake control of the world's energy supplies. Instead of conquering the oil-producing nations by force (which would not have been that difficult anyway), they would use a series of "bait-and-switch" tactics to achieve their purposes. They would use their Muslim allies' weaknesses and dependencies against them, just as they had done with the West for decades.

First of all, they must quickly get their Muslim allies to the south to become more dependent upon them militarily. This too would not be difficult, since the Russians had been supplying them with their best weapons for decades. The Muslims had a huge weakness in their fervent, rabid hatred of Israel. If Russia promised to deliver the complete demise and destruction of Israel, there would be little that the Arab nations would not agree to. The Iranians in particular were primarily focused on the destruction of Israel and America, and they would not see the Russians as any sort of threat until it was too late.

A group of Russian diplomats secretly met with their allies in Iran and put forward a plan to permanently wipe Israel off the map. The West's weakness had always been their compassion for others, and it had been their compassion for the downtrodden citizens of Iran that had prevented them from destroying Iran's nuclear programs in their infancy. The Russians would use the same international maneuverings that United States had used in the invasion of Iraq, and render them helpless to intervene. Also, the attack would not be a simple launching of nuclear arms, but would be one in which Israel's missile defense shield would be completely useless.

But Iran's part in the plan was crucial – if they did not agree to it and follow it to the letter, they would have to redraw nearly all their plans. Russia would partner with Iran much like the United States had done with Israel, and sponsor a United Nations resolution that called for the complete nuclear disarmament of the Middle East. Iran would agree to immediately turn over their entire nuclear arsenal and open their weapons facilities for in-spection by the United Nations. And then Israel and the rest of the other Middle Eastern nations must do likewise.

Besides Iran, Israel was the only other nation in the Middle East that had their own supply of nuclear weapons. The trap was that Israel would immediately refuse to follow Iran's lead and never turn over their weapons. After all, their nuclear arsenal really was their only true protection from a massive invasion from their enemies. The constant threat of Israel's nuclear arse-nal had prevented her neighbors from attacking her for decades.

When Israel refused to comply, Russia would then lead a coalition of nations to enforce the United Nations resolution, just like the United States had done when they invaded Iraq to oust Saddam Hussein. And this time the threat of WMDs was so much greater since everyone now knew Israel would use their nuclear weapons when threatened. This would give the Russians and her allies enough time to move a massive military force into the region surrounding Israel and coordinate the attack, all the while being completely justified in the international community. Russia, Iran, and the other Muslim nations would be viewed as being on the side of world peace, while the United States and the West would be silenced and ridiculed as hypocrites if they tried to interfere.

Once the resolution's enforcement deadline passed, the coa-lition would invade Israel, and disperse all her citizens to camps throughout the Middle East and Russia. Surely every Israeli citizen would fight to stay free, and that would give the coalition all the excuse they needed to completely destroy them. However, in the unlikely event that Israel did agree to the terms of the United Nation's resolution, the coalition would launch a surprise attack once all Israel's weapons had been turned over to the UN. But that was highly improbable – Israel would never give up her only sure defense of nuclear arms.

Either way, the outcome would be the same: Israel would cease from being a nation.

* * *

True to form, the Iranians agreed to the Russian plans to vanquish Israel. Even the Russians were surprised at how easily they agreed to the scheme. They were careful to not involve any others, and kept their true aims concealed and known only to their inner circle. The UN Resolution 3996 was received even better than they had expected, with nearly all the Muslim nations of Africa and the Middle East co-signing the resolution.

Soon even the larger nations of Europe, such as France, Germany, and Hungary joined in, along with Turkey and several central Asian states. Various Western countries signed on too, such as Canada, Venezuela, Brazil, Mexico, and even Cuba joined in the motion. The media and pacifists immediately threw all their weight and influence behind the resolution and claimed that if passed, there would be "peace in our time" at last.

But the United States, Great Britain, Australia, and of course Israel withheld their support from the resolution. Those nations had long distrusted Iran, recognizing that a violent, unstable nation would never voluntarily hand over the very weapons they had spent decades desperately trying to obtain. Israel saw that given the continuous threat from Iran, this was merely a ploy to disarm Israel and leave her virtually defenseless.

In the past, the only times Israel's enemies had ever wanted to make peace with her was when they were being beaten badly and needed to re-group or re-arm. Without the threat of her nuclear weapons to stave off a massive invasion, Israel knew she would not be able to survive the next joint attack. Her Islamic neighbors were now too sophisticated and too well-armed. And if Jordan turned and once again became her enemy, Israel would have no place to turn but to the sea.

The measure was put to a vote a week after its introduction, with less than three days of debate. The resolution nearly unanimously passed, with only Israel voting against the measure and the United States abstaining from the vote altogether. Jordan's ambassador had privately voiced concerns to Israel's ambassador, but said that they feared the consequences of military reprisals from Iran if they did not vote with them. Jordan knew that if Israel fell, they would be next because they had made (and kept) numerous peace treaties with Israel for many years.

In the weeks that followed the ratification of UN Resolution 3996, Iran allowed weapons inspectors from Europe, Russia, India, and China into all their nuclear facilities and missile factories. They combed over the sites and checked the inventories against their intelligence databases and weapons estimates. Iran was fully open about her programs after decades of maneuvers and deception. After the initial round of inspections proved successful, the disarmament groups moved in to secure, dismantle, and remove all the nuclear weapons and materials from Iran. Within three months, Iran was no longer a nuclear threat to the world, and the masses in America, Europe, the Middle East, and especially Israel breathed a collective sigh of relief.

Then it was Israel's turn to allow the inspectors into their country and disclose their nuclear arsenal. And as expected, Israel promptly refused. She contended that as soon as she turned over her nuclear arms, she would have no defense against all her enemies who would surely attack her in the future. The UN Security Council promised to protect Israel in the event of another attack, but Israel would have none of it.

Israel had relied on all the promises of the United Nations, Europe, and even the United States in the past, but they had always been betrayed in the end. They had signed dozens of similar treaties in the past, and they had always proved to be worthless. Now that her survival depended upon her nuclear weapons, Israel refused to rely on empty promises and mere paper any longer. The Israelis were adamant – they would never turn over their weapons.

Nearly unanimously, the supporters of the resolution accused Israel of being warmongers and standing in the way of peace. Even the United States pressured Israel to at least let the inspectors in and inventory the weapons. But Israel refused to back down – if the inspectors entered their facilities, their enemies would know their precise defense capabilities and the locations of all their weapons depots and military infrastructure.

The UN Security Council, led by Russia, immediately took a hard-line stance with Israel, and demanded that she allow the weapons inspectors into their facilities within thirty days or they would be forced to comply with the resolution.

*　*　*

Like most Israelis, Jacob smelled a trap carefully being set. After decades of Iran frantically pursuing nuclear arms, suddenly volunteering to give them up just did not add up. The mullahs cared little for their own people, much less anyone else in the Middle East. And had not Iran been preaching for years that their Islamic messiah could not come unless Israel was destroyed first?

Since the Islamic Revolution in 1979, Iran had never wanted peace with Israel, and had done everything they could to terrorize and slaughter Jews, both in Israel and abroad. Surely Iran had not given up her true aims! What were they up to?

And the injection of Russia into the Middle East as the primary sponsor of peace was very disconcerting also. Former Russian military officials had admitted only a few years ago that the Soviet Union had worked closely with Syria, Egypt, and Iraq to instigate the Six Day War, with the stated goal of destroying Israel's nuclear weapons program in its infancy. Russia had not only been prepared to bomb Israel's reactors and weapons factories, but to also launch an amphibious assault and destroy much of their military infrastructure. But when Israel had suddenly taken the offensive and surprisingly overwhelmed her adversaries, Russia backed out of the plan, leaving their Arab allies to fend for themselves.

UN Resolution 3996 was just the latest anti-Israel resolution put forth in the United Nations, along with the dozens of previous resolutions against Israel. The United Nations had been started with the best of intentions, but the Soviet and Arab influence of the previous decades had pulled it far away from its ideals and turned it into a harmful organization that provided cover for dictators and thugs, while constraining the influence of the freer nations. Over and over, the UN had turned a blind eye towards various genocides, while issuing condemnation after condemnation against Israel for the most trivial of perceived human rights violations and questionable offenses.

How could Israel survive without their nuclear weapons to keep their enemies from invading? She would still have her traditional arms and weaponry, but she was so small and so urbanized now that it would be hard to maneuver and defend themselves. Who would come to their aid? Who would stand with Israel if she refused to turn over her weapons?

Their staunchest ally since 1948, the United States, was sick of the problems in the Middle East. And now that nuclear weapons were involved, would the United States really risk their own future on behalf of Israel? America was too quick to trust in questionable alliances these days, and take Israel's enemies at their word. The idea of "trust but verify" had often given way to "trust and look the other way."

Would Israel be left all alone? The next days and weeks would tell, but Jacob was filled with trepidation about anyone coming to Israel's side. The thought of his beloved nation having no allies in the world sent a cold chill through him.

Israel could take on her surrounding neighbors and likely survive, but not against a coalition drawn from dozens of other nations, especially one backed and led by Russia.

* * *

Over the next thirty days, the tensions between Israel and the rest of the world escalated tremendously. Despite their long history of alliances and partnerships with Israel, even the United States became very critical of her stonewalling. They would not take Israel's side outright; otherwise the conflict could quickly turn into a world war in a matter of hours. And still Israel refused to comply. The United Nations had always been weak, divided and fickle, and Israel's leadership decided to gamble on that weakness. Surely the UN humanitarians would come to their senses and would not put nine million innocent people at risk of extermination. After all, hadn't Israel had been created by the United Nations in the first place?

On the thirtieth day after UN Resolution 3996 had been ratified, the United Nations once again repeated their demands for Israel to allow weapons inspectors into their facilities. And once again, Israel promptly refused. She would not be taken without a fight. Meanwhile, over the last month Russia had quietly organized what they called the "Coalition for Peace", and had been heavily arming and supplying every nation that volunteered to join their coalition. Russia would provide the arms, command-and-control logistics, and the leadership that the Coalition would need to seize the weapons of Israel. For the other nations that already had well-financed militaries, the Russians offered lucrative oil contracts and energy discounts.

The Coalition for Peace was enormous – the largest, best-equipped alliance of nations ever assembled. It was obvious to everyone that Russia and her allies were gathering all their forces to present such an overwhelming force that Israel would certainly back down. Iran, Turkey, Africa, and nearly all of Central Asia were in the Coalition, and even several South American and Indonesian nations had joined them. The Germans and the French, due to their numerous oil and weapons contracts with Iran, Turkey, and Syria, had also reluctantly decided to take part in the Coalition. Eastern Europe, due to the enormous pressure from Russia concerning their natural gas and oil supplies, also reluctantly signed on – they would contribute to the Coalition so their citizens would not freeze that winter.

The United States staunchly refused to take part in the Coalition for Peace in any way, along with Great Britain, Australia and a few other small nations in Western Europe. China also, surprisingly refused to take part in the Coalition – she was playing her hand carefully, and hoped that any conflict that arose would decrease Russia's power, opening the way for the Chinese to later easily move into the region. NATO had all but disintegrated, and now existed on little more than paper. Canada, Mexico and most of the Central and South American nations had very little in the way of military forces, and did not contribute forces either, though they lent support to the Coalition.

And though the United States would not directly help Israel, they did pressure a number of other nations to not join in the Coalition for Peace. Both Saudi Arabia and Iraq took the side of the United States and Great Britain, and claimed neutrality. Both were heavily protected and armed by the United States as a defense against Iran. The United States had also threatened to remove their military protection if they took part in the Coalition, and both nations knew they would be next to turn over their weapons to the United Nations after Israel. Iraq was still growing in stability, and her people, though Muslim, did not want to go to war after just getting their government and economy going again after many long years.

The next day, the Coalition for Peace and its long list of allies was made public on the floor of the United Nations. The sheer number of troops was unbelievable – their combined forces outnumbered Israel's by nearly thirty-five to one. Israel's leadership and people momentarily buckled at the announcement, and then recovered. The Coalition demanded that Israel immediately allow the inspectors into the nation, or they would be forcibly compelled to grant them full access within another thirty days.

If Israel did not unconditionally surrender within thirty days, the Coalition for Peace would then invade their country and permanently dismantle their government. The nation of Israel would cease to exist, martial law would be administered by the Coalition, and all her citizens would be dispersed throughout the world as they had been before 1948. And even if they did surrender within the next thirty days, martial law would be instituted and enforced by the Coalition until all the nuclear weapons had been removed from Israel.

Israel had called up all her reserves and put her military forces on standby ever since the UN Resolution 3996 had been ratified, and now called upon all of her citizens to prepare for war. All Israel (along with most of the other Jewish people of the world) knew that the Coalition for Peace would not hesitate from destroying them, given the rampant anti-Semitism throughout the alliance. They were knowledgeable enough about their own long history to recognize that billions of the people in the world wanted to see them slaughtered.

Yet Israel stood firm. And they stood alone.

* * *

The Coalition for Peace was the most terrible military force the world had ever known. As the Coalition forces gathered in the northern deserts of Syria and in the Sinai Peninsula, the Israelis increasingly prayed for a miracle. Rabbis throughout Israel, along with their Jewish and Christian counterparts all over the world, were expounding from their Scriptures, emphatically promising that God Himself would save them.

The Ezekiel 38-39 passage in particular was extremely accurate in detailing many of the nations involved in the Coalition, especially the strange involvement of Russia. But the Israeli people as a whole had little faith – after all, God had not saved them from the Holocaust and the other dozens of mass slaughters throughout their long history. Once again, they were all alone in a terribly hostile world. Why would this time be any different?

But the pressure upon Israel was on a scale that had never been before. Though nations had gathered against Israel on every front in the past, never before had such an enormous military force ever been assembled, and against such a tiny, insignificant nation as Israel at that. Israel had never attacked another nation for no reason other than when her immediate survival was stake. The air, land, and sea forces that were streaming into the Middle East were astounding, and a complete air and naval blockade had been established after the first deadline had passed.

Israel was completely isolated from the rest of the world, and the Coalition forces heavily enforced the blockade. It was as if the entire Middle East and the lands to the north had sent the full capacity of their military forces. Millions upon millions of faithful Muslims comprised most of the Coalition forces, and in such numbers that some even had to be turned away. The Sinai Desert and Lebanon had all but been turned into staging grounds for the Coalition forces. And from the size and makeup of the forces that were gathering, there would be little chance for even surrender once the Coalition began to move against Israel.

As the Coalition for Peace forces continued to gather, Israel began to falter and fragment. The liberals in Israel demanded that the government simply back down and comply with the resolution. They argued that though Israel would be disarmed at least they would still be alive. They could lose their government, nation, and their way of life, but at least they would be alive.

The conservatives argued that just before the Coalition entered Israel, she must use every weapon at her disposal against the Coalition and also against their contributing nations. The centrists fell somewhere in the middle, of course – they did not want to use the nuclear weapons until the nation's utter survival was at stake. They would not attack the Coalition until they entered Israel's defined borders, lest they provoke a nuclear attack themselves. The centrists appeared to have a slight majority over both the liberals and conservatives.

Over the next few weeks, all the financial markets uniformly dropped in double-digit percentages, and the media attention focused completely on the dire situation in the Middle East. The entire world was watching, and everyone was glued to their televisions, radios, and computers as the deadline approached.

Would the Coalition come to their senses and not invade, or would Israel surrender and let the inspectors in? As the Coalition forces continued to grow, it looked more and more as if the Coalition would invade Israel regardless of the decision she made. Anti-Semitism had also dramatically increased across the world, and even in traditionally Jewish-friendly cities such as New

York and Washington D.C. many synagogues were vandalized or burned.

Meanwhile, Israel's leaders and top IDF officials begged the President of the United States to use its veto power in the UN Security Council to intervene on their behalf. But the President and his Cabinet would not respond. The force had grown so large that even the United States was too afraid to intervene. But the President did attempt to become a mediator between Israel and the Coalition once again, such that the United States would ensure that Israel would be disarmed if the Coalition promised not to invade Israel.

Israel did not trust any of the members in the Coalition, especially Russia and Iran, but was open to the plan. Many of Russia's top scientists and educated class had fled to Israel in the waning days of the Soviet Empire, and the Russians viewed those Israeli immigrants as traitors. The Russians and the Coalition forces refused – they did not trust the United States to fully dismantle Israel's weapons, since they had been staunch allies since their founding.

And as Israel and the rest of the world entered the last day before the deadline passed, the synagogues, churches, and even the mosques across the world were full. Those in the synagogues prayed for the salvation of Israel from the hordes that had gathered against her. Those in the churches that still held to the Bible prayed for the safety of Israel and the Jewish people, while those in the liberal churches simply prayed for world peace. And those in most of the mosques prayed that the Zionists would finally be vanquished and that the Holy Land would be free of the Jews and pure once again. It was an abomination that the land once held by Islam had been infested with the Zionists for so many years.

* * *

Jacob knew the trap was set and about to be sprung, and Israel was indeed all alone. Her allies had all either turned away from them or were silent. On some small level, he didn't blame them. He had the sickening feeling that these would be Israel's last days as a nation. How many of his countrymen would live out the next twenty-four hours? Would any of his friends and family survive the week? Would he?

He was on the ground with the patrols in Haifa, while Ahban had been sent to the southern border of Israel in the Negev. Saul was nearby on the northern front with the tank brigades, and Naomi and Ruth were close to one of the new bomb shelters near their home. The troops at the borders were staggered in zones, so they would not all be overwhelmed at once when the invasion began. Israel's experienced military leadership still remembered how to fight when facing incredible odds, and that gave Jacob a tiny bit of comfort. Even in this ominous time, it was still Israel's policy to spread out family members in the military, so entire families wouldn't be wiped out. But given the current circumstances, there might be very few families left intact after the next several days anyway.

But even on this dark day, he was proud of his government for the first time in many years – finally they had not backed down, despite the tremendous pressure. It felt good to stand up for themselves for once. He and his fellow countrymen were afraid, but they had not surrendered, even in the face of the multitudes before them. They all seemed to know that this could very well be their last battle – possibly even their last day as a nation. He had a sense of underlying pride and courage in those around him – they would not give up either to the hordes before them. They would not surrender without a fight.

If they failed, what would happen to them next? Any soldiers who survived would undoubtedly be slaughtered, even if they surrendered. Their women and children would likely be scattered throughout the Middle East, and probably either put in internment camps or made slaves. Slavery! Only in the Islamic nations was slavery still a legal institution! How could slavery still be tolerated by the world? And yet it was, and it loomed over them if they failed to defend their nation. Their enemies would give them neither compassion nor mercy, and the Israelis expected none. After decades of war and terrorism, they knew exactly who their enemies were, and what they were capable of.

Israel still had her nuclear weapons, and they were no doubt already activated and targeted at the multitudes before them. The rumor was that they would not be launched until the Coalition crossed the Israeli borders. Israel would not launch a pre-emptive strike that day, but when they did attack it would be fatal. If the tiny nation did survive, life in Israel would not return to what it had been during the previous wars. This war was different, and everyone could feel it.

Where was God in all this? If He was indeed the God of Israel, where was He during this time? Where had He been during the last 2600 years? It seemed for nearly all of Israel's history they had been barely able to survive, and had constantly been either at war or brutally persecuted in foreign lands. Why did nearly everyone in the world hate them so much? What had the Jews or Israel ever done to cause such hatred? And now, even the Americans had abandoned them in the face of the enormous Coalition.

Jacob had been hearing more and more people discussing the Ezekiel 38-39 passage, but he remained skeptical. Most likely it would not happen, but a small part of him secretly wished that it would. However, his practical side reasoned that it was the rabbis' and the government's way of keeping their hope alive in the face of such overwhelming odds. They were now outnumbered at least forty to one, by the last statistics he had heard. And even though all of Israel was ready for what was coming, they all knew their nation would be left in a shambles even if they did manage to somehow repel the Coalition invasion.

What about all God's promises to bless them, much less protect them? As Jacob continued to think about it, he became angry, and especially angry at God. If He was real, how could their God be just when He frequently treated these Gentile barbarians so much better than the Jews, who where His own people, nevertheless! And what about the Russians, the Germans, and the Christians who had slaughtered millions of Jews and other people? God had not lifted a finger against them! Where was He now, and how could any of his fellow Jews believe in such an unjust and uncaring God?

He tried to think back to when he himself had last believed in God – it must have been 1967, during the Six Day War. At that time, he had been sure that God was on their side, but then came the Yom Kippur War several years later, and God had hidden Himself from them once again. Israel had been badly shaken, and had been worn down by the decades of brutal terrorism that followed.

Jacob was almost ready to die today, he felt just like his nation – tired of fighting, but unwilling to lay down and surrender. But what would happen to his children, even if they survived the invasion? Surely God was a Cruel Being, allowing His own people be trampled on by the bloodthirsty hordes once again.

No, he thought bitterly, the God of the Jews would not be coming to help them that day. He was sure of it.

*   *   *

The last hour before the deadline drew to a close – neither the Coalition nor Israel had made any pre-emptive strikes against the other, but both were at their top state of readiness. No specific time had been given for when the Coalition forces would begin the enforcement, but Israel assumed it would be immediately after the deadline passed. The multitudes that made up the Coalition were impatient and unstable, and if the invasion stalled even for a single day, it would likely fall apart into bands and factions that would attack Israel without mercy or purpose, other than to just invade them.

The minutes before the deadline seemed to slow, and all across the world, people were waiting for next phase to begin. In Israel, many of the young children, infants, and the elderly were in bomb shelters, while nearly everyone else who could hold a weapon was armed and prepared for the invasion. The deadline would pass at midnight, Israel Standard Time, but few in Israel would be sleeping that night. The protests of the peace activists had ended less than an hour before, and now the nation was united, even though it was united in fear.

THE TIME OF JACOB'S TROUBLE

One-third of all the Israeli air forces had entered the air within the last hour. Much of the Coalition's air power was still on the ground, presumably awaiting their orders from their commanders. Israel's renowned tank forces were spread out across the northern and southern borders in zone formations, and both her infantry and reserves were on full alert. Israel had imposed martial law on the West Bank and Gaza, in the event that Hamas and other Islamic terrorist groups launched surprise attacks against them. The West Bank was their largest border, and Israel could not afford to try to fight on all three fronts; four, if the Coalition also decided to invade them from the Mediterranean. As the deadline passed, the Israelis waited for the Coalition to make the first move.

But surprisingly, the Coalition did not begin moving into Israel immediately after the deadline passed, and in fact many of their airborne fighter planes turned away from Israel and streamed back to northern Lebanon and the southern Sinai. Israel's military leaders were stunned at the retreat even before a single round had been fired. Even the destroyers and the attack submarines moved back from the coastlands into deeper waters.

Suddenly all the skies above Israel lit up with hundreds of brilliant flashes of colored light. The Israeli people on the streets outside and on their rooftops instinctively looked up to watch the display, while the military leaders scrambled to find out what was happening.

But within moments, as all their monitors and military equipment failed, they realized what had happened. The Coalition had simultaneously blinded, deafened, and disarmed them in an instant. Israel had been hit with an electromagnetic pulse (EMP). They were not simply hindered or crippled, but completely paralyzed.

Any device or instrument that used electricity, such as cars, planes, tanks, trucks, and even the power plants that generated the electricity stopped working seconds after the flashes in the sky passed. Their tanks, jet fighters, and also their naval forces were rendered useless, as they suddenly lost all power and navigation. The airborne IDF jets began falling out of the sky but most of

25

their pilots punched out safely. The tanks stopped moving and their engines died, and the ships stopped dead in the water. A few of their submarines were still functional, but without the command-and-control centers, they too were mostly blind. Israel was utterly helpless against the invasion forces that would surely be moving against them soon.

And as the Israeli soldiers patrolling the northern and southern fronts left their worthless vehicles and stood next to them, the ground began to tremble and the sounds of distant rumbling filled the air. Smoke and dust in the distance across the fronts began to rise like a sandstorm, and the Israeli commanders began to shout for the soldiers to get their weapons and prepare for battle.

The clouds of dust were coming from the thousands of Coalition tanks that had begun moving towards them. Just as suddenly, the sky appeared to come alive as it was filled with jet fighters, and at first the Israeli soldiers thought they were their own, until they realized they were coming from in front of them, instead of behind. Then entire horizon was quickly packed with the hordes of the Coalition forces, and the Israelis trembled as they realized that this would be the end.

The invasion had begun, and Israel was defenseless. Even the air raid sirens had been silenced by the EMP, and most of the people in the pitch-black bunkers went outside. Without electricity, the bunkers were like mass graves. The Israelis quaked in fear as they watched the horizon, and many cried out to the Lord for help in their darkest hour.

But God still did not answer their pleas.

CHAPTER 2
THE FINAL JIHAD

N aomi was frightened just like everyone else in Israel. The rest of the world was watching what would happen now that the final deadline for Israel's surrender had passed, but only the people of Israel were truly afraid. She hated that her husband and sons were not there with them, but she knew the survival of the country depended upon all the people of Israel each doing their part in defending the nation.

At least Ruth was with her – she was surprised at how well she was dealing with their situation. It even seemed that Ruth was less afraid than she was! But Ruth had always been fairly light-hearted, and Naomi hoped today and the days to come would not steal that away from her. These were difficult times, and they were bound to have a deep impact on all Israelis, especially the young people. If the nation survived the day, would there be enough people and strength to rebuild, or would they give up and leave Israel for safer countries like the United States or Great Britain? Would they even be welcome elsewhere?

Ruth and Naomi were standing just outside the bomb shelter closest to their home. It was crowded, and a number of people had already gone inside. But they had decided to wait until the sirens went off – the shelters became hot and nauseating after a few hours with too many people. Since the War of Independence in 1948, Israel had required public bomb shelters to be constructed and maintained throughout every city. All the bombings and rocket attacks necessitated them, and they had saved many lives over the years.

The first gasps drew everyone's gaze up to the skies, where they saw the brilliant flashes of light like the northern lights high above them. But the gasps of surprise turned to shouts and screams of fear when all the lights turned off and all their phones went dead. Someone yelled out something about an "EMP" and a number of people quickly began moving away from the bomb shelter. No one wanted to be in a bunker with no lights and no electricity – it would feel like a tomb!

Naomi made a quick decision and grabbed Ruth's arm, and together they headed back to their home. They would just feel safer there, she reasoned, and there were plenty of candles they could light. It was likely that the invaders would go to the crowded shelters first anyway. Also, Jacob had loaded a handgun that he had kept hidden in case their home was burglarized. She had taken a couple of classes to learn how to handle it, and she realized that now she might have to actually put that training to use over the next few hours. She didn't want to think about what would happen if looters started roaming the streets, but she would be prepared. As for the invaders surrounding their nation – well, she didn't want to think about that either.

Ten minutes later, Naomi and Ruth reached their home safely and went inside, checking the doors and windows to make sure they were locked and secure. Ruth gathered some candles while Naomi found the handgun and a pair of binoculars, and then they went up to the rooftop to the patio. Their home had an excellent view of the north and west, and from there they would be able to see what would happen next. Naomi also took her Bible, a photo album, and some playing cards to help them pass the time. She had not read her Bible much, but she felt a little comfort in taking it with them upstairs.

On the roof, they lit several candles and sat down at the table, facing towards the north. Over the last few weeks, Naomi had heard a number of rabbis on the radio and television proclaiming that what could be happening was the fulfillment of some passage in Ezekiel, and that God would deliver Israel from the invaders. But most of the news outlets had treated them as extremists or fanatics, and just went on reporting the grim situation in the Middle

THE TIME OF JACOB'S TROUBLE

East. She hadn't read it yet, so it might be appropriate to do that now, she decided.

Instead of the rows of streetlights they were used to seeing, it was nearly pitch-black everywhere below them, even far out on the horizon. A gentle, cool breeze was blowing, and it created an eerie feeling – they were so used to the sounds of people and traffic around them, and now they could just hear faint voices and shouts every so often. There were no horns, sirens, or any other typical sounds of modern life. Just silence and darkness.

"Mom, I'm afraid," Ruth said, looking towards the north. "What are we going to do?"

"I don't know," Naomi replied. "But I know we'll be okay. Maybe the Coalition will negotiate with us now that the deadline has passed." She said it more as a remote hope than anything else; inside, she felt just as afraid as Ruth. "Let's read a little and take our minds off of it."

"Okay," Ruth said as she opened the Bible and began leafing through it. Soon she came to the Book of Ezekiel and then found the thirty-eighth chapter, and then she began reading. As she read, they recognized some of the more familiar nations mentioned like Ethiopia, Libya, and Persia, but most of the others they had not heard of before.

Ezekiel 38:1-17: Now the word of the LORD came to me, saying, "Son of man, set your face against Gog, of the land of Magog, the prince of Rosh, Meshech, and Tubal, and prophesy against him, and say, 'Thus says the Lord GOD: "Behold, I am against you, O Gog, the prince of Rosh, Meshech, and Tubal. I will turn you around, put hooks into your jaws, and lead you out, with all your army, horses, and horsemen, all splendidly clothed, a great company with bucklers and shields, all of them handling swords. Persia, Ethiopia, and Libya are with them, all of them with shield and helmet; Gomer and all its troops; the house of Togarmah from the far north and all its troops – many people are with you.

"Prepare yourself and be ready, you and all your companies that are gathered about you; and be a guard for them. After many days you will be visited. In the latter years you will come

into the land of those brought back from the sword and gathered from many people on the mountains of Israel, which had long been desolate; they were brought out of the nations, and now all of them dwell safely. You will ascend, coming like a storm, covering the land like a cloud, you and all your troops and many peoples with you."

'Thus says the Lord GOD: "On that day it shall come to pass that thoughts will arise in your mind, and you will make an evil plan: You will say, 'I will go up against a land of unwalled villages; I will go to a peaceful people, who dwell safely, all of them dwelling without walls, and having neither bars nor gates'— to take plunder and to take booty, to stretch out your hand against the waste places that are again inhabited, and against a people gathered from the nations, who have acquired livestock and goods, who dwell in the midst of the land. Sheba, Dedan, the merchants of Tarshish, and all their young lions will say to you, 'Have you come to take plunder? Have you gathered your army to take booty, to carry away silver and gold, to take away livestock and goods, to take great plunder?'"'

"Therefore, son of man, prophesy and say to Gog, 'Thus says the Lord GOD: "On that day when My people Israel dwell safely, will you not know it? Then you will come from your place out of the far north, you and many peoples with you, all of them riding on horses, a great company and a mighty army. You will come up against My people Israel like a cloud, to cover the land. It will be in the latter days that I will bring you against My land, so that the nations may know Me, when I am hallowed in you, O Gog, before their eyes." Thus says the Lord GOD: "Are you he of whom I have spoken in former days by My servants the prophets of Israel, who prophesied for years in those days that I would bring you against them?

As they finished the seventeenth verse, they looked at each other uneasily. It did kind of sound similar to what was happening, but it was hard to tell. Ruth happened to glance up and exclaimed, "Mom! Do you see that?" She stood up, pushing back her chair and pointing towards the northern sky.

Naomi jumped to her feet and fumbled to get the binoculars

out of their case. Far to the north, dozens of tiny pinpricks of lights were becoming visible. But when Naomi looked with the binoculars, she found that there were hundreds, if not thousands more lights appearing every second.

"What do you see, Mom? Is it them or us?" Ruth asked, her voice trembling.

"I see thousands of planes, but I can't tell if they are our fighters or theirs. I don't see any shooting yet, but it looks like most of them are coming towards us!"

The Coalition forces were streaming into Israel in the skies, quickly sweeping towards the border like a huge storm cloud.

With a sickening feeling, Naomi and Ruth knew they should run back down the street to the bomb shelter, but so would everyone else! They would be in the middle of the panic to get to safety, and they realized that they might as well just stay on the roof. If the planes headed directly towards them, they would go downstairs and find cover elsewhere.

Ruth took the binoculars and looked at the lights, and then gasped at all the jets that were gathering before them. The ominous cloud of lights grew larger and larger in the northern sky.

* * *

Saul was nervous; he had been on active duty before, but only on patrols and training exercises and such – but nothing like this. He was in one of the many tank brigades scattered across the northern border. The Israelis had tried to prepare for whatever was coming, but from the incredible amount of air power that the Russians had equipped the Coalition with, they knew they would be fortunate to see any of the Coalition's ground forces after the initial air strike.

As the massive Coalition forces had begun to gather at the borders weeks before, Israel had deployed as many of their new directed-energy systems as they had available. Saul and his team had set up dozens of them and were now safely behind them. The systems were spread out in zones, and it would take some time for the Coalition to clear them out. He was glad he was on this side of them, because when activated, they would make the invaders feel like they were already in Hell!

The directed-energy systems were one of the newer weapons in the Israeli arsenal. The systems had been developed as a nonlethal way to break up Palestinian demonstrations and riots, instead of always having to send in their soldiers and police. Intense, high-frequency beams of infrared-energy made the victims feel as if their skin was instantly being cooked, putting them in tremendous pain and rendering them defenseless. Rioting in Gaza and the West Bank had dropped dramatically after Israel began using them, and the military immediately requested hundreds more, but with a higher intensity, range, and control. The IDF saw a potential use for the systems in stopping any invading ground forces dead in their tracks. Once their enemies were paralyzed, the Israelis could quickly overwhelm and disarm them.

It had been relatively quiet on the northern front, even though the Coalition forces were now complete. The latest reports of the number of tanks and armory and troops were staggering, with the tanks alone in the tens of thousands. Like most of the citizens of Israel, the troops had the sinking suspicion that the Coalition would not be satisfied in simply removing Israel's nuclear weapons, but would most likely crush them. The Coalition did not want surrender no matter how many overtures they made. They were there to invade and crush Israel forever, and everyone knew it.

Saul had never thought of himself as being a particularly brave or courageous man. Before the war, he had simply wanted to finish his studies and get a decent job writing software (and get paid for it at that). But whatever happened during the next several hours or days would be over soon – either Israel would fight her hardest to survive and the Coalition would back off, or Israel would be quickly overwhelmed and wiped out. This would not be a long, drawn-out conflict like previous wars with Lebanon and the PLO had been. He had never pictured himself dying in a war like this, but then few of his fellow soldiers had either.

Suddenly he heard a loud, distant popping sound above him, like fireworks very far away. Then all the idling tanks, trucks, and hummers – everything electrical around him – fell dark and quiet along the Israeli battlefront. Then the IDF officers started shouting orders and everyone began rushing around to check their equipment and instruments.

All their systems were dead, and no matter what the soldiers tried, they could not get any of their vehicles started or their equipment reactivated at all. It was an EMP! There could be no other explanation for everything instantly failing! Of all the scenarios they had prepared for, an EMP was the one tactic no one could defend against. But how could their enemies prevent an EMP from damaging their equipment too?

And as the realization of their new situation and its implications sank in, the Israeli troops on the front knew this would be their final day. The directed-energy systems that would have kept the hordes of their enemies at bay (or at least slowed them down) were now worthless, along with all their tanks, communications, and most of their heavier weapons.

The Israeli northern front was now blind, deaf, and utterly defenseless against the innumerable Coalition forces. And then far ahead in the distance, the Israeli troops could see the horizon brighten slightly, and then heard a low, growing rumbling sound.

* * *

Far to the south in the deserts of the Negev, Ahban sat calmly in his tank with his small team. The kilometers in front of them were covered with nearly as many tanks, armored vehicles, and ground forces as there were in the north (at least there had been a few days ago). They had also set up hundreds of directed-energy systems and spread their forces out in zones so they could more-easily move about and attempt to contain the southern invasion. There was more room to move quickly in the desert, but also more ground to protect and defend.

Ahban had been in war only a few years before, but nowhere near this magnitude – none of them had. At first, some of the older officers said the Six Day War fronts were similar, but as more and more divisions were added to the Coalition forces, soon there was no comparison. For decades the Arabs and the Muslims had been promising to one day drive Israel into the sea, but had failed time after time. But perhaps that day had finally come.

Part of him was afraid of what lay ahead of them, but he was mostly just angry with Israel's enemies. Why couldn't they just leave them alone? Israel was always the one reaching out and making peace gestures, and where had it gotten them? There would be no more appeasement or treaties after this, not if most of the citizens had their say in the matter. You cannot live in peace when your enemies do not want peace, nor negotiate with those who want to bring about your annihilation.

Ahban considered himself somewhat brave during this time – many of those around him had seen action off and on in the years before, and they were nearly as angry as he was. If this was to be Israel's end, it would be a glorious end. Her troops would not surrender nor stop fighting until they either drove the Coalition forces back or were overrun and slaughtered. But they would not go down without a fight – there could be no surrender. There was an unspoken feeling growing all over Israel that today would be a turning point in their history. Whether it was life or death, their nation would forever be changed that day.

Inside the tank, he monitored the forces gathered kilometers ahead of them across the border. No one had moved, and the deadline had slowly ticked past. They were under orders to let the Coalition forces enter the directed-energy "kill zone" as they jokingly called it, and then activate the systems all at once and immobilize them before firing. It would be like a huge net that would instantly paralyze all the invaders and leave them defenseless, while the Israeli forces swept in to disarm them.

Suddenly without warning, the engine in the tank stopped dead and all the instruments darkened! What was going on? Their radios and all their communications were dead also!

"Find out what's happening outside!" Ahban shouted to the junior operator while he and the other tank specialist tried to diagnose the problem with the equipment.

"Everything's out, sir! All the tanks, all the vehicles, everything!" the young man shouted down at them, just a moment after he stuck his head out the tank hatch. They could all hear yelling and the shouting of orders by the other commanders and troops outside, and the sound of rapid footsteps to find out what had happened.

Ahban swore and climbed up the hatch past him, and sure enough, everything outside was as black as night. Outside troops were running around, trying to restart the equipment. He shouted to the operator in the tank next to his, and they were just as puzzled as he was.

Off in the distance, he heard a faint rumbling sound. He shouted for those around him to shut up and listen, and they heard it too. And then the rumbling in the distance slowly began to grow louder. Overhead, he saw swarms of aircraft rushing toward them, and he shouted for everyone to take cover. The Coalition forces were coming!

As he lowered the hatch and dropped back into the tank, he felt a cold shiver run down his spine. Presumably, the directed-energy nets were useless also – the trap they had laid for the Coalition was now worthless. There would be no glorious fight-to-the-death with the Coalition – only death.

The invasion had begun, and the Israeli troops on the southern border were completely helpless to stop it.

* * *

As soon as the EMPs had been detonated in the skies above Israel, the Coalition forces began furiously rushing across the northern and southern borders. As they poured forth like flood-waters bursting through a dam, they were filled with euphoria and glee. The celebrated IDF was defenseless, and the Zionists' day of doom had finally come.

Today would be the last day the nation of Israel would exist. The Islamic brigades were filled with anger and fury; they had vowed to let no Zionist soldier remain alive. They had been humiliated for decades ever since the British and Europeans had been meddling in their lands, and even more so when Israel had been declared a nation in 1948. They hated the Jews without

35

reason and were jealous of their freedom and wealth. Today all the Jews' riches would be theirs, and their humiliation would be turned to triumph. Allah was merciful to those who served him, but nowhere were they required to be merciful to their enemies.

Throughout the Islamic armies and over their military radios, verses from the Koran and the Hadith were read, chanted, and sung. Today was the beginning of the end – the day that would soon bring their Paradise to the earth.

The Prophet said, "You will fight with the Jews till some of them will hide behind stones. The stones will betray them, saying, 'O Abdullah (servant of Allah)! There is a Jew hiding behind me, so kill him.'"

The Prophet said, "The Hour will not be established until you fight with the Jews, and the stone behind which a Jew will be hiding will say, 'O Muslim! There is a Jew hiding behind me, so kill him.'"[4]

The verses repeated over and over, and rose to a clamor, urging the warriors of the Coalition onward, feeding their bloodlust. Today they would be heroes for generations to come, and their stories would be told to their children and their children's children. And if they died in battle, they would be in Paradise!

The millions of those filthy Jewish women and children would be made slaves and dispersed throughout the lands of Islam, and they would behead all who refused to bow to Allah. They would ensure that no one ever lived in that cursed land ever again.

Within minutes, they would overrun the Israeli tank zones and troops, and the great day of slaughter would finally begin. They were to rush across the border as far as possible and destroy any Israeli soldier or vehicle in their path. They would let the weaker, slower brigades behind them do a more thorough job of killing their enemies. And today they would offer the entire land

---

[4] The Islamic Hadith teaches that the Judgment cannot come until the faithful Muslims go to war against the Jews and slay them. Even the trees/rocks expose the Jews, according to their teachings. (Hadith Volume 4, Book 52, Number 176; Hadith Volume 4, Book 52, Number 177)

of Palestine as a lasting sacrifice to Allah.

But after several kilometers into Israel, the commanders of the tanks and other ground forces grew puzzled. Where were the hundreds of Israeli tanks and forces that had been there moments before? Before the EMP strikes they had seen them interspersed all over the countryside, but they now they didn't see any at all. Where had they gone? The IDF tanks and equipment should be clearly visible! They checked their instruments, and they were right on top of them! But their Jewish enemies just weren't there!

Some of the commanders popped their heads out of their vehicles and looked around – the entire land was barren, with no enemies in sight. They called their superiors, and were told it was a Zionist trick. "Keep going forward and destroy anyone you find!" were the orders, and the commanders were fine with that. But some of them did have a strange, uncomfortable feeling. Something just was not right.

The Coalition forces continued to pour into Israel, but none of them encountered any Israeli forces – it was like the Israelis had just disappeared! Those in the jetfighters did not see any Israelis from their positions either, but they kept going anyway. No matter, their officers thought, because today was the last day Israel would ever exist.

And by the time they were finished, no one would set foot in that cursed land for centuries.

*   *   *

The Israeli commanders shouted for all the troops to take cover and get back to their vehicles and their posts. The rumbling was now nearly deafening, and the ground was shaking from all the tanks and vehicles rushing towards them. An enormous dust cloud had formed in their wake and was sweeping towards them like a massive sandstorm. The first brigades of the Coalition invasion would reach them within seconds, and they had no artillery or weapons to use against them.

As the front of the enormous Coalition line quickly pressed

37

towards them, the thousands of Israeli troops hunkered down and waited for the inevitable to happen. Everyone was sweating and afraid, some wept quietly, and many prayed for the first time in their lives. Those with little cover would soon be shot or blown apart, while those in tanks and armored vehicles would most likely be torched alive from the anti-tank missiles and na-palm. Either way, within minutes they would all be dead. The invaders had no use for Jewish prisoners.

The rumbling had turned to a roar and was in their midst now, and Ahban could hear the armored vehicles rushing past them. He closed his eyes tightly, and then seconds later opened them in surprise. There were no sounds of what he had been ex-pecting: artillery, bombs, or even heavy machine gunfire. From what he could tell, none of the invaders had even stopped, but had just kept going past them – almost as if they weren't there.

"Why were they still alive?" he thought. Why hadn't the in-vaders even fired a shot yet? In shock, he climbed the ladder to the tank hatch and slowly eased it open. He snuck a cautious peek out, and the Coalition vehicles continued streaming past them. Thick dust and smoke was everywhere, blocking out much of the landscape around him. He slowly looked over to the near-est Israeli tank he could see, and one of the men in that tank was peering out from the hatch the same as he was.

Feeling suddenly brave, Ahban popped his head out of the tank, freely looking around. The Coalition vehicles kept stream-ing past without incident. Several times, he was sure some of the enemy had looked right at him, but they didn't even ac-knowledge he was there! He had the strange sense that he and all the other Israeli forces were invisible to the invaders. The exhaust from all the vehicles made him cough, and though he was probably only visible as a dim silhouette from all the dust, he knew he should still clearly be seen.

Soon, more troops were doing the same thing as he was – cautiously looking out from their hiding places and out of their tanks and vehicles. All he could see were their faint movements and outlines, but he knew they were there. A few of the braver ones even got out and stood on the tops of their vehicles waving around in surprise. But there was still no response from the Coalition troops – it was as if the Israelis didn't exist to them at all!

Was the Coalition blind, or under some bizarre orders not to engage them yet?

* * *

The United States, Great Britain, and many other nations had been continuously monitoring the satellite feeds and were as shocked as Israel when the skies all over the Jewish state had suddenly lit up. When the flashes faded, the entire nation of Israel that had once been filled with the lights from the cities, the streets, and the houses was completely dark. They realized immediately that the Coalition had launched a series of small nuclear missiles above Israel not to obliterate her, but to instantly paralyze her. All the radio signals and communications coming from within Israel had ceased into static, and all their video feeds from Israel turned to fuzz.

The President had been in nearly constant contact with the Israeli Prime Minister and his Cabinet, who had been living in bunkers for the last month. The Prime Minister had been begging the President to stall the Coalition or intervene in any way possible, but the United States had remained on the sidelines, primarily because of fear of starting an even larger conflict with the Russians and the Arabs. If the President had a strategy or last-minute plan to intervene, he hadn't told anyone – not even his own Cabinet. But when the communications and video feeds from Israel all suddenly went dead, the President of the United States realized he would be forced to make a decision.

Since the surveillance satellites were kilometers above the earth, they were not affected by the targeted EMP attack over Israel, but the pictures they transmitted were shocking. And as the President and his Cabinet watched in horror, they realized that the Coalition had not come not to merely disarm the tiny nation of Israel, but to destroy her. Over nine million Jews and an assortment of Arabs and others would most likely be slaughtered without mercy. The President and his Cabinet declared a state of emergency to Congress, and headed for the bunkers underneath the White House.

And as soon as he and his Cabinet were safely underground, the President called the chairman of the Coalition for Peace, the President of Russia, and the Secretary General of the United Nations and threatened to immediately intervene with deadly force unless the Coalition forces returned to the Lebanon and Egyptian borders. He understood why they were entering, but not why they were moving in with such speed when Israel was now clearly incapacitated.

The Russian President and Secretary General unanimously refused, citing that their enforcement had more legality and support than when the United States had invaded Iraq to enforce their own set of sponsored resolutions. The Coalition's intentions were clear at last to the President of the United States: the so-called Coalition for Peace cared nothing for peace. They had come to destroy Israel and completely reshape the Middle East, and perhaps even the rest of the world.

The President was furious at their response, quickly took counsel among his advisors, and then gave the order for the United States military to intervene on behalf of Israel. No one from Israel's government could be reached, except for their ambassador who was nearby (who couldn't contact Israel either).

The United States' naval, ground, and air forces in Iraq and Saudi Arabia that had been on alert for weeks suddenly went into motion, and rapidly moved to block the Coalition from further entering Israel, or at least cause them to turn away and confront them instead. The naval and air forces at America's disposal simultaneously launched long-range heavy artillery and ballistic missiles at the front lines of the Coalition forces, which were now so swollen with troops and equipment that few of the missiles could miss.

The Coalition demanded that the United States immediately cease their assault, or the cities and the citizens of the United States would be targeted with not only conventional weapons, but with nuclear weapons as well. The President was not bluffing any more than the Coalition was, and he understood that even though they were still the lone superpower in the world, if the Coalition was not stopped, the United States would be next on their list. The oil supplies and other interests in the Middle East were still critical to the United States, and once the Coalition took control, the entire free world would fall under the Coalition's control, first economically, and then militarily. Regardless of his decision of whether to back down or go forward with his counterattack, millions of people would die horrible deaths. There was no avoiding the day of decision any longer.

The President of the United States, with his Secretary of Defense and Chief of Staff as witnesses, slowly unlocked and opened the "nuclear football", the briefcase that had been in his possession every day since he had taken office. Everyone in the room with him was silent, and fear filled their faces as they watched him remove the code-book. While the President anguished over his decision, the Secretary of Defense stepped forward and asked him to consider just activating the entire arsenal, without actually launching them yet. Perhaps just activating a massive number of missiles (which of course the Russians and the Coalition were certain to be monitoring) would cause the Coalition to back down. And if not, at least they would be at full-readiness if and when the time came. The President agreed, and the others in the roof breathed a slight sigh of relief.

But the Russians had been waiting to engage her for decades. They had put on a good show after the collapse of the Soviet Union, and had begged the United States and Europe for financial assistance, which they had given in the form of loans and grants in the billions of dollars. She had always excelled at deception, and just as her spies had successfully infiltrated the United States during the Cold War to steal nuclear secrets, so she had successfully given the impression that she was now a peaceful, democratic nation no longer bent on conquering the world. But the Russian Bear had merely been sleeping, and now that she had awakened, she was hungry and angry.

As soon as Russian intelligence detected the activation of America's nuclear weapons, the President of Russia gave the order to go to the same state of nuclear readiness, and to also deploy their tactical nuclear weapons against America's military forces in the Middle East that were now meddling in their affairs. Today was the last day that the United States would be the world's lone super-power. Today, Russia would reveal her true strength, and this time there would be no long, drawn out Cold War to bankrupt them. Russia refused to call off the invasion forces, and continued their massive push into Israel.

The majority of the Coalition forces were already within Israel's borders, and would soon reach the cities. The real destruction of Israel had yet to get underway, but it would begin early within the next hour. The Coalition fighter jets and attack helicopters had already reached the population centers and had started carpet-bombing Israel's cities. The air forces would destroy the buildings, roads, and the infrastructure. But the infantry and the ground forces would be ones who would slaughter the Jews.

In this Holocaust, there would be no escape, nor would any liberating army save the remnant of Abraham, Isaac, and Jacob.

* * *

As the last wave of the Coalition for Peace troops entered the land of Israel and the bombs began to rain down upon her people, something bizarre began to happen within her borders. The tons upon tons of munitions that the Coalition had dropped upon Israel struck, but did not detonate – not a single one of them. The fighter pilots and the military analysts monitoring every movement of the Coalition forces were stunned, and furiously ordered more munitions dropped.

But those bombs had the same effect – nothing happened. And then the Russian planners decided to switch their arsenal from conventional to nuclear, chemical, and biological. All the treaties they had signed over the decades were now just meaningless paper. Today they would provide the world with the Final Solution that Hitler and his allies had longed for.

Suddenly the most massive, longest earthquake in the history of the world struck within the midst of the Coalition forces. The very ground on which they were driving, running, and walking shook with tremendous force and threw them to the ground. Many of the military vehicles went dead from the wrenching of their frames and engines.

In front of the invasion army's first wave, the ground opened up and swallowed them alive. In the midst of the Coalition forces, great sinkholes appeared at random, and thousands of soldiers, tanks, and trucks fell into them. And still the ground shook – even after five minutes the earth continued its ferocious upheavals. The seismologists monitoring the quake were as shocked as everyone else – the epicenter appeared to be the entire nation of Israel, instead of just being centered in a tiny area! And though the epicenter was in Israel, the earthquake was felt worldwide, and nearly every person in the world was awakened and ran outside. It was as if the very earth itself had risen to defend Israel against those invading her.

When the earthquake finally stopped, all the skies above Israel began to take on a strange faint glow. Both the people of Israel and the Coalition forces noticed the change above them and instinctively looked up. The glowing across the sky grew brighter, and faint pinpricks of bright lights began to appear and become distinct. Within moments, the sky looked as if it were filled with thousands upon thousands of tiny orange flares and streaks. And it appeared as if the lights were descending directly upon Israel.

But it wasn't until the first meteors struck the Coalition's fighter jets in the air, did anyone realize what exactly they were. The millions of lights were actually fiery bolides and flaming meteors that were streaming into the atmosphere above Israel.

And they were somehow all finding their targets – few missed striking Coalition vehicles and invading soldiers, but none were falling upon the Israeli forces that had gathered to defend their land. As the earth had done only moments before, it appeared that the very heavens had arisen to rebuke the invaders.

The brutal forces of the Coalition for Peace found themselves being destroyed not by Israel or any other nation, but by heaven and earth themselves.

CHRIS HAMBLETON

From their strongholds, the Coalition commanders and analysts mistakenly concluded that the United States had launched her nuclear weapons against the Coalition forces. Or perhaps they had a top-secret weapons system in a low-altitude orbit that the Russians had been unaware of. As for the massive earthquake, perhaps the Israelis or the Americans had developed some sort of directed seismic weapon that they had utilized against the Coalition front.

The Russians were furious – this was their day of conquest and glory, and they would not be denied. Then the President of Russia ordered the unthinkable: launch their nuclear ICBMs against the cities of the United States. Whether they were defeated or victorious in the Middle East, by the end of the day America would no longer be a significant military power in the world. Even if they were defeated that day, Mother Russia would rise again – she always did.

In the bunkers underneath the White House, the face of the Secretary of Defense suddenly turned pale, and he called for the President immediately. Russia had launched a full barrage of ICBMs and they were on their way to their targets: all the coastal cities of the United States, and a few apparently into the interior. The President wasted no time in reacting himself – they now had no choice – they were in this fight to the death. He was ashamed at not doing what he should have and stand with Israel. But now Israel's fate would be theirs, and the United States would stand alongside Israel and confront the Coalition, as she should have in the first place from the very first day that the UN Resolution 3996 had been introduced.

A verse came into the President's mind as he prepared to give the order to strike back at Russia: "those who bless Israel will be blessed, and those who curse Israel will be cursed."

And for the first time since the end of World War II, the President of the United States gave the order to use nuclear weapons against another nation. There was no chance the United States would escape unscathed in this new World War, but neither would her adversaries. If the United States and her long-time ally and friend Israel were to be no more, then they would destroy as many of their enemies as possible while they still could.

Sadly, the President and his Cabinet knew that many in their own country would die. He hastily called for the camera crew and made an emergency statement to America: the United States was now involved in a nuclear war with Russia; find cover and shelter, and take as much food and water to a safe place as quickly as possible.

The first global nuclear war had been unleashed, and given the ferocity of the nations involved, it would not last very long.

*   *   *

In the thirty minutes before the first nuclear missiles reached their targets in both the United States and Russia, miracle after miracle took place in the land of Israel. All the Coalition forces that had entered into Israel had either been shattered by the earthquake, sinkholes, or the bolides. And the rest were in the process of being destroyed. The few remnants of the Coalition that had not yet entered Israel or had turned back at the last minute were now fleeing for their lives as fast as they could. The Coalition forces themselves appeared to be going insane and were now frantically attacking one another, as if they had forgotten all their objectives in invading Israel. The ferocity of the Coalition's self-destruction was appalling.

Yet none of the Israeli cities were being destroyed, aside from some broken windows and fallen possessions from the earthquake. People across the world watching and listening to the news coming in from Israel were shocked, and many fell to their knees, praying for protection from what was happening on the earth. It was as if the entire world was coming unglued, and they had been so unused to the supernatural intervening in their lives that they did not know how to react.

But as the ICBMs finally reached their targets in the United States and Russia, the world news shifted away from Israel to cover the incoming nuclear missiles. The news commentators and reporters openly wept as they continued their broadcasts, even up to the last moments before the multi-megaton bombs struck. And then many of the news broadcasts were momentarily disrupted as they shifted over to other locations that had not been affected. In both nations as the nuclear bombs struck, the capitals, cities, and other major population centers were vaporized, consuming nearly all the buildings and their inhabitants.

And just as suddenly as the world war had begun, it ended quietly with a whisper, and silence fell upon the face of the earth. The people still alive emerged from their shelters and hiding places. And what they saw and heard shocked them all over again. In the United States, the cities that had been destroyed were Washington DC, New York, Atlanta, Baltimore, Miami, Tampa, Los Angeles, San Francisco, Portland, and Seattle – all the major coastal cities had been shattered.

Since the President of the United States, his Cabinet, and roughly half of the Congress had survived, the federal government of the United States was still able to function in an emergency capacity. The President had already declared a national state of emergency, and the world was shocked by what had happened. It would be weeks before anyone could fully understand the magnitude of the attack and its implications, but at least the war was over, as far as they could tell.

In Russia, the destruction was not as widespread since there were far fewer cities than in America, but nearly all their vital infrastructure and military facilities had been destroyed. Literally nothing was left standing or alive in Moscow and St. Petersburg. Much of their gas, oil, and energy infrastructure had been decimated.

Her military was no more – they had borne the brunt of the supernatural destruction that had occurred within the borders of Israel. They had contributed such a significant percentage of their military and equipment to the Coalition forces that they now had little more than a rudimentary defense left. Their first-rate military of the last hundred years had been reduced to that of a third-world nation in a matter of hours.

None of the other nations that had nuclear weapons in their arsenal had joined in with the nuclear exchange between the

THE TIME OF JACOB'S TROUBLE

United States and Russia. Once they had seen what was happening, the nations of Great Britain, China, France, and Japan stayed out of the conflict. They were witnessing the two great world superpowers destroy one another, and they wanted no part of it. They had endured many centuries of wars themselves, and they knew when to get involved and when to simply wait it out. America, the star of the West, had fallen nearly as quickly as she had risen.

But while the destruction of the major cities of the United States and Russia shifted the world news away from the annihilation of the Coalition forces, the Israeli media continued covering the incredible events still happening in the Holy Land. [5]

* * *

The earthquake and the destruction overhead had stopped, but Ruth's ears were still ringing. She and her mother had been crying and shaking since the earthquake had begun, and amazingly both were still apparently unharmed. Naomi rose to her feet and looked around, almost in shock at what had been happening for the last hour.

Ruth also stood up and went to her side, and they began looking around and up to the north – the carnage was unbelievable. Undetonated bombs, missiles, and other military equipment were strewn about all over their neighborhood. And yet few of the homes had sustained much of any damage, at least from what they could see. The ground and roads all around them were full of holes and craters, but the homes mostly were unscathed. The air was full of acrid smoke and the stench of burnt metal, plastic, and charred flesh.

The meteor strikes on the jetfighters and bombers all over the skies above them had clearly hit their targets. It was still the middle of the night, and they were both exhausted. As they sur-

---

[5] The wording of the verse implies a distant land far away from the other nations that are involved in the Magog Invasion. Also, the inhabitants of that distant land are dwelling securely or without care. (Ezekiel 39:6)

veyed the destruction from their rooftop, Ruth began to weep again. But as she bowed her head and fell to her knees, Naomi realized she was not crying out of fear, but out of thankfulness at being alive.

She heard her praying and knelt down beside her, and put her arms around her to comfort her. But what she heard stunned her – Ruth was praying to Yeshua! In Israel, most Christians were looked down upon, and Israelis who converted were especially despised by most of their fellow Jews. True, Christians from abroad (mainly America) had been pumping billions of dollars into Israel's economy in the decades since its rebirth, but most Israelis didn't really care for their beliefs. Naomi didn't say anything, but she knew her husband and sons (especially Ahban) would be angry if they heard about it.

Naomi didn't know what to say or how to react, given all that had happened that day. In New York, she had known people who had accepted Yeshua, but it had been years since she had heard of someone she knew doing that in Israel.

So for now, she continued kneeling quietly beside her and listening to her as she prayed.

*   *   *

Saul slowly stood up from his curled position behind the truck – it was raining! And he was still alive – it could only be a miracle. Was he in Heaven? No, one quick glance up convinced him that he was indeed not. Was he in Hell? No, he didn't think so – it all still looked like where he had been when the invasion had begun, except now was filled with destruction and carnage. The ground was soaking wet with blood and littered with mangled bodies and debris all around him.

As he got to his feet, he could see his fellow solders emerging also, looking as bewildered as he was. He could hear his commander and others calling out names and their owners responding. Every name had a response, and he replied in kind when his name was called. His group shakily re-assembled, and to everyone's surprise, not a single person had been lost from their company. Moments later, he heard chatter on the radio of other commanders calling for status reports. If he hadn't still been in shock from what had happened, he would have been relieved to realize that they had electricity again and that some of their vehicles had already been restarted.

He slowly began piecing together what had happened. He remembered the Coalition forces thundering towards them, and the air filling with dust and making him cough. He had shut his eyes and tucked his head down, waiting for the inevitable. He had expected to either be quickly shot or blown up along with the vehicle he had been hiding behind. But his inevitable fate had never come.

The earthquake had struck just as he was lifting his head to look around, and he had promptly curled up again with his head buried between his knees. He could still hear the tearing of metal, the bursting of tires, and the horrible screams of the invaders as they fell into the sinkholes and fissures. When the screams started, he looked up and couldn't believe what he was seeing! The earth was swallowing up dozens of armored vehicles, tanks, and even soldiers on the ground, whether they were standing still or moving. And just as suddenly as the earth would open to swallow the enemy, it would close again.

He was still shaking from the earthquake and the sinkholes when the meteor shower and the rains started. All above him, he could see fighter jets and attack helicopters being struck and streaking to the ground and crashing all around him. For what had to have been ten minutes at least, wave after wave of aircraft was struck and thrown to the ground, shaking everyone who had taken cover nearly as much as the earthquake.

Then the rains had started, drenching everything, and that was what had made him finally lift his head for more than a few seconds. At first, he looked at the ground to his left, and there was so much blood on the ground that when the raindrops struck, it looked like it was raining blood! Minutes later the rains stopped, and it left behind puddles and small pools of blood all over the land.

He was still alive – and apparently so were all the Israelis in his company. And from what he was hearing from the cheers and the pieces of reports from the other companies, they had not lost any troops either. But the Coalition invaders had been utterly decimated, and obviously not by the Israelis. Had the Americans or someone else stopped the Coalition? No, he thought – not unless they had done the impossible!

As he looked around in shock, he realized that he was in the midst of what could only be described as a miracle. God Himself had destroyed the invaders! There could be no other explanation for what had happened. Only the God of Israel could have (or even would have) made a distinction between Israel and the Coalition, and directed the destruction from the skies and the earthquake to only Israel's enemies.

He was excited and overwhelmed by what had taken place, and yet at the same time unnerved with fear and uncertainty. If God had finally come to save Israel from certain destruction, what would possibly happen next?

*　*　*

The shaking and thundering all around him suddenly ceased, and all was still. Was he still alive? Ahban opened his eyes, looked down and briefly checked himself over. There were no broken bones or wounds that he could see or feel. He slowly got to his feet and peered over at the others in the tank with him. They appeared to be uninjured also. What in the world had happened?

Then he remembered – he had been looking out through the hatch as the huge Coalition forces had been rolling past without firing a shot, and then the earthquake had suddenly struck. He must have fallen down the ladder and landed on the tank floor. The hatch had evidently slammed shut, keeping out most of the dust and muffling some of the thundering noise outside.

When he and his team finally left the tank and looked outside, they were stunned. The familiar, barren wastelands of the southern Negev had been turned into fields of carnage as far as the eye could see. All around them were wreaked military vehicles and sinkholes with Coalition vehicles and tanks sticking out of them. Covering the ground was thousands of small pools of bloody water and corpses, some whole and some torn apart. Innumerable weapons and supplies were strewn about them.

At first glance, it looked as if only the Coalition forces had been destroyed – Ahban could see Israeli troops, vehicles, and equipment that appeared to be unharmed. Minutes later, it was clear after the radios and communications started working again that none of the nearby Israeli companies had suffered any casualties. There were some minor injuries such as concussions and broken bones from the earthquake and the falling Coalition aircraft, but no Israeli soldiers in their vicinity had been killed.

Some in Ahban's company proclaimed it to be a miracle, but he was skeptical, in spite of what was clearly before him. He was very well-educated and therefore took an entirely rational approach to the world around him. And even though he could not explain what had happened yet, he would not come to any conclusions before he did some of his own investigation and lucid thinking.

*　*　*

Jacob stood up from where he had been thrown to the ground several minutes before. Time and time again he had tried to get to his feet but had been unable to stay standing long. His left hip throbbed in pain, and his arm hurt. His hands were scraped up and he knew his arm was bleeding slightly. But it wasn't serious, so he pressed his sleeve against it and began looking around.

The invasion must have stopped after the earthquake and the meteor shower and the rains. It was the only explanation he could think of for why he was still alive. He didn't hear any jets or bombers overhead, nor could he see any invasion forces approaching.

He rubbed his eyes and put his glasses back on. And then when he could see clearly, what he encountered took his breath away. There were numerous bodies and shredded metal scattered all about the streets where he had been patrolling. Fires were burning in the wreckages, and appeared to be slowly dying out. But oddly enough, few of the buildings or homes had been damaged, at least not as far as he could tell.

He pulled out his cell-phone and looked at it – it was still dead. What had happened to his wife and daughter? Were they still alive? And what about his sons at the borders? Had they been taken captive in the invasion, or worse? Luckily, Ahban and Saul were at opposite borders, one at the north and the other at the south, so there was hopefully a chance that one of them had survived. But with the size and ferocity of the Coalition, he almost didn't want to let himself hope.

Jacob had watched the entire supernatural destruction of the invasion. He had been awake through most of the earthquake and even the rainstorm. The Coalition air forces that had come upon them ahead of the ground forces had covered the skies like thousands of insects buzzing far overhead. The earthquake had then struck and the skies had turned a strange color just before the downpour. It all had happened so fast, and yet it seemed like it had taken hours! And then he had covered his ears as tightly as possible when the aircraft in the night sky began being thrown to the ground.

He gazed at the destruction with a glazed stare, and walked over to what appeared to be the wreckage of a helicopter lying in the middle of the street. The pilot was dead of course – it was so obvious that he didn't even need to check. There was a large portion of his skull missing, and he nearly threw up when he saw him.

There were fist-sized dents all over the outside of the aircraft. Most of the windows had been shattered, and he saw some large pieces of hail beginning to melt inside the wreckage. He also saw some burnt, black-outlined holes in the hull also, and dozens of smoking rocks interspersed among the hail.

He thought back to one of the Bible stories he remembered from his childhood, about how God had sent a huge hailstorm and meteorites against Israel's enemies during the day the sun had stood still for Joshua. Back then, Israel had been the invader and all the Canaanite nations had come out to destroy them. God had decimated the Canaanites and thrown them into confusion, destroying them all. And while their enemies had been wiped out, the hail and meteors had not touched Israel at all. The rabbis had quipped that God had literally stoned His enemies with the hailstorm and meteor shower, but not the Israelites.

As he looked around, Jacob realized that what had taken place 3400 years ago had just happened again. God had stoned His enemies: the Coalition of nations that had come up to destroy His people Israel. But while he saw meteors and melting hail in and about the wreckage, there was little trace of them on the rest of the ground. Perhaps the rains had been partly from the hail striking the planes and breaking apart in the sky.

And then another thought stunned him: he was kilometers away from the areas where most of the Coalition forces had been. If it was this awful here where very few Coalition ground forces had been, what was it like in the areas where the majority of the Coalition forces had gathered?

The God of Israel had indeed intervened to save the Jews from certain destruction, just like the old stories of his ancestors in the Bible. Then as now, their enemies had vastly outnumbered them, and Israel had been rendered powerless. But when all hope had been lost, God had stepped in and defended His people. And now their enemies had been supernaturally destroyed, but Israel had not been touched.

He hung his head and wept at his own stubbornness and bitterness towards God. In spite of their unbelief, He had kept His promises to save His people in the face of the inevitable.

Jacob's knees buckled, and he sat down next to the wreckage and put his heads in his hands, completely overwhelmed.

CHAPTER 3
THE BURIAL OF MAGOG

As the world began to digest the events that had transpired from the start of the Coalition invasion to the destruction of the American and Russian cities, few broadcasters found they could explain it without involving God or the Supernatural.

The mainstream media interviewed scientist after scientist, and spoke with many religious leaders to provide a reasonable explanation for what had transpired. The supernatural defeat of the Coalition was very difficult for them to accept, even though it had been visible for all to see. Most of their audiences who had seen and heard the footage for themselves knew that God in one form or another had intervened, and on behalf of the Jewish nation of Israel at that.

The Internet blogs were filled with first-hand accounts of what the Israeli people had seen and heard and experienced during the invasion and afterwards. The flaming meteors, hailstorm, and the huge earthquake were still unexplainable, not to mention about how the vast majority of the destruction occurred to only the Coalition forces and not to the Israelis. And no one could explain why the Coalition hadn't even bothered to engage the Israeli troops on the borders. Power had already been mostly restored inside Israel, and the Israelis immediately spread their stories all over the Internet as soon as they could use their computers once again.

But very few commentators and analysts had the insight (or at least revealed so publicly) that the supernatural intervention on Israel's behalf had been not only to protect Israel, but to also severely punish many of her worst enemies. For centuries, the Islamic nations had blasphemed the God of the Jews and proclaimed over and over that Allah would one day destroy them. But instead, the military forces of all the nations that had joined the Coalition for Peace in the enforcement of UN Resolution 3996 were utterly devastated.

The only survivors of the Coalition were the stragglers that had not crossed the borders of Israel. Less than ten thousand of all the invading troops had survived, and there were no wounded among those who had fallen in Israel.

All of the invaders had been slain by either the earthquake and the meteors, or by their fellow soldiers when they had turned against one another.

*　*　*

The morning after the failed invasion, the people of Israel awoke to discover that they had not been dreaming the night before. They were alive and well, relatively speaking. Only a few among them had been killed, and nearly all of those had been due to the tremendous earthquake that had shaken not just the land of Israel, but also most of the other nations. As unbelievable as it was, it appeared that the massive Coalition for Peace forces had not killed any Israelis other than a handful of soldiers who had not been able to take cover when their enemies had punched through the defenseless Israeli lines.

The EMP pulse that had rendered Israel defenseless had turned out to be almost a blessing for them, since few had tried to fight the Coalition forces with their remaining weapons. Many had abandoned their vehicles and larger equipment altogether and hid in the terrain, and then picked off small numbers of the Coalition forces as they had passed by. However, since they had been limited to machine guns, bazookas, and shoulder grenade launchers, they had not had much of an impact as the Coalition had rushed across the border. Perhaps their hampering fire had contributed to some of the confusion, but the vast majority of the damage to the Coalition had been caused from the earthquake, sinkholes, and meteor showers, and also from the Coalition forces themselves when they had turned against one another.

On the second day after the attack, the Israelis were startled to see huge flocks of birds streaming into their land. Millions of vultures, ravens, and other carnivorous birds from all over the Middle East flocked to Israel in the days that followed. They feasted on the corpses, which were starting to rot and fill the air with the choking stench of death. The contaminated northern and southern fronts were immediately declared hazardous areas and were completely fenced off where the Coalition forces had stopped.

The military secured the contaminated areas and ensured that no one – including the media – entered the areas to inspect the carnage. However, some video footage made it onto the Internet, and the viewers were shocked at what they saw. Most of the Israeli citizens (and the Israeli government) quickly helped relocate all the people who had lived in the contaminated areas.

The Israeli government immediately ordered that the all noncritical government departments and agencies be closed for two weeks so the people could learn of the status of their family members and friends, and recover from the aftermath of the invasion. Even more surprisingly, the secular government of Israel requested that all the people attend synagogue and give thanks to their God.

Israel immediately set up family location services and basic emergency relief and medical stations throughout the country. The IDF implemented a rotating plan for all the people in the military, so that one third were sent home on leave to help their families, homes, and communities, another third was assigned to patrols and military duties, and the last third was assigned to survey and quarantine the areas where the Coalition forces had been destroyed.

The people of Israel quickly started to help one another recover and begin rebuilding their nation. Israel had been greatly sobered by the miraculous events that had taken place before their very eyes. They knew they had been saved by God just as their ancestors had been in the ancient days. The synagogues were full of those who had not observed Shabbat (the Sabbath) in years, and there were so many that wanted to attend and pray that the rabbis began holding their services both inside and outside the synagogues at all hours of the day.

The Western Wall in Old Jerusalem was bursting at the seams with the throngs of Jews that worshipped at the last remnants of their Temple. All over the world, but especially in Israel the Jewish people talked about what had happened and often praised their God with tears and singing. It was like one of the miracles they had only read about in their Scriptures before.

The God of Israel had revealed Himself to them once again, and they didn't know what else to do except worship Him as they knew best.

*   *   *

Jacob was the first to return home three days after the invasion, and was relieved to find that Naomi and Ruth had not been hurt. He had heard the day before that both his sons had received only minor scrapes and bruises, which was incredible since that they had been so close to the front lines. His home and business had not been damaged either, except for some items that had been knocked off the walls and fallen on the floor. Most of the buildings throughout Israel had escaped significant damage, and the people were anxious to get back to their "normal" lives and their families.

Saul returned a week after Jacob, and he was soon posted at one of the local relief stations in Haifa. Later, many of the relief workers would be assisting the road crews and other teams in repairing the critical pieces of Israel's infrastructure that had been damaged by the earthquake. Many of the roads were still blocked and unusable from the earthquake, Coalition remains and equipment, and other debris.

A month later, Ahban came home for a week on leave also – he spent some of the time at his apartment in Tel Aviv, but most of it was in the family home in Haifa. Because of his construction expertise, he would be assigned to one of the infrastructure repair teams in Tel Aviv while Jacob would be supervising one of the Haifa crews. Naomi decided to close her floral shop for the rest of the month and help with the relief organizations, and would pay her handful of employees a supplemental salary while it was closed. Saul had been assigned to the decontamination division, and would be helping to remove the bodies and weaponry that had fallen over the northern front. The Israeli government tried to keep their military personnel relatively close to their homes, both for comfort and for familiarity of the region.

Ruth returned to school a month after the invasion, and said that it felt more like a children's daycare than a school. With all that had happened and all that was going on, no one was really interested in learning or doing schoolwork at that time. But the government understood the importance of getting their peoples' lives back to normal, and making sure the young people were in school was part of normal life.

In Israel, there were no idle hands, and the government increased the pay of the personnel who were on the decontamination teams, both to compensate them and make sure there would be enough workers to cleanse the land.

* * *

The destruction of the cities of Russia and those of the United States continued to take up most of the world news for the month that followed. In both nations, most of the cities were completely destroyed – and only the people on the outskirts and the suburban areas had survived. The highly centralized government of Russia had all but fallen, and the rule of anarchy began with a vengeance. The powerful Russian mafia was the closest entity to a government that remained, and they quickly took control of whatever companies and institutions they could. Much of their oil and natural gas infrastructure had been destroyed. The Russian Bear had finally been slain, and its many captives had fled away and gained their long-desired independence.

The United States had faired almost as badly as Russia, but

did not fall into anarchy because of their state governments and lower degree of centralization. With the destruction of New York and Washington DC, much of the federal government was in a shambles and the financial markets had all but collapsed. The economy was in turmoil, but would recover much faster because it was so large, diverse, and spread across a large area. Many of the larger companies and infrastructure of the nation had resided on the coasts, and it would be years before the nation recovered to its former level of prosperity.

With the loss of both their bloated federal government and their robust economy in a matter of days, the people of the United States wanted no more dealing with the international alliances that had forced them into taking part in war after war on foreign soil. The Americans now just wanted to rebuild their country and be left to themselves. The people demanded. independence from all the foreign problems, and with the absence of many of the regulatory agencies that had hampered and slowed economic independence from the Middle East, businesses offering alternatives sprang up and begin filling the need. As she had done early in her history soon after her birth, America returned to semi-isolationism, to focus on rebuilding her infrastructure and economy. The United States had gone from world's young policeman to retirement in less than a week.

Within the next month, most of the United States military was pulled from all parts of the world and recalled to the continental section of the nation. When a nation was as devastated as badly as the United States had been, no one could blame them for wanting to look after their own people and their own welfare first. Since the United Nations building had also been destroyed along with most of New York City, the United States requested that the United Nations relocate and rebuild somewhere else. And in addition to the request for the UN Headquarters to be relocated, the United States withdrew their UN membership altogether, as did Israel.

The militant Islamic nations of the world had been shattered, and the majority of their adult male population had been killed in the invasion attempt, since most had joined the Coalition forces in droves. It was as if the God of Israel had personally destroyed the followers of the god of Islam. It was now foolish even in the mainstream media to portray Allah as the same as the God of the Bible. The slaughter of the Islamic invaders in the land of Israel had been all too obvious even to most Muslims themselves.

Many of the moderate Muslim believers left their faith entirely and turned to the God of Israel, who had obviously shown Himself vastly superior to their god. Often, the imams and their accomplices would try to drive the people back to their former place, but they found that the people no longer feared nor would submit to them. Even in Saudi Arabia, people abandoned the mosques in droves, and rebelled against the authority of the religious police. Synagogues and churches sprang up all over the Middle East, and for the first time in modern history, Bibles were freely distributed there. After nearly five hundred years, the imams and their tight hold on the people was broken.

During the month following the invasion, the Westernized segments of the Iran population finally revolted and overthrew the mullahs who had ruled the nation for nearly thirty years. They immediately imprisoned the imams who had kept the tyrannical Islamic government in power for decades, and instituted a democratic form of government in which the people had a direct voice in their country, very much like their neighbor Iraq now had. A number of other totalitarian governments controlled by radical Muslims were also overthrown in the weeks and months that followed, and people all over the world began the long process of rebuilding their nations.

The long march of Islam to subjugate the world had not only been stopped, but had been turned back to the very place where it had begun.

The religion of the sword had been slain by the very sword it had drawn.

*   *   *

For the first time in their recent history, the Israeli people felt as if a great spiritual awakening was taking place. Many began reading the both the Torah and the Tanakh, often for the first time in their lives. The primary readings in the synagogues during the weeks that followed the invasion was Ezekiel 36-39, which emphatically spoke of the return of Israel from the Diaspora from among all the nations, and the incredible salvation of Israel from a massive invasion force led by the armies of the far north and their neighbors. All across the world, Jews and Christians alike studied the passage for themselves and listened to studies and teachings about it on the Internet, television, and radio.

Though the more conservative rabbis had been teaching on that very same passage in the weeks that had preceded the attack, few had taken it seriously. In the minds of most Jews, God had forsaken them long ago, and they were on their own in a horribly anti-Semitic world. Especially after the Nazi death camps of World War II, the majority of Jews across the world had cast off their faith and abandoned their heritage as they felt God had done to them. As a result, their children and grandchildren had become highly secular and agnostic – not really knowing if there was a God and at the same time, not really caring. If God had allowed the Holocaust to wipe out one-third of all the Jews – His own chosen people – then surely He could not be a loving God, or worthy of their devotion.

But now even the most secular and agnostic people among them studied the Ezekiel passages in detail, and given what they had just seen with their own eyes, they could not deny that God had indeed intervened on their behalf as He had promised. The fulfillment of the Ezekiel prophecies was too incredible to deny. All of the major nations that had led, joined with, and those who had stayed out of the Coalition invasion had been named in the Ezekiel passage thousands of years in advance. Not only that, but the very details of why and how the invasion would occur and then be thwarted were too precise to ignore.

While studying the Scriptures, the Jews and many others realized that the God of Israel had kept His promises in saving them in their darkest hour, and that perhaps He had not abandoned them. Or at least perhaps He was no longer angry with them and punishing them for their sins. Perhaps He was the God of salvation they had been longing for since the Diaspora had begun. The wrathful god of Islam had been utterly shamed and humiliated, and it was clear even to the most faithful of the Muslims that the God of Israel was superior to the god of Islam.

In addition to the Jews reading their Scriptures now, the Christians, Buddhists, Hindus, and even non-religious people all over the world began actively studying the Bible and seeking answers. Even Jewish Rabbis began seeking out Christian commentators who had long stood with Israel and had been predicting the Coalition invasion and miraculous defeat for years based upon those very passages in Ezekiel.

And not only did they take a second look at the Ezekiel passages, but they also studied many of the other prophetic and messianic passages of the Bible. If God had kept His promises in Ezekiel, what about the thousands of other prophecies? As a result of the dramatic increase in Bible reading and study, many Jews also began reading the New Testament and becoming Messianic Jews.

The rabbis and the Orthodox Jewish leadership began to soften. They no longer outright forbade the reading of the New Testament or ostracized messianic Jewish believers as harshly as they had for the past two thousand years.

*   *   *

The contaminated regions in the north and south of Israel were secured within the first two weeks. Many of the areas were still smoking days after the failed attack. The meteors had struck so many of the fuel tankers and vehicles that only a few were left unscathed. The sky had been black with all the smoke from the burning fuel and equipment even after the first week.

The Israelis sent in dozens of aerial drones to retrieve video footage that the IDF, the Mossad, and the other intelligence agencies could analyze. At first, they had wanted to send in their hazardous materials teams, but with all the undetonated munitions, they feared that the HAZMAT teams would be in too much danger. Much of the footage was immediately made public and put on the Internet for everyone to see, and what the footage revealed was utterly sickening.

The contaminated lands were literally blanketed with millions of uniformed corpses, most of which were scattered everywhere in a haphazard fashion. The ground under and around all the bodies was stained with their blood, and the ravenous birds and vultures had already heavily picked much of the bodies apart. Many looked as if they had turned their weapons upon their fellow Coalition soldiers and slaughtered each other, and not just with their machine guns and rifles, but with their artillery, shoulder weapons, grenade launchers, and even some of their tanks. It was as if all the soldiers had suddenly turned on one another, not just one group or nationality against another, but they had slaughtered each other individually.

In the video clips the mainstream media broadcast on television, most of the footage was far off so the images and clips would not have to be blurred. But on the Internet, there was no blurring or fading – the viewers saw the full, unedited footage. When the footage was first released, the remnants of Russia and many of the other nations that had taken part in the Coalition were both shocked and ashamed at what they and the rest of the world saw. Other nations were similarly shocked at the carnage, and the United States, Canada, and some of the nations in Europe promptly offered to send equipment, biohazard experts, and supplies to help Israel clean up the land.

In order to halt the spread of diseases from all the rotting corpses, the Israelis and the Jordanians decided to burn all the contaminated areas as quickly as possible. The area with the highest concentration of the dead was sprayed with large amounts of napalm and other flammable liquids, and then set afire. The objective was to burn away all the flesh, clothes, and any other contaminated substance that was already rotting. This would hasten the decontamination of the land, and also prevent them from having to bury the millions of decomposing bodies immediately.

And then they would wait. The rainy season was six months

away, and the Israelis and the Jordanians would wait while the heat of the desert summer and the monsoons that followed would further cleanse the contaminated zones.

*   *   *

Ruth took her steaming chai over to a quiet table in the back of the small café and sat down. She had just finished school for the day, and had some reading and other studying to do, but didn't feel like going home yet. She was months away from finishing the school year, but still had another year to go after that. It would be a long last year in school, but at least she had a few months off before it started. In her mind and heart, she had already graduated and just wanted to be done with school. It was typical for kids her age, she supposed – so close to being an adult and ready to start a new phase of life, but having to wait in order to finish Tikhon (Israeli high-school).

As she was reaching into her backpack to pull out her textbook, she changed her mind and took out her small Bible instead. She had been reading it off and on since the invasion, but today she felt like getting more serious about it. The world had changed dramatically since the attack, and she had found that reading the Bible gave her a renewed sense of peace and security in such an uncertain time.

She had felt somehow different ever since that night, as if she now had another purpose in her life, but she did not quite know what it was yet. She knew she felt differently about Yeshua than she had before, and still thought it very strange that she had called out His name during the invasion. She didn't know if she was a Christian yet, but she could feel herself being slowly drawn more in that direction every day.

For the most part, Ruth had kept her exploration of Christianity to herself. It was not just unpopular to be a Jewish Christian in Israel, but cause for various forms of persecution, (even though it was relatively mild compared to the persecution in many other parts of the world). Most of the time, the trials of Jewish Christians in Israel weren't as physical as much as social and emotional. She had heard about Jewish Christians being over-looked for jobs, scholarships, promotions, and even entry into the synagogues by the various factions of Ultra-Orthodox Jews. Ruth knew her father and possibly even her mother would not approve, but they would still love her – she was certain of that. And now since the invasion, it seemed like the persecution was decreasing, so maybe they would be more open to her new beliefs.

Her brothers were harder to read than her parents though. Saul had become more religious since the attack, and had been regularly attending synagogue. He had always been more thoughtful and considerate, like their mother, while Ahban was very quick-tempered and decisive, like their father. She had heard both of them, but mostly Ahban, rail against the Orthodox and Ultra-Orthodox and some of the laws they had pushed through the parliament and the local governments. Ahban was thoroughly secular after his years at the university, while their father was at least respectful of the old laws and traditions. And since the invasion, he had become even more so.

Ruth opened her Bible to one of her favorite passages and began to read.

Jeremiah 29:11-13: "For I know the thoughts that I think to-ward you, says the Lord, thoughts of peace and not of evil, to give you a future and a hope. Then you will call upon Me and go and pray to Me, and I will listen to you. And you will seek Me and find Me, when you search for Me with all your heart."

That same passage had been read by millions of her people over the centuries, and had given them comfort during their diffi-cult times. And as a young woman just discovering the personal God of the Bible for herself, that gave her hope because she wanted to find God now more than anything else.

She had already read the verses several times before, but like most of her readings, she just read some verses here and there, without doing a more in-depth study. Even though she had been reading the Bible for over two months, she still felt very much like a child in her new faith. Perhaps it was now time to become more serious about it.

So she continued reading Jeremiah's words from there, and

suddenly found herself becoming emotional about what she was reading. The tone of the passage was as if God was pouring out His heart to her and her people, promising to care for and re-gather the remnant that He had sent into Captivity because of their sins and wickedness. He loved His people – that much was obvious, but He hated their rebelliousness.

When she reached Jeremiah 31:31, the passage about the new covenant, she felt as if her eyes were starting to open, like waking from a dream or being able to more clearly see what had been written. God had made a new "deal" with her people – a law of the Spirit for their hearts, and no longer a law of Stone for their flesh. But most of her people were following the laws of works and deeds as they had for thousands of years, since the time of Moses and the Wilderness Wanderings, in fact.

And yet God had said in this passage that there was a new law and a new covenant, and it would be nothing like the old one. What could this mean, other than the New Testament that spoke of Yeshua?

She noted a reference to the Book of Hebrews near the verse, so she flipped over to it and continued reading. She understood it on some level, but much of it was foreign to her.

As she was reading, she felt someone watching her and she instinctively glanced up. A young man she had seen in the cafe several times before was looking up from his books at her. When she caught him, he smiled at her and turned back to his table. She thought little of it, and returned to her Bible too.

A few minutes later, she looked up in surprise as he came over to her table and introduced himself.

"Hi, my name is Nathan – I don't mean to interrupt you, but I couldn't help notice what you're reading," he said, pointing to her Bible.

Ruth smiled shyly and nodded. "I'm Ruth," she said.

"It's nice to meet you, Ruth. I attend a messianic synagogue nearby – are you a Christian?" he asked.

She looked around, apparently concerned about what others would think. "Well, I think so. Actually, I'm not sure yet. I'm reading Hebrews and I don't quite follow it," she replied

THE TIME OF JACOB'S TROUBLE

"Yeah, that's one of the more difficult books in the New Testament. Would you like some help with it for a few minutes?" he offered with a smile.

"Uh, sure."

She motioned to the empty chair across from her, and he scooted it over and sat down next to her, but not too close as to be rude or overly forward.

He asked her about her knowledge of the Torah, and began to explain how the Torah was intended to serve as both a guide to build a decent, orderly society based upon the rule of law rather than the rule of man, and also that the Torah was to be a guardian or tutor until the Messiah came. The Torah was designed to show God's standards of perfection and how far man fell short on every level.

That made sense to her, so he continued, and described a passage from Galatians in which Paul described the difference between a servant and an heir. An heir differs little from a servant while he is young, with the Law being his master. However, once the heir has matured, he is no longer under the Law but free to partake in the blessings of the home and then the inheritance.

Once Yeshua ratified the New Covenant by His death on the cross, He provided the way for people to become co-heirs with Him in the Kingdom by belief in Him alone, instead of mere servants as the Law had described. Where there is a change in the priesthood, there must also be a change in the law. When Yeshua arrived and became the new priest-king, He brought with Him the new law – the New Covenant.

The desire of God had always been to have a people He could call His own, and the means He had provided for this was through belief in Yeshua the Messiah. [6]

Nathan continued to walk her through the New Testament, describing the New Covenant and how the perfect sacrifice of Yeshua was required to take away sin forever, instead of just temporarily atoning for it as the animal sacrifices had done (since

---

[6] Paul describes the Law as our tutor or guardian until we spiritually mature. Once mature, we are no more under the Law but partakers of the Grace and Inheritance we have been offered. (Galatians 4:1-7)

they had to be done every year).

After he finished, he glanced down at his watch. "I have a class to go to soon. Do you mind if I give you a booklet from my church?" he asked.

"Sure – that would be great," she replied.

He went back to his table and gathered his books, then came back and gave her a small, neatly printed pamphlet.

"Well, it was nice to meet you, Ruth. I hope I've been able to help make things a little clearer for you."

"Thanks – it was very helpful," she replied. He said goodbye and left for his class.

Ruth watched as he left, and then returned to look over some of the passages he had cited for her, and read the pamphlet. On the back were basic instructions (with Scripture passages) on how to become a Christian.

As she read them over, her eyes began to well up with tears. The hope of being a permanent part of God's family was overwhelming – she suddenly felt as if that was now the most important decision she could make in her life. All of a sudden, it seemed like it was all that really mattered.

She read over the pamphlet again and a particular verse caught her attention:

Romans 10:12 – "For whosoever shall call upon the name of the Lord shall be saved."

She considered the verse again for a moment, and then with tears in her eyes, she bowed her head and asked Yeshua into her heart and forgive her sins, and asked to become part of His family. After she was finished, she opened her eyes and dabbed them with a napkin.

She did not understand all of what Nathan had told her fully yet, but she wanted to. But she felt at peace with her decision, and had felt no pressure from him, so she knew she had made the decision on her own.

But there were few Christian churches and teachers in Israel, and none that she felt she could openly attend. What about the Internet? And that thought made her smile – there were many missionaries, teachers, and new Christians sprouting up all over the world, with many from America on the Internet. Perhaps she could even find and download some free MP3 sermons or studies and learn more about it discreetly.

Ruth smiled at that thought, and put her Bible back in her bag. She had a lot of studying left to do, and if she didn't get started now, it was going be a long evening.

She decided to get on the Internet later that night and look around for some materials for new Christians, since she knew she was one now.

* * *

Over the next six months, Israel's government created a number of biohazard decontamination agencies, in preparation for the coming cleanup in the fall. The IDF had trained all of its regular and reserve forces in the decontamination techniques and procedures. They retooled and revamped as much of their older equipment as possible for use in the contaminated areas, and also purchased as much other equipment and supplies as they could.

After the first month following the attack, Israel had removed as many of the intact fuel tankers and supply trucks as they could before they began the burning, and tried to burn just the areas that had bodies. At first, many environmental groups protested the mass burning of thousands of square kilometers, but given the alternative – the massive spreading of disease and bacteria from the decomposing bodies – the groups didn't push too hard. Though it was Israel who had been attacked by dozens of other nations, it was up to them to clean up the mess that had been left behind.

The vast burning of all the contaminated areas filled the skies to the west of Israel with thick, black smoke. But since there was only the Mediterranean Sea to the west of Israel, few other countries were affected. The Israelis had thoroughly mapped all the areas to be burned and had coded them with varying degrees of contamination based upon the data from the drones and the other reconnaissance equipment. Their decontamination plan involved burning all the contaminated zones on the maps, and then re-burning the worst areas additional times until they could be reasonably sure that no rotting flesh remained.

Civilian bomb-squads and the IDF also used mine detectors and bomb-sniffing dogs to find and then either remove or detonate the thousands upon thousands of missiles, bombs, grenades, and other munitions that were scattered all over the inhabited parts of the land. When the air forces of the Coalition had flown ahead of the ground troops, they had dropped thousands of tons of munitions upon Israel, but none of them had exploded. A number of buildings and homes had incurred damage, but only from the bombs crashing upon the roofs and going straight through. The civilians were a tremendous help in the cleanup process, and would phone or email the IDC (Israel Decontamination Center) whenever they found an undetonated bomb.

Being instantly overwhelmed with calls and vague, often erroneous information, the IDC began distributing RFID markers. Whenever someone would find a bomb, they would simply place and activate an RFID marker next to it, which would transmit its precise GPS coordinates to the IDC. The IDC would then remove the bomb as they swept through the area. The system worked so well that within four months, all the land that was not within the contaminated areas was cleared of Coalition bombs. After their thorough sweep, it was rare to find any additional undetonated munitions.

Israel continued to burn, test, and re-burn all the contaminated areas in the north and south border regions of Israel. After six months, the IDF stopped the napalm drops and let the areas lie so the HAZMAT teams could begin entering the areas to bury the bones and other biohazardous debris.

* * *

Six months after the attack, Israel had finished the burnings and began entering the contaminated areas. Nearly every citizen of Israel who was able to help in the cleanup did so, along with a multitude of foreign workers. The task of gathering, transporting, and then burying all the bodies was enormous, and HAZMAT crews worked around the clock to cleanse the land.

THE TIME OF JACOB'S TROUBLE

The work went slowly for the first few weeks, but after the workers and various groups had grown accustomed to the process and coordinating their efforts, their efficiency greatly improved.

Since the larger population centers of Israel were in the north and the lands of the south below the Dead Sea were mostly arid wilderness, Israel had set aside a huge parcel of land for the burial zone. The hot winds from the Arabian Desert blew from the east and the numerous mountains and canyons south of the Dead Sea blocked much of the winds from passing over the mountains to the coastlands. Also, winds from the Mediterranean blew against the eastern side of the mountain range stopped much of the east wind that had passed through the mountains. So the Israelis buried as many of remains in the region immediately south of the Dead Sea among the mountains.

The Israelis carefully selected the driest, lowest, and most arid sections of the area for the great burial pits, and had sent the hundreds of bulldozers and earthmovers in months earlier to prepare the burial sites. At more than five kilometers in diameter, it would be the largest tomb on the face of the earth. Inside the valley, they had also dug hundreds of smaller pits. And they called it the Valley of Hamongog, which meant "the multitude of Gog", taken from one of the verses in Ezekiel 39, which described how the Israelis would cleanse the land.

Also in holding to the passage, the Israelis constructed a small, makeshift city to the east of the Valley of Hamongog and called it Hamonah, meaning "multitudes." Hamonah was where the workers would rest when their shifts were over and also served as the command-and-control center for the IDC. Mechanics flocked to Hamonah from all over the land to work on the equipment, and HAZMAT teams set up mobile-trailers and small buildings where they would spend their off-time in. Israel paid top-wages for HAZMAT specialists and workers, and people from all over the region came for the high wages.

The burial teams methodically combed through the contaminated areas and separated the bodies, the weapons, and the equipment. They catalogued nearly everything they found, and whatever weapons and equipment could be salvaged they set aside for refurbishment. There were vast amounts of guns and ammunition that were relatively undamaged, and Israel's targeted burnings had appeared to be very successful. Not only did the Israelis recover tons of reusable weapons and munitions, they found massive quantities of nuclear, chemical, and biological weapons that had also been unused in the attack.

Israel immediately destroyed all the chemical and biological weapons, but saved the nuclear weapons for conversion to nuclear energy in their power plants. The world was shocked all over again when it saw the evidence that Israel and her supporters had been correct: the Coalition for Peace had not invaded Israel to simply defang her, but to completely exterminate her and all her people.

The disposal of the millions of bodies and bones was more tedious than the equipment had been, and the HAZMAT teams piled the bodies into huge dump trucks and sealed them tight, and then the dump trucks would take their loads down to the Valley of Hamongog and dump them into the designated burial pits. Few attempts were made to identify the dead, since the burnings had made that nearly impossible. The Coalition forces had kept extensive lists of the soldiers who had joined in the invasion, and few of them had survived. It was simply taken for granted that no Coalition soldiers who had set foot into Israel had made it out alive. If there had been any survivors, they weren't coming forward, lest they be arrested and punished.

* * *

After the land and the borders had been thoroughly decontaminated, the IDC issued another set of RFID markers, but these were colored red, instead of the black markers that had been issued for the undetonated weapons. Later when the tourists and citizens were allowed into the decontaminated areas, they would take handfuls of the RFID markers with them, and whenever they discovered a bone or scrap that the HAZMAT teams had missed, they would not touch it, but would set up a marker next to the fragment and activate the marker. Israel was awed at the number of tourists and visitors from all over the world who came to see the destruction firsthand for themselves, and they distributed maps of the destroyed areas for the tourists to pass through.

Many of the tourists were Christians or Jews from America. The vast majority of the more-observant Christians in Europe and the Middle East had migrated to America long ago, and their Jewish brethren had followed after them before 1948. After the creation of the nation of Israel and during the decades that followed, most of the remaining Jews from the Middle East, Africa, Russia, and Eastern Europe had typically migrated to Israel, while their brothers and sisters in Western Europe had moved to America. At the time of the Coalition invasion, nearly as many Jews were living in the United States as in Israel – over six million in each nation.

But the destruction of the United States' coastal cities had dramatically changed those numbers, and since the Jews living within the borders of Israel had been so miraculously saved, many of the remaining Jews from Western Europe and also the United States began migrating to Israel. There was plenty of work waiting for them in the cleanup and rebuilding industries, and Israel once again began to feel as if her land was not big enough for all her people, especially with all their brothers and sisters from across the sea coming back to their native land.

So Israel took the opportunity that she had neglected after the Six Day War and the Yom Kippur War: she annexed the West Bank and Gaza. The IDF quickly cleaned out all the pockets of resistance, which were now feeble and bankrupt without the support of the United Nations, Russia, and the other Islamic nations. The Palestinians, who had suffered for over sixty years in the UN refugee camps, were given a clear, immediate choice: either become peaceful, productive Israeli citizens, or move to the land that had been set aside for them before 1948: Jordan. The majority of the Palestinians became Israeli citizens, mostly for the opportunity to have a better life. They were humiliated that their long hatred of the Jews had kept them in bondage to their Islamic neighbors, and were now ready to accept the state of Israel as a nation.

The cold, hard reality had finally set in for the Palestinian people, and they acknowledged that their Islamic brothers had cared nothing for them – they had been despised pawns in the Islamic goal of destroying Israel. Thousands of their people had been killed in their misguided quest for the genocide of the Jews, and their own leaders and fellow Muslims had kept them starving and enslaved just to foster world hatred against Israel.

* * *

Like many others in the land, Ruth found she was starting to slip back into a few of her old habits and routines after less than a year after the invasion.

The return to normalcy and the busyness of life had made everyone start to grow comfortable again. Synagogue attendance had been steadily declining for the past few months, even though many more were still attending than before the invasion.

Most of the damage to Israel's roads and other infrastructure had been repaired or rebuilt, and businesses of all sorts were running at their usual pace. The awe of the miracle that God had worked in their land began to fade and shift to the background of the nation's thoughts, and an element of pride crept in, similar to what had happened after the Six Day War.

Saul would return to the university in the fall, and Ahban had returned to his old position at the architecture firm. Naomi's floral shop was back to normal, and with all the added tourism from America, was actually thriving. Her father's business was thriving too from all the extra construction projects for homes and businesses.

Ruth had finished the school year and was now on summer vacation. She had taken a part-time job at one of the local coffee shops within walking distance from their house. Most of her friends had found summer jobs also, but they usually tried to get together every few days, especially since they were going into their last year of school.

Sometimes they talked about what had happened with the invasion, and often Ruth spoke with her mother or Saul about it. She tried to get them interested in the Bible, even if it was only the Tanakh (the Old Testament). She knew they would be much less receptive to the New Testament portion, as nearly all Jews still were.

Her family and friends listened to her with some interest, but at times she felt that they were just being more polite than anything else. At times she became discouraged – how could they live through such an incredible event and still not be interested in what their own Scriptures said about it?

But from her Bible studies, Ruth was learning that it took time for the spiritual seeds she was now planting to grow and bear fruit. So she would continue planting and watering, and leave it up to God to do the growing.

* * *

Fourteen months after the Coalition forces had been supernaturally destroyed, the cleansing of the land was finished. The Israelis threw a huge celebration and a national holiday to commemorate the completion of the enormous cleanup.

The Israeli government and a number of groups set up memorials and other markers in the areas where significant destruction had taken place. In all the areas where the IDC had found the worst contamination and had feared biohazard problems for decades, they were shocked at how quickly the land was recovering. But the entire Valley of Hamongog remained desolate and barren – even the weeds and desert vegetation could not grow there.

After the dramatic events of the previous year, millions of the Jewish people had turned from their secularism and had begun to follow the practices and ordinances of Judaism once again. Many had been brought up with the holiday rituals and such, and practiced them simply as part of their cultural heritage. But there had been a subtle change in the collective spirit of the Jewish nation. They had clearly seen how God had kept His promises to protect them as His chosen people, and down to the last detail, in fact. Now that the Jewish people had begun to awaken from their long spiritual slumber, the political power and support of the Sanhedrin increased dramatically.

The Sanhedrin was the ancient ruling body that had governed Judea from their return under the Persians in the 5th century BC to the destruction of the Temple in 70 AD. It had all but vanished for over 1900 years, and then in 2004, the Sanhedrin was restarted as a political party in Israel. However, due to the secular beliefs and background of most of the Jews at that time, the Sanhedrin had little political clout.

But the massive invasion and the miraculous events that had subverted it had changed not only spiritual nature of Israel, but also its politics. Throughout Israel they officially stopped referring to the failed invasion as the "Coalition for Peace Invasion", but as the "Magog Invasion", after the Ezekiel passage that had surnamed the Russian invaders long before by their ancestors: the Magogians.

During the course of the cleanup of the land, the Israelis discovered the remains of the 1st Century Jewish Temple slightly south of the Dome of the Rock. Once the discovery was certified, the evidence was so overwhelming that even the Wahabi Muslims in Saudi Arabia could not dispute it. The borders of the Temple remains were just south of the Dome of the Rock, so the entire area of the Muslim temple was actually in the outer courts of the ancient Jewish Temple, which in the Scriptures had been set aside to be given to the Gentiles anyway.

And for the first time in nearly two thousand years, a faint glimmer of hope appeared that the Jewish people would once again rebuild their beloved Temple.

* * *

Saul walked into the bookstore and began browsing the computer books. He had taken a summer internship as a programmer at a small software company nearby, and was living at home that summer. He had borrowed a little too much on his credit cards last year, and wanted to pay them off so he wouldn't have to deal with them during his last year in school. He was doing some interesting work (at least for a summer job), and was seeing what his life would probably be like once he got his degree, after he got out into the workforce.

The software industry was always changing as new languages, machines, and frameworks were constantly being introduced, and that was something he liked. He became bored after awhile doing the same thing day after day, and the ever-changing technology would keep him interested. He couldn't see himself working for his father's business at all, and he had a streak of independence in him that made him not want to stay too close to home. It might be a long summer living at home, but hopefully his job would make it go by quickly.

He picked up a book on software engineering practices, and another one about a new framework that had just been released, and headed towards the counter. As he was walking to the front of the store, he passed a rack of Bibles and hesitated. His sister had been talking more and more about the Bible and what had happened in Israel, and it somewhat bothered him that she knew more about it than he did. He loved to read, and since he had recently become interested in the long, rich history of his nation, he decided he should at least read through the Bible once.

With all the American tourists and Christians flocking to Israel recently, Bibles with New Testaments were much more common now, even in the local bookstores like this one. Before, they had mostly been just the Tanakh, and the New Testaments had been sold separately on a back shelf, if at all. What could it hurt to buy one, he figured – then he could at least learn about what the Christians believed and thought about Israel and the Jews. It never hurt to broaden one's horizons, he supposed.

He decided he would see for himself what the Bible was all about, as objectively as possible. He picked out a small one from the rack and went to the nearest checkout counter.

CHAPTER 4
THE RETURN OF THE WATCHERS

R uth carefully put in her ear-buds for her MP3 player, pressed the Play button and then gathered her backpack to go home for the evening. The small printed page she had been reading was discreetly hidden away in one of the thicker books at the bottom of her pack.

She said goodnight to the young man at the espresso machine and the older woman behind the counter. Everyone needed a place to relax at away from home and work (or school in her case), and this small coffee shop was hers.

This was her last year in Tikhon, and it felt like it was taking forever. The holidays would be approaching soon, and she had always looked forward to that time, but especially more-so this year. She had continued working part-time at the coffee shop, and that helped break up the monotony of the school year. Many of the modern holidays that Israel celebrated had been derived from the ancient Biblical feasts, and she had just finished an MP3 series on their original meanings and prophetic nature.

Ruth frequently examined her own faith and wrote down any questions she thought of during her listening and reading times. Later on her laptop, she would look them up or go to one of the message-boards and post her questions there. When she had started her last school year, her parents had bought her a laptop since she was always on their computer. She also had more papers to write for school that year, along with college entry and scholarship forms to fill out online all the time.

She was very grateful for the gift, and used it nearly every evening. Most of the time she just used it for her schoolwork, but lately she had found herself browsing some of the Christian forums, looking for information and asking questions about what she was studying.

She had been making a point to read the Bible nearly every day for the last year, along with listening to studies on one or two specific books on her MP3 player. When she wasn't in the mood for a study, she would listen to some of the Christian music albums she had downloaded instead. She still had not told her parents or even her two brothers about her faith. She felt bad about hiding her faith from her parents, but she still felt like she wouldn't know how she would handle her parents if they confronted her about it. At times, she thought herself foolish to worry – after all, there were many worse things she could be doing, especially at her age.

The young man who had spoken with her many months before at the café had not returned, even though she had often looked for him. She found it odd that he had been there quite frequently for weeks until the day he talked with her about Yeshua, and then had not been there again. Perhaps he had been sent to help her along on the road to faith. She thought about that day often, and regularly thanked God for sending him to help bring her into the Kingdom.

The printout she had hidden away earlier was from the Zion's Harvest website that contained some basic information on who they were, what they did, and how to join. The Zion's Harvest ministry was mostly active in America where they had started, with major offices in San Francisco, Los Angeles, and New York. They also had small branches in various European countries and slightly larger ones in Israel. Their ministry had been growing dramatically in Israel after the Magog Invasion, but it still had not attracted a huge, mainstream following.

Ruth frowned as she walked home, thinking once again about what she would do after she graduated. She had never been very career-minded and couldn't really see herself being a professional like a doctor or lawyer or someone like that. She loved being around people and interacting with them. As she had been growing in her faith, she had begun to realize that she wasn't that interested in going to college, at least not right away. Lately, she had found herself more excited about joining a ministry full-time and sharing her faith with others, especially among her own people. Perhaps that was her calling, she often mused.

She grimaced as she thought about how her parents – particularly her father – would react if and when she told them she wanted to join a ministry instead of going to college. After they had stopped laughing and realized she was serious, her father would probably blow his stack! She feared the consequences of telling her own parents more than anyone else – she had read stories about others – even in Israel – that had become estranged or even disowned by their families when it became known they had converted to Christianity. It was still almost better for a Jew to convert to any other religion than Christianity if they lived in Israel!

But deep down, she knew that one day she would have to tell them – if they didn't figure it out before she got up the courage. Until then, she would keep reading, learning, and praying. Sometimes she would play out different scenes in her head. She felt herself growing in the knowledge and the love of her Lord, and He comforted her fears when she became too overwhelmed with them.

She loved her parents and hated to upset them, but she understood that one day she might have to make a choice between them and her faith in Yeshua.

* * *

Naomi heard the quiet sound of a jiggling key at the back door, and looked up as Ruth walked in. The sun was low in the sky and the smell of early autumn flowed in behind her.

"Hi Mom, do you need some help with dinner?" Ruth asked as she kissed her mother on the cheek.

"Sure. You can set the table, if you don't mind. Your father will be home soon," Naomi replied with a smile, returning to stir the sauce in one of the pans.

THE TIME OF JACOB'S TROUBLE

Ruth took the dishes out of the cabinet and began properly arranging them on the table. Saul was back at the university, so there were only three places to set now.

"How was your day at the shop, Mom?"

"Good – we had a slow day today. Maybe tomorrow will be more exciting. How was school?" Naomi asked.

"Okay, same as always. I have a Modern History test tomorrow and some homework. It will be great when I don't have to do that anymore!" she exclaimed.

Her mother smiled and said, "It won't be long before you're finished. A few years from now, you might miss those late nights studying and getting together with classmates to cram."

"Maybe, but I doubt it." Ruth smiled wryly as she finished setting the table and went back to get the glasses. "I'm going to get changed – I'll be back down in a few minutes," she said as she put them on the table.

"Alright – I'll call you when your father comes in," Naomi replied. Ruth left the kitchen and headed upstairs to her room.

Naomi looked over the pans and turned down the heat on the stove. She sighed – cooking after a full day at work seemed like even more work at the end of the day to many, but she found it relaxing, and it helped her settle back in at home.

Her thoughts returned to her daughter – now Ruth was almost grown up, and becoming more like an adult every day. She had been expecting a tough year, with this one being Ruth's last one in school and all. Saul hadn't been too difficult a few years earlier, but Ahban had thoroughly prepared them for what could happen during the last year at home. He had been on the wilder side, and had rebelled almost as often as he could. But a year or two later after he had moved out, he had calmed down, and now he was nice to be around again. Oddly enough, Ruth's personality had always been somewhat of a mixture of her two brothers, and her mother had been preparing for the worst.

Naomi was probably the first to notice the various minor, yet curious changes in her daughter. If Jacob or her sons had detected them before she had, they had kept silent about them. The changes had been trivial at first, but they had steadily grown over the last several months. She often thought about when exactly the changes had begun, and whether they were just because of her age and all the changes that happened to older teenagers. But she kept coming back to that pleading prayer that Ruth had whispered on the night of the Magog Invasion.

The first of the changes were mostly outward – she had begun to wear less-revealing clothing, such as longer skirts and shorts during the summer. She found this change in modesty curious, since Ruth had previously liked the shorter, trendier clothes and usually wanted to wear the same styles as her friends. She had also been wearing more mature clothes, which still showed her as very attractive, but without a lot of the sexual overtones and suggestive nature that had been there before.

The next change she had noted was that Ruth's language had improved, even though she had never been very crude or mouthy. Her language became cleaner and less sarcastic, even when Naomi overheard her talking on the phone with her friends. Several times, she had noticed that Ruth was more reserved and respectful to her and Jacob, even when they denied her something she wanted or in getting permission to do something.

Surprisingly for a teenager, Ruth appeared to be much more in control of her emotions and responses than mere weeks earlier. When Naomi had braced for an argument or a fight on an issue, Ruth responded with some disappointment but also with respect and acceptance for their authority. As a result, Naomi had found herself seeing her as being more adult-like and responsible, and thereby giving her more independence.

Perhaps as a result of the invasion, Ruth had become religious, even though she had never seemed to give Judaism much thought (or any other religion, for that matter). She had not really mentioned any new beliefs, but she did talk more about the Bible.

She would have to ask her husband and maybe even some of Ruth's friends if they knew anything about it. Since Israel was widely secular, different religions of every sort could be found and freely practiced within its borders. The only group most Israelis did not really accept was the messianic Jews, which Naomi had always found to be somehow ironic, coming from America. After all, Yeshua was the most famous Jew that had ever lived.

Something had definitely happened to her daughter to bring about these new changes, but she wasn't sure if she should be worried yet – they had all been those of maturity, and she did not want to hinder that, of course. This was still a volatile time in her young life, especially with everything that was happening to Israel and the world around them.

Naomi decided to watch her behavior closely and ask questions if a situation arose that warranted it.

* * *

The industrialized nations of the world regained their bearings late within the first year after the attack on Israel. The United States of America had all but withdrawn to her hemisphere across the Atlantic. Though still very active in promoting and encouraging world-trade, the Americans no longer wanted anything to do with the numerous problems and conflicts across the ocean, and especially in the Middle East. The devastation of her capital and the larger coastal cities had firmly pushed her back to her isolationist upbringing, and her people wanted to keep it that way.

The United States had immediately tapped the vast oil resources in Alaska and the Gulf of Mexico and made economic treaties with her neighbors to secure and expand their oil supplies and refining capabilities. Canada and Mexico felt much the same as the United States, and quickly formed the North American Union to provide for their common defense and help their economies recover.

Other nations quickly followed suit and formed large coalitions of neighboring nations. As the number of coalitions began to grow, the more powerful nations decided that these movements needed to be quickly brought under control before another large-scale war broke out due to entangling alliances.

CHRIS HAMBLETON

The North American Union and the European Union moved to replace the defunct United Nations with a new organization called the World Union, which would be made up of a small number of democratically-elected representatives from each of the newly forming unions. One of the major problems with the former United Nations was that over the years it had become filled with many pseudo-democracies, which were just dictatorships hidden behind worthless elections.

The original vision of the United Nations had been all but lost soon after its inception, as a place where democracies could flourish and nations could hopefully resolve their issues rather than go to war against one another. But too many delegates who were too concerned with only their own interests had quickly poisoned the good intentions of the organization. Within its first decade, the UN became inefficient, ineffective, and constantly embroiled in bureaucracy and scandals of its own.

The model of the World Union would immediately correct many of the problems inherent in the old United Nations' charter. Instead of hundreds of delegates with one appointed delegate per nation, there would be only one delegate who was democratically-elected from all the nations in each Union. Far fewer Union members meant much less bureaucracy and faster decision-making and action.

An elected Union member could be recalled at any time by another vote by the citizens of their Union, and elections were to be held once every three years. The greatly reduced number of delegates would help them stay focused on the issues that mattered, and the creation and enforcement of resolutions that had teeth, instead of pointless resolutions that could simply be ignored at will. There would be no more bloated bureaucracy that did little other than draft and vote on resolutions that meant nothing.

Instead of a Secretary General elected from among the general assembly, the World Union would unanimously select one of their own to be the Secretary of the World Union. The Secretary would then be confirmed by two-thirds of the nations in all the Unions. For the World Union headquarters, there would be no single location where it would reside. Since the World Union was such a small body, the delegates would spend a year in a different nation in which each Union member government was based, and it then would change locations after each election of a new Secretary. The Americans and Europeans had created and implemented a federal government on a global level.

The World Union military would be a completely separate body, with each Union member contributing a number of troops proportional to their collective population, along with the financial backing from each Union. There would be no more of the ragtag national contributions to the world military peacekeeping forces as there had been with the United Nations. The World Military would be controlled by and accountable to the elected World Union leaders, and many of its military leaders would be contributed from each of the Union nations.

Each Union member would be responsible for policing their own territories and member nations of course, and if one or more nations rebelled against their Union, the entire World Union could immediately move to put down the insurrection to maintain a united front against rebellion. In order for a potential Union member to join the World Union, 75% of all the weapons from all the Union's member nations would be placed under the World Union's jurisdiction. Rogue nations would be forced to comply and join their respective Union or face certain, swift economic sanctions, isolation, and perhaps even invasion to replace their rebellious government.

Over the course of the next year, the nations coalesced into ten solid Unions and would elect members in the following year. The ten Unions that were formed were: the European Union (which already existed), the African Union, the Eastern Asian Union, the Central American Union, the North American Union, the South American Union, the South Asian Union, the Central Asian Union, the South Pacific Union, and the Middle Eastern Union.

In the end, only a handful of tiny, insignificant nations or states had refused to join their collective Unions, but they were quickly forced to comply by the threat of sanctions or an attack.

The World Union was very serious in its mission: there would be world peace, whether certain people wanted it or not. [7]

* * *

In Israel, the people and the government had grown increasingly confident with the ending of the cleanup. Israel had gained worldwide renown from the miraculous salvation and their cleanup efforts. In many nations, the Jews also had the sympathy of the populace similar to what they'd had after the horrors of the Holocaust had been revealed. The Israelis seized the opportunity to require that Jerusalem be recognized as only true capital of Israel, which irritated some of the nations, but they ended up agreeing to the demands and moved their embassies.

In addition to increased political capital, Israel also now had an incredible military arsenal, most of which had been plundered and refurbished from the vanquished Coalition forces. Israel had promptly destroyed all the chemical and biological weapons, but had converted as many of the atomic missiles over for nuclear energy use in power plants.

After the nuclear weapons had been reprocessed, Israel had so much energy from the conversion that they began selling both the nuclear fuel and the electricity to their neighbors and Europe, and stored as much of the rest as they could. They found that not only did they have enough surplus energy for reselling and distribution, but also they would have just over seven full year's worth of fuel, even with a rapidly expanding population and economy. Many noted that the infamous Ezekiel passage also stated that Israel would be burning the weapons for seven years.

Since Israel was a democracy and most of the Jewish people now wanted to see their Temple rebuilt, the Israeli politicians in the government used a small portion of the energy sales to begin

---

[7] The Anti-Christ will eventually have authority over the entire world, not just one or two large regions such as Europe or the Middle East. There are increasing calls for groups of neighboring nations and entire continents to coalesce into unions similar to the European Union. (Daniel 7:24)

rebuilding the Temple. The Temple Institute in Jerusalem had created extensive design plans and models years before, and the Israeli government simply evaluated and then adopted their plans. The Temple designs were largely based upon the last Jewish Temple that had existed during the Roman period, and the existing Temple Mount foundation would accommodate the previous model the best. But of all the expenditures of Israel's political capital, this one was the most costly.

On the surface, the issue of rebuilding the Temple was very straightforward: every nation had their own religious centers and buildings, except for Israel. It was absurd that the Jews could not worship their own God in their own way in their own land, especially when it was one of the oldest, most widely known religions in the world. Of course, the various Islamic leaders and groups howled that the new Temple would be too close to the Dome of the Rock, which would immediately lead to renewed violence between the Jews and the Muslims.

But their protests largely fell upon deaf ears – the Israelis were tired of giving into the Arabs and the other Muslim groups, especially after the powerful Islamic military forces had been destroyed less than two years earlier. But they listened to their complaints to be cordial, and then went ahead in rebuilding their Temple. They also offered to give the Muslims a significant donation to renovate the Dome of the Rock, which was badly in need of repair after years of neglect. But the Muslims refused, and so the Dome of the Rock was left as it was.

For the first time in over nineteen hundred years, it appeared that the Jews would once again have their beloved Temple. The task would take at least a year to complete, but the Jewish people were committed to having their Temple once again.

*   *   *

Just days after the Jewish Passover in the year following the cleanup in Israel, a team of Christian archaeologists from the United States discovered the remains of Noah's Ark in the Zagros Mountains of Iran. Since the demise of the mullahs and the

Islamic government, Iran had opened her doors wide for commerce, tourism, and foreign investing. Second only to the shock at the supernatural intervention on behalf of Israel, the world was startled with this new discovery in such an unexpected location. Teams of both secular and religious archaeologists flocked to the site, and all confirmed that the discovery was indeed Noah's Ark.

To their amazement, the Ark was still recognizable for the most part, even though it had been split in two and somewhat deteriorated. The wood was black from the pitch that had been evidently spread over its entire surface, and the wood was mostly petrified and as hard as stone. The two inner floors were still intact, and many of the cages and the stalls inside were undamaged. The dimensions of the Ark – once they began to account for the structure separation and the scattered timbers – were very close to those given in the Book of Genesis. At roughly 475 meters long by 80 meters wide by 40 meters high, the Ark was amazing to behold.

As for dating the barge-shaped Ark, the archaeologists discovered a strange etching that appeared to be a large star map on the upper level where Noah and his family had evidently lived at one time. The star map showed where the sun rose and set in the sky in relation to the various constellations (the ecliptic), and using that information the archaeologists were able to date the time of the Flood at about 2500 BC, very close to the genealogical dates given in the Bible.

Also, the construction and some of the tools and other items they found in the Ark proved conclusively that it had been built at the same time as the earliest known civilizations of the world. To the surprise of many of the archaeologists, thousands of iron fittings and fragments were found embedded within the structure of the Ark as rivets. Iron fittings and castings over a thousand years before the supposed start of the Iron Age and hundreds of years before the Bronze Age upset most of the traditional dating models of archaeology.

The discovery of the Ark occupied most of the news for the first two weeks after the initial announcement. In addition to the star map of the constellations, the archaeologists also found a detailed map of the world as it apparently had been in Noah's day. All the continents appeared to be much different, but the northern and southern edges of the landmasses were still very similar to the current continents. Some of the major differences were that Antarctica was connected to what appeared to be India, and the Americas were connected to Europe and Africa. However, a huge section of the map was missing on the modern globe, in the area that appeared to occupy most of the Pacific Ocean. Many of the areas now occupied by oceans were simply not on the map, yet the map appeared to be complete and accurate.

Near the cages and stalls inside the Ark, usually above or along the sides of the doors that remained, there were strange pictographs which appeared to have been used to designate which animals lived in which areas. The pictographs looked similar to ancient Egyptian hieroglyphics but were used like letters from the alphabet.

A handful of scholars familiar with ancient languages and hieroglyphics examined the images of the word-pictures, and they quickly concluded that they were actually very similar to ancient Hebrew, and were close cousins of the earliest inscriptions that had been found in Iran and Iraq before cuneiform writing had been invented. Once translated, the inscriptions were clearly the names of the various animals that resided in each cage or stall. Shockingly, some of the inscriptions were of small reptiles that had been previously classified with the dinosaurs, along with many of the other animals that had become extinct during the Ice Age that followed the Flood.

The Theory of Evolution had been under fire for over forty years from what most mainstream scientists and the media deemed "religious extremists" – namely, the Creation Science movement and then later the Intelligent Design movement. The evolutionists had grown increasingly frustrated over the decades with their inability to find conclusive evidence and transitional fossils to bolster their theory. It seemed as though the harder they looked and the deeper they probed, the more absurd the Theory of Evolution became.

All the cellular, genetic, and biological evidence pointed to an incredible genius of a Designer who had constructed living organisms in such a way as to make dramatic genetic shifts impossible, whether they were small changes over a long expanse of time or huge changes over a short burst of time. Evolution was finally seen for what it was: spontaneous generation over an extremely long period of time, which of course was impossible.

Given the maps that had been found and the incredibly preserved remains of the Ark itself, the evolutionists finally acknowledged that nearly all of their theories and models concerning the beginning of the world, the ascent of man, and even much of their history of man up to about 2500 BC was blatantly wrong.

Between the saving of Israel from the Coalition and the discovery of Noah's Ark, secular scientists quietly but reluctantly abandoned the theory in droves. However, they did not turn to Creationism or necessarily Intelligent Design, but took more of an agnostic approach to the issue of man's beginnings.

*   *   *

Ruth was very excited about the discovery of the Ark – the images and videos on the Internet were stunning! She had been looking for an opportunity to speak with her parents about her faith for months, and perhaps this would finally give her a good opening. She had spoken to them several times about the Magog Invasion, but it felt as if they were still being polite more than anything else.

She only had a few months of school left before graduation, and she had shared her beliefs with several of her friends. Some wanted to talk about it more than others, but many seemed as if they just wanted to graduate and move on with their lives. They cared about what was happening in the news about as much as they cared about school at this point. She felt ashamed at times because she still hadn't really spoken to anyone about Yeshua other than her best friend Rina, and given her reaction, she probably would not. They were still friends, of course, but Ruth could tell it was one of those topics that would hurt their friendship more than anything else.

Her parents were pressuring her more about college and her plans for the next year. They would be completely shocked when she told them about what she really wanted to do. She had been chatting with various messianic Jews for months, with several of them being members of Zion's Harvest. The Israeli branch had continued to grow tremendously over the last year, and a number of other messianic ministries had sprung up also, with most of them being planted by the American churches and evangelical Christian groups.

Ruth had made up her mind to join one of the groups as a full-time missionary to her own people as soon as she could, which would probably be early in the fall after she had saved up some money over the summer. She knew her parents would be upset at her decision, especially since both her brothers had immediately gone off to college after graduating. It was just assumed that she would also.

Her parents and friends typified what was happening in Israel and the rest of the world: they had seen with their own eyes the miraculous destruction of the Coalition forces, and were awakened spiritually to some extent, but were now going back to sleep as they settled back into their normal lives. Perhaps the news of Noah's Ark would re-awaken them before they lapsed into a spiritual coma again and all the new spiritual growth would be wasted.

When Ruth spoke to her mother about the discovery of the Ark, the reaction was close to what she had expected, but it was still disappointing. Then later the same held true with her father, but he was even less interested than her mother had been. Ruth thought about her brothers – Ahban would be skeptical and completely disinterested, but Saul might have a much better reaction. Ahban had always been disinterested in religion and probably spiritual matters altogether, while Saul had been more curious about them.

Saul would be coming home in another few weeks for Shavuot – it would be nice to have him around again for a few days, even if it wasn't for very long. Even though he was her brother, she felt like she did not know him as much as she wanted to, since he had been away for most of the last several years in college.

They had talked for a while when he had been home for the Passover week, and it had been fun for them to catch up with one another. He seemed nicer than she had remembered when he had lived with them the summer before – perhaps he would be even more open to deeper spiritual discussions on this visit.

What more could she do to share her faith with those around her? She sometimes found it ironic that she wanted to become a missionary to her own nation, yet she couldn't even talk about her faith with her own family! But she tried to keep in mind that it was up to Yeshua to decide who to invite into His Family. He was the one who called people to Himself, and no one could come to Him unless they had been first called.

Those thoughts gave her more confidence and somewhat lifted her spirits, but she still felt saddened at being unable to talk with her friends and family about the most important Person in her life.

* * *

It was a time of monumental changes for everyone on the earth – as if the planet itself was preparing for something huge to happen. There was a general feeling of uncertainty throughout the world, in spite of the new World Union and the ceasing of most of the wars since its inauguration. The failed Magog Invasion and the discovery of Noah's Ark had thrown everyone off-kilter, and many people were longing for a time of peace and stability. The financial markets were returning to their previous levels and most of the industrialized nations were thriving again.

On the first of January, nearly six months after the inauguration of the first World Union body, widespread reports about strange moving lights in the sky began circulating in the media. High-quality video footage of the lights (or spacecraft as some declared) swept the Internet, and were so well-documented that the vast majority of people began to believe that the earth was being "visited" by beings or spacecraft from outside the solar system. The numbers of so-called "alien abductions" increased dramatically, and nearly all the reports were consistent in that the abductees had been willing participants and their abductors had been very friendly and inquisitive. Some of the abductees had reported that the beings appeared to be preparing to reveal their existence to all mankind very soon.

On the last day of March, the leaders of the World Union were visited by three extraterrestrial creatures. In many ways, they appeared to be very similar to humans, with each having two arms, two legs, two eyes, etc. – nearly all of the main features that humans had. The creatures were tall, thin, and pale gray in color, and had large black, tear-shaped eyes. They moved in a smooth, flowing fashion, very similar to how people move as when walking in a full swimming pool – almost as if the air of the world seemed exceeding thick and heavy for them to move through. [8]

Their voices were very beautiful when they spoke, and they had a certain calming, melodious tone that immediately set their audience at ease. In fact, nothing about them was threatening in the least, and they had soft, white, flowing clothing that covered similar areas as the humans did, namely their chest, arms, midsection, and legs. What also set their human audience at ease was the soft glow of light that seemed to be emitted from their skin, surrounding them with what could be described as a heavenly

---

[8] The frequency and variety of sightings and alleged abductions by "extraterrestrials" continue to grow. While many sightings are hoaxes or can be adequately explained, many cannot. Those who have researched this phenomenon from a Christian/Biblical worldview have found many similarities between alien abductions and cases of demon-possession. Many ancient cultures (such as the Sumerians and the Hebrews) describe "gods" that come to the earth from the stars and interact with mankind. Many of the demigods of Greece and Rome described unnatural offspring that came from the coupling of a male god and a human female, but rarely the reverse. (Genesis 6:1-2; Daniel 2:43; 2 Peter 2:4-5)

aura, as if they were standing in front of a brilliant, yet invisible light source.

The creatures did not simply walk into the conference room where the ten World Union leaders had gathered, but they also did not appear instantly in a sudden flash. The members had been discussing the latest status reports of each of their respective Unions when three strange lights began to appear in the front of the room, to the right of the Secretary's chair.

The lights had started as faint glowing spheres and then slowing took on three distinct humanoid shapes. As the members stared in surprise at the shining lights taking shape before them, three elegant creatures stepped out of the light to stand next to the Secretary. They each raised their right hands in a gesture of friendship and peace, and greeted the members in several of their native languages.

The delegates nervously rose to their feet and greeted them in a similar gesture, and immediately introduced themselves. The creatures of light likewise introduced themselves – they called themselves the "Anshar", which meant "the Foremost of the Heavens".

The Anshar lost no time in stating their purposes for appearing to the World Union leaders. They had come to seek permission to reveal themselves to all mankind, and to help man move into a time of complete peace and prosperity. Once perfected, man would then be able to leave the confines of their own planet to begin exploring the stars as the Anshar did. They had come to help man finally move beyond earth and seek new homes in the stars beyond.

The Anshar mesmerized the delegates of the World Union – their appearance and mannerisms seemed so much higher than their own. When asked their names, the Anshar stated that they had no individual names, but were all known simply as the Anshar. Individuality was a source of conflict that they had long ago expelled from their natures, and had evolved towards a collective consciousness. Though separate and distinct, they were completely one in thought, word, and deed – complete unity.

They had long ago discovered the secret to immortality, and

had been interacting with man for thousands of years. Sometimes they had appeared to mankind in the past as they were to the delegates, but more often they had worked quietly, invisibly on behalf of humanity.

But they had chosen this time to finally reveal themselves to mankind since humanity was now at a critical juncture in its evolution. Either it would progress and move forward towards the path the Anshar had been on for millennia, or they would regress back to barbarians and enter a vast era of darkness. In ancient times, the Anshar had been known by their general term of "the Watchers", but they had also revealed themselves to other cultures and peoples in the past by other names.

Rather than stay hidden and simply watch mankind any longer, the Anshar had decided to present themselves first to the leaders of the world and work with them to help all of humanity progress to the next great chapter in the story of man.

*   *   *

The World Union immediately welcomed the Anshar and promised to provide them with any support they would need. The delegates moved quickly, and began leaking information to the media and pushing studies about how extraterrestrial contact would help unify the peoples of the earth in peace and prosperity. Also, the Anshar began appearing in the skies more frequently and for longer periods of time. The number of video clips posted on the Internet increased dramatically, and there was little doubt even among the skeptics that something extraterrestrial had indeed come to earth.

Both the World Union leaders and the Anshar carefully gauged the public's responses and noted that the general population was not frightened of the increased contact. In the majority of surveys, it appeared that the people were ready for the extraterrestrials to be revealed. Not only were the people ready, but it was also shown that their revelation would help the World Union further win the peoples' trust.

Prominent astronomers consulted with the World Union

CHRIS HAMBLETON

leaders, and they reasoned that if a race of beings were capable
of traveling beyond their own star system and come to the earth,
then they must be a peaceful, brilliant race that was far superior
to mankind. And from the recent nuclear exchanges that had
killed millions of people, the world was desperate for some sort
of external, superior guidance. With such overwhelming statistics, the World Union and the Anshar jointly decided that mankind was ready to take the next step.

On June 1st, the World Union leaders held a press conference and formally introduced the Anshar to the populace. The
news immediately filled all the news networks, radio stations,
and the Internet. There was a small amount of panic and even
several thousand suicides across the world. The Anshar had been
prepared to withdraw if the response suddenly turned over-
whelmingly negative, but the general population had received
them just as warmly as the World Union had.

The Anshar were welcomed by all the peoples, and the hope
of a better future for all mankind was rekindled.

*   *   *

Ruth watched the television in stunned disbelief, and felt a
tremor run through her as if the ground was shaking. But it
wasn't another earthquake – it was her very faith being shaken.
Incredible creatures from beyond the solar system had come to
the earth and had been introduced the public. Her parents seemed
anxious too, but not for the same reasons as she was.

She had been so sure of what had been written in the Bible
and what she had been studying and listening to. But now with
the arrival of the Anshar, was everything she believed mere fables and stories? Her faith had grown tremendously over the last
year, but now it no longer seemed to matter.

The Anshar were not ghastly or too unnatural as they had
been portrayed in movies and comics for decades, but very much
like humans. The creatures were not frightening in the least, and
they genuinely seemed to want to help mankind through these
difficult times. They said they had come to bring humanity into

96

the next phase of existence – the eternal phase – and after the last few years, it seemed like everyone was ready for that.

Somehow, it still seemed so surreal – like everyone in the world suddenly knew they were no longer alone and something larger and greater than themselves existed, and they could now see it as clearly as the sun. On some level, it even felt more real than when the Magog Invasion had been thwarted, since they could now see the force behind the supernatural occurrences in the world. She could almost feel that the people, tribes, and nations would realize that many of their problems and differences were insignificant and petty now that Others had come.

How would the world change with their very presence? She had a thought that the greatest changes would be in what people believed and the collective worldview. The public had been so unstable ever since the Magog Invasion, and the arrival of the Anshar would give them renewed hope for a better future. Mankind would unite and move forward together, fully embracing the new future that was being offered to them.

In some ways, it felt like the world was in the middle of a game of supernatural tug-of-war, going from the Magog Invasion, to the discovery of Noah's Ark, and now to the revelation of the Anshar.

But in some odd way, she felt as if she had been preparing for this latest revelation, but it was still shocking to her that it was actually happening. She had listened to several recent Bible studies that predicted that Satan might present himself or his angels as aliens of another world or galaxy. At the time it had been produced, it had been highly speculative, of course, yet now these extraterrestrials had come.

Many cults and strange teachings had begun with revelations from "beings of light" or other "heavenly visions". One Bible series had also gone over all the passages in the Bible describing the strange signs in the stars, sun, moon, and sky that would accompany the End Times that had been prophesied, which many Christians believed that the world was now entering.

She went to her room and quietly closed the door, and knelt down beside her bed to pray. Slowly, her mind and her heart became calm, and His familiar peace came back in. She asked Him to give her clarity, wisdom, and peace during these strange times, and for the ability to discern truth from lies.

Ruth then petitioned Him for her family and friends, and that He would approach them soon and that they would each be awakened to Him. And then she simply waited in His presence and the calmness of their time together. When she opened her eyes, she realized that over an hour had passed.

She rose and retrieved her Bible from her desk drawer and opened it to Matthew 24 and then read and reread the chapter. One verse in particular jumped out at her – the 24th verse: *"For there shall arise false Christs, and false prophets, and shall show great signs and wonders; insomuch that, if it were possible, they shall deceive the very elect."*

These were the words of Yeshua Himself, and He was warning His followers to be very cautious and skeptical of what would happen in the last days. From the passage, it was clear that the very sights that they saw could be deceptive.

How could she know if the Anshar really were who they said they were? And then her hours of Bible studies came back to her – she would know whose side the Anshar were on by how they regarded Yeshua, His incarnation and His resurrection.

If they dismissed Him as just another religious teacher or magician, or even if they said He had been one of them, she would know that they were false and should not be regarded as anything more than lying spirits or false teachers. From numerous passages in the Bible, she knew that the Anshar would probably even work miracles and perform signs and wonders to convince mankind to follow them and their teachings.

She carefully considered His Words again, and felt as if she were one of those elect who was on the verge of being deceived. But then she reread it again, and focused on the "if it were possible" phrase, and the implication made her smile. Indeed, if she were truly one of His own, then she could not be deceived, no matter what strange occurrence took place on the earth or in the heavens.

And then she shuddered as she contemplated the opposite

case: those who were not believers in Yeshua would most likely be deceived by the Anshar. Her friends and family were all vulnerable, and it would be up to her to help them see what was really happening.

And if talking to them about Yeshua had been difficult, speaking against the Anshar might be even worse.

* * *

The Anshar were very open and frequently available to the press and the public, but they always stayed together, and would not appear alone or even in twos. Some religious scholars immediately came to the conclusion that the Anshar were the foundation of the concept of the Trinity, since the Three Beings operated in complete unity as one, yet all three were distinct.

The scholars and the media began speaking of the Anshar as perhaps being God, since they were so much greater than mankind and had been apparently living for thousands upon thousands of years. The Anshar presented themselves to the public as man's savior, helper, and even their creator, to some extent. They had come to protect the human race from another horrific destruction, and to help them make the transition from the earth to the stars.

Both the secularists and the more liberal religious people quickly began to view the Anshar as the Supreme Beings that had formed the basis of all the religions of the world, whether it was the God of the Jews and Christians, Allah of the Muslims, or the gods of the Buddhists, Hindus, or the other many religions.

When asked about both the recent and ancient historical events that had been miraculous, the Anshar took credit for many of the supernatural events throughout history, such as many of the miracles in the Bible and the Koran, and even the recent destruction of the Magog Invasion armies. Several times, mankind had nearly been destroyed, and the Anshar had always intervened to save them from certain destruction.

The Anshar provided many details concerning their interaction throughout man's history. They had been in existence for several hundred thousand years, and had slowly guided the earth's creatures in their onward, upward path of evolution. Nearly ten thousand years ago, the Anshar had finally helped man reach self-consciousness, and had dwelt alongside him. They had taught the ancient humans many of their sciences and mathematics. Mankind was quickly evolving towards immortality. Great strength, long life spans, and incredible intelligence were common among men.

But the Elohim and their leader Yahweh, had vowed to prevent man from ever reaching eternal life except through them. Yahweh was selfish and terribly jealous, and had waged a long war against the Anshar. If man became immortal and joined the Anshar, they would overwhelm Yahweh and his armies. He and the Elohim drove the Anshar from the earth after destroying their laboratories on the planet of Nibiru, which thereafter became the asteroid belt.

After forcing the Anshar to retreat from the earth, Yahweh had sent the Great Flood over the earth to completely destroy everyone and everything in it, and force the earth back to its primordial state. But the Anshar had saved and protected a man and his family in a large boat, along with many of the kinds of creatures that roamed the earth.

After the Great Flood had destroyed the earth, the Elohim withdrew and prevented the Anshar from returning to renew their efforts to help mortal man evolve into immortal beings. But the handful of survivors of the Great Flood remembered the Anshar and their knowledge of science, mathematics, and history for many years and preserved them in the ancient writings of the Sumerians.

When Yahweh returned to earth a few centuries later, he was enraged to discover that man had been saved and was once again thriving and evolving. But instead of destroying them again, he confused their languages and changed their skin colors to cause them to war against each other. Also, he greatly damaged the environment to shorten the life spans of all creatures and mankind, forcing them to spend most of their energy just trying to survive.

But now the Anshar had returned to the earth to save mankind from fulfilling the curse that Yahweh and the Elohim had placed upon them. Man had now reached the same knowledge of science and mathematics and knowledge of the universe that they had achieved before the Great Flood.

The Anshar had come to protect them from any future threats by Yahweh and his cohorts. Once mankind evolved into their immortal state, they would no longer need to fear Yahweh or the Elohim. The Anshar valued freedom and democracy above all; any other form of government – especially kingdoms – was of Yahweh and the Elohim, who wished only to enslave others or enslave them for their vile purposes.

By joining with the Anshar, mankind could prevent the terrible destruction of the Great Flood from being repeated.

* * *

After the people had grown accustomed to the presence and all the media coverage of the Anshar, they began teaching about the next steps that the human race would be going through in their evolution. Just as with childbirth, both the infant (the people) and the mother (the earth) must go through a traumatic time of transition from their current existence in mortality to their next phase of existence: immortality.

Both the earth and its inhabitants were about to enter a time of refinement and trials, and they must persevere and unite if they were to succeed. The Anshar were there to help guide and protect mankind through the most challenging time in their history, but when the times of trial were completed, the people would be just like the Anshar in body, in mind, and in spirit. To their mortal eyes, they would become as gods.

The people of the earth must also fully embrace their future. They would all be tested to help them prepare for the day when Yahweh and the Elohim returned, which they surely would. Before the Great Flood, the Anshar had not asked mankind to help them in their own struggle against their Enemy, but this time they would. It would take both the Anshar and mankind to defeat the Elohim and forever overcome them. If they failed, they could expect either barbaric enslavement or complete destruction of the human race and the entire earth.

The Anshar only requested that they be provided with a permanent location from which they could counsel the World Union and the peoples of the earth during the time of transition. The World Union, with the full support of most of the world, offered them any location and any accommodations they would require.

The Anshar decided to take up residence at Babylon, one of the oldest cities on the earth both for cultural significance and for strategic significance. The Anshar would honor the Sumerians, the last group of people who had remembered them with much clarity.

Babylon also happened to be at nearly the exact geographical center of all the lands of the earth, and was also within a nation that had just recovered from a brutal history of terrorism and tyrannical rule. Iraq was a living example of how different warring peoples uniting for a common cause against insurmountable odds. Iraq and Babylon would help give everyone hope.

Iraq would be the best place to demonstrate just how much the Anshar could help the earth through her time of trial.

*   *   *

For the second time that year, the entire Rosenberg family was gathered together. Ruth was happy that Saul was home, and Ahban had also surprised them at the last minute by stopping by just before the evening meal. She had never been very close to her oldest brother, since he was nearly ten years older than she was.

She had been a small child when he had left to go to college. He was very opinionated and frequently boisterous, and from his obvious skepticism, she knew it was pointless in talking to him seriously about God. Arguments and debates rarely led anyone to Christ, and frequently caused more to divide than unite.

They had a wonderful Shavuot dinner and celebrated the holiday in the traditional Jewish way. Ruth celebrated it in the Christian way silently, and after dinner they all relaxed on the patio on the roof. The news of the Anshar took up most of the conversation, and Ruth did not say much about them; she just listened, for the most part.

Ahban seemed to be very excited about them, while most of the others were curious but still unsure what to make of them. Ruth chatted with Saul for a while about his job hunting, and they stayed on the roof long after the others went back downstairs.

"So, what do you think about them?" Saul asked her. "I noticed you clammed up during dinner whenever they were mentioned."

"Who? The aliens?" she said. He nodded. "Well –" she started to tell him and then hesitated. "Can you keep a secret?"

"Sure – from who? Mom and Dad, or just everyone in general? If it's just Mom and Dad, you can count on me," he said, joking around with her.

She smiled. "Mainly Mom and Dad, and probably Ahban. I don't think he would understand or agree, and I want to tell them myself."

"Okay. What is it?" he asked.

"Well, I've become a Christian," she said quietly. "After the invasion, I started reading the Bible, and a few months later I was saved."

"Wow!" he said. "You're right – you shouldn't tell Ahban!" He wasn't quite as shocked as she had expected him to be, and that was a relief.

"How do you think they'll react? Mom and Dad, I mean?" she asked.

"I don't know – they don't talk about Christians much, or Yeshua at all for that matter. Mom will probably be okay with it, but Dad might have a tough time. You know, from his family background and all."

She nodded, remembering that several of her father's relatives had been slaughtered in the Holocaust. Much of what Hitler had done had been overlooked, if not publicly sanctioned, by many German churches, and then they had helped give sanctuary to the war criminals later.

"What do you think about it?" she asked.

"I don't know. I mean, it's your choice and all. To be honest with you, I've been reading the Bible here and there over the last few months too. I sort of stopped after the news of the Anshar, and I'm not really sure what to do with it next. It's all so confusing," he said in a half-joking tone.

She nodded and smiled. "I know. I guess I'm the opposite – I've been reading it more since they've come!"

"Really? So, what's your verdict?" he asked.

"Well, I've been reading everything I can about them and what they're saying, and also checking out what some other Christians think about them. Some think they're satanic – that they're just lying and saying they're advanced creatures instead of being evil spirits. Others think they are who they say they are, and that they're from another star system and all that."

"That's interesting. But what if God and a lot of the things that happened in the Bible really are the Anshar or the Elohim?"

"I thought about that for a while," she replied, "and the Bible talks a lot about 'signs in the heavens' and 'lying wonders' and other strange things in the End Times. The Bible says that in the last days, the whole world will go after Satan and follow him. Few people would willingly worship Satan if they know who he is, but if he disguises himself as an extraterrestrial, most people would. Just look at how everyone is so enamored with the Anshar!"

"What about evolution and all that?" he asked. "You know, the Anshar have been saying that they helped us evolve and gave the ancient civilizations all the skills and knowledge they needed to get to where we are today. How does evolution fit into the Bible and the Anshar?"

Ruth smiled. "That's something else I've been reading a lot about. Evolution has always contradicted the Bible, and it's been interesting to see how the Anshar have tied it in to their story of our history. Several people in the forums have advocated that the entire theory of evolution was just a stepping stone for the Anshar's false account of our history."

"I'm not following you – what do you mean?"

"Well, for many years the schools taught that random

chance and many mutations over millions or billions of years had brought about our evolution, instead of being supernaturally created. But over and over, the evidence and biochemistry proved them wrong, and the theory was in decline. Yet now the same people that peddled evolution have completely bought the Anshar's story, even though it opposes their own theories."

He nodded thoughtfully, and she continued.

"Both the Anshar account and the Biblical account are supernatural, but one is acceptable to the world and one is not. What if the real purpose of the theory of evolution was to just break down everyone's faith in God and relegate that to only religion and myth? But when it became clear that there had to be another supernatural force at work in the world, it opened everyone up to accepting the Anshar and their story. But they are not open to God any more."

Saul scratched his chin. "I never thought of it that way. You might be onto something, I suppose. Do you have a book or something I could borrow to read up on that stuff?"

"No, but I can send you some websites and some of my MP3s. I didn't want Mom and Dad to find any books lying around before I was ready," she said.

"Okay. Are you alright with everything that's happening around here?"

"Actually, I am now. I was pretty upset when they first arrived. But after I did some reading and prayed about it, I feel a lot better about what's going on." She paused for a moment. "Hey, Saul? I'm serious about not telling anyone, especially Mom and Dad. I don't want them to know until I'm ready."

He nodded, and then they continued talking until they were too tired to speak anymore.

CHAPTER 5
THE GREAT VANISHING

S oon after the Anshar had gained the public's trust, they began to provide more details of the times that would soon be coming upon the earth. Most people trusted them implicitly, and the more the Anshar described of their previous interventions in human history, the more secure the people were in their beliefs that the Anshar had indeed come to help and protect them.

There had not even been a hint of violence or hidden motives on their part, and the people had been watching them very carefully on television and the Internet for weeks. And now the people had grown comfortable with their presence and with the fact the human race was no longer alone in the universe.

But the Anshar began to make more and more strange, metaphysical predictions. They warned of a series of widespread natural disasters that would befall the earth over the next few years, and the emergence of a great World Leader who was destined to rise and be their representative on the earth. This man would represent mankind before the Anshar, and the Anshar before all mankind.

The Anshar had promised this great leader many millennia before, as recorded by the Sumerians and other ancient cultures. But Yahweh had attempted to deceive man two thousand years before with his own counterfeit, namely Jesus of Nazareth. They warned that even his name was evil and should not be spoken, even as curses.

This counterfeit leader had caused millions of deaths from

his false teachings of submission and unquestioning obedience. The Anshar warned the public emphatically about him and his teachings, and not to believe his followers or his disciples' writings, primarily the New Testament of the Bible. Christians were shocked at the implications, and immediately Bibles began being pulled from the bookshelves and removed from the Internet.

This promised World Leader would be fully Anshar and also fully human – the very order of Supreme Being that all people would evolve into once the times of trial were completed. He would have the authority of the Anshar to act on their behalf, and also have the authority of the World Union. The supreme goal of this great leader would be to unify mankind in mind, spirit, and soul as much as possible, so they could make the next leap in their evolutionary progression.

The arrival of the World Leader would then immediately be followed by a seven-year period of trials and conflicts that would envelope the world. Nation would rise against nation, and Union against Union, and even brother against brother and sister against sister. But this World Leader would guide them through these conflicts and would help them continue the evolutionary process.

Even the earth and nature would seem to rage against mankind and itself, as it struggled to move into the realm of the metaphysical. The remnants of Yahweh's previous corruption of the earth must be purged before the earth could move forward. Even the stars and the heavens would appear to change as the earth and her creatures entered into the next phase of their existence. But in the end, the earth and mankind would unite as one and move into the Golden Age – the greatest time the earth and its inhabitants had ever known.

Of course, there would be some people, tribes, and even nations who would refuse to conform and adapt, and these would have to be re-educated and re-trained, so they could then accompany the rest of humanity. There would be no one left behind in the evolutionary process. The Anshar described it as removing the slower children from a classroom in order to unburden the other students, to allow them to move ahead faster. Thus the "less-conforming" people would need to be removed from the earth to help the rest of mankind press forward. After the seven years of trials, the Anshar would help mankind build the world anew from the destruction of the trials, and then they would begin dwelling in the heavens above.

The children of the earth held the future of mankind, and these would be the easiest to train and unify for the common cause of moving onwards. The Anshar declared that nearly all the children would be removed from the earth before the trials began, so they would be completely protected during the perilous days ahead. For their own safety, they would be taken to avoid any violence and resistance from their parents and others.

Instead of mourning their children, the parents should rejoice that they were safe, and that the World Leader would soon come. While away from the earth, the children of the earth would all be trained to think, feel, and live as one – they would be the first of the new race of man, destined for eternal immortality among the stars. They would be the first and foremost of the new race – a great privilege. They would no longer be pre-disposed to hatred or war or disunity by the corruption of the Elohim. And their removal from the earth and seven years of special training would be critical to the evolution of mankind.

As expected, many of the parents were frightened and protective of their children, but eventually the continuous speeches about the coming trials and the comforting approval of the media alleviated many of their fears. The Anshar revealed a few of their massive spacecraft orbiting the earth and showed everyone the beautiful living quarters that the children and the others would be living in. Of course, every parent wanted their children protected from harm and danger, and once again the Anshar provided reassurance for those on the earth. Parents would be selfish and evil if they wanted their children to remain with them during the trials – which was why they would have no choice in the matter when the time came.

When exactly the children and the others would be taken not even the Anshar would tell. But the earth was now rushing onwards in its evolution, and when it was ready to begin its trials, the Anshar would know and remove the children to complete comfort and safety. The Anshar reiterated time and time again that the earth itself was a living, conscious organism, and she had to evolve into her next phase so she and her inhabitants could fully dwell with one another in peace.

*   *   *

Ruth stared at the laptop screen and drew a deep breath. She had double-checked the enrollment form several times already, but was still hesitant to click the "Submit Application" button. How incredible, she thought, that with the simple click of a button on a web page, her entire life would change. She closed her eyes, said a short prayer, and then clicked.

Filling out the online enrollment form to join Zion's Harvest and become a missionary had been the easy part. But now she would have to tell her parents, especially since she would have to move in a few weeks. She had prayed over her decision for weeks, and the Lord was clearly telling her to be unafraid and honest with her family and friends. Now that the form had been submitted, she knew she couldn't put it off any longer.

She decided to start with her parents, but only one at a time. She would tell her mother first, since she had been an American for the first part of her life and had been exposed to a wide variety of Christians. Christians were a mixed bag in Israel, especially in Jerusalem – many were on the extreme side and frequently disruptive and rude. The latest pronouncements from the Anshar had increased the anti-Christian attitudes throughout the world, and had made it difficult to find Bibles and other Christian literature. But they weren't being persecuted, at least not yet.

Her mother's reaction would help determine how she approached her father, unless her mother became too upset and told him first. After she told them, she wasn't quite as concerned about telling the rest of her family – Ahban and some of her other relatives would be upset, but they weren't nearly as close to her as her parents were.

"What was the worst that could happen?" she thought, trying

to bolster her courage. "Kick me out of the house?" But she prayed it wouldn't come to that.

She wanted to leave with the relationships intact as much as possible. Her feelings for them had not changed since she had converted – in fact, her feelings for many of them had grown. As she had matured in her faith, she became acutely aware of how hard her parents had worked and sacrificed to give her and her brothers a decent life, especially in the midst of all the terrorism in recent years. She was very grateful, and had grown to love them on a much deeper level, even though they probably had no idea of how she felt.

Some of her "comfort verses" while she had struggled with the issue were the passages of Matthew 10, which spoke of how if anyone loved their parents or spouses more than Yeshua, then they were not worthy of Him, and about how they would receive many more brothers, sisters, mothers, and fathers in Heaven.

She also knew (almost by heart), the verses about how God is a father to the fatherless, and a protector of the orphaned. As she had grown in her faith and struggled with the impact her new beliefs would have upon her life and her family, she came to understand that she had already traded her earthly family for a heavenly family when she had become a believer. It was just that her earthly family did not know that the spiritual exchange had already taken place.

Ruth took another deep breath and gathered her courage. It was now or never. She went downstairs, where she found her mother reading a magazine. Her father was working on the computer in his home office, and she could hear the television playing quietly in the background. He always liked to keep the news on while he worked, and even did so at his office.

"Hi Mom – can we talk for a minute? It's kind of important," Ruth said nervously.

Naomi looked up and saw the serious look on her daughter's face, and promptly put the magazine down. "Sure. Would you like to go for a walk?" she asked.

Ruth nodded. "That would be great." She knew she appeared nervous, and tried to calm her emotions.

THE TIME OF JACOB'S TROUBLE

Naomi got up from the couch and they headed for the back door. "We'll be back in a minute, dear," she called to her husband. He muttered a reply to acknowledge that he had heard and they stepped outside.

After they had walked half a block, Ruth decided to just go ahead and tell her. "Mom, I've decided not to go to college in the fall." Immediately after she had said it, she chided herself for not telling her mother about her faith first, and then her decision.

"What? When did you decide this?" Naomi replied with surprise.

They hadn't really talked about much about college lately, since Ruth had been accepted at several good schools already. With all that had been happening in Israel over the last year, they had figured she would simply choose one that summer and enroll.

"Well, about a month ago, to be honest," she said.

"Oh, what are you going to do next year then? Of course, you're welcome to stay at home, but sooner or later you'll need to decide what you're going to do with your life." Naomi turned gave her a very serious look.

"I know," she nodded. "Actually, I've enrolled in a program in Tel Aviv," she admitted.

"Really? What program is that?"

"Well, it's for field work with Zion's Harvest." She realized she could have said 'missionary work', but 'field work' didn't sound quite as intense.

Naomi stopped walking. "Zion's Harvest? Aren't they one of those fringe groups?" she said.

The look on her face was one of both shock and concern, as if her daughter had just mentioned that she had joined a neo-Nazi group.

"They're not a fringe group, Mom. They're just a messianic ministry that witnesses to Jewish people."

"But they're Christian, right? You know how unpopular they are, especially now." And she was right.

Ruth nodded, "I know." The Anshar seemed to have a particular disregard for Christians, which sometimes helped her know that she was on the right path.

"How will you take care of yourself? Will they be providing food and housing for you?" her mother asked.

"Yes, for the most part. The Israel branch is largely supported from the other branches, especially from the United States. But since the invasion, many others have joined them here and it's been growing, so they pay for a lot of it. At least it was until recently."

Naomi sighed and then fell silent. "This is quite a surprise. I'll need to talk to your father about it."

"Actually, Mom, can you let me tell him on my own? It's something I think he should hear from me, instead of someone else."

"Alright," her mother said.

They walked in silence for another block or so, letting the announcement sink in, and then Ruth began to speak again.

"Mom, I'm sorry I didn't tell you sooner. I just wasn't sure how to break it to you and Dad," she said

"I understand – it's just some very big news. We thought you'd be going off to the university soon; I guess we had no idea you had other plans, especially since you had such good grades your last year."

Ruth nodded. She had received decent grades through most of school, but the last year, she had gotten the best ones of her entire time in school.

"So, I assume you're a Christian now, right? When did you decide that?"

"Well, I started reading the Bible soon after the Invasion, and a few months later I decided to accept Yeshua as my Savior." Ruth paused for a moment before continuing, "Mom, I'm really sorry – I feel like I've been keeping this big secret from everyone for the last year, and it's a big relief to finally be able to tell you."

And then for the first time on their walk, Ruth finally smiled and began to relax somewhat. She was so glad she had told her mother first, who was much more understanding than her father probably would be.

"I did notice that you seemed different over the last year. I had attributed it to you just growing up, but I guess it was something else," she said.

This time, her mother smiled also, and as they walked by a frozen yogurt shop, she offered to buy them dessert, and Ruth agreed.

They finished the rest of the evening reminiscing over the last year and talking about Ruth's upcoming plans. If her mother was unhappy or displeased with her, she hid it well.

* * *

Later that night after returning from the walk, Naomi thought about the news that Ruth had shared with her. She was a little disappointed that Ruth wasn't going straight off to college, but she felt a little better about her decision than she first had.

Ahban was in Tel Aviv, and maybe he could check up on her every once in a while, or at least give her a hand if she needed it. That thought gave her some comfort.

Maybe it was just a phase Ruth was going through – the invasion and its repulsion had been truly miraculous, and many in the nation had turned to religion after it was over. And now with the arrival of the Anshar and all their strange predictions, she could understand how Ruth needed something solid to cling to.

Surely joining a ministry was better than her messing around or doing nothing the first year or two out of school.

All things considered, Naomi felt a certain sense of peace about it. Ruth was not really prone to extremes, and her behavior over the last year had been wonderful. At times it had felt like a well-mannered adult was living with them, instead of a typical emotional, erratic teenager.

But Jacob probably wouldn't feel that way about it, and that made her uneasy.

* * *

Ruth knocked on the door of her father's home-office. "Hi Dad, are you busy?"

"Come in, sweetheart. No, I'm just looking over some invoices." Jacob looked up from a small stack of papers. He was wearing his reading glasses, and looked like he needed a break.

"Okay. Do you have a few minutes?" she asked.

"Sure. What's on your mind?" he said, putting the papers down in front of him on the desk, among the other piles of papers and binders that were scattered about. He had never been one for much of an organized desk, but he did know where everything was (unless someone tried to tidy things up for him).

Ruth was nervous, even more than she had been when she had spoken to her mother about the same subject only a few days earlier. Her mouth was suddenly dry, and her voice was shaky. She had decided to try a slightly different approach than she had with her mother, and maybe that would help.

"Dad, I've decided not to go to school here this fall. I'm going to move to Tel Aviv and find an apartment there."

"Oh, really? Well, that's some news. When did you decide that?" he asked, taking off his reading glasses and putting them on the stack of invoices.

"A couple weeks ago. I told Mom a few days ago," she said. So far, so good.

"What will you be doing there? You're going to school there, right?" he said, in his serious, fatherly tone.

She nodded and swallowed, deciding to push forward with it.

"Actually, I've decided to join a ministry working with people there."

"A ministry? What are you talking about? I thought we were talking about college."

She could feel herself starting to tremble, "I know, Dad. But I don't think it's the right time for me to go to college right now. It's not that I never want to – just not next year."

His eyes narrowed, and he began to get past his initial surprise at her news. What was so bad about taking a year off before starting college? Not much, he supposed – as long as she did something worthwhile. He would not be paying for her to have a long vacation for the next year or two.

"Alright – a year off isn't that bad. What are you going to do for work? We can't really afford to put you up in an apartment and pay your bills in Tel Aviv," he said, matter-of-factly.

"Well, the ministry gives us a living allowance, and I figured I'd get a job at another coffee shop or something. Besides, I'm sure I'll get a roommate or two."

She had debated on how to refer to the ministry for awhile, but in the end, she figured that it would be best to just call it what it was.

"Hmmm," he grimaced, rubbing his brow. "Now, what exactly is this ministry about? Is it for them?" he asked, pointing to the sky – probably referring to the Anshar.

"No. It's not for them. It's for a regular ministry – you know, like for a church." She was speaking a little quieter now, trying not be get too much on the defensive.

"A church? You mean for Christians?" he said, reacting with much more surprise than when she had first broke the news of not going to college.

Ruth nodded. She had figured that if they had gotten this far, this would be the issue that put him over the edge, figuratively speaking.

"Do you mean to say then that you're a Christian too? When did this happen?"

He was visibly irritated now, and he could feel his face growing hot. Jewish Christians were typically regarded as traitors or lunatics in Israel. With the arrival of the Anshar, the number of Christians and the affiliation of people in other religious groups was dropping rapidly. And now to think that his own daughter was now one of them was almost more than he could take.

She nodded again, and then took a breath and plunged ahead.

"I became a believer about a year ago. I'm sorry I didn't tell you sooner, Dad. It took me a while to figure things out."

He did not say anything further, but just shook his head in disbelief.

"I'm sorry, but I'm still surprised about all this. For God's

CHRIS HAMBLETON

sake, how can you be a Christian, after all that's happened? I mean, they're here now, and they've explained where all the religions came from in the first place," he stated.

And they had – the Anshar had been telling the world that they had founded all the religions, but many of them had gone astray over time, and now they had come to set them straight again. All that is, except for Christianity.

"I know, Dad. I know that it sounds weird, but I just don't believe them. I hear what they say, but I don't think they are who they say they are."

"So who are they then?" he asked, still upset.

"I think they're evil – or worse." She said the last part very quietly. She didn't really want to have that discussion at this time, and she hoped it would just go away.

"Well, that's what they say about Yeshua and the Christians!" he exclaimed. "The Anshar were the ones that saved us during the invasion! If you want to call them evil, you should read what the Christians have done for the last two thousand years!"

He paused for a moment and then began in a low, serious voice, "You know, if you're going to go off and join some cult, I can't stop you, but you may find yourself to be on your own."

He was almost as surprised as she was to have heard those words coming out of his own mouth, but it was too late to take them back.

At that, Ruth began to cry – it had gone about the way she had expected, except worse. She had prayed it wouldn't end that way, but it had.

"I'm sorry, Dad. I didn't mean to disappoint you, but I have to do what I think is right for me," she said, her voice breaking. She turned and rushed out of the room.

Jacob sighed and leaned back in his chair, rubbing his brow. How had this all happened just now? Why had he reacted that way? But he was still stunned that she had become a Christian, let alone her joining a ministry instead of going to college.

* * *

116

THE TIME OF JACOB'S TROUBLE

The next week passed quickly, and Ruth began packing to move to Tel Aviv. She and her mother seemed to be back to normal, but her relationship with her father had been strained. They hadn't really spoken much since she had broke the news to him, in fact. They didn't avoid each other, but there was clearly an air of tension whenever they were in the same room. That made Naomi irritated and sad, and she spoke to Jacob several times to him to try to make peace, but he was being too stubborn.

Ruth was regretful about what had happened too, but she had told him as gently as she knew how. It wasn't the delivery of the message that he had rejected, but the message itself. She could almost understand how he felt, but she still found it hard to believe he felt that way about something she loved. She knew that much of the history of Christianity was sordid, especially towards her own people. But they that had acted in the name of Jesus or the Church had not been following the Bible, but whatever worldly power that was acting on its own authority. The Church leadership had often acted in stark opposition to the doctrines put forth in the Bible, and often they had even supplanted the Bible with their own teachings.

She wouldn't be taking much with her when she moved, other than clothes and a few personal items such as some books, her laptop, and a small envelope of pictures. For the most part, her room in her parents' house would be left as it was. Eventually, they would convert it into a guest room or something else, but her mother had promised her that they wouldn't be doing anything with it for at least a few years. She hadn't said so in as many words, but Ruth figured that was so they could leave it available for her in case she changed her mind or needed to move back home. And that gave her some measure of comfort, just knowing that she still had a familiar place to call "home".

"Hey, Ruth – moving somewhere?" a familiar voice asked, coming from the doorway. Ruth looked up to see Saul standing there. Instantly her face brightened and she looked up at him with a big smile.

"Hi! What are you doing home?" she exclaimed, walking over to give him a sisterly hug.

"Well, Mom called me the other day and said that you were moving out, and I figured I'd see you off before you left home."

"That's nice. How have you been?" she asked.

"Good. I'm getting settled in at the new job – so far, so good," he said. A few weeks before, he had accepted an offer at a technology company in downtown Haifa, and hadn't had much time to talk with her lately.

"You like it then?"

"Yeah, we're working on a release for next month, and that's keeping everyone very busy. I should've negotiated to be paid by the hour – I'd be making a ton of money!" he said wryly. She smiled at his comment; he was the same old Saul.

"Thanks for coming – things have been rough around here lately." She looked away and went back to her packing.

"I heard. Do you want me to talk to Dad about it?" he asked.

"No – it's okay. He'll come around sometime," she said, more out of hope than anything else.

"Are you alright?" he said with serious concern.

"Yeah, I'll be okay. It's just sad sometimes when I think about it. He couldn't understand how I could still believe in God with the Anshar here and all."

He nodded and hesitated for a moment, as if he had been thinking about the same questions lately.

"Hey, I started listening to some of those MP3s you sent me," he said. "There's some interesting things in there."

"Really? That's great!"

"Can I ask you something?" he asked. She nodded and then he continued.

"What do you think about those things the Anshar are talking about? You know, with the big disappearances that are supposed to be happening one of these days. Isn't that kind of bizarre?"

"Yeah, it is kind of surprising. But did you know that many Christians believe the Bible says the same thing, but with a different explanation?" she stated.

"No kidding. What's that?" he asked.

"Well, in Christianity, it's called the 'Rapture'. The Bible's explanation for it is that all the faithful believers in Yeshua are to be instantly removed from the earth and taken to Heaven, so they will not experience the Tribulation."

"The Tribulation?" he asked, with a puzzled look.

"You know, when the Anti-Christ comes and institutes the Mark of the Beast, '666', and all that. You've heard of Armageddon, right?" He nodded that he had.

"Do you believe all that?"

"Yes, I do. Something's just not right about them," she said, referring to the Anshar. "When I see them on TV or listen what they're saying, it just doesn't sound right. I mean, what they say sounds reasonable and all from one point of view, but I get a weird feeling about it. It's like they're not quite telling the complete story, or that they're not telling us the whole truth."

"Huh," he said, as if not knowing what to say next. "I haven't really made up my mind about them yet. I guess I want to just wait and see what happens."

"Some of the Christians I chat with on the web think that they're telling everyone that the vanishings will happen beforehand, so everyone will be prepared for them when they actually occur. They've been talking more and more about them, too."

"Hmm. That kind of makes sense, I suppose," he said, starting to get a little uncomfortable. "Anything I can help you with?" he asked, changing the subject.

"Sure," she said, pointing to some of her books. Ruth could tell that he didn't want to talk anymore about the Rapture and the Anshar, and she didn't really blame him.

Saul helped her finish packing, and they chatted mostly about where she would be living in Tel Aviv and what she would be doing. She would be leaving tomorrow, and it was nice for them to have one last talk before she moved out.

She had felt alone in her own home for weeks, and it lifted her spirits to have her brother there.

*　*　*

Ruth had just come home from her classes for the day, and

was going through her mail when she heard the doorbell ring. Her new roommate was supposed to be moving in tomorrow, but maybe she had arrived early.

She put down the mail and went to answer the door. She was about to open it when she remembered to look through the peep-hole first, which she had rarely done back at home. Even though she was living in a safe area of Tel Aviv, you could never be too careful as a single young woman.

It was Ahban! He had been away on business when she had moved in, and he must have just come back. She opened the door and gave him a huge smile.

"Hi, little sister!" he exclaimed, and gave her a hug as she welcomed him inside. He glanced around for a moment. "How do you like this place?" he asked.

The apartment was small but comfortable, and quite average for a typical student in Israel. The carpet was cheap and the lino-leum in the tiny kitchen had seen better days, but at least it was fairly clean.

"It's been great. You know, it's a little scary being out on my own and all, but I'm getting used to it. My roommate is supposed to be moving in tomorrow, and I thought it was her at the door."

He smiled and said, "Cool. Sorry I didn't drop by sooner – I got in last night and had meetings at the office all day today."

"That's okay – it's great to see you!" She offered him a cold drink, since it had been warmer than usual for September, and she could see he had been sweating a little.

"Thanks," he said, taking a seat on one of the cheap chairs clustered around the kitchen table. He smirked to himself as he looked around at her apartment, thinking that her sparse furnish-ings looked much like his when he had first left home. But at least she had a real table and chairs – his had been a folding table and plastic lawn chairs.

"So what are you doing now – are you going to school?" he asked. "Dad didn't give me too many details, but he mentioned that you'd be looking for work or something. Do you want me to check around the office and see they have any openings?" he of-fered.

THE TIME OF JACOB'S TROUBLE

"That would be great!" she said. But she didn't think she would be able to since his office was located on the other side of town, and since she didn't have a car, any commute would be somewhat limited.

"What's this?" he asked, looking at one of her binders on the table.

"Oh, it's for one of the classes I'm taking," she said quietly.

"'An Introduction to Zion's Harvest'? Don't tell me you're mixed up with those people," he exclaimed, looking up at her in stunned surprise. Then he glanced down at the rest of the binders and books, and it was clear what kind of school she was attending and the curriculum.

"Yeah, that's what I'm here for," she said.

"Wow – I guess that is big news." No wonder Dad hadn't given him many specifics on why she had moved out or what exactly she was studying in Tel Aviv. They were embarrassed – his sister had turned into a Jesus-freak!

"I guess they didn't tell you, huh?" Ruth said.

"Nope – Mom and Dad just said that you were going to school here now and had just moved out." He was still quite surprised, of course: it wasn't some lunatic in Jerusalem that had decided to convert to Christianity, but his own sister!

"Are you okay?"

"Yeah, I'm just surprised. I mean, don't you remember what they did to us? You know, like the Holocaust? The ghettos and the gas chambers and all that?" He was sounding irritated now, much like their father had been, except that Ahban was usually a little better at hiding his feelings.

"Of course, but they weren't really true believers, at least as far as the Bible is concerned."

"Oh, I see," he said with sarcasm. He hated religious discussions and debates – they only made him angry and upset. He took a long drink from his glass, and set it down.

Ruth could tell that he was uncomfortable now too, so she decided not to continue the discussion.

"Would you like to see the rest of the place?" she asked.

"Sure – I need to get going after that, though. Stuff at work

121

is really crazy right now," he said.

"Okay – I understand."

She felt a little sad and lonely all of a sudden, but she brushed her feelings aside. He stood up and she showed him around the small apartment. One bedroom was empty, and hers was a little messy already. Other than basic furnishings, there wasn't all that much to see. A few minutes later, he had emptied his glass and headed back to the living room, trying to appear a little too much in a hurry to leave.

"Thank you so much for stopping by, Ahban. It was nice to see you again!" she said, giving him another hug. But it didn't feel as comfortable or cheerful as the first one had been.

"Sure – anytime. Here's my cell-phone number – give me a call whenever you need anything, okay?" he said, holding out a business card.

"Alright. Thanks!" she said taking the card, and then waved goodbye to him as he turned to leave.

As she closed the door, tears filled her eyes and she suddenly felt very alone and homesick. Her parents had helped her move just over two weeks before, and she hadn't been too homesick since she had started school a few days later. But these feelings came more from being isolated from her own family than from being in a new apartment all by herself.

Why did it have to be so tough? Why couldn't they see Christianity the way she did?

She wiped away her tears and found her Bible, and turned to one of her familiar comfort verses. Later that night, she set aside her books and spent a long time praying for strength and comfort.

*　*　*

On the thirteenth day of September, every child under thirteen years old instantly vanished, along with millions of the elderly, adults and adolescents from all over the world. Although most of the people on the earth had been prepared and had somewhat expected the vanishings to happen at any moment, they were still shocked when people around them suddenly disappeared.

The parents were those who were most visibly upset, and many wailed and wept openly for their children. But the religious guides, the media, and the Anshar were soon there to comfort and reassure them that the children were indeed safe in the Anshar spacecraft on the far side of the moon. [9]

* * *

"Pick up the phone!" Naomi whispered in desperation.

But there was still no answer. Even though it was early in the morning, it was the ninth attempt she had made in the last hour, and she was growing very concerned. Jacob had already left for the office, and had tried to reassure her that everything would be fine.

From the news reports, the disappearances had all happened at precisely the same time – in Israel they had been just past sundown the night before. Ruth usually had her cell-phone with her, and was typically very prompt about returning messages, especially those from her mother.

---

[9] There are many of the Second Coming passages that cannot be adequately resolved with one another, much like how many of the descriptions of the First Coming of the Messiah (the Suffering Servant vs. the Messianic Conqueror) could not be resolved. This, along with several New Testament passages leads many to believe that "the Rapture" will occur first, when the Messiah physically removes His Church before the Tribulation begins.
Rapture Passages: John 14:1-3; Romans 8:19; 1 Corinthians 1:7-8,15:1-53,16:22; Philemon 3:20-21; Colossians 3:4; 1 Thessalonians 1:10,2:19, 4:13-18, 5:9,23; 2 Thessalonians 2:1; 1 Timothy 6:14; 2 Timothy 4:1; Titus 2:13; Hebrews 9:28; James 5:7-9; 1 Peter 1:7,13; 1 John 2:28-3:2; Jude 21; Revelation 2:25,3:10
Second Coming Passages: Daniel 2:44-45,7:9-14,12:1-3; Zechariah 14:1-15; Matthew 13:41,24:15-31,26:64; Mark 13:14-27,14:62; Luke 21:25-28; Acts 1:9-11, 3:19-21; 1 Thessalonians 3:13; 2 Thessalonians 1:6-10,2:8; 2 Peter 3:1-14; Jude 14-15; Revelation 1:7,19:11-20:6, 22:7,12,20

What if Ruth was one of those who had vanished? Even more concerned now, she called Ahban – he was closest, and she asked him to check in on Ruth as soon as he could. Unfortunately, it would be later that day since he was on the other side of Tel Aviv from where she lived, and he wouldn't be able to get away from the office until the afternoon. He told her not to worry – that she was probably at school or something and had simply forgotten her phone. That didn't help reassure her much though, but she thanked him anyway.

Then Naomi remembered Saul – he was further away than Ahban, but maybe he would be able to check up on her sooner. Then she thought of how Saul and Ruth had been talking more frequently lately – nearly every chance they had, come to think of it. She called him, and thankfully he answered on the second ring. He immediately offered to take a sick day from work and go find his sister, even though he was in Haifa and would have to drive to Tel Aviv. At first she protested, since he had only been at his job a month or so, but he reassured her it would be fine. That gave her some consolation, and he promised to call her the instant he found Ruth or any update as to her whereabouts.

Saul called Ruth's cell-phone and received the same response his mother had time and time again: no answer. After his third attempt, he began to grow worried too.

He quickly stopped for a coffee along the way and then drove as fast as he could to her apartment in Tel Aviv. He rang the doorbell several times, but no one answered.

He walked over to the apartment manager's office, and told her that they were unable to reach Ruth and were quite worried, and she was kind enough to let him in. She finally left him alone after he showed her a picture of his family from his wallet (with Ruth in it) and then one of the family pictures in her apartment.

At first, Saul started looking around for signs of when she had last been there. Apparently her roommate had moved in and had unpacked. He checked the sink, and it looked like the dirty dishes in it were from the evening before. Then he checked the bathroom – all the towels, sink, and shower were completely dry, which he interpreted to mean that no one had used the bathroom or shower that day.

He went to her room, and found it more or less in order, except for a small pile of her clothes and shoes lying crumpled in the middle of the floor. Her books, backpack, and purse were still in her room, along with her identification, checkbook, and credit cards. The same was true for her roommate, except her clothes were on her bed instead of in the middle of the floor. It was very strange – it looked as if they had last been at the apartment the night before and then suddenly left, without taking anything with them at all. Even their keys were still there, yet the apartment door had been locked.

His mother had given him the address of the ministry training center/school she had been attending, and he decided to head over there next. He took her keys and left a quick note for her on the door, telling her to call his cell-phone if she came home. The school was close by, but most of the parking lot was empty; it was now late in the morning, and there should have been more than just two or three cars there. He began to get an uneasy feeling about what was going on, but he didn't want to jump to any conclusions yet. When he ran out of options, he would stop and consider what it could be.

The entrance to the ministry office was locked, and from the window, it looked as if the office was closed. But as Saul was leaving, a broken, anguished voice startled him.

"They are not here – they have been taken," the stranger said.

"What?" Saul said, turning to find the source of the voice.

He must have not noticed the middle-aged man who had been sitting off to the side of the entrance when he had walked by. The man looked somewhat disheveled, and it was obvious that he had been crying. But his clothes were decent and on the newer side, just wrinkled and dirty, as if he had been sitting on ground for hours. Lying next to him was a mostly empty bottle of liquor.

"I said, 'They have been taken'. Everyone, that is except me. I should have believed what they were saying! Why didn't I listen to them!" he moaned, weeping again and covering his eyes in shame.

"I don't understand," Saul said. "Who took them where?"

"Yeshua. Took 'em all to Heaven! Don't you get it? It was the Rapture! All the children – and all the Christians, just like they've been saying all these years! Oh, God – why didn't you take me too?" he cried out.

"Everyone?" Saul asked incredulously.

"Of course! Everyone who believed in Yeshua! I had been checking them out after they had come to my synagogue, but I thought they were all crazy. Then last night – 'poof!' – they're all gone!"

Saul swallowed hard, and then backed away from the distraught man. He had to find out exactly what had happened before he would tell his mother and father anything. He jogged back to his car and jumped in. He would go back to the apartment and look for more clues. If what the stranger had said was true, then he and countless others had missed it too!

As Saul drove back, he didn't know what to think anymore. He had more or less accepted the Anshar's explanation at face value, even though it seemed more mystical than he felt comfortable with.

But now that his own sister had vanished (especially after warning him that she might), he knew he would have to soon decide which explanation he believed: the Anshar's version, or the Rapture.

And he had the distinct feeling that whichever path his search led him down, it would change his life in a dramatic way.

*   *   *

Saul spent the next nine hours straight combing over his sister's apartment. He did his best to stay out of her roommate's bedroom, but he did go through her papers, books, and some of her binders from the ministry. They were about the same as his sister's school materials. Since he had set up his sister's computer over a year ago, he still had the administrator login, and was able to go through all her files, documents, bookmarks, and her web browser history.

Nothing was too out of the ordinary though – most of her

files and browser history were for music, ministries, and other Christian information. He put together a list of the forums, sites, and groups she frequently visited, and began browsing them. After two hours, he became thoroughly convinced that the man at the ministry office had been correct: all the children and all the Christians had been taken by God, not by the Anshar.

Another confirmation of his theory was that most of the Christian forums were silent, other than a handful of users asking where everyone was. Over and over, he saw chatter about the Rapture having occurred, and the Anshar propaganda explaining it away.

Later that night, he called his parents to tell them what he had discovered at Ruth's apartment and school. When his mother answered, she said that Ahban was supposed to have stopped by, but he had not so far, at least not during the time that Saul had been there. At that news, he could tell his mother was irritated, and his father was too (who was on the other line), and he vowed to call Ahban later.

When it came time to tell them his conclusions, Saul was surprised that he was suddenly nervous, but he went on to tell them everything he had learned, along with his theory.

His mother wept, and his father was silent. Both said repeatedly that they couldn't believe that she had been taken. They listened to him explain what he had found with great interest, but when he concluded that it had been the Rapture that had occurred, it was clear they did not agree.

And why should they? The Anshar were all over the media, and they had explained in advance that the mass removal of people would be for their own protection and re-education. In spite of all the vanishings and the turmoil that had occurred, the news was remarkably upbeat.

Saul reiterated what he had found, especially concerning his sister's browsing history and message boards, but it still didn't convince them. His mother might have possibly believed his account of Ruth's disappearance, but his father remained very skeptical.

Saul hung up the phone in frustration, and turned on the

television. He had been so busy investigating that he hadn't even bothered to check the news that day. His parents had been right: the news coverage was portraying the families of those who had been taken as being relieved and sometimes even elated that they had been taken to a better place. Millions upon millions of people were no longer on earth, and there was evidently no trace of them other than their clothes and other personal items being left behind where they had been during their last moments on earth.

Numerous mothers, fathers, siblings, friends, and other relatives were interviewed and few of them were sad at the loss (at least on television). According to most of the news-anchors, the mass vanishings had been a wonderful event, with little if any grief by those who had been left behind.

*   *   *

Saul awoke early the next morning, only to find he was lying on the couch in Ruth's apartment still fully dressed, with one of the news channels still playing.

Dazed with sleep, he looked around and rubbed his eyes – he must have fallen asleep in the middle of the night. He remembered watching the news and flipping through the channels for hours, until the same clips began replaying over and over, and he had finally nodded off.

He rose and went to the bathroom to clean up and splash some water on his face. He had dark circles under his eyes, but he found that he didn't notice them as much as the frightened expression on his own face.

If Ruth had been right about what she said would happen (namely the Rapture), what would happen next? She had obviously checked into all this Bible prophecy stuff and had tried to tell him about it, but he hadn't really listened to her. At least, not as well as he should have, he thought regretfully. He looked back at his reflection a moment later, and then took a deep breath.

Saul went back to his sister's room and found an empty box in her closet, and put all her pictures, laptop, books, and materials in it. He decided he would take the rest of the week off from

THE TIME OF JACOB'S TROUBLE

work and find the answers to what he was looking for.

* * *

The rest of week after "The Great Vanishing" had occurred, as the media had called it, most of the roads of the cities, and other infrastructure services were gridlocked. The World Union immediately declared a world holiday – the first of its kind – so that people could attend to their families and adjust to what had happened.

Emergency crews all over the globe worked around the clock to remove the abandoned cars from the roads, whose drivers had suddenly disappeared. People were encouraged to check up on their neighbors and notify the authorities of anyone they found to be missing. The cars, belongings, and property of those who had vanished were registered, inventoried, and immediately taken into state control. The animals, flocks, herds, and pets of the departed were also inventoried and given to whoever would take them. If the departed individuals had left a will, the legal process was followed to distribute their belongings as if they had died.

The Anshar broadcast their message of reassurance over and over, and after the initial shock wore off, the majority of mankind were relieved to know that their children were now safe and protected. People of every age had been taken from all over the earth, but in some regions there were more disappearances than others. Millions of people in the Americas, China, India, and Africa had been taken from the earth, while mere thousands had been taken from most of Europe, Russia, the Middle East, and the myriad of tiny nations scattered abroad. A number of the people who could not accept the vanishings of their loved ones or their children committed suicide.

When the demographics of the people who had vanished were finally analyzed, most of them were found to have little else in common other than their religion, which happened to be typically on the more-traditional or conservative side of Christianity. However, many of the mainstream denominational churches remained intact, and only a few of their members were taken. Most

129

people in the other religions were not widely affected, but there were handfuls missing from them also. The smaller churches and the often-illegal house churches had large numbers of their members removed, and sometimes entire congregations had vanished.

But for most of the people who remained on earth, the Anshar and the World Union continued to provide comfort and reassurance, and encouraged everyone to look beyond the immediate loss and towards the next phase with joy and anticipation. The World Leader would be coming soon to guide them through the coming times of trial.

CHAPTER 6
THE MAN OF PEACE

David Medine had just turned thirty years old when the Anshar had revealed their presence to the world. An Assyrian Jew from Iraq,[10] he had been through some of his country's worst days. His parents had been among the handful of Jews who had not immigrated to Israel during the reign of Saddam Hussein and the years of terrorism after the brutal dictator's fall.

The Medine family had always been careful to hide their Jewish background for fear of persecution, and they had been among the wealthier families in the area for centuries. But a few years ago, his parents had been murdered in one of the suicide bombings during the violent times that followed Saddam's fall, and David Medine was all that remained of his family.

He had been employed as a mid-level assistant to the Prime Minister of Iraq for the last three years, and now he was considering leaving his job and taking a position in the Middle Eastern Union Administration Office. He was tall, dark, trim, and very handsome – the very model of a Middle Eastern man. He had a cheerful, yet driven look and a deep sense of unfulfilled destiny. David had always been a clear, rational thinker, and had long pondered mankind's future.

There in the ancient birthplace of civilization, he had the ink-

---

[10] The coming world leader will most likely be an Assyrian, but also be Jewish in order to be accepted as the Jewish Messiah (at least at first). Also, Nimrod is mentioned by many records as the first world tyrant/dictator – this world leader will be the last. (Micah 5:5-6)

ling that Iraq would be where the next phase of man's destiny would begin. He had never been very religious personally, but he had found its influence on society interesting, especially the ancient religions of the Sumerians and the Assyrians.

Like many others, his outlook on life had dramatically changed after the Anshar had come. Though he had been shocked like the rest of the world when Israel's enemies had been miraculously destroyed, it had not influenced his life all that much. Like most, he had thought of the initial extraterrestrial sightings as a curiosity, but not something to be taken very seriously.

But the revelation of the Anshar had changed his mere curiosity into something much more substantial. He had immediately believed nearly all of their teachings, but also felt as if he had heard it all before, even the stranger details such as the mass vanishings and the coming World Leader. He felt strangely drawn to the Anshar, and even had a feeling of familiarity with them.

Medine relentlessly began studying the ancient legends and myths of both his own land and the other ancient cultures of Elam (later called Persia), Canaan, and Egypt. He found many similarities between them, and also a number of records of what appeared to be visitations by the Anshar. The most frequent occurrences seemed to be in the earliest records of the Sumerians, and then the number had dramatically decreased over time, especially after the rise of the Assyrian Empire and then the Babylonian Empire later.

The Anshar had also interacted with the Egyptians for centuries, and had recently claimed to be the builders of the Great Pyramid of Giza, and provided detailed evidence to support their claims. The Great Pyramid had been built as a symbol of unity, a monument to unite the Upper and Lower Kingdoms of Egypt, and never a simple tomb for the Pharaoh. And the Great Pyramid still stood strong to show that one day man would be united, just as Upper and Lower Egypt had been united thousands of years earlier.

One evening nearly two weeks after the Great Vanishing,

while he was in his study reviewing the ancient accounts, three brilliant shining figures surrounded by light appeared in front of him. He nearly fell out of his chair when he realized who stood before him: it was the Anshar – they had come to visit him in his own home!

He had so many things to ask them, but suddenly all his questions left him in their awesome presence. The Anshar introduced themselves, and then to further add to his shock, they bowed down before him and prostrated themselves on their faces! After he recovered from his astonishment, he protested and told them to stand, but they ignored him.

When they finally rose from their faces a long minute later, the Anshar announced to him that he was the Chosen One, the World Leader who would soon rule over all the earth. His destiny was to become the Mediator who all mankind had been longing for.

And his vital destiny would be fulfilled very soon.

* * *

Saul rubbed his tired eyes, placed a pen in the book to mark his place, and then stood up to stretch and move around a little.

He had been doing little other than absorbing Bible prophetic literature for the last four days since the Great Vanishing. When he needed a break, he would turn on the television and listen to the news. What he heard continued to astound him. As he learned more about what the Bible said and its prophetic nature, he felt as if he was beginning to see what was really happening. And the emerging picture was becoming increasingly terrifying.

Since the Anshar had come, the media had become more of an extension of the World Union than an independent entity. The news coverage was extremely slanted towards the Anshar and the analysis was typically consistent between news outlets. Any mention of the Rapture explanation was always scorned and deemed as the excuse of the fringe extremist religious groups to subvert the World Union and the Anshar. Spokesmen for the Anshar were all over the news, telling the people not to worry, and

133

showing video clips of some of the children playing happily in some of the rooms of the Anshar ships, and even hugging and laughing with their caretakers. Not only that, but numerous parents came forward to say how happy they were that their children were in a better place and becoming the first of the new race of mankind.

As Saul learned more and more about the Bible's predictions he realized that his sister had been correct: the Anshar were merely masquerading for Satan and his fallen angels. Some of the maneuvers of their ships and the bizarre, almost magical properties they displayed simply defied the laws of physics; but they happened nonetheless. The ships could zip through the sky in any direction at lightning-fast speeds, jumping and darting about at impossible velocities and angles. Sometimes the ships would instantly vanish and then reappear thousands of kilometers away only seconds later. [11]

One of the books he had started reading yesterday had explained that extraterrestrials had been gradually revealing themselves to mankind over the last century, and how many of the characteristics of alien abductions were the same as in cases of demon possession. Several of the books also mentioned the Watchers and the Nephilim – the unnatural offspring of fallen Watchers (or angels) and women they had taken for themselves.

These "beings from the stars" had visited earth in previous times, like before the Flood and during the early days of Israel. The media and secular education systems had ignored much of the information or simply neglected to mention it, and therefore little of the historical evidence was widely known. And yet the Biblical account of the ancient Watchers was the best explanation for what was happening now. The Anshar were recreating what had happened before the Flood, in an attempt to once again change (some commentators had said "corrupt") mankind, or help the human race "evolve" as they described it.

It was getting late, and he didn't realize how hungry he was

---

[11] The End Times will be filled with deception and signs in the heavens. Many of the alien encounters are metaphysical and very "New Age" in nature. (2 Thessalonians 2:8-12)

until he began moving around. Saul decided to go out to eat and do more reading over a long dinner, so he gathered the book, his wallet and keys, and headed for his car.

As he drove, he thought about what he should do next. He was still surprised at his father's skepticism at his explanation for Ruth's disappearance. He was even surprising himself at how interested he was becoming about all this prophetic stuff from the Bible. He had heard the basic stories from the Tanakh and ancient Israel before as a child, but he had never really connected with it until now. And while he had always felt Jewish, he now felt as if he had a much deeper connection with his homeland and his people.

What would be the next move by the Anshar, he wondered. And while he was fairly certain that it had been the Rapture that had taken all the people, how could he know for sure if the Bible was truly reliable? He was determined to finish the alien-prophecy book that night, and perhaps that would give him some of the answers he was looking for. He had poured over the materials all that day, and he had become increasingly grateful to Ruth for how much information she had gathered in such a short time. He was beginning to see her in a different light now, and found himself wanting more and more to talk with her about what else she had learned. But that was no longer possible, he sadly acknowledged.

Surprisingly, he was finding that his grief at her disappearance was turning into something else, something almost akin to relief and happiness for her. But he also felt a pang of jealousy towards her in that she was in Heaven now while he was still on the earth. He found himself beginning to yearn for the answer to a question he had never really given much thought to: what would happen to him after he died?

But something inside was still making him hesitate from going down the path that she had chosen. Part of it was the fear of losing his friends and family if he converted to Christianity, but a bigger fear was what if he was wrong and everyone else was right? Whereas he had once felt fairly certain about his own future, now everything was being turned upside down.

He would put the Bible to the test, he told himself, just like the prophecy book had challenged. If the Bible was indeed accurate in the prophecies that had already been fulfilled, then surely there should be more that would soon be fulfilled too, especially in the bizarre time he was living in.

He would make a list of all the prophesies that were to happen next (if they were in any order in time), and then keep track of which ones came true and which ones did not. He would approach it logically and systematically. But at the same time, he felt a certain odd tugging inside his soul, like a quiet voice that was telling him there was little time for that now, that he had to step out and make a decision for Yeshua or for the Anshar.

Saul took his time eating his dinner, and didn't read as much as he had wanted to. However, he was able to think more clearly about what was happening. How he wished his sister were here – he had so many questions to ask her! The urgent whisper to make a decision was growing louder inside him, and he had a sense that he would have to choose sides very soon.

He finished his dinner, and then ordered a large coffee to go. He figured he would be up for the rest of the night like the one before. He didn't want to return to his old routine, at least not just yet. The routine and busyness would only cloud his thinking again, and he wanted some clarity to what was happening.

When he got back to his apartment, he returned to reading the book and finished it a few hours later. When he came to the section on how to accept Yeshua, he still felt unsure of whether to or not. Maybe Ruth had had the same questions as he did, he thought. He remembered that she frequently posted questions on the Internet; maybe he could find some of her old posts. He sat down on the sofa with his laptop and turned on the television with the news in the background, and then began searching for her username in some of the forums and other sites he had found on her computer.

Several minutes later, Saul stumbled upon one of the usernames she had used. And as he began reading some of her posts, he was suddenly overcome with grief for her once again, and his eyes filled with tears.

THE TIME OF JACOB'S TROUBLE

Why hadn't he taken her more seriously when she had tried to tell him about Yeshua and the Anshar, when she was still there? How he wished that he was where she was now – perfectly content and at peace, with no more fear of the future and of the terrible times ahead. He set the laptop aside and put his hands to face.

Then almost without realizing it, he found himself slipping to the floor onto his knees, with his face buried in the cushions, crying out to the Lord to forgive him and to protect him. He confessed his sins and his foolishness at ignoring his sister's warnings, and then he begged Him to take him too, to be with Him forever.

And in that moment, he accepted Yeshua as his Messiah and Savior. A calming peace flowed over him, and his fears and sadness slowly melted away, and then he fell into a restful sleep for the remainder of the night.

*   *   *

The Anshar took David Medine to their main ship that had been orbiting the earth since their arrival. As he boarded the vessel, he again felt a certain, unmistakable sense of déjà vu. A flood of memories came rushing back, and he began to remember images, sounds, and smells from his childhood.

Had he been there before? How was that possible? And as he toured the ship with his hosts, he found it becoming more and more familiar. The Anshar, upon noticing his expressions and wonderment, began to tell him more of his own personal history – his past that had been carefully hidden from him until the proper time.

The Anshar brought him to a wide room that contained what looked like a dentist chair, with a large, thick cable that hung from the ceiling. All the walls, floor, and ceiling were covered with dark panels that were slightly curved and almost seamless. Most of the time, the panels seemed transparent, showing all the stars in their constellations, along with the huge earth below and the moon above.

David wandered over to the chair and sat down – he felt it shift underneath him as it morphed and re-molded itself to perfectly fit his contours.

As he sat in the chair, he remembered a phrase that always came into his mind as he recalled sitting there before: "the Seat of Knowledge". Vaguely he began to remember the days, weeks, and months (or was it years?) that he had spent in that very room in days past – but they seemed to be in another time and in another life.

His surroundings gradually began to change and morph, and many of the panels in front of him began displaying numerous scenes from his past: the moment of his birth, him learning to crawl, then him walking and speaking, his childhood, and then his early adolescent years. Then he watched as some of his old lessons in that very room started once again. And then as the room swirled and refocused, his long-suppressed memories came flooding back all at once, making him gasp at their clarity and vividness.

For the first time in his existence, David Medine realized who he was – he was the creation of the Anshar. He was fully man and also fully Anshar. He remembered his training and his years of lessons in that very room. He remembered all the tests and the images, and now understood what had happened to him.

The Anshar standing in the doorway were watching his reaction carefully, and they began to speak to him for the first time since he had entered the room. He was the pinnacle of their creation – their merger of the best DNA fragments and genetic reconstruction, along with all the knowledge and capabilities of the Anshar. But if his early life and parents had been mere fabrications, then who really was he?

The Anshar seemed to read his mind – indeed, since they used telepathic abilities among themselves. Since he was fully Anshar, they could read his thoughts, and he could read theirs, he would soon discover. But those capabilities would take some time to re-awaken after years of dormancy and neglect. They told him of his conception and infanthood. His mother had willingly lent herself to the Anshar in secret for them to implant their creation in her. He had no earthly father, for it was through the male genes that the inability to interact with the Anshar from one generation to the next had been passed. This defect was yet only one of the genetic errors introduced by the Elohim to reduce mankind to the level of beasts. And with his enhanced genetic makeup by the Anshar, he would interact with them unlike any human had for thousands of years.

The Anshar told him again that he was the Chosen One – the first and foremost link between the Anshar and the human race. His gene sequences had been carefully constructed from the best of mankind's history. He had genetic material from the greatest leaders in history: Alexander the Great, Albert Einstein, Napoleon Bonaparte, Genghis Khan, Cyrus the Great, Saladin, Peter the Great, Nebuchadnezzar, David, Solomon, Mohammed, Abraham, Moses, and many ancient other kings and pharaohs. His potential was limitless, and he had been thoroughly trained years before in their ways, but his skills and knowledge had been hidden for his own safety until the proper time.

The Anshar pointed to the portion of the room showing the earth below. Around the outside of the globe, images began to be displayed and slowly transitioned from one scene to another. The images were of the most beautiful scenes, mansions, palaces, and luxuries of the earth. He saw himself, and multitudes of people adoring him, and even bowing low before him. He saw millions of soldiers standing at attention, awaiting his orders. He saw unrestrained beauty and glory and power – the greatest of all that the world had to offer.

A shining, beautiful creature suddenly appeared before him, and he turned away from the display. Light flowed from the new creature, who looked much like the other Anshar, but seemed much greater than they were.

And then the creature began speaking to him in a wonderful voice, which sounded like soothing music, "All this will be yours, if you let me teach you."

David Medine nodded.

"All this will be yours, if you obey my every word," the creature continued.

Medine promised he would.

"All this will be yours, if you bow and worship me!" the creature of light exclaimed.

And David Medine fell forward out of the chair and prostrated himself on his face before him as low as he could.

"Excellent," he said. The creature turned to the other Anshar. "He is ready. You may continue."

And then the creature of light vanished as quickly as he had appeared. The Anshar beckoned to Medine, who was still lying facedown on the floor, and he went back to sit in the chair.

Awestruck, he asked who that incredible creature was. It was their master, they replied: the master of the Anshar, and of all the dominions that were not controlled by Yahweh and the Elohim.

And now, the Anshar told him it was time to for him to take his rightful place in history, as the king of kings and lord of lords. The same procedures that had been used to bury his memories and training would be reversed, and his suppressed abilities would soon be instantly re-awakened.

As well as the retrieved memories, he would undergo an extensive DNA revitalization procedure, and also another huge knowledge transfer. The DNA transfer would "refresh" his DNA and repair any genetic errors that had accumulated in his system since his last session as an adolescent. The knowledge transfer would also help him regain all the knowledge and wisdom that he had long ago forgotten.

A transparent helmet was lowered over his head as he sat comfortably in the chair. He instinctively closed his eyes, and felt himself quickly drifting off to sleep. And then volumes upon volumes of information – terabytes of data – were uploaded directly into his brain while he was slept, bringing his mental capacity to within 99% of his full potential.

Within hours, he would literally be an entirely new man – indeed, a god among men.

*   *   *

Saul closed the last of the books he had taken from Ruth's

apartment, and looked over at her in the last family picture they had all taken together. He smiled – she would have been so proud of him for the decision he had made last night.

All the doubts he had had the day before no longer seemed important, since he had accepted Yeshua. He still had some questions here and there about what would be happening next, but there were no longer any huge roadblocks to his faith. He had found it ironic (and a little sad) that Ruth had asked many of the same questions he had before, and obviously she had gotten the answers in time. But it was still comforting to read the notes she had made in some of her books and even finding posts she had made on the Internet. It was as if part of her was still there.

From the Bible literature and the information he had gleaned from the Internet, it appeared that the so-called "Anti-Christ" would be making his appearance very soon now that the Rapture had occurred. Once that man came on the scene, the prophetic events would begin taking place one after another as detailed in the Book of Revelation and the Tanakh.

Bible scholars had gone back and forth for centuries over how this incredible leader would make his grand entrance and be identified, but after even his brief study, it almost seemed silly to Saul. The Book of Daniel was very clear on how the tyrant would be identified: he would be the one who would make (or enforce) a seven-year treaty with Israel. In the middle of the seven-year term, he would break the treaty and declare himself to be God inside the Temple.

But now that he was a Christian in this peculiar time in history, he didn't know what he should do with his life. He no longer felt as drawn to the software industry or any career path as he had only days before. This was such an important period in the history of the world, and he felt an urgency to make up for lost time. After all, he only had seven years to make his Lord proud of him – and there was so much to do! What was the point of spending the rest of the short time he had left doing anything other than serving his King and helping gather as many other souls to Him as he could?

There were millions – no, billions – being systematically deceived every day, and he felt an urgency to speak to as many of them as he could while there was still time.

And then a thought occurred to him: he had all the training materials from the ministry program that Ruth had enrolled in. Why couldn't he just enroll in the same school as she had? However, he realized that most of the people who had been involved in the Christian organizations and ministries had been taken. But their materials were still there for the most part, and it was very likely that no one would be using their offices. Maybe he could find some like-minded believers and start up where those ministries had left off?

Excitedly, he logged onto the web and within minutes found a messianic group that had just been restarted in Haifa, and he decided to go visit them the next morning. However, who knew if they would be open, with most of their members probably missing.

He was still so new to his faith and understanding of the New Testament (or much of the Bible, for that matter), but it wouldn't hurt to check them out. Maybe they needed help as much as he wanted to get involved. And with that thought, he went to bed and got a full night's sleep.

The next day, Saul drove to the offices of the Haifa branch of "The Way". From his research online, it appeared to be a ministry similar to Zion's Harvest. As he drove into the parking lot, his spirits fell when he saw only one other car. He feared that whoever was left might be like the distraught man he had met at Zion's Harvest earlier that week. But he didn't see anyone outside and the lights inside were on, so that was a good sign.

He opened the front door and a small doorbell chimed, alerting the office that there was a visitor. A normal-looking man in his late thirties came out from the back.

"Welcome to 'The Way'. How can I help you?" the man asked.

"Hello, my name is Saul Rosenberg. I'm looking for a messianic ministry to get involved with. Are there any openings here?" he said.

The man smiled and replied, "There sure are – I'm Daniel

Hershel. One of my friends used to work here, and it seems that everyone is no longer with us."

He reached behind the front desk and pulled out an information sheet about the ministry.

"I'm new here myself," he said. "When the vanishings happened, I stopped by to check up on my friend, you know, to see if he had been taken. He had been talking about the Rapture for years, but I always thought he had been exaggerating or something. When I got here, the office was open but everyone was gone, except for their clothes," Daniel said.

Saul remembered the same being true of Ruth and her roommate, and most of the other vanishings that had been described on the news.

"So are you running the office now?" he asked.

"I don't know yet. No one else has come around since the vanishings, but I only became a Christian a few days ago. I'd like to get this place going again – they have a decent supply of materials and it seems like everything's in good shape."

Saul began looking around, evaluating the office. It did seem like it was quite organized and modern, and even the receptionist's computer looked only a year or two old. From the information sheet, the ministry had been named after the very first messianic movement that had occurred in Judea after the resurrection of Yeshua the Messiah.

"That's cool," replied Saul. "Mind if I check the place out?"

"Go ahead – I found this here yesterday," he said, picking up a DVD from the desk. "I've watched it a few times – it's more or less what the ministry is about, and there's another one about the Rapture. Do you want to watch it?"

"Sure."

Saul followed Daniel into the meeting room nearby, and they both watched it several times. There was no doubt to them any longer that the Rapture had occurred and that they had been left behind.

The office was empty the rest of the day, so they had plenty of time to further exchange backgrounds. When Saul re-iterated his interest in getting involved, Daniel gladly accepted his offer, and they began talking about how to restart the ministry.

First, they would have to go through all the files and papers in the administrator's office, and locate any information concerning the ministry's bank accounts, finances, and management practices. Daniel had managed one of the clean-up teams after the invasion, and had a decent amount of managerial and sales experience. Saul had more computer and technology skills, however, and would have to learn bookkeeping and other skills that would get the ministry running. Saul quickly restarted the computers and the network, and found most of the information they needed. Then they spent the rest of the day learning about the internal workings of the ministry.

The two men quickly became good friends, and both spent long hours at the ministry office for the rest of the week learning all they could about it. The ministry was well-stocked with books, DVDs, CDs, and many other witnessing materials, and it looked like they had been stocking up on them, or perhaps had just been unable to distribute them after the Anshar had arrived. Fortunately, the previous administrator had been very well-organized, and it didn't take them very long to figure out how everything was run.

By the end of the week on Friday, the ministry was back up and running, and Saul found himself surprised at how much they had accomplished in such a short time. But now his vacation was over and on Sunday he would have to go back to work.

Immediately, he got a sinking feeling about it, and talked it over with Daniel. Daniel was no longer employed, and had saved plenty of money from his years in private industry – enough to fund the ministry if need-be. But when they had gone through the ministry's bank accounts and books, they found that there was enough budgeted for them both to draw a small salary, and still have plenty left over. After all, there were no more employees left there to pay other than themselves!

Saul went back to his apartment late Friday night, tired but excited. He had a big decision to make that weekend, one that would change the entire direction of his life. Would he go back to his good-paying job at the software company, or would he quit to go work for the ministry full-time?

His parents would be upset if he chose the latter, but after the last week, he knew that it was the right choice to make. People needed to know the truth, and there would be much suffering in the years ahead. It would be a grave mistake for him not to do the work of his King while he still had the opportunity to do so.

On Saturday morning, he got up early and went to one of the northern beaches that he loved, and took a long walk. By the end of the day, he had confirmed his decision.

* * *

Saul was nervous as he rang the doorbell of his parents' house. It was about an hour after dinner, and he had just left the ministry for the day. He didn't have to tell them the news, he supposed, but they would find out sooner or later anyway, so he figured he might as well just get it over with.

If something bad happened to him, his parents would need to know what he was involved in and what could have occurred. At first, he had resisted the very idea of telling them, but after prayerful consideration and talking it over with Daniel, he resolved to take the initiative and tell them in person. After all, his life had been radically changed in a very short time, and they should know what was going on.

"Hello, Saul! What are you doing here at this hour?" his mother asked with a huge smile as she opened the door.

"Hi Mom! Well, I was over on this side of the city and hadn't been home in awhile, and thought I'd drop by," Saul said.

"Well, please come in," she motioned, waving him inside. He followed her back to the family room where she had been reading a magazine. "Jacob – Saul's here!" she called out, who was watching the news as he usually did late in the evening. He was sitting in his easy-chair, leafing through the newspaper.

"Hello, son! How have you been?" he asked, taking off his reading glasses with a welcoming smile.

Saul sat down on the plush sofa at the other side of his

mother, and Jacob muted the news.

"Good. How's things at the office?" he asked, suddenly a little nervous.

"We've been fine. We have lots of new contracts starting up soon. How's your job going?" he asked.

Saul hated small talk and for the most part, he just wanted to get his announcement over with. And he had figured that sooner or later that evening, the subject of his job would come up.

He had been praying that they would take the news well, but with his father typically so concerned about business and money, they probably would not. After all, he had just finished four years of college and they had paid for it (thankfully). He might as well just go ahead and tell them.

"Well, that's one of the reasons I dropped by," he said nervously. "I've resigned at the company, and will be leaving at the end of this week." The easy part was over, but from the look on his father's face, he thought he was going to have a coronary.

"What?" Jacob exclaimed. "What happened? Did you find a better job or something? I didn't even know you were looking!"

"Sort of – I've decided that I want to take my life in a different direction."

"Oh. What's that?" he asked.

"I don't know an easy way to say it, but I'm partnering with another guy at a ministry close to my apartment." With that part out, the rest should be easy, Saul thought with a grimace.

"What? You're not staying in engineering? Why not just find another software job?" Jacob demanded.

Naomi sat nearby, as surprised as Jacob, but she wasn't saying much, at least not yet. He knew she didn't like his decision either, but she at least usually listened first and then reacted later. Besides, she would get over it much faster than his father would.

"Because that's not what I want to do with my life. I've given this a lot of thought, and after the Rapture, I've really had to re-think what's important."

"The Rapture?" Jacob said, almost flabbergasted. "Don't

tell me you still believe that nonsense! They've told everyone what happened!" he declared, pointing at the news.

Out of the corner of his eye, Saul could see his mother shifting in her seat uncomfortably, waiting for his response.

"I do – the Anshar are lying, Dad. Can't you see that?" Saul said, standing his ground. If he could be strong with his father, he could handle just about anyone.

"The Anshar are the best thing that's ever happened to us!" Jacob said emphatically. He paused to let himself cool off a little. "How will you pay your bills? Your rent? We aren't going to pay for your apartment while you go out and preach every day! We just finished paying for four years of school!" he exclaimed.

"I know, Dad. I'm not asking you to. The ministry has enough funding to pay for my living expenses." Saul replied.

"What about retirement and savings?" he asked.

Saul held back a sarcastic retort about the last question, since clearly his father had no idea what the world was in for in the near future. He paused and lowered his voice.

"Dad, I don't think we're going to be around to even see your retirement!" he said.

"What do you mean by that?" his mother asked.

"The Tribulation is coming – you know, Armageddon, the Anti-Christ, 666?" he asked.

"Oh, for God's sake!" his father yelled out in frustration. "Don't tell me you've been converted like your sister too! One Christian in this family was enough. Didn't you learn anything from her? It was because she got converted that she was taken away – to be re-educated from her crazy, stupid thinking!"

"But that's not true, Dad!" Saul found himself shouting back. "You're right in that she was taken because she was a Christian, but not to be re-educated. She was taken to spare her from what's going to be happening to this world soon! She's not the one who's going to be put through hell – we are!"

"This is unbelievable! You know, we didn't put you through four years of college only to have you graduate and then throw it all away!" Jacob said angrily, his face very red.

"I know. And I'm sorry – if it were any other time and all this stuff wasn't going on, I would have stuck with it, at least long enough to pay you back." Saul tried speaking in a softer tone, since both their tempers were running very high.

"But what if you vanish too? Don't you know that they may take you too? Is that what you want?"

"Of course not – but it's not going to, Dad," Saul explained. "It happened just once and won't happen again. Haven't you noticed that the Anshar aren't speaking about it anymore?" he said.

Jacob shook his head, appearing to regain control of himself. "I've heard enough," he said quietly, but with more of a controlled fury than gentleness. "I think you'd better leave."

"What?" Naomi asked, stunned and getting to her feet. Saul was dismayed also, but had somewhat expected it after what had happened after Ruth had told them.

"You heard me – I want him to leave. I don't want any more trouble in this house!"

"Jacob! You can't be serious!" she exclaimed, moving to Saul's side in his defense.

"Mom, it's okay – he's right. I don't want to cause any more problems than I already have," he said as he stood up and headed for the door.

He looked back at her apologetically as he opened the door, "I'm really sorry, Mom – I'll call you in a few days, okay?"

"Alright. It'll be okay – I'll talk to him," she promised. Saul nodded as she watched him walk over to his car.

As he drove away, tears filled her eyes, and she shook her head in sadness and disbelief. What was going on with everyone? First Ruth had suddenly changed her life, and now Saul! Who would be next?

* * *

Thirty days after the Anshar had taken David Medine to their starship, they accompanied him to the World Union headquarters and introduced him as the promised World Leader.

THE TIME OF JACOB'S TROUBLE

He would represent the Anshar before all mankind, and conversely represent all mankind to the Anshar. The Anshar would soon be withdrawing from the earth to oversee the training and re-education of all the children and the others who had been removed from the earth during the Great Vanishing.

After they had introduced David Medine to the World Union leaders, they withdrew to the back of the room to let him speak for himself.

During the thirty days of his intensive retraining, all of Medine's long-dormant memories, knowledge, and previous training had been completely re-awakened. His knowledge of technology, history, and human nature were unsurpassed, as was his mental sharpness, clarity of thought, and his confidence, all of which he demonstrated to the World Union leaders, who sat in silence before him.

He had also acquired an incredible capability to read minds to a significant extent, which he also demonstrated to the leaders of the World Union. A certain aura surrounded him – some would even say a faint glow – which seemed to brighten when he spoke. Clearly, he was not just a normal human being any longer. After only a few minutes in his presence, his esteemed colleagues recognized that the power and knowledge of the Anshar did indeed rest upon him.

David Medine was also now an eloquent, charismatic speaker. They hung on his every word, drinking in his rich tone and words, spoken in the even, measured tones of the Anshar. He spoke at length of his plans to unite the world with such peace and prosperity that it would last a thousand years.

But if the world was to permanently unite, there would need to be significant changes throughout all areas of the society. Everything from their currencies, religions, economies, banking structures, markets, languages, and their degree of technology was different. These barriers to unity, peace, and prosperity must be torn down and relegated to the trash-heap of history. He re-iterated what the Anshar had been telling the world since their arrival: if mankind was to achieve its immortal potential, they must first unite into what they really were – a common race of man.

David Medine also confided that even the World Union was still not enough to achieve that potential – they had merely reduced the scope of the problem. Instead of a World Union made up of ten separate federal entities, there should be only one.

He recommended merging as many of the Unions together as quickly as possible, followed by putting the permanent cultural changes into effect, and then lastly bringing in the remaining Union groups incrementally. While merging all the Unions at once would have been ideal, he recognized that the world was still too fragile for that to be accomplished realistically. Even with his divine guidance and the assistance of the Anshar.

He convinced them that time was short, and this unique opportunity for peace and prosperity might not come again for another five thousand years.

*　*　*

Unbelievable! Jacob thought to himself as he drove to his office. Two of his own children had become Christians! Where had he gone wrong? After all, he had raised them to be logical and sensible, hadn't he? Look at Ahban – he hadn't lost his mind with all the phenomena going on; why had Ruth and Saul? How could they deny what was clearly visible to everyone else, and that the Anshar were already making the world a better place?

He regretted throwing Saul out of the house last night, but he was still simmering about the whole incident. He tried to put it into the proper perspective. So what if his son believed in Yeshua – millions of others did, and he got along with most of the Christians he encountered anyway.

Yet something still rankled deep within him about the notion of his own flesh and blood converting to Christianity. It was almost unthinkable! The Christians had been slaughtering the Jews for nearly two thousand years – and to have his son join them was almost more than he could handle. He could somewhat understand Ruth's conversion, since she had been young and naïve, and hadn't been to the university to learn Jewish history yet.

But at least Saul was still with them, he thought, not like

THE TIME OF JACOB'S TROUBLE

Ruth. He missed her terribly – she was so much like Naomi, especially during her last year at home. She would light up the room by just walking in, regardless of what was going on around them. He didn't really believe in the afterlife, even though a slight fear ran through him when he thought about his own death and the remote possibility of Hell. But he didn't think about those things very often.

Naomi had been extremely upset with him since last night. And though they had gone to bed together, they hadn't said much at all. When Naomi was unusually quiet, she was angry. Nearly thirty years of marriage had taught him that much, he grimaced.

He would apologize to her later, and then find a way to make it right. Perhaps flowers would at least help take the sting out of it, especially since he rarely bought them for her anymore. Maybe she was more upset about losing Ruth than she was letting on. He did need to pay more attention to his wife and less to the office. That much he could acknowledge.

At least Ahban was still normal, he reflected. He was proud of his oldest son – he was so much like he had been in his younger days: handsome, confident, witty, and very driven to succeed. He was doing very well these days, and he wasn't even thirty years old yet! His own career had started out rather slowly, and Ahban was far ahead of where he had been at his age.

Upon thinking of Ahban and what had happened with Saul, he decided to give him a call later and see how he was doing. They hadn't spoken in a few weeks, and it would be nice to find out what he was up to.

Jacob decided that he needed to focus more on his family than his business for once. He knew it was something that would be uncomfortable at first, but it was an adjustment he had to make.

Before it was too late.

* * *

As David Medine continued speaking to the World Union

151

leaders, he could feel them falling further and further under his spell.

He laid out his financial plans in detail: all the nations must immediately begin replacing their antiquated currencies with one of the three largest currencies (the Euro, the Dollar, and the Yen), which would dramatically improve and unify the economies of all nations.

After three years, the primary currencies would all be replaced by the World currency, which would be managed by the World Bank. To prevent counterfeiting, the new currency would be completely cashless and counterfeit-proof, which would save them trillions. Each citizen would receive tamper-proof identification, which would also enable them to buy and sell goods and services. Also, they would be able to borrow against their future credits just like a credit card for whatever they needed. This would enable the poorer people to immediately buy food and health services.

Medine also recommended that three of the Unions be immediately combined to begin the unification process, and the three he wished to join were those that were the most dependent upon one another, namely Europe, Central Asia (formerly much of the Soviet Union), and Africa. His basis for these choosing these three Unions were that Europe could provide the technical and economic foundation, Central Asia could provide the petroleum resources and industrial strength, and Africa could provide the raw materials and man-power. As to who would oversee and supervise the first joint Union, David recommended that he personally manage it, since this one was the most important and would also be the most difficult.[12]

Another significant reform (although perhaps a few years away) was the establishment of a new religion that would encompass all the religions in the world. Granted, there would be a number of people who would refuse to join, and these obstacles would be handled as they arose. Once the currencies and econo-

---

[12] The world leader will initially take over three of the ten "kingdoms" of the earth. (Daniel 7:24)

mies were all united, the people would be much more willing to alter their long-held religions also.

The new religion would be designed with tolerance and acceptance as its greatest pillars, and once the traditions, holidays, and grandeur of the new belief system were firmly established, all the people would naturally gravitate to the new religion. Since religion tended to be such an emotional, traditional issue to most of mankind, the world religion would be one of the last major pillars to be established.

Eventually the lesser pillars of society would need to be established also, such as marriage that was no longer restricted to a single man and woman, and the raising of all children over six months old by the state. The new race made up of the children from the Great Vanishing would probably be the first generation in which these changes would take effect.

For the last of his proposals, he suggested the most surprising reform of all: the introduction of a new era: the Age of Peace (and as such, abbreviated "A.P."). If the world was to cast off its violent, divided past, then they must all commemorate it with a new era, and one that would constantly remind them of their new world. The old designations such as B.C.E. and C.E. would remain of course, but the archaic B.C. and A.D. would be completely removed from existence.

Yes, the reforms were wide-sweeping and incredible, but so was the era they were living in. The world could not afford to squander this unique opportunity for peace and prosperity. [13]

The World Union leaders immediately accepted all of his recommendations and began discussing how to turn them into reality.

But first, they made plans to introduce him and his impressive plan for unification to the world.

---

[13] The world leader will seek to change the times and the laws; a likely change will be the introduction of a new era denoted by a new name that has nothing to do with Jesus Christ. Part of this change has already occurred in many school textbooks, universities, etc. (Daniel 7:25)

CHRIS HAMBLETON

* * *

On the last day of October, the World Union leaders gathered and held another worldwide news conference. Every television and radio broadcast was interrupted for their important news. All work in nearly every factory, office, and business ceased, and the people watched and listened.

The Secretary of the World Union rose to his feet and walked confidently to the podium. His face was beaming, and that helped relieve everyone's fears that another frightening development had taken place.

"Noble citizens of the world," he began. "As you all know, four months ago we were visited by the Anshar – the supreme beings who gave life to earth and who made it possible for us to arise, and who have promised to take us to the next step in our evolution." He paused as the journalists and news media clapped wildly and then waited for the applause to subside.

"For the last four months, the Anshar have been revealing many truths to the world, and they have provided tremendous assistance during these times of change. They have also given us great hope in promising to send a great leader who will guide humanity through the perilous years ahead as we throw off our constraints of time, space, and matter as we begin our journey to the stars. And as they have foretold, I am pleased to present this great leader to you at this time – the Chosen One."

He attempted to continue speaking, but the wild cheers and applause from the media drowned him out, so he graciously waited for it to quiet down. He had thought about announcing his resignation at that time also, but they had decided against it. He would stay on as an advisor during the passing of leadership duties to David Medine.

"And now, I am most pleased to present to you the new Secretary of the World Union: His Excellency, David Medine!" he said, turning to a tall, very handsome man who had been seated next to him among the other World Union leaders. If the applause had been tremendous before, it was nothing compared to the uproar that resounded now.

THE TIME OF JACOB'S TROUBLE

David Medine rose confidently and strode to the podium to stand next to the outgoing Secretary, smiling graciously and shaking his hand. And as he began to speak, the audience noticed that his aura began to brighten, and they became mesmerized by his mere presence. He was a phenomenally charismatic speaker, with every word being eloquent and articulate. He spoke with such charisma, confidence, and authority that people almost stopped listening to what he was really saying. The words almost didn't matter – the people immediately loved this new powerful, confident leader. The world needed someone who could guide them, someone who could shepherd them.

And Medine promised to do just that. He proclaimed that no longer would individuals have no say in their government. As the foremost of the Anshar principles, democracy would flourish everywhere. In their eternal bodies, they would all be kings, and servants never again.

He would favor no particular group, race, gender, tribe, or nation. Since his awakening, he no longer saw himself as Jewish nor Iraqi, but as Anshar. He would seek the peace and prosperity of all. Equality would rule the earth as the Anshar had always intended. Once equality was reached, the entire human race could move forward together in their evolution.

Above all, he would be merely their servant, their prince – he would shepherd them according to their needs and desires. He declared he would not use the title of "World Leader" or "World Chancellor", but would be referred to as their "Sarrim" – their prince. The Anshar would no longer communicate directly to them except through him, and he would mediate with the Anshar on their behalf. Once the human race was ready to take the next step of evolution, the Anshar would come and live among them, ushering them into the final phase of immortality. Together they would even conquer death itself.

After he finished speaking, every news channel played and replayed his speech, and analyzed every part. All of the commentators raved about the Sarrim. There was not a word of criticism about him – not even questions about what would happen to the former Secretary. People all over the world seemed immediately more at peace after his introduction. Humanity had now been given their ultimate leader – the prince of princes – the one who would lead them into eternity. [14]

* * *

"Hello?" Naomi answered as she picked up the phone.

"Hi Mom – it's me. Hey, have you been listening to the news?" Saul asked.

"No. What's going on?" she asked, quickly going over to the small television she kept in her office. She had always kept one there, in case there was an emergency or an attack. During the long years of the Intifada, it had come in valuable several times.

"Go to the news channel – you know, the one Dad always has on," he said.

"Okay. What's happening?" she repeated.

"It's all starting, Mom! Just like the Bible says!" exclaimed Saul.

"What is?" she asked.

"The Tribulation! The man all over the news today, David Medine – I think he's the Anti-Christ!" he said, almost frantically.

"Are you serious? Why do you think that?" she asked, trying to keep the skepticism out of her voice.

"Mom, I know it sounds crazy right now, but you have to believe me. This man, this super-man – he's not who he seems to be. He's very dangerous, just like the Anshar. The Bible says the Anti-Christ will be an incredible world leader, and that he will change the times, just like what Medine is proposing. Also, the Bible alludes to him having some strong connection to angels or aliens or something else supernatural. Just watch the news for a few minutes – everyone is going crazy over him!"

Naomi started flipping through the channels and sure

---

[14] The coming world leader will be a great speaker and conquers by prosperity, unity, and peace. Often in the Bible, God allows evil or a ruler to reach their worst before He judges. (Daniel 7:25, 8:23-25, 11:36-39)

enough, David Medine's introduction or a newscaster talking about him was nearly on every channel, and not just on the news channels either. Even the movie channels had been interrupted and the commentators were talking about him there too.

"How can you be sure if he's really the Anti-Christ?" she asked. "People have been saying that about every great leader for thousands of years," she stated, trying to bring some common sense into the conversation.

She remembered well about that kind of foolishness in the United States, such as when some religious extremists decades before proclaimed that President Reagan was the Anti-Christ simply because he was very eloquent and just happened to have exactly six letters in his first, middle, and last names. And when he had quickly recovered in his old age from a nearly fatal wound, they said it had proven their case all the more.

"I know, but this is different," he said. "The way to be certain if Medine is the Anti-Christ is if he signs a seven-year treaty with Israel. The Bible is very specific about it – watch for some type of seven-year treaty, peace deal, or 'covenant' that protects Israel or the Temple. On the day the treaty is signed, the seven-year Tribulation will begin – and you need to be ready for it!" he said emphatically.

"Alright, I'll try –" she began.

"Oh, and Mom?" he broke in. "Sorry to interrupt. But be sure you tell Dad about what I told you, even if he doesn't want to hear it," he said. "Since he won't listen to me, maybe he will be more open to hearing it from you."

She promised she would (even though she didn't want to), and he said he would call her in a few days when things calmed down.

CHAPTER 7
THE RISE OF BABYLON

T he nation of Iraq had captured much of the world's attention for years, starting with the invasion of Kuwait in the 1990s by the Butcher of Baghdad, Saddam Hussein. For the next twelve years, Iraq had been turned into a virtual prison camp for its dictator and citizens alike, with hundreds of thousands of people dying of either inadequate food or medical supplies, or at the hand of their dictator and his regime.

In 2003, the United States invaded Iraq to finally dethrone the dictator and the Baath regime because of its denial and subterfuge of its WMD programs and stockpiles. Years of terrorism and reconstruction followed, and the initial reconstruction policies took a high toll on both the Iraqis and the Americans while Iraq was rebuilt under a democratic government.

Four years after the invasion and nearly continuous terrorism, the American people had finally had enough, and threatened to leave if the Iraqi government did not make widespread, sweeping changes to fight the radicalism within its own borders. To assist them, the Americans dramatically increased their troop levels, and the Surge overwhelmed the terrorists and drew the various factions of the country together.

Saddam Hussein had been apprehended and convicted of genocide and other crimes late in 2006 and then hung early in 2007, but the terrorism had continued. The war had grown increasingly unpopular in the United States, and there had been little progress in Iraq. Based upon the recommendations (and increased pressure) by the Americans, the Iraqis instituted an oil-

THE TIME OF JACOB'S TROUBLE

revenue sharing model for all its citizens. Each citizen would own an equal share in the oil revenues. Once a month, and also once a year each Iraqi would receive a deposit from the government for their share of the oil revenues. But the success of the plan rested primarily on the numerous factions coming together to stop the terrorists living among them.

The reduction in terrorism was nearly immediate after the revenue-sharing plan was announced. The first month saw a minor decrease, but after the first oil revenue checks were sent out, the reports of hidden terrorists came flooding in. The Iraqi security forces responded promptly and harshly against the terrorists and other rebels. Often, firefights would erupt and the terrorists would all fight until they were killed, with very few of them ever being taken prisoner. Within six months, nearly all the IED explosions and suicide bombings had ceased, especially in Baghdad and the other urban areas.

Once the nation had ridden itself of the terrorists among them, tourism began in earnest, to everyone's surprise. Soon money was flowing into the country from a multitude of sources, and not only from the oil industry. Saddam had spent millions of dollars excavating and rebuilding the royal palaces and temples of ancient Babylon. The oldest city in the world enjoyed throngs of tourists and the businesses that came to tour the places they had been hearing about on the news for years. And the recent selection of Babylon by the Anshar had greatly increased the attention on the tiny, but quickly growing ancient city.[15]

For the first time in decades, the people of Iraq began making real progress in the rebuilding of their nation. With the destruction of many of the nations around them in the Magog

---

[15] The literal city of Babylon will rise in last days to be overthrown in a very short time by a combination of God and several armies. There is also a "spiritual Babylon" which many surmise is the city of Rome (or the Vatican), which may also be moved to Babylon. There are many strong parallels between Babel and Babylon, and Nimrod and the world leader. Judgment of the post-Flood age comes full circle from Babel back to Babylon. (Zechariah 5:11; Revelation 17-18)

Invasion, the Iraqis found themselves once again becoming the center of attention, as the world sought their plentiful oil supplies. Iraq quickly became the vital link between India and China in the east and the commercial nations to the west in Europe.

After the Anshar had selected their ancient city of Babylon to be the new center for world unity, the Iraqis were filled with pride that their nation was once again a rising star.

Babylon would soon be the crown city of the world – the jewel of kingdoms – as in her days of the Babylonian, Persian, and Greek Empires.

The Iraqi people were sure of it.

* * *

Jacob grimaced as he pulled into his parking space. After days of guilt over his reaction towards Saul about his religious conversion, he finally decided to reach out to his son.

He had refused to speak with him even on the phone, but he had finally come to realize that he was being foolish at ostracizing his own son. He had already lost one child in the last six months, and he realized that he was causing another one to become lost to him too, but this time by his own doing.

He had never been good at apologizing, except probably to his wife. Usually when he said something, he meant it, and would refuse to back down. He never knew where to begin, especially with Naomi, so he typically started with flowers and a groveling "I'm sorry."

But this was different, since it was his son and not his wife. He had always appeared reserved and strong to his children, especially his sons. Ruth had always been his little girl, and he had been softer with her. And part of being strong in his eyes meant never apologizing. He wanted them to be tough and strong, and to get used to the unfairness of life, especially in Israel. But he had been wrong to say what he did and had made it even worse since he had thrown Saul out of his house.

He got out of the car, took out his briefcase, and then walked up to the front door of the office. He chided himself for not calling Saul sooner – in these uncertain times, who knew when someone's last day could be?

He went straight to his office and then locked the door behind him, leaving the lights off. His assistant would know from the closed door to leave him alone as long as he needed. If he didn't take care of this before his day started, he wouldn't have another opportunity to call him until later that evening. He set down his briefcase on the desk and dialed Saul's cell-phone number.

"Hello?" Saul answered.

"Hi Saul. It's your father. Do you have a few minutes?" he said, in a softer tone than he usually had.

"Uh, sure. How have you been?" Saul was actually very busy that morning, but this was more important than anything he would have to do that day.

"Okay. Listen, I don't know where to start here, so I'll just go ahead and say it." He took a long pause before continuing. "I'm very sorry for what happened between us the other night. I was wrong to react the way that I did. I made a bigger issue out of it than it really was. Anyways, I'm sorry." There – he had said it – the hard part was over.

"Thanks, Dad – that means a lot," Saul answered. Jacob felt as if a huge weight had been lifted off his shoulders, and that somewhat surprised him.

"I also wanted to tell you that I'm proud of you for stepping out on your own. I may not agree with your decision or your beliefs, but I know it took guts to do what you did. Are you doing okay?" he asked.

"Yeah, I'm fine. I'm still getting used to everything. We're getting more people coming in now. At first, it was pretty quiet most of the time."

"Would you like to come over for dinner tonight? I'll have to let your mother know, unless you just want to surprise her," Jacob said with a grin.

"That'd be great – I'll be there, Dad. Same time as usual?" he asked.

"Of course," Jacob replied. They had been eating at the same exact time every night for decades, and it wasn't a pleasant evening when dinner was late.

"I'll call your mother and let her know. I'll see you tonight, son," Jacob said, drawing the conversation to a close.

"Okay, Dad. Thanks for calling – it means a lot," Saul said.

"Same here – we'll see you at dinner then."

"Bye, Dad. See you tonight."

Jacob hung up the phone and breathed a sigh of relief. It hadn't been as bad as he had thought, but it still hadn't been enjoyable.

Sometimes that was the price one had to pay to keep a family together.

*   *   *

In the months that had followed the Magog Invasion, the demand for Iraq's oil and natural gas supplies had skyrocketed, since most of the other major oil producers in the region had been destroyed. Saudi Arabia was still the primary oil exporter to the industrialized world, but its equipment was aging and most of its reserves were already heavily developed, whereas Iraq's were not. For the most part, the resources of Iraq were still untapped, and new oil fields were discovered on a regular basis. With the huge disruption of both Russia's and Iran's petroleum industry, the world turned to Iraq to meet their critical oil needs.[16]

Not only was Iraq now a major raw petroleum supplier, but was also quickly becoming one of the top refiners in the world. The practices, principles, and technology the Iraqis had acquired from the United States during the years of rebuilding had laid the foundation for their incredible future growth and prosperity. While most of the land of Iraq had significant oil deposits, ancient Babylon had been built directly on top of one of the largest reserves. And Babylon's central location and close proximity to the Tigris and Euphrates Rivers also provided efficient shipping routes to both the north into Central Asia and south to the Persian Gulf.

---

[16] Babylon grows very rich in the last days, though the entire region has been very poor for many centuries. (Revelation 18:11-13)

THE TIME OF JACOB'S TROUBLE

Between the sheer economic potential and the richness of its long history, Babylon was officially designated the permanent world capital by the World Union. Since the Anshar had already chosen it to be their primary residence, the World Union had followed suit and began planning a city that would be worthy of its designation, history, and importance. The ancient part of city would be completely restored to its former glory, and the new city would be built all around it.

All the buildings, roads, gardens, parks, and infrastructure would be state-of-the-art, and Babylon would soon be the envy of the world. Just as the city of Dubai rose like a glittering oasis out of the desert, so the great city of Babylon would rise from the barren wilderness of Iraq and blossom to become the greatest city in the history of the earth.

Construction crews and companies flocked to Iraq for the lucrative contracts and quickly began building the new world capital. Labor from Asia, Africa, and all over the Middle East migrated by the tens of thousands to Babylon and the surrounding areas. The amount of foreign capital that poured into Iraq was staggering, and much of the investment capital was also pulled from other modern nations such as the United States and even India to invest in Babylon. The Iraqis, along with the World Union, intricately planned nearly all the infrastructure of Babylon and took massive future growth into account from the onset.

The first and foremost of the buildings to be built were those that would belong to the World Union. The new Tower of Illumination would be the tallest building on the entire earth, and would be built directly on top of the ruins of the ancient Tower of Babel (at the suggestion of the Anshar). The World Union also decreed that no other building on the earth could be built taller than the Tower. It would be nearly two kilometers tall, surpassing even the mile-high tower the Arabs had recently built.

The gardens and parks that encompassed the capital structures would be immaculate, and many of them would be placed on the terraces of the buildings similar to the ancient Hanging Gardens of Babylon, during its prior days of glory.

Some quipped that it would be the new Tower of Babel,

since it was so tall and because it had been built directly on top of the ruins of the original tower. David Medine thought it rather fitting, since the Tower of Babel had been the last time the An- shar had regular, intimate contact with mankind before the peo- ple had been scattered.

While the Tower of Illumination was being constructed, buildings and roads all around it for kilometers sprang up like grass and trees from the ground. Within a year, the entire area would be transformed from barren desert lands into the most beautiful city on the face of the earth.

*   *   *

The executives at the architecture firm had just announced being awarded the largest contract in the history of the company, which was quite significant since it was already nearly twenty years old.

Ahban had been working there for over five years and was considered one of their rising stars. He loved his work (his mother said that he loved it a bit too much) and would do what- ever was asked of him to move the company forward. And if his career continued to take off also, that would be fine too.

He smiled and raised his champagne glass as the CEO made a grand toast after making the announcement. It would be a good year – actually, it would be a good five years, if not longer. Since his last promotion, he was now entitled to annual bonuses and other incentives when the teams beat their deadlines. He often worked long hours – typically twelve or more hours a day, and usually the same amount from home on the weekends. But it would all pay off, he thought; at not even thirty years old, he was already making more money than his own father. And this con- tract and the opportunities it presented would translate directly into an even earlier retirement for him later.

The contract his firm had just been awarded was to design and construct a significant number of the government buildings and other municipal structures for the new city of Babylon. It was astounding to see how much money had been invested in that city in such a short amount of time. The firm was now so prominent and respected that it had been in the running for the Tower of Illumination, but they had come in third in the final tallies.

The firm's executives had been disappointed, but they made up for it after they won the Babylon municipalities' bid, which was just as large as the Tower of Illumination contract. But it would have nowhere near as much visibility, nor generate as much publicity as the other contract would have.

His first thought was to tell his father about the announcement – he would be so proud. Ahban waited until the celebration was finished and then went back to his office and closed the door. He pulled out his new cell-phone (just two days old) and called his father.

"This is Jacob," his father answered.

"Hi Dad. This is Ahban – I have some great news!" he said excitedly.

"What's that? You're getting married?" he joked.

"Ha – I'm afraid not, but it may be just as good. My company just won a huge contract to design many of the government buildings in Babylon. This is really big for the company."

"Congratulations – what part will you be playing in that?" Jacob asked.

"Well, that's the other good news – I'll be heading up one of the teams that will go over there."

"That's great! So that means you'll be traveling there quite often then?"

"Actually, Dad – it means I'll be moving there. I'll probably have to put my condo up for sale and buy one there instead. With the real estate market booming over there, I could end up doing pretty well when I sell that one too."

"Oh, I see," he replied. Ahban could tell from his tone that he was disappointed at the prospect of him moving away.

"Have you talked to Saul lately?" Ahban asked. "I heard from Mom that he left his job to become a street preacher or something. Is that true?"

"Yeah, that's about right, for the most part. He's working in a ministry, but I don't think he's a preacher – he's much too shy for that."

"Either way, it sounds kind of stupid to me," he said, matter-of-factly. He still couldn't believe that his younger brother had just became a Christian and quit his job. It ran completely counter to everything they had been raised to believe.

"I agree. But he's still my son and your brother, and we'll do our best to accept his decisions and get along," he said firmly.

Ahban agreed and replied, "Sure – I'm just still surprised, that's all. Anyway, I have to get back to work. Talk to you later, Dad."

"Okay – goodbye, son. Stop by the house before you leave – we'll all have to get-together for a going-away dinner or something."

"Thanks, Dad. I will," he said, and he flipped the phone shut.

* * *

David Medine's supernatural skills and abilities were already paying great dividends in his quest to remold and unite humanity, but the growing problems in the religiously-oriented Middle East might become a serious threat to his plans.

It was the same old story there: the Muslims and the Jews again. It would have been almost comical if the situation wasn't so frustrating. From an early age, he had always distrusted religion, especially the more fanatical sects of the various religions. They usually were so exclusive – it was always either their way or no way. The arrival of the Anshar had all but disproven that foolish, antiquated thinking. But some continued to stubbornly hold onto their old beliefs.

But religion did play a critical role in the lives of billions of people in the world, and had been frequently used throughout history as a tool of the state to influence and sometimes even control the masses. Perhaps he could devise a means of harnessing the wealth, power, and zeal of the Middle East into a system for the benefit of all humanity. Islam was still a significant belief system in nearly all the Middle East, but its power and influence had been greatly diminished after the annihilation of the Magog Invasion forces. But their tribal and national pride was still strong, and perhaps their zeal could simply be redirected and put to better use.

One impediment to using religion as a tool was that it often spun out of control, especially the monotheistic religions. This had occurred in both Christianity and Islam, and even Judaism to some extent. There was just something about the worship of a monotheistic god that seemed to draw out a particular zeal and fervor in people that was hard to set aside later. And while the separation of religion and state had its own set of advantages and freedoms, it had led to division after division – Europe and the Americas were prime examples of that, even though they were now stable and peaceful, for the most part.

Also, he must choose carefully the figurehead of this new religion. The man also had to be controlled to some extent, without him being fully aware of it, lest he use his power and authority for himself instead of the cause. He must be an incredibly charismatic leader, good looking, intelligent, and wise. He must be one who fully supported the goals of unifying mankind and moving forward in their evolution. He would exert an enormous influence over a huge part of the world, and would be second to only David Medine himself.

If he was to harness the power of religion to unify mankind, then it had to be one of complete tolerance and inclusion. The primary moral law would be that intolerance would simply not be tolerated. After all, they were all of one race with many physical, mental, and emotional differences – why wouldn't the same hold true with their spiritual differences also? And mankind was already off to a head-start in this area, since most of the belief systems in the world were fairly tolerant and quite accepting of the Anshar and all they had to offer. Christianity and Orthodox Judaism seemed to be the ones that were most suspicious of the Anshar, and even wary about himself to some extent.

But he felt he had little to fear from either of them, especially from the Christians. Millions of the most extreme Christians in their ranks had been taken from the earth at the same time the children had, and so a major source of disunity had been instantly removed without him having to do anything.

The Orthodox Jews presented a similar problem as the Christians, but there was a major difference: hundreds of thousands of Jews had migrated back to Israel because of the cleanup and the new Temple project. Perhaps he could increase the migration and confine them to mostly Israel, instead of having them scattered all over the world.

Yes – that was it: he would encourage the Jews from all over the world to move back to their homeland to unite with their own people first. And then once the Jews were isolated, the new World religion would stand a much better chance of permanently taking root and then sprouting throughout the rest of the world.

And after a period of segregation and marginalization, perhaps the "radical" Jews would realize how silly and exclusive they were, and would grow to embrace the new belief system as the rest of the world had.

David Medine smiled as he looked out the window and watched the foundation of the Tower be laid.

*   *   *

Hundreds of kilometers to the west in Israel, another historic construction project was underway: the rebuilding of the Jewish Temple. Security was extremely tight around the entire Temple Mount, especially on the Jewish side of the site.

While world opinion had shifted to support Israel (more or less) after the Magog Invasion, it had recently begun to turn antagonistic towards Israel as the Temple project progressed. There were often lies and rumors spread that the Jews were planning to destroy the Al-Aqsa Mosque or even the Dome of the Rock. As a result of the false rumors, resentment from Muslims and Arabs in the area had began to simmer and steadily increase.[17]

The Temple Institute had thoroughly designed and modeled

---

[17]   The Jewish Temple will be rebuilt and exist in the last days. (Daniel 9:27; Matthew 24:15; 2 Thessalonians 2:3-4)

the entire new Temple years before any construction had begun. The Temple design had been largely modeled after the previous one, often called Herod's Temple. All their plans and specifications had been checked and revised, and many of the materials had already been purchased even before the Magog Invasion had occurred. Nearly all the aspects of construction had been planned far in advance, and when authorization to build the Temple was finally granted, construction rapidly moved ahead.

Compared to other modern architectural tasks, many aspects of the Temple design were relatively simple. The Temple itself was composed of a two-story, rectangular building made of glistening white marble. Directly in front of the Temple was a porch with pillars in front. Surrounding the Temple and the porch was a huge open area for the priests.

In front of the porch was an open area for the Jewish worshippers. Much further away from the porch was another wall that divided the Temple grounds nearly in half, and outside that gated wall was the Outer Courts, where the Gentiles could worship. Another huge wall surrounded the Outer Courts, with several gates along each side facing outward. Artisans and craftsmen from all over the world were contracted and flown into Jerusalem to sculpt the Temple features and artwork, strictly according to the Temple Institute's designs.

For the Dedication ceremonies that would commemorate the completion of the Temple, the Temple Institute planned to invite hundreds of Jewish and Christian groups who had supported them with contributions and resources over the years. They were quickly granted the permission to invite their supporters first, since the Temple Institute had been the foremost contributor in the rebuilding of the Temple.

All the priests who would serve at the Dedication had already been chosen by lottery, and were busily preparing for their ceremonial duties. The Dedication of the Temple would occupy a full seven days of activities and celebrations at the Temple, and the local government of Jerusalem expected the city to be bursting with people during the Dedication Week.

Most of Israel was filled with excitement as the Temple

quickly began taking shape. This was the event their people had been looking forward to for over nineteen hundred years.

*   *   *

Saul looked through the small pile of mail that had been delivered for the day, and began separating the junk mail from the bills and catalogs.

At the bottom of the stack, he noticed a pamphlet that he had almost put in the junk pile. "Come Worship at the Temple!" it said in bright gold lettering, and it showed a color photograph of the new Jewish Temple. The Temple was nearly completed, and its progress had been all over the news recently. He smiled and set it aside.

After the rest of the mail was sorted, he picked up the pamphlet and knocked on the door of Daniel's office. He was busy with paperwork and bookkeeping that afternoon, but fortunately he only had to do it once a week.

"Hi Saul. Come in – I could use a break," Daniel said, sliding back from the desk and rubbing his eyes. "What's up?"

"Check out what came in the mail today – an invitation for the Dedication of the Temple. Want to go?" asked Saul. He handed the brochure to him to read over.

"Sure – do you have time to sign us up? I'm swamped today," he said.

"Yeah – I'll look around for a place for us to stay while I'm at it, too," Saul replied.

From the time they had restarted the ministry, Daniel and Saul had formed a great working relationship. They had divided most of the office work according to their skills; Daniel did the books and speaking/preaching, while Saul did most of the computer and technical work, pamphlets, and the rest of the miscellaneous office tasks.

"This is going to be big – do you think there will be riots or something?" Saul asked.

"There might be, but security has been so tight there from the start that I don't think they'll be able to pull off anything significant. I'd be more concerned at the time of the next Passover or Yom Kippur," Daniel said.

"He'll be there, won't he?"

"Medine? I'd assume so. I'm sure he'll make a big deal about giving us the Temple and the seven-year treaty. But I doubt we'll see him – they will probably just have World Union leaders and the media at the signing of the treaty," said Daniel, thinking out loud.

Saul smirked. "That sounds like him. I'll make sure we get reservations and lodging," Saul said confidently and picked up the pamphlet.

He went back to his own office to make reservations right away. If they couldn't find a hotel to stay at, they'd probably have to call a local church or ministry in Jerusalem and ask to stay with them instead.

They had been studying Bible prophecy everyday since they had restarted the ministry, and were now well-versed in those books and passages. While the events leading up to the End Times had been written about long-before in the Tanakh, many of the New Testament prophecies concerning the Church itself had no definite time as to when they would occur.

However, the New Testament prophecies about the End Times after the "Anti-Christ" signed the seven-year peace deal with Israel were very precise as to when and where they would occur in the prophetic timeline. But the event that would start the End Times clock was the signing of a seven-year treaty with Israel by an unnamed great world leader.

Both men were very grateful to those who had set up the ministry before them. Christian commentaries and studies were becoming harder and harder to find, especially in the bookstores. There was still a huge amount of Christian books and such available, but few of them followed the Bible any longer, especially the more recent books. The Internet was becoming a greater threat to the World Union, since it was so difficult to regulate and censor. But certainly the various secular groups were working on hard to restrict true Christian content and the availability of Bible resources.

The Way and other ministries had foreseen that sooner or later the government would censor their materials, and Biblical literature would become more difficult to find. At first the censorship would be quiet and in the background, but would become more public after the Judgments began. Therefore many of the Christians and ministries began downloading and copying as much of the online Bible notes and literature they could find.

Some younger Christians who were more technology-savvy found clever ways to hide documents and other files, and often hid large audio sermons and files all over the Internet.

Those resources would become vital in the long years ahead.

* * *

When the Temple was nearly finished, the local Muslims and Arabs launched a huge protest against the Temple. While they were not entirely happy about the Temple being rebuilt as a national symbol, they were emphatic about it never being used as a place of worship.

They began to spread rumors again and put their propaganda machines into action, saying that they had been under the assumption that the Jews only wanted to rebuild it for tourist or historical reasons, but not at all for religious ones. They raised such an outcry against it that the threat of violence against the Jews once again became common.

David Medine, not wanting to see the Middle Eastern Union split apart over the Temple, had begun holding joint negotiations between Israel, Saudi Arabia, and the Palestinian Arabs in an attempt to calm the rising tensions. He was furious that foolish religious problems there kept coming up. Those groups had been fighting for thousands of years over such petty issues.

He decided that he would have to push the World Union to accelerate the establishment of the new religion and force all these fools into it, before they started another war. He had too many other critical issues to attend to in Babylon to permanently solve the Middle East problem.

THE TIME OF JACOB'S TROUBLE

Medine decided to postpone the permanent decision concerning the Temple and the Jerusalem dilemma in general. He quickly drew up a plan that would hopefully placate all the groups involved.

The Jews would give up some of the land they had reacquired in the West Bank in exchange for a seven-year guarantee of peace and security. The Palestinians and the Arabs would be less likely to raise further problems over the Temple if the full weight of the World Union was behind it. The seven-year postponement of the lasting solution would buy some time to spread the World religion in that area, along with the establishment of the global economy. All he needed was a little more time.

To enforce the treaty, if Israel did not live up to their side to provide decent land and infrastructure to the Palestinians, then the Temple would immediately be placed under international control. And if the terrorism did not stop from the Palestinians, then they would be relocated to Jordan. He knew that this would be the point that would be more difficult to enforce, since the Palestinian groups could always deny being involved in any terrorist acts, but still support them nevertheless. But perhaps the new economic and religious changes would come in time to reduce the terrorism to acceptable levels to prevent the region's tensions from boiling over again.

David Medine brought the Muslims and Jews back to the negotiating table, and the Jews readily signed onto it. The Israelis' return to Judaism and the fervor of their desire for the Temple bothered him.

But perhaps in several years their zeal would decrease so they would be better able to work out a permanent solution. The West Bank had not been fully redeveloped anyway, and there was still plenty of land to negotiate with.

The Palestinians and other Arab groups initially opposed the proposal, but when they talked it over among themselves, they realized that the solution was by no means permanent, and perhaps they could find a loophole or exploit some aspect of the treaty to benefit them. They had been practicing the art of media manipulation and propaganda for decades, and they were masters at portraying Israel as the primary obstacle to peace, no matter who was causing the problems in the region.

In the end, both parties verbally agreed to the seven-year peace treaty, and would formally sign it just before the Temple's Dedication.

*   *   *

On the day Israel signed the treaty that Medine had brokered, ominous dark clouds filled the skies over the entire land of Israel, causing most of the population to turn on their televisions, radios, and computers to find out what was happening.

And at the moment David Medine signed the treaty, lightning flashed over the new Temple, and struck it on its uppermost tower. Part of the roof caught fire and was promptly put out by the emergency crews nearby. Lightning was very rare over the city of Jerusalem, and it was quite odd that only one huge bolt had struck.

But Medine shrugged it off as if it was just a bizarre coincidence, and proudly held up the signed treaty and showed it to everyone. Suddenly a downpour of rain began and drove everyone to find shelter. The treaty signing ended as quickly as it had begun, and within moments the entire area was deserted except for the chairs. Some video clips showed Medine clearly angry about the unnatural rainstorm, but they were quickly pulled from the Internet.

After watching the live coverage of the lightning and the signing of the treaty, many Israelis were left with an uncomfortable feeling in the pit of their stomachs, even though most didn't want to admit it.

The rainstorm was quite extraordinary, since it rarely rained at that time in Jerusalem. Many witnesses also said it had rained only over the Temple Mount. Medine was immensely popular all over the world, but especially in Israel. In some parts of the world, small statues of Medine had been made and sold in large numbers, and millions of people included him in their list of gods and worshipped him. Of course, many in the secular nations did not do that, but he was highly revered among them. They worshipped him without bowing or offerings, but gave him their utmost reverence and respect nonetheless.

Now that the treaty was signed, an air of electricity ran through Jerusalem, and throughout most of Israel. The Jews finally had their beloved Temple. Many of them still couldn't believe it, and even the secular Jews were surprised at how proud they felt that it was finally rebuilt. The Orthodox Jews could be frequently seen dancing in the streets and in front of their homes. The synagogues were bursting with activity, and it seemed like everyone was trying to get to Jerusalem to see the new Temple for themselves.

And after nearly two thousand years, the Jewish Temple was ready for its rededication and the offering of sacrifices once again.

*   *   *

On the same day the seven-year treaty was signed, far off in the wilderness of Judea, two figures arose from the sands of the desert.

They strode steadily with an air of authority, solemnity, and purpose. Immediately after leaving the vicinity of Mt. Nebo, they began walking west towards Jerusalem. They had only met on earth once before that day, but they knew one another very well. These two men had been given the same mission: to usher their people back their Lord, remove the veil from their eyes, and open their ears to their God.

Both men had not walked these lands in nearly three thousand years. Both were great prophets who had been ignored and even hated by their people at the time, yet revered by those who had followed later. They knew their destiny and the outcome of their mission. But they were resolved to accomplish that which had been given to them.

They had been given a second opportunity to turn the hearts of their people back to their God. Their ministry would last for three and a half years: one thousand, two hundred and sixty days, to be precise. One had tasted death while the other had not, but both would after those days were finished.

One appeared much younger than the other, but both were heavily bearded and wiry looking. They were wearing the same robes and garments they had worn on their last day on earth, and they would wear them until their ministry was completed.

They walked side by side, neither moving ahead of the other, for both had a singular, common purpose. They would not merely preach with words, but with curses, plagues, and signs. Incredible power and authority had been granted to them, and they would use whatever means necessary to get their message across to their people.

The wilderness lands of Judea had not changed much over the last three thousand years, but the rest of Israel had, mostly in just the last century. Much of Israel was now covered with paved roads, office buildings, industrial complexes, homes, apartment buildings, restaurants, and the like.

But those aspects of modern life would not affect them much, since they knew the days ahead and what would happen soon to the people of Israel. When they had been alive many centuries before, their previous ministries had not been completed. They had been brought back to finish the task that the Lord had decreed for them.

And then three days later, the greatest of the ancient prophets of Israel – Moses and Elijah, alive once again – entered the city limits of Jerusalem.[18]

* * *

Naomi walked in through the back door, put her purse and keys on the counter, and then went into the living room to sit down on the sofa.

She hadn't been feeling well that day. It wasn't that she

---

[18] The Two Witnesses testify against Israel with preaching and judgments. The judgments they bring upon Israel closely parallel those wrought by Moses and Elijah, who also happened to be at the Transfiguration of Jesus. (Matthew 17:2-4; Revelation 11:3-13)

really felt sick, but uneasy and anxious about everything that was going on. Perhaps she just needed to slow down for a day or two. She was starting menopause, so maybe that was the source of her discomfort. She decided to go to her doctor if she didn't feel better in a few days. Business had been slow that afternoon, and she knew it was in capable hands for the rest of the day.

For now, she just wanted to figure out what was bothering her. Ahban was moving to Babylon, and she didn't like that. She couldn't quite put her finger on why, since it was a great opportunity for him and his career. Babylon was a great city that had suddenly risen from the middle of a scorching desert. In just one short year, it was well on its way to becoming another world wonder.

Saul and Daniel were in Jerusalem attending the Temple Dedication ceremonies for the next seven days, and she had been worried about that too. They would be coming back late next week, staying a few days longer than they had initially planned. They had found a similar ministry with some members that had offered to let them stay with them during the celebration. Naomi was relieved that Jacob and Saul had reconciled their differences months before.

She could tell that Jacob had been affected from the incident too, but now he was spending more time with her in the evenings and less in his office. She was glad for that – now that all the children were gone, she felt lonely more often, and Jacob had seemed more sensitive to that lately.

Probably Ahban's moving away was weighing on him too, but it was a bit strange that he wasn't throwing himself into his work when things were rough at home. He had always been a creature of habit, and when there were domestic problems, he usually escaped from them (in some sense) by working more hours. But this time he had not been doing that, even though life at home was very unsettled.

Maybe a cup of hot tea would help, Naomi thought. She went to the kitchen to put on a kettle of water. As she turned on the stove, she smiled at how Jacob and the boys had always given her a hard time about heating water the "old-fashioned" way. It was a waste of electricity and much slower, they had always complained – why couldn't she just microwave it like everyone else?

But Ruth had always understood, and they had had many teas together when she had lived at home. It was one of their mother-daughter activities that they had both cherished. At times, a good tea could easily take them an hour, and they usually tried to have tea together about once a week.

There was just something comforting about doing certain things the old way, like she had done with her own mother when she was growing up. Even the little things, like waiting for the kettle to whistle when the water came to a boil.

Staring at the beautifully hand-painted kettle, tears suddenly came to her eyes and she began to weep. Ruth had given her that kettle a few years ago for her birthday, and every time she saw it, she always thought of Ruth. She missed her so much – why did she have to be taken? They had always been close, and the last year with her had been among the best they had ever had.

And yet she had been a Christian the entire time and she hadn't even known it! What had drawn her to those beliefs? It wasn't as if she and Jacob had ever pushed religion on their children, and none of her friends had been religious either.

She remembered back to the night of the Magog Invasion, and how she was sure that Ruth had called out to Yeshua – that must have been when it happened, she thought. From that time on, Ruth had been different. Not in a bad way, but somehow she had nearly instantly changed about how she behaved and treated those around her.

And now Saul was a Christian too! Ruth's disappearance must have been what caused him to convert to Christianity also. Would Ahban be next, she wondered, and then shook her head. She just couldn't ever see that happening – that would be a miracle!

The kettle began to whistle. She wiped her eyes and rose to turn off the stove. She reached for a tea bag, and then decided to make the whole pot instead of just one cup. A long afternoon tea might be just what she needed.

THE TIME OF JACOB'S TROUBLE

She put in the bags, and flipped the lid of the kettle closed. She turned on the small television in the kitchen, and saw the clip of the lightning hitting the Temple and the people scattering from the downpour. News commentators were interviewing meteorologists and analysts trying to explain what had happened.

After a few minutes, Naomi turned it off – she just wasn't in the mood for the news today. But she still felt unsettled, and found herself going to get her Bible. She had never much been one for Bible reading, but had kept one around mainly for nostalgic reasons. Seeing that old Bible always reminded her of her childhood, and America. Her family back in America had always had one lying around, and it made her feel connected to them in some way.

She poured herself a cup of tea, and opened the Bible to one of the few verses she remembered from her childhood Sunday school class: John 3:16. *"For God so loved the world that He gave His only begotten Son, that whosoever believeth in Him should not perish, but have everlasting life."*

And as she read that famous verse, she thought again about Ruth, and began sobbing. If only she had taken more time with her when she had been there before.

*   *   *

Saul and Daniel arrived in Jerusalem earlier than they had expected, and quickly found their host's residence. One of the leaders of Yeshua Ministries in Jerusalem had kindly offered to house them during the Dedication Week, and they had come a few days early to get settled in and do some sightseeing.

They had a list of many of the Christian and Jewish holy places that they wanted to see on the trip. But the main event would be going to see the Temple and participating in the Dedication Week ceremonies.

Daniel had stayed up late the night before and decided to turn in early that evening, so he would be ready for their first full day in Jerusalem. But Saul was too excited to sit still for long – he wanted to see the Temple as soon as he could, even if he could only catch a distant glimpse of it.

He wanted his first time seeing the Temple to be a solemn occasion, and he had been thinking about it for weeks. He wanted to pray over it, before its new era in history began. So much would be happening there soon, even though most of its destiny had already been written thousands of years before.

Saul drove over to the Temple, parked the car, and then showed his Dedication Week pass to the guard at the main gate. The gate was promptly opened and he walked on through. It was very late in the evening, and there were only a handful of people there.

No one was allowed in without a pass, and that was only to get through the main gate, but not all the way to the Temple itself. The Outer Court of the Temple was the furthest the visitors could go, but after the Dedication began, Jews would be allowed into the Inner Courts, while the Gentiles were strictly limited to the Outer Courts.

When he passed through the gate and finally allowed himself to look up the magnificent Temple, its very sight took his breath away. It was so beautiful! He had seen the models of what the various ancient Temples had looked like, and drawings of what the new one would be.

But those models and pictures couldn't come close to how it actually looked. The high gates and walls and the wonderful artistry of the Temple made it seem awesome and holy – a sober place for the reverent to worship their God. He had a sudden overwhelming surge of patriotism and courage, not just for his nation, but also for this place. Yet he also knew its terrible fate in the days to come, and the thousands of his people who would die defending it.

As he entered the Outer Courts, his heart pounded loudly, and he could feel himself almost shaking. He would go as far as he could, and then pray. He stopped at the edge of the Outer Court and bowed low to the ground, with his face towards the Temple. How many millions of his brothers and sisters had longed to do the very act of worship that he was!

For centuries, the Jews had dreamed of praying at their restored Temple. How fortunate and blessed he was to be living at this time, seeing these sights, and kneeling on this holy ground! He was overcome with emotion, especially when he considered what this time meant for his people and his nation. Even in this strange time and knowing some of the terrible days ahead, he would still be grateful and praise His Lord.

A commotion off in the distance behind him shook him out of his prayers. He wiped his glistening eyes and turned to see what happening. The guard at the main gate appeared to be shouting for assistance, and there were two strange-looking figures that the guard was preventing from entering.

Another two guards hurried to join the group to prevent the two from overpowering the first guard. They were yelling at the two men, ordering them to step away from the gate, but the two refused to turn around and retreat.

The guards drew their weapons and shouted for the two men to lie facedown on the ground, and put their hands behind their heads. But they did not even respond, and turned to go on through the closed gate.

The guards fired a warning shot into the air, but the two did not even appear to hesitate. Then one of the guards pulled out what looked like a taser and shot it at one of the men. Even from as far away as he was, Saul could see the electricity arc into the man's body, but it appeared to have no effect on him either!

Another guard drew his nightstick and tried to club the other man over the head, but it merely bounced off him to no effect. The guards resorted to their firearms and began shooting the two men, who still had not responded to their orders. But the bullets bounced off them just as the taser and the club!

The two men slowly turned to face the guards and a huge stream of fire shot out of their mouths and instantly consumed them! The guards didn't even have time to scream before they had been turned into flaming masses. Saul immediately took a step forward and then stopped, deciding it was better to just wait and see what happened next.

When the fire from their mouths finally stopped, the blackened bodies of the guards toppled over and collapsed into dust as their remains struck the ground. And then the two men turned, and the main gates were opened without either of them laying a hand on it. They walked into the Outer Courts of the Temple, heading in Saul's general direction.

Saul trembled with fear, even though he remembered from the Scriptures what he was seeing and who the two men were. He stared at them as they walked towards him. He didn't know whether to greet them or run away as fast as he could!

So he just stood there, and watched them as they approached and then walked past him without saying a word. They were dressed in almost-ancient clothing and both seemed quite old, but one of them appeared to be much older. Neither of them smelled like smoke nor looked affected by what had just transpired – not even their hair or beards had been singed.

He could do little but stare at them, and they both solemnly looked him in the eyes as they passed by. He was too afraid to say anything to them, so he just kept staring.

Saul turned to see where they were going, and it appeared as if they were making their way for the Golden Gate – the eastern entrance on the side of the Inner Courts.

He watched them stop to stand in front of it, taking their places on either side, like the sentries they had just consumed only moments before. He shook his head with wonder at them and left the Temple, staring at the remains of the guards as he passed by.

He knew who they were: the Two Witnesses of the Lord.

CHAPTER 8
THE WRATH OF THE LAMB

The first sacrifices at the new Temple were initiated with great ceremony and celebration. Years earlier, the Temple Institute had painstakingly reproduced all the Temple artifacts and tools for use in the sacrifices and offerings, down to the minutest detail.

The new Jewish priests were primarily from the clans of Cohen and Levi, who could still trace their roots back to the times of the last Temple. The priests were careful to follow all the traditions and requirements put forth in the Talmud and the Torah. Most of the rituals and rededication rites were performed inside the Temple, in which the reporters and journalists were not allowed.

The month before the Dedication Week, the priests and the rest of the priesthood had been rededicated and their duties assigned. The sacrificial animals were stabled underground just inside the Temple grounds, where they were inspected and prepared for the rituals. But the media was gathered by the hundreds outside on the portion of the Temple grounds which had been set apart for the Gentiles and others who were not there to worship.

Hundreds of demonstrators from the various animal rights groups protested loudly outside the Temple grounds, calling the worshippers "bloodthirsty" and "barbaric". Along with them were many Muslim protestors who were there simply because they despised the Jews and hated their new Temple.

Daniel and Saul stood among the hundreds of other Jews who were crowded into the Inner Courts, full of emotion and reverence. Both courts fell silent as the ceremonies began. They heard the goats, rams, and lambs brought out and prayed over. Though they couldn't see the actual sacrifice because they were too far away, they would still be able to still hear the sounds, see the smoke, and smell the burning flesh.

As the first sacrifices began, smoke began rolling out from the Brazen Altar, and the smells of the burnt offerings filled the air. Once all the instruments, furnishings, the Holy Place, and the Most Holy Place had been rededicated, the priests moved outside and then purified the rest of the Temple grounds. There were no interviews allowed from the priests, except for the High Priest alone, who only spoke with the media briefly.

The High Priest had been chosen from among the most senior members of the Sanhedrin, which had grown in both popular support and political power in Israel over the last two years. While many of the people still disliked some of the more rigorous religious rules of the Sanhedrin, they were in general pleased that the Sanhedrin was behaving with much more prudence and morality than the other secular parties.

When each animal was sacrificed, everyone in the Inner Courts bowed low to the ground and worshipped the Lord. They gave Him thanks for finally allowing the commencement of the daily sacrifices after so many years. Frequently many of the worshippers wept with joy and uttered quiet prayers.

After the Temple was rededicated, there was great rejoicing throughout all Israel. After nearly two thousand years, there were once again sacrifices at the Temple in Jerusalem – an event that few Jews had believed would ever happen again.

*   *   *

Saul opened the door to his apartment, wearily dragged his luggage across the threshold and left them just inside the door.

He and Daniel had just come back from their trip to Jerusalem for the Temple Dedication Week. Both were exhausted, but still very excited that they had been given the privilege to witness those historic events first-hand. Many of those who were either messianic Jews or had messianic tendencies had found it incredible that more of their fellow Jews did not seem to recognize the visible warning from God when Medine had signed the seven-year treaty with Israel's leaders. God Himself had shown them that the treaty was ominous with thunder and lightning striking their beloved new Temple, but they pressed on with the peace treaty anyway.[19]

He would be going to his parents' house for dinner in an hour, so he decided to take a shower and clean up beforehand. That would give him some time to think about everything that had happened over the last few days and contemplate the next set of prophetic events. If his studies were correct, the so-called "Anti-Christ" had just been identified and revealed, and the last seven-years of Israel's history and of the current age had begun: the 70th Week of Daniel the Prophet. But those years ahead would be the worst in the entire history of earth – even worse than the days which had led up to the Great Flood.

From a careful study of the Bible, Saul and Daniel had been surprised to learn that Israel's history was apparently made up of four distinct periods of 490 years each. The Bible referred to each of these periods as "seventy sevens" or seventy "weeks" of years.

The first period was from the covenant with Abraham to the Exodus under Moses' leadership. The second 490-year period was from the time of the Exodus to the inauguration of the Temple. The third period spanned the first Temple period to the fall of Jerusalem in 586 B.C. And the fourth period had been from the return of Israel after the end of the Babylonian Captivity to the crucifixion of Yeshua in 32 A.D., with the last seven years being interrupted by the Church Age for nearly two thousand years.[20]

---

[19] The world leader signs a treaty with Israel that either authorizes or guarantees the protection of their worship at the Temple. The Bible refers to a "covenant with hell" that the Lord later annuls. (Isaiah 28:15,18; Daniel 9:27)

[20] Israel's entire history is comprised of four distinct 490 year periods (Abraham to Exodus, Exodus to Solomon's Temple, Temple to Exile, and Exile to the Millennium). Dr Chuck Missler

The Church era had lasted nearly as long as Israel's entire four 490-year history put together into one block of time: over 1960 years, and had only concluded months before with the Rapture. The Church – figuratively called the Bride of Christ in the Gospels and the rest of the New Testament – had departed in a similar fashion as she had arrived: very suddenly with a great wind and a tremendous moving of the Spirit of God.

On the Day of Shavuot in 32 A.D., the Holy Spirit had suddenly come upon a handful of Yeshua's followers who were cowering in an upper room. But the Holy Spirit had taken from the earth a Church that was full of people from every "tongue, tribe, and people", just as Yeshua had prophesied in His last days on earth. Everyone left on the earth had known someone who had been taken in the Great Vanishing, as a witness to them.

And now with the signing of the seven-year treaty, the man the Scriptures referred to as the "Beast" or the "Anti-Christ" had been revealed, and the last seven years of Israel's history had finally begun. The countdown had started, and there was much for the followers of the Messiah to do.

Terrible, horrific times would be coming upon the earth – much worse than had ever taken place, even worse than if the Magog Invasion had been successful. But this time, the calamities would encompass the entire world, not just a tiny nation in the Middle East. No nation, tribe, or people would be spared, for now this was the time of God's wrath and judgment upon all the earth. All the evil that had been done in that age would soon be judged and be punished, from the time of the Flood to the time when the Messiah would return.

Saul showered and managed to take a short nap before he left his apartment. His parents had always expected promptness from their children, and it was a habit that Saul was often grateful they had instilled in them at an early age. His mother opened the front door and gave him a hug and a smile, and welcomed him inside. Since his father had kicked him out months before,

---

(http://www.khouse.org) has extensively documented the Scriptural basis for these periods. (Daniel 9:24)

Saul had decided to use the front door from then on, not presuming to be anything other than a welcomed guest in their home.

At first it saddened him, but it helped him keep in mind that things had changed since he had become a Christian.

*   *   *

"How was your trip, Saul?" Naomi asked.

Jacob looked up from his food, interested in what his son would say.

Saul wiped his mouth with his napkin and replied, "Great – we stayed fairly close to the Temple, mostly in the Old City. We went to the Temple every day, and we were able to see the offerings and the sacrifices and all that. There were tons of people, and most of us couldn't believe that we were actually there, you know, seeing all those things again."

"Was it kind of disgusting watching the sacrifices and such?" she asked.

"I was afraid of that at first, but they were performed very humanely, and we were far enough away that it wasn't much of a big deal. When the animals are put on the Brazen Altar, it smells kind of like a big cookout. It made me hungry the first day, and then I made sure I ate before going the rest of the week so I didn't get distracted," he said.

"Were there many protesters?" his father chimed in.

"Yeah, but they were restricted off to the west side, outside the perimeter. We could hear them when everything was quiet, but other than that they didn't really cause too many problems. It was kind of funny: the animal rights protesters were more of a nuisance than the Arabs were," Saul said with a grin.

"Really? I heard they threw some pig blood and all that. I can somewhat understand where they're coming from, I suppose. It does seem a bit barbaric when compared to most modern religions these days," Jacob added.

Saul slightly nodded his head without saying any more, acknowledging the statement but not really agreeing with him.

He was purposefully being very careful in his responses. He

didn't want to re-open any old wounds between them. Few people had ever been argued into the kingdom of God. He didn't have much of an action plan for witnessing to his father. It would take time, he supposed, even though there was precious little of it left. He would simply be a decent son and be available to talk if and when his father ever wanted to. He felt certain that God would get his attention sooner or later, especially given the terrible days ahead.

Witnessing to his mother was a different story, though. Saul could tell that she was much more open to discussing Yeshua and the Bible than his father was, and he had already decided to talk to her later that evening if he had the chance. He had told her about who he thought Medine really was weeks before, and he had the inkling that she had some questions about that. After all, she had been the one who had invited him over for dinner anyway.

The rest of the meal passed with the three of them talking about less-divisive subjects, such as how Ahban was doing, his father's company, and his mother's flower shop. Ahban was in the process of moving to Babylon, and he was currently there on a business trip. He was also apparently looking for a condominium or even a house there. The real estate market in Babylon was the hottest market on earth, and it seemed like everyone who was anyone was trying to move there, or at least invest in property or businesses there.

After dinner was finished, Saul ended up talking to his mother for over an hour, mostly about what he was doing in the ministry and more details about the Temple. She asked him a number of questions; at first they were more "surface" questions about his faith, but they soon grew deeper.

He also told her much about Bible prophecy, and described a number of passages that were currently relevant. She was very curious about the man that the Bible referred to as "the Beast" and specifically why he thought that person was David Medine. He gave her all the reasons why he had come to that conclusion, and wrote down some websites where she could learn more about it.

THE TIME OF JACOB'S TROUBLE

After a while though, Saul could tell that it was time to change subjects, so they went into the living room where Jacob was watching television, and then they spent the rest of the evening just having a pleasant family time together.

* * *

After Jacob went off to work the next day, Naomi called her shop and told her assistant Shoshanna that she was taking the day off, and asked if she would be all right being there by herself. It would be a slow day, her assistant said, and that she'd be fine handling it by herself that day.

Naomi turned on the computer in Jacob's office and began visiting some of the websites that Saul had recommended to her. Some of them had audio files, and she decided to download them to her MP3 player to listen to them later when she went on her afternoon walk. She had always loved being outdoors, and the last few years she had gotten in the habit of taking a long walk at least once a day, usually either early in the morning or after dinner. The walks helped her set aside the events of the day and put things into perspective, not to mention give her some exercise. Before she had been taken, sometimes Ruth had gone with her, but Jacob rarely did.

The more websites she read about Bible prophecy and the End Times, the more it seemed plausible that what was happening was indeed what the Bible had predicted. She didn't fully grasp how Bible prophecy worked, but she was interested in what it had to say about the immediate time they were now in. The prophecies about the coming world leader and his identification with signing the seven-year treaty fit David Medine perfectly.

She went to the website of Saul's ministry and found it to be very helpful, and downloaded more audio files and more articles to read, along with more Bible passages to contemplate.

Naomi was still a bit uneasy about the idea of Yeshua being the Messiah, but not nearly as much as her husband and oldest son were. As a matter of fact, she didn't even think they believed in any Messiah at all. As for the Tribulation and End Times coming, she half-believed it, but wanted to wait to see what happened next and see how it compared with what she was reading. She had always been quite careful about staying away from extremes. Moderation, she believed, was one of the keys to a happy life. Saul didn't seem extreme though, especially not like some of the charlatans she had seen on television back in the States.

She spent the rest of the morning browsing the different websites and considering what they had to say. Sometimes a tremor of fear would run through her when she let herself think too much about what was supposed to be coming next: namely massive wars, disease, famine, and death.

But these had not happened yet, and she felt there was not much sense worrying about something until it actually occurred. Her mother had always been consumed with worry, and Naomi had determined long ago not to be ruled by worry or the fear of the future. However, it couldn't hurt to learn about what her son thought would be happening soon, and the references he had recommended had been very insightful and convincing.

When it was time for lunch, she went to a small nearby café with her notes to think about all she had read.

*   *   *

For the forty days that followed the rededication of the Temple, there was peace upon the face of the earth. It indeed felt as if the world was uniting at last, and even the skeptics were growing optimistic of the future. There were a few religious skeptics on the fringes who decried this time as a false peace and that the End Times were about to come upon the earth. But most of the press and the public regarded them with scorn and derision.

In addition to those on the fringes, were those two peculiar men that stood shouting and preaching just outside the Jewish Temple. The Israeli media and authorities kept a close watch on them, but they had done no violence except to the two original guards. The world media had mentioned them several times, but since they were doing little more than preaching, there was no need to cover them in the global newswires.

The Two were always dressed in the same outfits of sack-cloth and they had long, unkempt beards and shaggy hair. Some said they never slept nor ate, but no one knew for sure. When one would be speaking, the other would be facedown on the ground in prayer, and then they would change places after every hour or two. Oddly enough, there had been no rain or even morning dew in all the land of Israel since these two old men had come to the Temple, and they were proclaiming that they had stopped the rains as a curse upon Israel for signing the treaty. [21]

On the forty-first day after the Temple had been dedicated, war suddenly broke out on the earth with an unprecedented fury. There had not even a tremor or a rumble before the global wars erupted; all the hotspots on the earth exploded during the same week.

The first conflict was the long-running dispute between China and Taiwan, and then India and Pakistan followed within two days. Many of the troubled nations in Africa erupted in civil and national war, and a few in South America and Central America flared up also. It was as if an invisible wall that had been holding back the floodwaters of war had suddenly collapsed and then burst out all over the earth.

In the days that followed the initial eruption, the wars weren't just confined to nations, but also broke out among people groups, tribes, cities, villages, and even down to individual families and households. People seemed to be turning against each other across all levels of society.

Husbands turned against their wives and beat them, and some even were killed. And many wives turned against their husbands and families and attacked them without warning. Complete strangers on the street even turned on one another and sought to maim or kill. If the children had not been taken from the earth in the Great Vanishing, many of them would have been slaughtered in their own homes or schools.

---

[21] The Two Witnesses prevent any rain over Israel, similar to Elijah's famine of rain. (Revelation 11:6)

Peace had been taken from the earth, and now the earth was engulfed in war and destruction. But the Anshar, the guardians of the world, did not intervene in any of the conflicts.

And David Medine seemed powerless to make peace also. [22]

* * *

At the Temple, a larger and larger crowd began to form, composed mostly of the media. Being journalists and reporters, they had a particularly liberal, skeptical mentality of most things religious, especially when it came to the street-preachers.

But now that much of what these two strange men had been proclaiming were befalling the earth, the media was suddenly interested in covering them. If anything, they could serve as scapegoats. They had been dubbed by many as the "Two Preachers" or Two Prophets" since that seemed the best way to describe them. But off-camera most of the journalists and skeptics referred to them as the "Two Madmen."

The Two typically took turns praying and preaching, but since just before the first war broke out, they both had been preaching and shouting nearly nonstop. They had taken no food, no water, and no sleep – impossible to believe but it was indeed happening. The journalists were tired of listening to the same messages from them over and over, but it was their job, and many soon wanted to be reassigned. Some of the media outlets set up a rotating schedule so their journalists could cover more exciting news, like some of the disaster areas and war-zones and such.

"Peace! Peace! The peace of the earth has been taken! Why will you not turn from your sins, O Israel? You are a stubborn donkey that refuses to turn away from your own destruction!" the younger of the Two shouted. "Why do you rage against your Maker, O you nations?"

The older one then cried out, quoting Yeshua in the Book of

---

[22] Peace is taken from the earth soon after the world leader enters power. (Revelation 6:4)

THE TIME OF JACOB'S TROUBLE

John, "'I have come in my Father's name, and you receive me not; if another shall come in his own name, him you will receive.'"

And then the younger one spoke again, "Wherefore hear the word of the Lord, you scornful men, that rule this people which is in Jerusalem. Because you have said, 'We have made a covenant with death, and with Hell are we at agreement; when the overflowing scourge shall pass through, it shall not come unto us: for we have made lies our refuge, and under falsehood have we hid ourselves.'"

Many of the journalists rolled their eyes and sighed; they were so tired of hearing of the gloom and doom over and over, day in and day out. Many of them complained continually about their assignment, except when broadcasting, of course. And most openly mocked the Two as a means of relieving their boredom and frustration.

But that day, one of the reporters had finally had enough, and walked up to the Two and shouted back at them to shut up or they would call the police. No one was listening to them, yet they kept spouting the same garbage every day. The reporter was red-faced and belligerent, and most of his colleagues quietly agreed with him.

He turned to face his fellow journalists, and began shouting nonsense and gibberish, mocking the Two that were behind him. At first, they laughed and cheered, but when they realized that the Two had fallen silent, an awkward uneasiness came over them.

But many kept smiling and rooting him on. Seeing that he was providing some amusement and relief, he became bolder in his mocking, and backed up so he stood nearly in front of them.

Suddenly a tremendous stream of fire shot out of the mouths of the Two and enveloped him, and all the journalists screamed and covered their mouths. The mocker had not even had an opportunity to cry out in pain, or fall to the ground.

Seconds later, what was left of him collapsed on the ground in a pile of ashes. The fire that had come from them had been so terrible that it had instantly consumed his flesh and bones entirely, and left nothing but dust and ashes!

The journalists screamed and frantically scattered, but the Two would not let them escape unscathed. Fire shot out of their mouths once more and struck all the journalists who had participated in the mocking. The remainder were merely singed, for the most part.

In the end, over two-thirds of the media audience had been turned into smoldering piles of ashes, quickly blowing away in the East wind.[23]

* * *

Naomi and Jacob sat down in their living room, ready to watch the evening news. They typically had the news on after dinner, but had not really watched it with interest until the last several weeks. Now they were almost glued to it all the time and had even been eating dinner in front of it, watching what was happening to the nations all over the world and the destruction that the wars had wrought. There were so many wars and catastrophes happening all at the same time that they wanted to stay informed in case it spread further.

Incredibly, Israel had been spared from any of the carnage since the first of the new wars had broken out. Some thought it was because of the prior destruction of the Magog Invasion that had wiped out most of their more formidable enemies. Some mused that there was simply no organized movement to go to war against Israel. Others thought that because of the previous supernatural destruction of the invaders, everyone had left Israel alone out of fear of a similar destruction. And yet others thought that God Himself was watching over them and protecting their tiny nation.

"Did you hear about that today?" she asked, as another report of the Two Prophets came on the news.

"No – can you turn it up, please?" he said.

---

[23] The Two Witnesses consume others by fire that comes from their mouths. (Revelation 11:5)

THE TIME OF JACOB'S TROUBLE

She did and they watched the news coverage of the massacre that had taken place between the camera crews and the two men at the Temple. The news media had taken a break from reporting on them for a few hours as additional details had been gathered, and now it appeared they had better video clips and reports of what had occurred.

"Dear God!" Jacob exclaimed. "Did you see that?" he said, as they watched the fire consume the first reporter, and then moments later many of his colleagues.

She nodded as the news played the clip again, and then zoomed in on the smoking remains of the reporters. They both gasped at how little was left – they had been expecting something like the victims' clothes being on fire or even them having severe burns. But instead there was nothing that remained except smoldering piles of dust and ashes.

"What on earth did those reporters do to deserve that?" he exclaimed.

"I don't know," she replied, shaking her head.

And then she remembered something she had read earlier – something from the Book of Revelation. Maybe she had heard about it from Saul. She rose and retrieved her Bible and then sat back down, going to the back of it and flipping through it. Jacob looked up and glanced over to see what she was doing.

"What's that?" he asked.

"I heard something about this in the Bible the other day and wanted to look it up. Here it is – Revelation 11," she said, putting her finger on the passage.

"And I will give power unto my two witnesses, and they shall prophesy a thousand two hundred and threescore days, clothed in sackcloth. These are the two olive trees, and the two candlesticks standing before the God of the earth. And if any man will hurt them, fire will proceed out of their mouth, and will devour their enemies; and if any man will hurt them, he must in this manner be killed. These have power to shut up heaven, so it will rain not in the days of their prophecy: and have power over waters to turn them to blood, and to smite the earth with all plagues, as often as they will. And when they shall have finished

their testimony, the beast that ascends out of the bottomless pit shall make war against them, and shall overcome them, and kill them," she read.

When she was finished, she looked up again at the television, where some of the journalists who had not been attacked were being interviewed.

Jacob was silent, thinking about what he had just heard from her, and what he was seeing on television.

"That's very strange," he finally said. "I wonder how they did it."

"What, the fire?"

"Yes – maybe they have napalm or flamethrowers under their robes or something."

However, from the zoom-ins on the news coverage, it was clear that the fire had come straight from their mouths. Even stranger, there was no sign of scorching or fire on either of the Two Prophets. From the enormous flames that had come from them, they should have had at least minor signs of fire on them.

But there were none. And immediately after they had torched the journalists, they had mercilessly continued preaching, picking right up where they had left off when they had been interrupted. As if the entire incident had never occurred.

Surprisingly, even though the news media had aptly named them the "Two Preachers", none of them had apparently connected them to the Two Witnesses mentioned in the Bible. Yet it was clear even to Jacob that these Two Preachers were indeed the ones described in the Bible. From the fire, to the plagues, to their behavior, and even to their clothing, they perfectly matched the description in the Bible. He didn't really want to admit it, but the similarities were undeniable. But perhaps someone was merely copying what had already been written in the Bible.

The police and Temple authorities had set up a heavily-armed perimeter around the area soon after the massacre had taken place, but the Two were still there preaching. Perhaps the police were not prepared to engage them yet, or perhaps they were just afraid. Maybe they were just there to keep the angry crowd away from the Two, so no additional people would be killed. The Two had been watched constantly for weeks, and no one had seen them doing anything other than preaching and praying. Until that day.

They watched the news coverage for a while, and talked some more about the Two Witnesses and the passage. However, Jacob still thought that they were a couple of crazy men who were copying what was written in the Bible. For what purpose, though, he had no idea. Maybe it was a protest or some publicity stunt. He was still somewhat skeptical of the "supernatural", even after all he had seen and lived through.

Deep inside him, there was a slight fear slowly rising. He didn't want to change what he thought or how he had ordered his life. But with everything that was going on in the world, how long could he hold on to his old life?

* * *

In the midst of all the wars, Ahban had found the perfect condominium in Babylon. He could well-afford it, and it was in one of the new high-rise towers that were springing up all over the city. Many of them had grand terraces with incredible gardens outside, emulating the Hanging Gardens of old, one of the Ancient Wonders of the World. But the new Hanging Gardens were incredible, and far surpassed the originals that had been constructed by King Nebuchadnezzar.

His condo wasn't up in the penthouse, but it was close enough. He had a corner unit, and a large portion of the walls were constructed of thick, darkened glass that provided a wonderful view of the Euphrates and overlooked most of the city.

He could see the Tower of Illumination just across the way and the Promenade, along which many of the other ancient ruins had been rebuilt. Some of the ruins had been started and even completed by Saddam Hussein before his fall, while the rest had been completed in the years after the Iraqi War. The newer construction had mostly taken place after the failed Magog Invasion, when trillions of dollars had been channeled into the Iraqi economy from the demise of its neighbors.

Incredibly, the entire nation of Iraq had escaped the recent wars and turmoil much like Israel. The Anshar had promised the World Union and their constituents that they themselves would protect the new world capital, and it appeared that they indeed had. But it was also likely that no one nearby wanted to risk open war with the Iraqi Army, who had been highly trained from the American forces over the last decade.

Another reason that the raging nations were probably leaving Iraq alone was because they greatly feared any interruption of their oil supplies from the World Union. Though some had significant reserves and inventories, they knew that their oil supplies could become scarce very quickly during wartime or other periods of unrest. Not only that, but Iraq was also home to many of the world's new petroleum refineries, which were critical to every industrialized nations' economy and war-machine.[24]

Ahban's new projects were both going very well. He spent long hours at the office, but that had been typical since he had been hired out of college. Sometimes he grew tired of it, and went for a run or a drive, depending on his mood. Other times when he began feeling burned out, he knew it was time to take a few days off or some vacation time. His father had always spent many hours at work, and Ahban understood that to get to the top in his profession, he must devote as much of his time and energy to it as possible.

He thought about getting married sometimes, but not very often – there was too much to do at this point in his life. He would probably wait until he was forty or forty-five, if at all. His parents had a decent marriage, he supposed, but with the divorce rates so high and the unfairness of the courts towards men during divorce settlings, he was almost inclined to not marry at all. Why should he work all these hours and build his financial portfolio, and then have most of it taken away in a divorce? Relationships were so unpredictable, especially in these difficult days. In his mind, marriage just wasn't worth it.

---

[24] Babylon grows to be an economic superpower in the last days. (Revelation 17-18)

THE TIME OF JACOB'S TROUBLE

Taking one last look out the window at the Euphrates far below him, Ahban smiled and turned from the awesome view. Babylon was truly incredible at night, with all the lights and the towers and gardens sparkling like jewels against a black velvet background.

Yes, he would be satisfied here in Babylon – very busy of course, but still very satisfied. He would live like a king.

* * *

When most of the smoke cleared and the nations finally ceased fighting, the World Union estimated that over one-tenth of all the people on the earth had been killed either by bombs, war, or other violence. But while peace slowly came back to the earth, the awful consequences of the conflicts on every level of society began to take their toll.

At the behest of the Sarrim, the World Union instituted worldwide martial law, and sent in whatever Union paramilitary forces they could muster. The World Union peacekeeping forces seized tons upon tons of nuclear and conventional weapons from every nation that had gone to war, and demanded that every other nation hand over all their weapons also. The idea was that if all (or at least most of) the weapons of the world were confiscated and put under World Union control, then they could not unleash destruction on such a huge scale as they recently had. There were still some hotspots, but most of the fires of war had died down. The World Union peacekeeping forces had to move quickly if they were to take permanent control of the weapons of the world.

Disease and famine quickly followed in nearly all of the major regions that had erupted in war, and these diseases soon spread to the neighboring lands because of the wide extent of the damage. Most of the water supplies were also contaminated, and adequate food was difficult to find over much of the earth. Numerous conflicts broke out again between neighbors, friends, and relatives over water and food, and many people died in domestic violence in the weeks that followed. And a few weeks later, millions more people succumbed to cruel deaths by thirst, starvation, and disease than had been killed by the wars and violence.[25]

In the highly technological and industrialized areas of the West, food, water, and often even luxury items were still abundant and widely available. While they still had money and technology, they often had little natural resources, since so much of them were imported from the poorer nations of the world. Inflation began spiraling out of control, and soon people were spending whatever it took to buy food.

Whatever assets, savings, and retirement investments the wealthier people had was soon depleted just for basic necessities. As they watched their wealth quickly evaporate, they began to demand assistance from their governments and the World Union.[26]

And just as shrewd businessmen take advantage of the weaknesses and vulnerabilities of their clients, David Medine and the World Union moved quickly. They used the financial crisis to further debase currencies all over the world, so they could later rebuild the world economy according to their plans. The peoples' money was worthless and they were starving – the perfect time to put the new financial and banking systems into place. And then in addition to the economic reconstruction, they would also be able to unify most of the governmental and social service programs across every nation of the world, for efficiency's sake, of course.

Medine realized that these disasters would greatly help unify the world, which was most likely why the Anshar had not intervened. They were indeed most-wise, and he understood that he still had much to learn from them and their higher ways.

The time of the nation-state was over. The time for the permanent global government to rise from the dust of war had finally come.

* * *

---

[25] The other Three Horsemen of Revelation that come after the world leader appears: War, Inflation/Famine (economic problems), and Death. (Revelation 6:3-8)

[26] In the Tribulation, there is massive inflation, famine, and shortages, yet luxuries are still available to the rich. (Revelation 6:5-6)

THE TIME OF JACOB'S TROUBLE

Naomi turned off the morning news and went over to sit down at the kitchen table. Scattered all over the table were printouts from various websites. Some were from Christian and messianic sites, while others were from secular news sources.

Also there on the table was her Bible, opened to Revelation 6 – the chapter that concerned what most Bible commentators had named the "Seal Judgments" and the "Wrath of the Lamb". What was written in those pages was terrible, but not nearly as terrible as what was now happening on the earth.

Nearly every day for the past month, she had been staying home in the morning after Jacob had left for work. She had been busy studying religious and news sites on the Internet, and going through many of the more detailed prophetic passages in the Bible. Every day that she studied, she became more and more convinced that Saul and Ruth had been correct all along: they were in the End Times, and that both the Anshar and David Medine were not who they portrayed themselves to be.

It was increasingly difficult to deny that something supernatural was not happening all over the world. The Anshar had promised the world unbridled peace, but it now was enveloped in war, destruction, and death – and they seemed unable to do much about it. But over and over, they explained that these were the times of trials they had repeatedly warned about.

But for all this, Naomi still had not become a Christian – that still seemed too much for her. The idea of a literal, eternal hell repulsed her, yet it seemed that the world itself was turning into that very place. But she was more open to God and the Bible now, and that was a start, she supposed.

When she first began reading the Bible, she was very surprised at how historically accurate it was. It was a little cryptic and strange to read in some places, but what the prophets and Yeshua had said had indeed come to pass in history. The cities and nations that they had proclaimed would be rebuilt indeed had been, and those that the Scriptures had said would be destroyed and never rise again had not, even though people had tried in some cases.

And then as she began studying more of the prophecies, she

found them to be usually very clear and detailed, not like those of the other religions or "prophets" such as Nostradamus and the like. Starting with the more-detailed prophecies in the Tanakh and then moving on to the Book of Revelation, she began to get a clearer picture of where the world had been and where it was going.

If she understood the Scriptures correctly, the world was quickly heading for a truly terrible time that would make the last few months look like a minor skirmish. The world would be turned into a horrible place both because of the Beast and because of the Judgments that would be raining down upon it.

There were still a number of passages that she didn't really understand, but perhaps Saul would be able to help her with them. She was more ready to listen to him now and could better understand what he would say.

But she still wanted to wait a little while longer and see what else would happen. The entire world had turned upside down, and she wanted to find a place of stability.

* * *

Jacob locked his office door behind him with his briefcase in hand, and said goodbye to his assistant, who was nearly bewildered at the sight.

It was a Sunday, and he was leaving hours before he usually did. She couldn't remember the last time he had left before her, especially at the start of a busy week. She said good night in reply and watched him leave. Maybe he was finally taking her advice and slowing down a little to smell the roses.

As he got into his car and drove away, he decided to do something he hadn't done in years: take a long drive down the coast. With all that had recently happened to the world, he was increasingly aware that life was short, and that his plans for the future might quickly amount to nothing. Part of him wanted to do his best to hold on to them and get everything back under control, but another part of him was just tired – tired of working, struggling, and pushing all the time. What was the point when the entire world was blowing itself up? What was the use?

The drive down the coast helped lift his melancholy a little, and the sight of the ocean with the brightly shining sun raised his spirits. And then he decided to do something else he hadn't done in years.

He found himself pulling over into one of the public beach parking lots that were scattered up and down the coast. He parked his car and made his way to the beach. He took off his shoes and socks, and rolled up his dark slacks. They needed to be washed anyway, and a little sand on them wouldn't hurt too much. He hadn't been to the beach in so long – since it was always there, he had just always taken it for granted and therefore rarely went. The sand sparkled under his feet and its warmth made him smile.

He loved the smell of the sand and the salt air, and found it very refreshing. He had done some sea-fishing with his sons when they had been younger, but he hadn't been to the beach in years. There was a strong breeze, and the sand was warm in contrast to the cool seawater. The sea gulls would scurry towards the water in front of him, and then would dash back as the next wave rolled in. As he began walking down the shoreline, he looked out over the horizon and began thinking about his life, his family, and this land that he loved so much.

How long had these waves been rolling and pounding on these shores? How many of his countrymen had taken this same walk over the centuries they had been there? There was so much history in this land – good and bad, triumph and catastrophe – so much that had befallen his people and his nation. What if there was some sort of divine plan in all of this? What if God was who He said He was, and what if Israel really was His chosen people. Why had they been so mistreated and abused these many centuries? And why had God forsaken His own people for so long up until just the last few years? Why all the pointless suffering?

He and Naomi had been talking a lot about the Bible lately, and he found himself slowly softening to it for the first time in many, many years. He was still very adverse to the New Testament, but was becoming more interested in what the Torah and the Prophets had to say. It was hard to deny that there weren't blatant parallels with what the Bible had said would happen and what actually was these days. Even though they had started going to synagogue again soon after the Magog Invasion, he still felt somewhat cool towards God.

But now that two of his children had converted to Christianity, maybe he should at least look at what the New Testament had to say, even if he didn't believe it. After all, no one could force him too! He didn't like Yeshua, or even the thought of Him being the Messiah, that was for sure. He was just getting comfortable with the idea of a messiah again, and the incredible nature of David Medine had a lot to do with that.

What if Medine was the Messiah? He was such a powerful, charismatic leader, and he was governing the world wonderfully through these difficult times. How could anyone tell for sure if he was the Messiah or not? And what if Medine was the so-called Anti-Christ that the Christians were always warning of? How could someone who seemed so good really be so evil?

Could they really be in the End Times, he wondered. Increasingly he was beginning to think so, but he hadn't really let on to Naomi, or anyone else about it for that matter. He knew that Saul believed Medine to be the Anti-Christ, as he would have called him. But Jacob had not made up his mind yet. David Medine had protected Israel and had secured their Temple.

So far, Medine had been one of their greatest allies. How could he possibly turn against them after all he had done?

* * *

Soon after the world had begun to recover from the previous devastations of wars, an eerie silence suddenly fell across the earth. People everywhere stopped what they were doing and looked around, and then they finally looked up. And what they saw caused them to tremble with fear.

Suddenly the globe shook with a massive tremor, and every creature on the earth was thrown to the ground. Most were unable to rise for more than a brief moment, and then were thrown back to the ground again. As the people once again looked up, they were confronted with another shocking sight: the moon was rapidly moving from its place in the sky, until it stopped between the earth and the sun, enveloping the whole globe in darkness like an eerie night. But unlike most solar eclipses, this one did not pass after a few moments – and the moon stayed positioned exactly between the earth and the sun.

Around the globe where the sun was still somewhat visible, the bright skies above them had dimmed, and a great blackness began growing above them and spreading down towards the horizon. It was as if the blackness was eating away at the blue sky, and all the stars were beginning to appear, except that it was starting from the sky directly above them. Day gave way to night all over the earth, and all the stars became brighter than they had ever been. The backlit moon took on the color of blood, and its edges appeared to blaze with fire.

Just as quickly as the sky had appeared to collapse above them, another tremor struck the earth that was even stronger than the first. Many of the mountains on the earth shook and crumpled, creating great avalanches on the land and seventy-meter high tsunamis in the seas.

The people on the islands gasped as the water levels began to quickly recede from the shoreline. Those who realized what was happening began to run inland as fast as they could, because they knew the terror that would be coming in a matter of minutes. Moments later, the huge waves began methodically pounding the islands and the coastlands all over the earth. Any buildings, cities, and people that were less than several kilometers inland were obliterated and quickly swept back out to sea. The tsunamis relentlessly pounded the coasts, pulverizing the thousands of cities, villages, and buildings that lined the seas.

If the inhabitants of the earth could have watched the scene from the heavens, they would have observed a sight nearly as shocking as that of the moon streaking across the sky. They would have seen the earth and the moon rapidly being moved thousands of kilometers closer to the sun, back to the place where it had not been for over six thousand years.

And not only was the earth and the moon moved closer to the sun, but their orbits were also slightly altered back to what they had been at the first, for like most orbits, they had slightly shifted and elongated over the centuries. It was as if a great, unseen force was undoing the effects of thousands of years of orbital shifting in only a matter of minutes.

As the people far inland began to recover from the earthquake, they gasped and screamed as the moon seemed to suddenly draw closer to the earth. Not by much, relatively speaking, but those near the equator noticed the change most dramatically and the shadow that the moon cast upon the earth steadily grew larger and larger.

And all over the earth, the people and creatures scurried about, trying to find whatever cover or safety they could: behind rocks, in caves, and near any trees that remained standing.

They cried out and screamed, and millions yearned to die just to put an end to their terror and fright.[27]

*　*　*

"What are you doing? Are you trying to kill us all?" David Medine shouted at the two shining figures standing before him.

The Anshar had not responded during his initial outburst, and they remained silent before him as his questioning continued. He was not fully aware of what was happening yet, and they did not want to make him unstable. He would not be "complete" in their master's eyes for another three years, and they had been ordered to bide their time.

The Anshar knew their role in their master's grand scheme: they were to protect, counsel, and reassure Medine during these difficult times. He was of utmost importance, and would one day be their master. It would be better to stay on his good side now so it would go well with them later when he had been perfected.

---

[27] The Bible consistently uses 360 day years in its prophecies, as did most ancient calendars. Over time, a planet's orbit gradually shifts. It's possible that during the Tribulation, the earth will be moved back into its former orbit. (Isaiah 13:13)

But they also knew that once Medine had served his purpose, their master would discard him like the fleshly, pathetic worm he really was. They would remain, but he would be consumed. Perhaps they would even be allowed to partake in his feast.

"Reassure your people," they advised. "Provide them comfort and solace. Remind them that this is a required stage of their evolution. They must learn to let go of their hold on this world and change with it."

"I have!" Medine exclaimed. "But they want answers now! When will this end? When will there be peace again so they can rebuild their lives?" He was frustrated, but there was little he could do other than vent and rage and curse at them.

"If you can protect this city and these lands, why can't you protect more of the earth?" he demanded of the Anshar.

"We will send for additional resources immediately. What is happening at this time is the earth being brought back into perfect balance with the rest of the solar system. This will help you comfort your people and reassure them that this is the earth moving back into perfect harmony with the rest of the system."

"Very well," Medine sighed. "I will speak to the people again. Send for your reinforcements immediately," he ordered.

The Anshar bowed to him and left the room. As they left, David Medine cursed them under his breath and sulked. He noticed he was frequently having more outbursts of rage and losing his temper lately. He felt an inner anger and hatred he had never known before; but it felt good, and it comforted him.

He was beginning to hate them, along with all these sniveling, whining people he had to tolerate. But he would continue working with them and playing his part, biding his time.

One day soon, he would rule over every square centimeter of earth and all flesh, and all would belong to him.

CHAPTER 9
THE STARS OF HEAVEN

During the several hours that the earth and the moon were moved into their new orbits, those on the earth who dared look up discovered another shocking event taking place: some of the stars were falling away in the south, exploding, or simply vanishing.

And even though the stars were all many light years away, it was clear that the events were all occurring in real time, as if the very speed of light itself had been suddenly dramatically sped up. But how could they be seeing all these stars falling away at the same time, given that they were many light years away from one another?

After the earth and the moon were in their new positions, the moon once again began orbiting the earth. Bright sunlight once again flooded the earth as the moon slowly moved from the place where it had been fixed. People and creatures all over the earth crawled out from where they had been hiding, and looked up to the sky. Those on the dark side of the earth found several of the familiar constellations slightly different. Some of the stars were simply no longer there, while there were faint murky blobs where some of the other stars had been.

Later when the skies were re-catalogued by the astronomers, many of the missing or destroyed stars were found to be in the "serpentine" constellations – the constellations which had been named after dragons, serpents, and such in the ancient zodiacs.

Soon after the dramatic sights and movements of the heavens had ended, people began searching through the rubble of the buildings, rocks, and the debris around them, and small rescue teams were put together to help survivors who were trapped.

And then they noticed something peculiar – many did not even realize it until someone else mentioned it or they heard it on the news. All the winds on the earth had completely stopped, even those near the coasts and at the poles. The sails of all the boats on the rivers, lakes, and seas stood still and straight, and the sailing ships slowly stopped moving in the waters. The waves of the seas and lakes decreased and flattened, and were it not for the tides, the seas would have had few waves on them at all.

While the ceasing of all the winds did not seem to be too terrifying at first, within a few days the plague began to take effect. The air began to stink and reek of foulness, and the temperatures steadily rose all over the earth. The normal winds that flowed from the poles to cool and refresh the earth were no longer there, and life all over the globe became miserable. With no winds to clear the air and blow away the pollution, dust, and the hazardous gases, the air of most cities reached poisonous levels within the first week.

All over the earth, but especially in the densely populated cities of China, India, Mexico, America, Europe, and other nations, people and animals began to suffocate and die. [28]

* * *

Ahban looked down to the streets far below him, and then out towards the horizon, where the grid of streets and roads stretched on for kilometers seemingly without end.

There were very few pedestrians to be seen, but they would be out in a few hours when night had fallen and the temperatures had cooled. If it had been hot in Babylon before, the lack of wind had turned it into a blazing furnace. The sun's heat upon the black pavement and the golden-brown sands was relentless, and no one could escape the scorching heat. But Babylon was not

---

[28]   Revelation 7:1

alone, and most of the great cities were suffering likewise.

He turned away from the window, and looked over the condominium, which was empty except for several cardboard boxes that he had brought from Israel. The furniture he had recently bought would be delivered over the next several days, and he hoped to be settled in by the end of the weekend. At one point, he had decided to lease a furnished apartment, but given the state of the world, he realized he would just be better off just buying everything outright. Even though he worked long hours, he still wanted a comfortable, familiar place to go home to. One of the rooms would be set up as an office, but he wasn't sure how much he would be use it. Often he worked on his laptop in the living room, especially late at night.

The new, glistening city of Babylon – the pinnacle of mankind's ingenuity and greatness – reeked from the scorching heat and the smells of hot sand, body odor, and raw sewage. Ahban thought it was somewhat ironic. Enormous blowers had been set up near the Tower of Illumination and throughout the historic district to bring some relief to the people. However, they really did little other than blow the hot, rancid air around. The Euphrates and Tigris Rivers also contributed to the stench, and as more animals and fish died, the stench grew more and more overwhelming.

Most of the people of Babylon worked in offices or other air-conditioned buildings, where they were usually sheltered from the worst of the smells and the heat. It was a testimony to the builders' prowess that the power grid had held together under these extreme conditions. Ahban was thankful he wasn't one of the groundskeepers, construction workers, or day laborers that had to work outside all day. There was talk of changing the shifts of all jobs with outdoor-exposure from primarily daytime to nighttime, just so they could continue working and the great city would continue to grow. A number of other cities had already switched their city services to night, and people were quickly adjusting to doing everything at night instead of during the day.

The next month would be very busy for him, he thought

with a grimace. His designs for several of Babylon's government offices were due by the end of the month, and he expected to be putting in at least sixteen hours a day. Hopefully the heat would be lessened by the time he was finished, so he could take a short vacation. He was already feeling the pressure from the project, but he actually thrived on it. He would work twenty hours a day if need be, and do everything humanly possible to meet his deadlines.

Babylon was still very new to him, but even under these tough conditions, he was very excited to be there. He had tired of all the problems in Israel, especially all the religious and cultural conflicts. The entire Middle East had more than its fair share of religious troubles, but in Babylon, it seemed that the people had finally set them aside, much like New York, London, Paris, and many other major metropolitan areas. And he hadn't been away from Israel long enough to miss it yet anyway.

He unpacked a few of the boxes and found that it was nearly sundown. He put down the box he was holding and moved back to one of the thick glass walls.

For a long time, he looked over the incredible city as night fell, and then went out to one of the nicer restaurants close by.

* * *

Seven days after the winds had ceased, a wind of a different sort began to blow over the earth – but only a tiny number of people on the earth felt it.

The majority of those who felt the strange wind were within the borders of Israel, but a number of others scattered over the earth felt it also. As the wind gently swept over them, small flames about the size of a hand appeared just over their heads for a moment and appeared to touch them, and then moved down into their bodies. But the flames did not burn them, and as soon as the flames had entered their bodies, they all began looking around as if they had suddenly been awakened from a deep sleep.

From the expressions of the people around them, the strange

flames had been visible to everyone, and not just those who had felt the wind. And moments after those who had been touched by the strange fire had come to their senses, they began speaking to everyone nearby. And even though these anointed men were speaking in one language, everyone else was apparently hearing them in another. Some listeners would hear the speakers in Hebrew, while others heard the same speakers in Russian, English, Arabic, etc. – whatever their language happened to be. Some among the speakers immediately realized that what was happening was very similar to the Day of Shavuot (also known as Pentecost) as described in the Bible.

All the people who had been indwelt by the flames were all chaste, unmarried Jewish men. These men were from all over the world, and of various ages and backgrounds. Some were Orthodox Jews, some Ultra-Orthodox, some semi-Orthodox, some liberal, and even others were non-religious (with regards to Judaism). None were betrothed, married or divorced, and they were from all different environments and upbringings. Some did not know what was happening until after the wind had passed over them and their spiritual eyes were opened for the first time.

The Holy Spirit of the Lord had come upon them, and He had given them new life the moment He had touched them. They were now His servants, and they belonged to Him. These had been marked and sealed by God Himself, and the winds that had fallen still upon the earth were immediately released and began to flow as they had in times past.

The anointed men continued speaking to those around them and then began spreading out, traveling from place to place and speaking as much as possible, to Jews and Gentiles alike. They were consumed with reaching the world with the Gospel of the King. Some in the crowds would demean and persecute them, and some even tried to kill them.

But no one could hinder them from delivering their message. When these men were insulted, spat upon, struck with rocks, or even shot, they continued to preach until they were finished, and then they would move on to the next place. Try as they might, their enemies could not stop them, kill them, or even silence them. Their message would be declared to all the world, and no power on the earth could stop them.

These were the 144,000 who had been chosen from each of the twelve ancient tribes of Israel. Along with a spiritual awakening, they also received full knowledge of their ancestry all the way back to the time of their tribal ancestors. And when a small census of the 144,000 anointed was taken in the weeks that followed, it was discovered that there were exactly 12,000 men from each of the ancient twelve tribes of Israel, except for the tribe of Dan.

On a few of the Internet forums, some commented that the tribe of Dan might have been excluded because it had been through that tribe that idolatry had entered the nation of Israel in the time of the Judges.[29]

And the 144,000 began their ministry to the world.

*　*　*

Saul and Daniel were in the ministry's office talking when Saul felt a strong, cool breeze blow over him. He looked up, startled – maybe the winds had started again and had blown the front door open.

He went to the front door and found it to be shut, but the wind was still blowing all around him. Papers, pamphlets, and other office items were not moving at all, but he could clearly feel the wind. Then he looked up at the vents in the ceiling to see if the air was on, but it was a cool day and they had turned off the air the night before. Somehow, it seemed as if the wind was blowing directly through the walls themselves.

Daniel had turned away from Saul for just a moment when he noticed a sudden change about the room, with shadows quickly growing sharper and darker all around him. He looked down to the floor, very puzzled, and realized that it seemed as if a bright light was shining behind him. He turned around in surprise only to see that Saul was standing very still, with a strange

---

[29] Revelation 7:2-8; 14:4-5

CHRIS HAMBLETON

look upon his face. A brilliant flame was sitting on the top of his head, but there was neither smoke nor burning. Saul was glowing and there was no fear in his eyes, but rather a look of contentment, revelation, and wonder.

Daniel was about to say something to Saul, but found himself speechless. He had an idea of what he was seeing, but didn't want to ruin the moment with words. It was apparent to him that the Holy Spirit was visibly ordaining Saul but not him (at least not that he knew of). He had read the passage in Acts many times before, and it quickly dawned on him what was happening: Saul was being baptized as one of the 144,000 Jews who would preach the Gospel to all the world.

"Saul – are you okay?" Daniel said, half-stuttering with amazement.

He nodded slightly at Daniel with a smile, and then the flame appeared to sink directly into his head, and the shadows in the room returned to their normal shapes and shades.

"What are you feeling?" Daniel asked him, but he waited a moment to reply.

"I don't know how to describe it," Saul said. "I feel fine, but well, much better – like I can see everything around me much more clearly," he exclaimed.

"Really? What else?" Daniel asked.

"What do you mean?" Saul asked.

"Well, you know, like what else can you do?" Daniel thought for a moment, and remembered about the speaking in tongues from the story in Acts. "Here – can you understand this?" he said, tuning the office radio to one of the Arabic-only stations. Daniel knew for a fact that Saul did not know even basic words in Arabic.

"I can understand them!" Saul exclaimed, and then repeated several of the sentences from the radio.

"Whoa – that's wild! What about French?" said Daniel, and he spoke a few lines, to which Saul easily replied in kind.

Daniel picked up the Bible off his desk, and then flipped over to Revelation 7 and 14, which described the 144,000 men chosen by Yeshua to be His special witnesses until He returned.

214

THE TIME OF JACOB'S TROUBLE

"Saul, look at this: it says here that you cannot be hurt."

"Really?" Saul said. He then slammed the back of his hand against a nearby wall, first with medium strength, and then much harder.

It was true – he still felt the initial pain from the blow but the redness from the impact quickly faded. He grimaced and said that it still hurt. Apparently, the word "hurt" in the prophecy meant "no lasting damage" rather than "lack of pain".

Saul heard a loud voice, and then immediately bowed low to the ground and replied in a language that he had never spoken before. Yet somehow, he knew how to speak it. Daniel had a puzzled look on his face, and it was obvious that he had not heard the voice, but did not understand Saul's reply.

"What was that?" Daniel asked.

"It was the Lord. He just told me what I am to do," Saul said, raising himself off the ground.

"Wow! You spoke to the Lord? What did He say?" he asked.

"He greeted me and told me that I was one of His 12,000 Witnesses from the tribe of Naphtali. He told me to leave this ministry and go to Babylon immediately," said Saul.

"How are you going to do that? Drive? Fly?" Daniel asked.

"I don't know yet; maybe I'll just go to the airport and buy a ticket at the counter. Money doesn't really matter I guess, does it?"

Daniel smirked and replied, "I guess not. Well, looks like I'm on my own then, huh?"

"I know you can handle it. You can always call me if you need help with something," he replied with his familiar grin.

Saul began moving towards the front door, not even bothering to pack his belongings in the office. The Lord had told him to leave immediately, and he would do exactly that.

He couldn't even comprehend doing otherwise now. He had been completely transformed in an instant, and even though he was still in the world, he was no longer part of it. He did not yet have his glorified body, but he had been given new gifts and abilities he had never had before. And he had a new perspective.

Saul and Daniel went outside together and noticed that

something else was now different too. At first, neither could quite figure out what had changed. And then Saul held up his right hand and smiled. The familiar winds that had been stopped for days had returned and a gentle, cool breeze was once again blowing in from the Mediterranean.

He turned to Daniel and bid him farewell. He promised to visit him if and when the Lord granted, and shook his hand with a big grin. He wished him well, and as soon as Saul had said a last goodbye, he promptly got into his car and sped away.

Daniel shook his head with a smile, and then went back into the ministry's office. Once inside, he put up the "We're Closed" sign and turned off all the lights. And then he got down on his face and began to pray. When he finished, it was nightfall.

* * *

At the Temple Mount, the Two Prophets clothed in sackcloth continued rebuking the people who entered the Temple. They were merciless with their words, especially to the Orthodox Jews and priests who frequented the Temple grounds.

The Two would hurl insults at them quoting directly from the Bible, calling them "white-washed tombs", "thieves", "deceivers", "idolaters", and the like. Every day they became more and more hated by not just the Temple worshippers, but also by the Israeli people, especially since it had not rained in all of Israel since they had begun speaking months ago. And the sudden torching of the journalists months before had not endeared them to the press either.

Ninety days after the Two Prophets had taken up residence at the Temple, the authorities decided that they had finally had enough of their abuse, and decided to remove them for good. They had called the Israeli police many times to have the Two banished from the Temple grounds, but there had been no outright action to remove them from the premises. After all, the Temple was a public place and there were no laws against public speaking. The Two weren't really disturbing the peace, as much as antagonizing the Temple authorities and worshippers, and after all, the Muslims outside had been doing likewise (and usually worse). The press called the police cowards for letting the Two stay after what had happened to their colleagues.

The Temple authorities conspired together and fabricated a security video of the Two beating and harassing worshippers as they made their way into the Temple, and then had Temple attendants from among them come forward to the police to authenticate the video. The police were tired of the constant complaints and now that there was clear evidence and witnesses of harassment, they decided to arrest the Two. They were also prepared to place officers on the Temple grounds to ensure that they did not return and that others would not take their place and stir up even more trouble.

A squad of Israeli police officers responded to the Temple grounds to arrest the Two Prophets, and sent ten officers forward. The Two warned them not to come closer, but as soon as they approached to escort them away, fire shot out of their mouths and burned the police officers up!

The others drew their weapons and began frantically firing at the Two Prophets, but they were quickly consumed also. More police were called in, along with SWAT teams and reinforcements, but these were promptly dispatched by the Two as effortlessly as the previous ones had been. Finally, the police and the Temple authorities gave up their attempts to remove them from the grounds and left them alone. And so the Two Prophets became more hated than ever.

The following Shabbat after all the attempts to remove the Two had failed, they began calling down more curses and plagues upon Israel and other areas all over the world. They commanded extreme weather upon specific cities, along with swarms of flies, locusts, grasshoppers, frogs, and even lice. Tornadoes and hurricanes would suddenly appear in areas where they had never been before, and then leave behind great swaths of destruction. Mice, rats, and other vermin would quickly appear and ravage a city, eating all the food they could find, and then vanish as suddenly as they had come.

Then the Two began turning the water to blood. They started

first in the cleansing basins in the Temple when the priests were performing their ceremonial washings. Then they turned various streams, rivers, reservoirs, and then even the Sea of Galilee, Jordan River, and the Dead Sea to stinking, putrid blood. Fish and other marine life died by the millions because of the polluted waters. And then they began sending the plagues to other lands outside of Israel, even to the most remote parts of the earth.[30]

The more plagues they sent forth, the more news coverage they received. The World Union began to blame them for much of the world's problems, which in one sense was true. The Two became more and more vocal in their accusations of the World Union, David Medine and his cabinet, the Jews, and the very Temple they stood next to.

They also continued to proclaim that Yeshua the Nazarene was the only messiah of Israel, and that everyone should repent of their sins and follow Him. They cited hundreds of Tanakh passages, and had spoken the entire New Testament dozens of times for all to hear. They spoke against Jerusalem and Babylon as being equally wicked (which neither city wanted to hear) and proclaimed that both would meet their doom in the days to come.

If the Two Prophets had been hated during their first ministry thousands of years before, it was nothing compared to the animosity they had aroused this time.

* * *

The front doorbell of the flower shop rang, and the clerk at the counter looked up. She greeted the visitor cheerily, and then called to the back for Naomi.

"Hi Saul – what brings you here?" his mother said, seeing him as she came up to the front of the store.

"Hi Mom, I have some news. Do you have a few minutes? It's important," he said.

She could tell that it was serious, just from his mannerisms and the fact that he had shown up at the store out of the blue.

---

[30] Revelation 11:6

"Sure – want to go to the cafe?" she asked

He nodded, and she went back to her office for a moment to lock her computer and get her purse.

They walked a few doors down to the café, and soon they had gotten their drinks. Saul chose a table near the back where it was quiet and out of the way. Naomi was concerned now – she hadn't seen him this solemn for as long as she could remember. Even more than when he had told them he'd become a Christian.

"Mom," he started. "I'm leaving for Babylon immediately – as in tonight. I don't know how long I'll be there."

"Oh. Well, that is some news! Are you moving in with Ahban?" she asked.

"No," he said, shaking his head. "Have you heard of the 144,000 Witnesses in Revelation?" She nodded, and he continued, leaning forward to speak more softly. "The Lord came to me while we were at the office and chose me to be one of them. Know what?" he asked. "We're of the tribe of Naphtali – well, just Dad, actually. You're from Benjamin," he said with a grin.

That made her smile a little, but she was thinking about exactly what all that news meant.

"What about your ministry with Daniel?" she said.

"The Lord told me to leave it at once. Daniel was not one of the 144,000, because he was previously married," he said. "I said goodbye about an hour ago."

"Are you going to tell your father that you're leaving?" she asked.

"No – I asked the Lord about it and He said that it was not my place to speak to him this time, but yours. Can you do that for me? I'm afraid it might start another argument and set him back even further," he asked.

She nodded and looked down at her drink. The argument was still a sore issue at home, and she would have to find a gentle way to break the news to Jacob. She thought for a moment, and remembered she had many questions to ask Saul about what she had been studying, and then she realized that this might be her last chance.

Naomi asked if he had some more time before he had to

leave, and he said he did, but only for a few hours. So she began to ask as many of her questions as she could remember. They stayed there for over an hour and a half, and he answered them all very clearly, and he was also able to show her from the Scriptures what would be coming next.

After they had finished their drinks and said goodbye, he promised to visit them when he could, and told her not to worry about him any longer. Instead, she should worry about herself and her husband, and also Ahban. He pressed her to make a decision for Yeshua before it was too late. Israel would be free for only a bit longer before the long night of the Tribulation descended.

And with that said, Saul hugged his mother goodbye and then turned and walked towards the street. He would be taking nothing with him other than a small carry-on that contained his Bible and a few other items.

* * *

Forty days after the 144,000 Jewish evangelists had been empowered by the Holy Spirit, a deafening blast from what sounded like a horn rang out over all the earth. People everywhere covered their ears in pain and many fell to the ground at the paralyzing noise.

Moments later, the skies darkened with deep red-tinted clouds, similar to those that are seen just as the sun goes down behind an overcast horizon. But the reddening skies were not a forecast of good tidings to come, and the sun was not setting – the massive dark red clouds were blotting it out, even though it was still high overhead.

The entire earth took on a peculiar blood-red hue from the reddish light, and the landscape and all the waters looked like the color of blood. Many of the people on the earth looked up at the sight, and quickly headed for whatever shelter they could find. But moments later, they were frantically running for cover.

The red clouds had continued to grow darker, and it began to rain. But instead of clear raindrops of water, the rain was dark red and had a terrible pungent smell. And people all over the world screamed and shrieked as they realized that it was literally raining blood.[31]

And then as quickly as the bloody rains had started, the rain changed to hail and snow, mixed with small flaming bolides from the skies above. The entire earth was being pelted with the blood-hail and fire mixture. Huge portions of the land caught fire, and in scattered locations all over the earth, a third of all the trees were soon burned up, and then all the green grass was burned up. Three days later, the sickening hailstorm of blood ceased and the reddish clouds cleared out.[32]

While the earth-dwellers were still reeling from the plaque of blood and the fire, another deafening trumpet blast sounded from the sky. And as the blast stopped, an asteroid over five kilometers in diameter tore through earth's atmosphere and struck the middle of the Atlantic Ocean close to the equator.

Huge tidal waves quickly followed in its wake, and sent tsunamis upon all the western coasts of Africa, Europe, and the United Kingdom, along with the eastern coasts of the Americas. Nearly all the ships in the Atlantic capsized and then quickly sank into the ocean depths. And then the entire Atlantic Ocean turned to reeking blood, and all the fish and the other marine life died and floated to the top of the terrible waters.[33]

Exactly one hour after the first meteor had struck, another trumpet blast boomed. A blazing comet suddenly appeared and entered the atmosphere over the Western Hemisphere, and was descending much faster than the last one had. But instead of striking the earth in one place, it broke up high in the atmosphere and several huge pieces streaked to the earth below.

The largest piece struck North America at the top of the Great Lakes region, and all the Great Lakes quickly turned bitter and sulfurous. And hours later, the mighty Mississippi River and all its offshoots had turned bitter also, and all the fish were poisoned and died.

The other pieces of the comet struck the source of the Ama-

---

[31] Revelation 6:12; 8:7
[32] Revelation 8:7
[33] Revelation 8:8-9

zon in South America and the other major rivers of the continent and contaminated them also. Within hours, nearly all the fresh-water sources in the Western Hemisphere were rendered com-pletely undrinkable and useless. In the days that followed, many of the inhabitants of the New World died because of the polluted water, or from dying of thirst.[34]

When the forth trumpet sounded upon the earth, every light source in the entire world was suddenly dimmed to one-third of its normal luminosity, like the entire earth had entered into twi-light. The sun, moon, stars, fire, and even the man-made sources of light such as streetlights and flashlights were dimmed also, and could not be made brighter no matter what people tried. And a chill swept across the face of the earth.[35]

And then what appeared to be a huge man was seen flying through the skies all over the earth, saying in a loud voice, "Woe, woe, woe, to the inhabitants of the earth because of the other voices of the trumpets of the three angels, which are yet to sound!" [36]

*　*　*

On the same day that the fourth trumpet had sounded, a fifth one boomed, and once again the earth-dwellers ran for cover, even though most had not left their previous shelters because of all the plagues that were still coming upon the earth. And when nothing had appeared to happen after the trumpet blast, the peo-ple began peeking out from their shelters and looking for food and water.[37]

But those in the land of Russia west of Moscow saw a bril-liant light streak from the blood-red sky, and then strike the ground and explode in a massive flash of fire and smoke. How-ever, when those in the vicinity of the strike journeyed to the crash site, they did not find a smoking crater as they had expected

---

[34] Revelation 8:10-11
[35] Revelation 8:12
[36] Revelation 8:13
[37] Revelation 9:1

– they found huge, gaping hole in the ground with smoke and flames billowing out of it.

It was as if a great hole had been opened up far into the interior of the earth and massive amounts of gas, steam, smoke, and fire was blasting out. And the skies above the hole for kilometers around were blackened from the emissions of the deep pit.[38]

Out of the midst of the billowing smoke came huge swarms of creatures that were like locusts, and they immediately attacked all those who had come to look at the crater. People screamed and fled in terror as the tails of the locusts stung them, and they fell to the ground writhing in pain. The creatures appeared and sounded like normal locusts, but these swarms left all the green vegetation of the earth alone, along with every other creature upon the earth – everything except for mankind. Billions upon billions of locusts streamed out of the pit, and quickly spread all over the earth.[39]

The shapes of the locusts were like horses prepared for battle. On their heads, it looked as if they were wearing crowns of gold, and their faces looked like the faces of men. They had long, flowing hair like that of women, but their teeth were fanged like the teeth of lions. They had glittering, iron-like plates covering them, and the sound of their wings was deafening, like the sound of a massive stampede. The locusts had curved, stinger-pointed tails like scorpions, and they used their tails to sting and torment mankind. And try as they might, the locusts could not be crushed or killed, and no gas or insecticide could frighten them.[40]

In the days and weeks that followed the fifth trumpet blast, every person on the face of the earth who was not a believer in Yeshua the Messiah was repeatedly stung and bitten by the locusts that had emerged from the pit. Once bitten, the people could do little but lay on the ground, screaming and writhing in pain. Many were in such torment that they tried to commit suicide, but they found they were unable to die and end their torment. Drugs,

---

[38] Revelation 9:2
[39] Revelation 9:3-5
[40] Revelation 9:7-11

narcotics, and alcohol had little effect on their pain too. The victims jumped off buildings, hung themselves, shot themselves, and tried a multitude of other suicide tactics, but they remained alive and unable to die. [41]

And so their torment from the locusts and their stings remained, and only grew worse the more the people tried to lessen it or take their own lives. Mankind was getting a genuine taste of what Hell was like while they were still alive, and just like in Hell, they were unable to change their fate.

Those who repented and became genuine believers in Yeshua were immediately relieved of their torture. But the vast majority of mankind cursed God because of the plagues, His 144,000 witnesses, the Two Prophets, and the rest of those who proclaimed the gospel across the face of the earth.

While the other plagues gradually subsided, the terrible locusts remained to torment mankind for five months. At the end of the plague, the locusts suddenly vanished back into the pit as quickly as they had come.

And mankind still refused to repent of their wickedness. [42]

* * *

The very hour that the last of the locusts had gone back to the pit from which they had come, another tremendous trumpet blast sounded above the earth, followed by a thundering voice that commanded, "Loose the four angels which are bound in the great river Euphrates." And as with the preaching of the 144,000 Jews, each person on earth heard the proclamation in their own language – even the deaf heard the voice, and for many it was the first sound they had heard in their entire lives.

A tremendous rumbling went up and down the entire Euphrates River, and the waters of the great river bubbled and shook. Out of the foam arose huge horsemen arrayed completely in black, and all were riding great black stallions as terrible and

---

[41] Revelation 9:6
[42] Revelation 9:20-21

fearsome as their masters. As they rose from the river, half the group turned towards the east and the other half towards the west. When they reached the shoreline, they began galloping at full speed in separate directions. Each had been assigned to destroy specific nations, tribes, families, and individuals – and nothing would stand in their way. [43]

The horsemen numbered two hundred million, larger than any army of man that remained upon the face of the earth. The dark riders were covered in thick, black armor, and metallic breastplates that seemed to blaze with an unnatural red fire. The horses they rode appeared even stranger than their masters – instead of normal horse heads, they had lion heads, and instead of long tails of hair, they had venomous black snakes. Out of their mouths came a devouring fire, and out of their nostrils snorted thick black smoke. Whenever the horsemen came upon one of the individuals marked for slaughter, fire exploded from the horse's mouth and burnt them alive. And if the victims weren't killed from the fire, the serpentine tail of the steed bit them and they would immediately die from the deadly venom. [44]

The horsemen tore through fences, walls, buildings, and even galloped over waters regardless of the depth. Some even took flight for long periods of time when encountering mountains or other rough terrain. Their steeds ran with a maddening fury and a hunger for death and destruction that could not be quenched. The air around them reeked of rotting flesh, smoke, and sulfur, and whenever their foul smell suddenly filled the air, men and women ran for shelter wherever they could find it. But no shelter could protect them – not bunkers, caves, nor even bank vaults. The horsemen were not constrained by mere matter, and nothing could stop them from accomplishing their purposes. [45]

They were called the Slayers by the media, because they slew multitudes of every race and group on the earth. They took no bribe and showed no mercy. The only survivors were those

---

[43] Revelation 9:13-15
[44] Revelation 9:16-18
[45] Revelation 9:18-19

who the horsemen were not allowed to touch. In the end, the Slayers slaughtered over one-third of all mankind. Yet no one who had remained cried out to God or repented of their evil deeds and their worship of their gods and the Anshar.

From these two plagues of "eternal torment" and fiery death, mankind had been given a taste of just two of the witnesses of Hell, and yet they refused to turn from their sinful ways.

* * *

Jacob and Naomi sat in their living room in silence, numb from what had been besieging them. The world they had known was quickly crumbling all around them. Many they had known had been either stricken or slain by the Slayers. The plagues and judgments upon the earth had been devastating.

During the plagues, the rains of blood and fire had colored the ground and waters in an eerie tint of reddish-orange, but many of the people had been able to find some form of shelter. However, the fires on the trees and grass had quickly driven them out into the midst of the storm. The meteor strikes had briefly poisoned much of the water supply in Israel, and both the Sea of Galilee and the Jordan River were unusable for a time. A significant portion of the Mediterranean Sea also had been made toxic, and billions of the fish and other marine life had died.

But then had come the demonic locusts, and both Jacob and Naomi had been bitten severely. They were in such pain that they were bedridden most of the time, yet looked after each other the best they could. Several times, Jacob had talked of them ending their torment with the handgun, but both knew that no one could die at that time, and refrained from the futile attempt to cease their suffering. He hated the Two Witnesses vehemently, and cursed every time he saw or heard them on the news, which was quite often. Naomi did not feel quite the same hatred for them, since she had read about what was coming on the earth from the Scriptures and understood that their suffering wasn't from the Two.

On the same day the locusts had left and a surge of relief returned to the people, the demon-horsemen had been sent out and swarmed over the earth. Jacob and Naomi had left their home soon after their torment had ceased to see the extent of the damage to their neighborhood and businesses.

Both their offices had been closed since the locusts had come, and both were very much like they had left them. Near Naomi's shop, a handful of other people were out surveying the damage and evaluating what needed to be repaired. There was some exterior damage from the meteorites and hail, but for the most part, they had escaped the firestorms and looting that had ravaged many of the cities.

As they were about to enter Naomi's shop, they both heard a terrible snort and looked up to see one of the Slayers rushing toward them. They both dove into the shop to escape and peered through the bottom of the front window. But at the last moment, he turned aside from them and attacked several of the others nearby.

The people outside fell to the ground, crying out for mercy, but the Slayer ignored them and roared. His mount attacked a young man who had fallen in front of him, and he was quickly mauled by the ferocious lion-teeth and the fire that poured from its mouth. The Slayer drew his long sword and struck a fleeing woman with his flaming blade, splitting her in half from her shoulders to her waist. The snake-tail of the Slayer's horse had curled around yet a third victim to crush him, and a fourth had already succumbed to its venomous bite.

Within seconds, everyone outside was dead, and he appeared about to move towards three more people cowering inside one of the shops, but abruptly turned away and left them unharmed. The Slayer turned his horse back and walked right past Naomi and Jacob, who had been hiding behind the front window of the shop. As he strode by them, the Slayer looked directly into Jacob's eyes as he passed by, and Jacob saw nothing but death in his face.

Then seeing more people in the distance, the Slayer galloped away for another slaughter. Jacob and Naomi came out from their shop to help the fallen victims, but soon found they could do little for them other than cover their bodies.

Naomi knelt over one of the bodies and began weeping – it was the owner of the small café a few doors down from her shop. He had been slain by the venom of the serpent-tail.

Why had she and Jacob been spared yet again? They surely did not deserve it, she knew. Why were they given mercy when others were not?

*   *   *

The Anshar had been seldom seen publicly during the terrible times of the plagues, but David Medine had been at the forefront of the media attention throughout the world. As Sarrim, he had instituted widespread, far-reaching reforms as a result of the plagues and trauma that had encompassed the earth.

Worldwide martial law had been in effect for months, and he had used those new executive powers to all but render the ten World Union leaders powerless. But he had manipulated them carefully – they had all but begged him to take their authority from them. The nation-state system had finally been dethroned after five thousand years, and would soon be little more than a fading memory. The World Union leadership was now in control of most of the world's land and resources, and national governments and borders had little if any real governing power. And he was firmly in control of the World Union.

David Medine's skills as a public speaker and incredible charisma had only increased during the times of the plagues. He explained that it was the birth-pangs of the earth and the heavens, which were rapidly evolving in preparation for the everlasting peace soon to come. The people and the earth would suffer, unite, and then thrive together. This time of difficulty would be horrible but short-lived. He promised that the time of peace to come would be so incredible that they would forget all about the current time of trauma.

But when the last two plagues had overtaken the earth, David Medine changed his propaganda from one of perseverance and encouragement to that of criticism and blame. He primarily faulted the subversive 144,000 Jewish preachers and the Two Prophets in Jerusalem. When people began being tormented from the demonic locusts and then later when the Slayers came forth, Medine placed the blame directly on the Two Prophets. They had already withheld the rains from all Israel and caused other plagues and problems throughout the earth, but these last two plagues had been so devastating that surely they must be from the Two. And the animosity the world felt towards the Two Prophets and the 144,000 rose dramatically.

In the middle of the plague of the Slayers, David Medine reiterated to the world that the Anshar had a great Enemy, the Elohim, who was now tormenting the earth through his servants. He explained that the Anshar had been absent from the earth during its darkest hours because they had been viciously attacked by Yahweh and his armies again, and were trying to keep them away from the earth.

The Two Witnesses were merely two of the Enemy's ambassadors. If just two of the Enemy's henchmen could wreck such destruction upon the earth, what would millions of them do if they came to the earth? He convinced them that the locusts and the Slayers had also come from the Elohim, and any ill-feeling the people had towards David Medine and the Anshar quickly evaporated. The enemies of Anshar wanted to halt the evolution man by completely destroying them, and the Anshar were fighting ferociously to save mankind.

David Medine convinced the peoples of the earth that they must unite faster if they were to survive the transition and the terrors of the Elohim. Mankind must fully join forces with the Anshar to defeat the Enemy. They must also unite themselves with the Anshar in mind, spirit, and body, who would soon be living among them in their cities, villages, and neighborhoods.

The Elohim was surely coming to attack the earth, and the rest of the Anshar were now gathering to protect the earth from their common enemy. [46]

---

[46] Genesis 6:1-5; Daniel 2:42-43; Luke 17:26

CHRIS HAMBLETON

* * *

David Medine brooded alone in his lavish suite on the penthouse floor of the Tower of Illumination. He increasingly felt little but anger and frustration towards the Anshar, though he would never show it or say so publicly. How did the Anshar expect him to keep everyone united when they were seemingly helpless against the plagues and disasters that kept striking the earth? Were they really powerless to stop them, or were they simply biding their time?

He fixed himself a drink and walked over to the glass wall overlooking the Euphrates. The view of the city from the Tower was incredible. The new Babylon. His Babylon.

Suddenly the room was filled with a brilliant light and Medine spun to see what was happening. He assumed it was the Anshar and was about to rebuke them for their rude entrance, when he saw that his visitor was indeed none of those he knew. The light was so blinding that he was nearly forced to turn away. But gradually his eyes adjusted enough for him to see that it was indeed one of the Anshar, but not any of those he typically dealt with. This one was much more glorious and powerful.

After a moment, he realized that he had encountered this particular being once before. He was the one who had questioned him as to his allegiance and commitment when he had first been brought onto the Anshar's ship. He was the one who he had embarrassingly prostrated himself in front of out of fear and apprehension in his mere presence. He was immediately filled with terror once again and flung himself on the floor in obeisance of the mighty creature.

The being of light left him facedown for what seemed like an hour, and then he finally spoke with the voice of terrible authority. "Excellent. You have shown yourself to be mindful. And that you have not forgotten who your master is."

"Yes my lord," Medine meekly answered.

"You may now rise. I will conceal much of my glory to prevent damaging your feeble eyes," continued the creature. "The time has come to reveal what will soon come upon the earth, and how it concerns your evolution. Soon you will be made complete."

Medine didn't quite understand – wasn't he already the perfect human being? How could he then be made complete? He decided it best to remain silent.

"You will go to the Jewish Temple and take control of it. Those followers of Yahweh must not be allowed to continue their rebellion. Turn their abhorrent religion against them."

"Yes, my lord," answered Medine.

"Also, one of those rebels will soon assassinate you, but do not fear. I will be with you, and I will heal you from your death-wound," he paused for his servant to absorb the knowledge. "And after you are revived, you will be endowed with all my power, instead of the tiny amount which you now possess."

"If you are careful to obey me and follow all my commands, I will indwell you forever. You shall be the King of Kings, the Lord of Lords, and the God of Gods."

Medine remained silent, shaking from the delightful thought of possessing even more power than he already had.

"My lord, may I humbly ask you but one question?" Medine asked.

The creature of light waited for a moment before answering, and then told him to continue.

"What is your name, my master?" he asked in a trembling voice.

Suddenly the room blazed with blinding light again as the creature cast off the restraints on his power and glory.

"I am Lucifer, the Morning and Evening Star!" he declared. His voice rang out like thunder and shook the walls. He was terrible to behold, and spoke with power and authority.

Upon hearing his master's name, David Medine threw himself on the floor again and worshipped him, trembling with fear.

CHAPTER 10
THE ABOMINATION OF DESOLATION

The time of the Jewish Passover was approaching. This would be the third Passover celebrated at the Temple. The protests during the first year had been fairly peaceful, but because of the plagues over the last two years, violence at the holy site and in Jerusalem had increased dramatically.

The Muslims and other groups were constantly blaming the Jews and their Temple for all the plagues and troubles of the earth. After all, there had been growing peace and prosperity all over the earth until just after the sacrifices at the Temple had resumed. Many Jews feared Islam was on the rise again, and they began putting restrictions on the protesters and Gentile visitors at the Temple. The Middle East was falling apart again, and peaceful relations would need to be re-established quickly or the entire region would lapse back into war.

David Medine had selected Franco Pontiffica[47] to be the head of the new Ankida religion. Pontiffica was the last pope of the remnants of the Roman Catholic Church, and had been selected after his predecessor had disappeared in the Great Vanishing. Through Pontiffica's influence in the Vatican, the Ankida religion had quickly risen from the ashes of the Roman church infrastructure.

The Ankida Temple had been dedicated in Babylon less than two months before, and was located at the very top of the Tower of Illumination, which had a brilliant-crystal pyramid at its peak. David Medine had appointed a commission to create a religion

---

[47] Revelation 13:11-12

that would be based upon the Anshar's vision for mankind, their wisdom for evolving, and their history of the earth. The commission had already successfully unified all the traditions and religions of the world, except for Orthodox Judaism and evangelical Christianity. This new religion was called "Ankida", from the Sumerian word that meant "the joining of heaven and earth", a perfect picture of mankind's dreams of immortality.

Before the inception of the Ankida religion, the World Union had taken extensive surveys which indicated that the Christians and Jews were the only two groups who would actively refuse to unify with the rest of the belief systems. In their opinion, many of the Jews were simply stubborn and stuck in the past, which was why they would refuse to change. But the Christians presented an even more difficult problem – they had very strong beliefs against the World Union and David Medine himself. Many of them believed that he was the alleged Anti-Christ, who would subjugate the entire world for his own personal power and gain.

With the appointment of the supreme leader and the selection of his archbishops, the Ankida religion quickly began to grow. The plagues and wars had left many of the churches, mosques, temples, and synagogues all over the world in ruins. Those not in ruins were having terrible financial problems, since so few people were contributing to them any longer. It was the perfect time for the Ankida religion to take root.

The establishment and spreading phase would be simple: the World Union would send cities and villages financial aid and re-construction supplies, as long as their religious entities joined the Ankida religion and adopted their principles and beliefs. The general public would be much more open to a modified form of their current worship place and religion rather than new religious buildings alone. Once fully implemented, the Ankida religion could be shaped and molded in any form Medine and Pontiffica would see fit. It would be a dynamic, powerful arm of the state.

David Medine and Franco Pontiffica had recently devised a plan for getting the Jews and Christians to adopt the Ankida re-ligion. Both were heavily attached to the rebuilt Jewish Temple, so that's where they would begin. They would go into the Temple and publicly worship there also, and then soon after would renegotiate the terms of the seven-year guarantee of the Temple worship.

If the Jews joined the Ankida religion, the peace treaty would be made permanent, instead of for only the current seven years. But if they refused to join, then their precious Temple would be closed until they decided to change. As for the extremist Christians who refused to recognize any religion other than their own – well, they would be compelled to change, or suffer the consequences.

*   *   *

Saul pulled out another set of tracts as a small group of businessmen in expensive suits walked towards him. He smiled and held some out, but they completely ignored him and continued walking on by.

He sighed and shook it off, and then looked back up the street. No one was around, so he put the tracts away and then sat back down on the curb. One of the men in the suits reminded him of Ahban. He had gone back to work a few days ago, and was now back in his old routine of long hours at the office and at home.

Ahban had been bitten by the locusts and had stayed in his home, much of the time in torment. Like most businesses throughout the world, his company had shut down for weeks during the worst of the plagues. The Slayers had devastated his office, with only one-third of all the employees left alive. Ahban had been good friends with several of the victims, with two of them killed just as they had left the office.

He considered Ahban to have been very fortunate to have survived both the plagues and the Slayers. They had been merciless when they swept through Babylon, and had left less than half the city inhabitants alive. Many of the richest people in the world had been slaughtered there. But even with all the plagues and the wars, the world economy was still functioning, and no doubt the slain would be quickly replaced and life in Babylon would continue as normal.

Of course, Saul had been spared from both the locusts and the Slayers, though he had seen them face to face several times. On each occasion, they quickly fled away from him, probably because of his inclusion in the 144,000. Perhaps that was why they had not touched Ahban, he thought to himself.

He had seen Ahban often during the plagues, bringing him food and medicine, and doing as much as he could to ease his pain from the locusts. He had been in such misery and complained incessantly, but at least he hadn't tried to hurt himself or take his life as many others had attempted.

Saul was often gone most of the time during the day, preaching on the streets of Babylon or in the hospitals, even though no one really wanted to hear him. But his responsibility was to preach the Gospel to everyone, regardless how or if it was received at all.

Several of the 144,000 were there in Babylon, which was more than were assigned to most other cities. They usually gathered together once a week on Sundays for a brief time together for encouragement and prayer. None of them had permanent shelter in Babylon, and would stay with whoever invited them in. Some even slept outside in tents in whatever park or campground would allow them to. Some slept on park benches like homeless people. Saul had been staying with Ahban most of the time, especially when he had been suffering from the locust bites.

Weeks ago, they had divided the city into small sections and ministered in each section for a week, and then would change sections every Sunday. Sometimes they worked together, but most of the time they were on their own. Their task was to minister to the entire city until the Lord told them to go elsewhere.

Babylon was much richer than it had ever been in its history, but was also growing even more evil than it had been during its former days. Witchcraft, sorcery, gambling, prostitution, and every evil known to man (and even some others) were prevalent and had skyrocketed since the plagues had begun. The window of opportunity to minister in Babylon was short, and the handful of the 144,000 knew the day would be coming soon when they would be either imprisoned or cast out of the city.

Saul saw a young couple approaching. He stood up and pulled out the tracts once again, and smiled as he waited for them to approach.

* * *

Nearly three and a half years had passed since the Temple had been dedicated, and there had been few problems between the Jewish Temple Authority (the JTA) and the World Union.

But to Medine's dismay, the JTA refused to grant Franco Pontiffica permission to enter the Temple to worship, primarily because he was a Gentile. Both Medine and Pontiffica were outraged at the refusal – after all, they were the two most powerful people in the world!

This was completely unacceptable to Medine. If the JTA was successful in preventing either of them from accessing the Temple, soon other religions, groups, and entities would follow – and all the progress they had made in tearing down the ancient divisions and unifying the world would fall apart. Medine was Jewish by birth, so giving him access was not the problem, but letting him bring Pontiffica in with him was the sticking point. Medine was a reasonable man, but the refusal by the JTA could not be allowed to stand.

The coming Passover would be an event covered by world media (to some extent) and observed by the entire Jewish community. Both Medine and Pontiffica found the Israeli Jews to be quite stubborn and inflexible, especially the Orthodox. The Jewish resistance to the Ankida religion was a growing problem, since their defiance encouraged other groups and religions to not join in also. Perhaps Medine going to the Jewish Temple in person would exert enough pressure to cause the JTA to cave and let both Medine and Pontiffica into the Temple.

They would use media pressure first, and if that did not yield the desired results, then more drastic measures would force the Jews to comply. Though he was an Assyrian Jew, Medine cared nothing for the Temple, and it was becoming more of an obstacle than anything else.

Unity and equality were policies to be enforced, not just suggestions to be followed half-heartedly.

* * *

"Hi Ahban – how was work today?" Saul asked as he walked into Ahban's condo. He had only his keys with him, and he stuffed them back into his filthy pocket.

It had been another hot day, and he knew that he smelled of sweat, body odor, and dirt, but a long shower would take care of that. He was tired that night, but still mentally full of energy.

Sometimes his work in the mission field was discouraging, especially when no one listened and it seemed that he wasn't making much of a difference. Today though, several people had become believers, which was more than most days. Babylon was a thoroughly secular city; the people worshipped money, power, pleasure, and to a growing extent, David Medine and the Anshar.

"My day was good. How was yours?" his brother replied.

He was tapping away at his laptop in front of the television. He had been working more and more since the last plague had ended and the Slayers had left. Some said they had simply ridden back into the Euphrates River, and there were several video clips to validate their claims. But few had been brave enough to follow them to closely, just in case the Slayers changed their minds and came after them.

"Great! It was a pretty good day today," Saul said.

"Oh? How's that?" he asked, half-listening while he continued typing. Ahban always had a ton of email to go through from the day, and he usually did that in the evenings over a bottle of wine or a couple of beers. And from the several bottles on the coffee table next to his feet, it looked like it was a beer night.

"A few people accepted Yeshua today. They're coming back tomorrow to talk to me some more, and they promised to bring some of their family members and friends, too."

"Oh. That's good, I suppose," Ahban said, but not really meaning it.

The expression on his face betrayed his true feelings, and Saul watched his brother's face harden. Saul could have said "God" or "the Lord" instead of "Yeshua", but that would have been the trouble-free way. The name of Yeshua had always been a point of division between people, and always would be. Saul sat down on one of the other sofas and glanced at the television.

"Why do you do that all the time – the preacher stuff?" Ahban asked with a touch of irritation, glancing over to him.

Saul paused before replied; his brother had been increasingly intolerant towards him over the last week or so. Saul had managed to keep their conversations about his work on a pleasant level, rather than being too pushy. Witnessing to Ahban was about as easy (and as pleasant) as defusing a bomb. But the tensions had been rising over the last few days, and Saul was afraid that soon it would reach the boiling point.

"Because that's what He told me to do. Yeshua has given me a purpose and a gift, and I need to use it as best I can," he replied.

Ahban smirked and shook his head.

"Well, I think you're wasting your time. There is so much to do out around here, and you're nothing but a dirt-poor street preacher in the richest city in the world! No one really listens to you – why can't get a job like everyone else?" Ahban's tone was clearly angry now, and Saul didn't know quite how to respond. He wanted to reply in kind, but the Lord would not approve; so Saul held his tongue before he replied.

"Because that's what I've been told to do. Can I ask you a question?" Saul asked. Ahban nodded with somewhat of a sneer, but it didn't phase him that evening.

Saul continued, "Why can't you just listen to what I preach and honestly think about it? What if all the stuff you're doing is a waste of time in the light of eternity?" he said.

"Because I think it's stupid! How can you believe that religious nonsense with the Anshar and Medine here? You'd have better luck if you were telling everyone the world was flat!"

THE TIME OF JACOB'S TROUBLE

"Why can't you see them for who they really are? They've made everything worse, not better!" Saul exclaimed.

He could feel his temper rising, and he struggled to control himself. "Don't you see they're trying to control everybody?"

"That's ridiculous! Medine is the best thing that's ever happened to this pathetic place! And if the Anshar hadn't come, we'd have all been dead by now! If it wasn't for all you Bible-thumpers, we wouldn't be going through all this crap right now. This world will be much better off when all the religious nuts are gone," he shouted, without really meaning to. But that was what he felt, and it just came out.

"I'm sorry you feel that way," Saul said quietly, back under control. Indeed, tonight was the night the boiling point had been reached.

Ahban sighed and looked up at him. "You know, I didn't want to do this, but I'm tired of how things have been going between us the last few days. I think it would be better for both of us if you moved out."

Saul was surprised that Ahban had finally said it, but he had been feeling the same way himself. He slowly stood up from the couch and took the house key off his key ring, and left it on the table.

And then without a word, he went to his room and gathered the small bag that he had come with, and walked out the door.

Ahban looked up as the door closed and didn't say a word.

* * *

The Temple grounds were swollen with people – along with all Jerusalem. The Passover had come, and all the towns, villages, and cities surrounding Jerusalem were packed with observant Jews and Christians from all over the world.

The visitors in Jerusalem were some of the most religious, devout people throughout the earth – the perfect place for the foremost political leader of the world and his own priest to make their push for the Ankida religion. And if the meeting with the JTA went badly, then it would serve as a warning to the rest.

239

CHRIS HAMBLETON

On the day before the start of the Passover Week, David Medine and Franco Pontiffica announced their presence to the Jewish High Priest, the JTA, and the Sanhedrin. They were warmly welcomed and given a full tour of the Temple's outer grounds, but the reception turned cold when Medine and Pontiffica re-iterated their intentions to worship inside the Jewish Temple, as if they were both fully-observant Jews. And again the High Priest and the JTA denied Pontiffica access – the only way they could be allowed to enter the Temple together would be if he converted to Judaism and renounced his current religion.

And this was perhaps the one thing that the leader of the Ankida religion could not do. But unknown to the High Priest and the JTA, their meeting had been more about creating an incident than a simple request and rebuff.

Now that the two leaders had been firmly refused once again, they decided take a more direct, forthright approach: they would surround themselves with their security contingent and enter the Temple by force, if need be. They were not asking to be ordained as priests and enter the more-restricted areas of the Temple, such as the Most Holy Place. At least not yet.

The two leaders were both extremely popular throughout the world, with approval ratings for them both well over eighty-five percent in nearly every poll. They had an incredible amount of political capital, and the time had come to start spending it – or rather investing it, as Medine often put it. He had much more natural charisma and adoration by the people than his counterpart in Franco Pontiffica, but that would change as Pontiffica became better known and more influential.

On the first day of the Passover, David Medine and Franco Pontiffica made their way to the Temple early in the morning for the beginning of the day's festivities. The media had been stirred up by Medine and his powerful allies and was exerting enormous pressure upon the JTA and the rest of the Israeli government.

As the motorcade approached the Temple grounds, the JTA finally caved and granted them access to the Temple. Thousands of Jews were already inside the Temple compound, and were shocked that their holy place was being violated as they watched the limousine enter. David Medine was sending a clear message to them and all the world: that he was the supreme authority on the earth, and not God or any other religious entity. But after awakening from their two thousand year spiritual slumber, the Jews would not stand for any desecration of their beloved Temple, even though their leaders had compromised.

The motorcade stopped just inside the Temple grounds, and David Medine and Franco Pontiffica left their limousine and began walking towards the Temple. The Two Witnesses were nearby, and also watched the motorcade drive up and stop without incident.

Medine and Pontiffica left their heavily armed security detail behind with the vehicles, since surely no one would risk killing the Sarrim and his high priest. If anyone tried anything stupid, their precious Temple would be leveled to the ground, with many of them along with it! But both men were clad in bullet-proof vests underneath their traditional Jewish robes, which they had adorned in order to worship at the Temple. However, on both of their robes the Ankida symbol had replaced the Star of David, and by the looks on the Jews' faces, they recognized the alteration and its significance.

The Temple grounds fell completely silent as Medine and Pontiffica passed through the Outer Courts and made their way to the entrance of the Inner Court.

Suddenly, gunshots rang out from near the entrance to the Inner Court of the Temple. One of the Orthodox Jews standing next to the entryway in front of Medine had drawn a handgun and was firing at him!

The first bullet struck his chest, and when Medine staggered backwards from the impact, two more shots were fired, with one striking him in the head and the other blasting a hole in his hand as he had raised it to protect himself. [48]

Medine crumpled to the ground and his security detail leaped forward to surround him just before he lost consciousness, only seconds after he had been shot. His bodyguards shot the assassin

---

[48] Zechariah 11:17

in the leg and arm first, but when he resumed firing, they were forced to kill him.

Near the Golden Gate of the Temple, the Two Witnesses bowed their heads, as if something had suddenly called them to cease their preaching and pray instead.[49]

Medine and Pontiffica were rushed out of the Temple grounds and taken immediately to the nearest hospital in Jerusalem. Pontiffica had not been shot at all, probably because he had no real power or authority yet other than what Medine had given him.

If Pontiffica were killed, he could simply be replaced. But finding another David Medine would not be easy, if not impossible.

* * *

"My God!" Jacob exclaimed at the television. "Medine's been shot!"

A shiver of fear swept over Naomi – he had not reacted that way since Yitzhak Rabin had been assassinated years earlier by another radical Israeli citizen, over the signing of the Oslo Accords.

She rushed into the room to see what was happening on the news, and immediately covered her mouth in shock. On all the television channels, the regular programming had been interrupted for the breaking news of the assassination of David Medine at the Temple.

Swarms of cameramen scurried about the Temple grounds, interviewing eyewitnesses and reporting exactly what had occurred only moments before. The video footage of the shooting was being continuously replayed, with close-ups and stills to show precisely where Medine had been shot. Since the World Union would probably not be releasing any details of his condition for several hours, the video enhancements and analysis were the most complete information they could give the public.

---

[49] Zechariah 11:17; Revelation 13:3-4,12

THE TIME OF JACOB'S TROUBLE

David Medine had definitely been shot at least once in the head, and also in the right hand. There was a relatively small amount of blood where Medine had fallen just before being rushed into his armored car. Part of Medine's security detail had accompanied him while the rest secured the immediate area.

The Jerusalem police and Temple authorities were still sweeping the crowd, making sure that no one else had any weapons or was trying to flee the area before they could be questioned. The blocks surrounding the Temple had been sealed off also, and no one had left the Temple Mount or even Old Jerusalem except Medine's security forces.

The police initially tried to protect the body of the dead assassin, but they were too late. After he had been killed by Medine's bodyguards, the frantic mob had attacked his corpse with punches, kicks, and beat him with whatever they could find. It had taken the police longer to get the people away from the corpse than it had to seal off the entire Temple area.

The angry World Union supporters had beaten the assassin into a bloody pulp in a matter of minutes. Most of his teeth were still intact, but he had no identification. Analysts conjectured that he probably hid his ID or threw it away after he had passed through security, since everyone at the Temple complex had been thoroughly screened. But how he had been able to smuggle a gun into the complex was still a mystery.

Jacob shook his head in disbelief. "He was one of our biggest supporters!" he said. "What will happen to us now?"

Naomi nodded, but looked very pale. She was thinking about one of the passages in Revelation that spoke about the beast having a deadly head-wound but then being miraculously healed.

She hurriedly left the room and went to get her Bible. She quickly found it and flipped to the passage she was looking for. And what she read made her sit down and re-read the passage several times.

Revelation 13:3 – "And I saw one of his heads as it were wounded to death; and his deadly wound was healed: and all the world wondered after the beast."

243

She was certain that part of this prophesied event was happening before her very eyes. She wanted to cry and fall on her face, but she maintained what was left of her composure.

From the passage, it was clear that the assassination and the subsequent healing – some said resurrection – of the Beast would be the watershed event that would turn the entire earth into the equivalent of a Holocaust death-camp.

And at the deepest dungeon that death-camp would be the nation of Israel.

* * *

Following the shooting of the Sarrim, the Temple immediately closed and postponed all of the Passover festivities, while the world waited for news of his condition.

As far as anyone knew, David Medine was still alive, though badly wounded. From the analysis of the video footage at the Temple, he had been shot three times: once in the chest (from which he was protected by his bulletproof vest), once very close to the right eye, and once in the right hand as he had attempted to shield his face. The Sarrim's press office had not released any status as to his immediate condition other than "critical" or "life-threatening."

The world media and the vast majority of people on the earth were outraged at the assassination attempt. If Medine died, revenge would not just be demanded of the shooter, but also of all of Israel. Many of the Israelis felt the same towards the shooter and even towards the Orthodox Jews, to some extent. They had been very critical and distrusting of David Medine, in spite of all he had done for them.

The animosity of the world towards Israel was enormous, as it had not been since just before Magog Invasion. "Burn the Temple!" they cried. "Kill the Jews!" was another phrase heard and seen frequently all over the Internet and the news.

Later that day, the Ankida religion leader, Franco Pontiffica held a world press conference and announced that David Medine the Sarrim had indeed been assassinated.

THE TIME OF JACOB'S TROUBLE

He openly wept, along with many of the journalists who were covering the event. The bullet that had struck him in the face had pierced his right eye and lodged deep in his brain. He had died several hours after arriving at the hospital, and the remaining time had been spent planning how to tell the world.

A week of mourning was immediately declared for the entire globe, which would last from that day until their beloved Sarrim was finally laid to rest.

*   *   *

David Medine's body had been entombed in an immaculate, airtight crystal casket. It was tipped back at a high angle, so the body almost appeared to be standing upright. The leaders of the entire world had gathered in Babylon for the funeral, and if Babylon had been full before, now it was overflowing.

There was now no question that Medine was dead – cameras had been broadcasting the images and video of the transparent casket for over a day, and the multitudes that were gathering to walk past his corpse and pay their respects. His head-wound had been incredibly concealed, and his hands were covered with expensive dark gloves.

The day after the assassination, Medine's body was put on display and the multitudes of politicians, bankers, corporate leaders and other privileged people gathered to honor him. The multitudes would continue to file past around the clock for another two days, and the funeral would take place at noon on the fourth day after he had died. The media focused on little else other than the funeral procession, the casket, and the tons of flowers and gifts that were quickly piling up, along with the numerous eulogies.

The greatest leader in all the world – some even said all of history – had been murdered before their very eyes. Millions were still in shock that his brilliant light and glory had been so quickly extinguished from the earth. But after their grief wore off, many in Israel knew the mourning would likely turn to anger and thoughts of vengeance against the Jews.

Ironically, neither Medine nor anyone else in the World Union had put together any contingencies for what would happen in the event of his death. Everyone simply assumed that he was so popular that no one would even consider murdering him – even many of the religious fanatics who spoke ill of him had been considered such non-threats that they had not been taken seriously.

But they would be monitored much more closely now, of course, yet that still did not resolve their immediate problem. How could the world proceed with David Medine's ambitious plans to unite the world if the Sarrim himself was no longer with them? The World Union leaders and Franco Pontiffica had been trying to contact the Anshar for guidance, but they had been unable to so far. They realized that they could use an extended period of mourning to buy them some time to figure out what to do next.

At noon on fourth day after David Medine had been assassinated, the funeral ceremonies began. The World Union declared it a permanent global holiday, the first of its kind in history, and that no work should be done except for critical services. Everyone on earth was required to observe the funeral ceremony and mourn for the first great world leader. The entire funeral grounds and outlying areas were nearly silent; in fact, much of the world was somber as well. The normally clear skies of Babylon were cloudy and overcast, as if the earth itself was mourning him.

Millions of men and women openly wept and grieved for David Medine, their Sarrim, and prayed that one would soon rise to take his place and restore their hope.

* * *

The funeral ceremonies commenced, and twelve of the most powerful speakers in the world were slated to give their eulogies. The speeches would last hours, but no one seemed to mind the length – it was a mournful, solemn day for the people of the earth.

THE TIME OF JACOB'S TROUBLE

The entire auditorium was silent, except for the sounds of heartfelt weeping and the mourning. Just before the first eulogy began, a steady rain began to fall outside. The long eulogies were moving and beautiful; it was a perfect day for the reflection and honor of the greatest man in history. Like so many who'd held such promise, his life had been tragically cut short before he had barely begun to live.

Towards the end of the sixth eulogy, a strange light began streaming in from the huge glass panels in the auditorium's ceiling. Though it was the middle of the afternoon and still raining, the brilliant beam of light was much brighter than normal sunlight. Even stranger, the light seemed to be centered on the upright casket. The speaker briefly hesitated to observe the light, and then continued speaking. The audience and the others viewed the beam of light as a supernatural acknowledgement of David Medine's greatness and glory. As a result of the strange light, more people began focusing on the lit coffin, instead of the speaker.

Suddenly David Medine's eyes flashed open, first blinking, and then moving back and forth. Few noticed it because the brilliance of the light shining upon him.

But the first gasps were heard from the front of the audience when his right hand suddenly began to move. And then he raised it to press upon the thick glass lid in front of him. At that movement, even more people gasped and cried out, and the speaker stopped his eulogy in mid-sentence. Everyone turned their full attention to the coffin to watch the miracle that many were whispering of.

Before their very eyes, David Medine appeared to fully come alive as he leaned forward and pushed upon the lid of the coffin. With a tremendous kick, he knocked the lid open and then suddenly stepped out onto the stage. Many people shouted and cried out, and some even fainted. Everyone in the audience was filled with fear and wonder at what was taking place before them. Along with those in the auditorium, everyone else on earth was watching the miracle too.

David Medine was indeed alive in the flesh, and as he began

walking from his coffin to the podium, the speaker fell away in shock and rushed back to his seat next to the other speakers. And then David Medine himself began to speak.

He pronounced with complete authority that he had indeed died, and that he had brought himself back to life. Since he was fully Anshar and also fully human, he was therefore capable of living in both dimensions. The Anshar could journey back and forth to the eternal dimension which many referred to as "heaven" at will, where Medine had just returned from.

Though his earthly body had died, his eternal body had not, and he had used his knowledge and power to resurrect himself. And soon he would endow all mankind with the same power to stop death that he had just used and demonstrated for all to see.

His work was not yet complete – he had been tasked to bring immortality to mankind, and not even death could stop him from fulfilling his destiny.[50]

When all the people in the auditorium realized they were in the presence of a god, they simultaneously fell upon their faces in obeisance to him. And rather than blushing or looking awkward as to the outright worship of him, David Medine welcomed it and basked in it, as if it were perfectly normal for how they were honoring him.

He let the worship continue for a long while, and then he gave the most visionary speech the world had ever heard.

* * *

Jacob woke up early in the morning covered with sweat – he must have had a nightmare. He had not been sleeping very well since Medine's death, and now that the David Medine had been raised from the dead, he found himself to be even more restless.

He didn't feel like doing any work or reading to help him go back to sleep – he needed to get out and think for a while. Until the last week, the world had seemed to be settling down after all

[50] The world leader (or Satan) counterfeits the Resurrection to convince the world he is the Messiah (or God). (Revelation 13:3-4)

the plagues and problems of the past few years. The economy was starting to recover and hope seemed to be returning, but he still felt uneasy.

Dawn was just over an hour away, and he decided he might as well just get up and take his morning shower. It was Sunday, and his schedule would be slow that day. He decided to take a drive down to the beach again – maybe that would help calm his nerves and give him some measure of peace. He shaved, showered, and dressed in his usual fashion, and then kissed Naomi softly without waking her, and drove away.

He made his way south along the frontage road near the shoreline, and soon found a quiet beach a few kilometers south of Haifa that had public access. He was the only one out that day – perfect for contemplating and relaxing. As soon as he began walking along the water's edge, he began feeling calmer and more at peace.

Jacob walked for nearly a kilometer before he began thinking about the day ahead, just being content to breathe the salt-air and feel the cool seawater wash under his bare feet. The sea gulls scurried about and eyed him curiously, hoping for the first hand-out of the day. There weren't as many birds as there used to be before the plagues, he thought, but more were coming back now. Even the annoying birds like crows and pigeons were a welcome sight now, yet another sign that life was returning to normal.

The recent events came rushing back into his mind, and he began to process them from the beginning. He had been deeply saddened when David Medine had been assassinated, and almost felt as if the hope of the world had been torn away from them once again.

But then came the greatest of wonders: David Medine's resurrection. Jacob had been nearly overcome with emotion, and felt that all the hope that he had lost had instantly returned. Perhaps it was the emotional roller-coaster and all the "ups and downs" that were making him restless. But deep down, he felt an odd sort of fear, as if somehow he would soon be forced into a future against his will. Somewhere terrible and frightening. Was it his own evolution he felt trepidation about?

Who was David Medine, he wondered. How could he do those miracles if he wasn't God, or even some lesser god? Not only that, but how could he resurrect himself as he claimed if he wasn't God in the flesh? Many Jewish leaders all over the world were now claiming that Medine was the Messiah – after all, he had restored their Temple and its worship. And now he had conquered death itself. He was Israel's greatest supporter, and had often stood up for her in the World Union and the press when she was denigrated.

Could Medine indeed be the long-awaited Messiah of Israel? On the surface, it sure seemed that he was. Everything seemed to fit. He was the very image of the Messiah that the Jews had always pictured.

And he met many of the criteria from the ancient Scriptures concerning who the Messiah would be and what he would do. He was so handsome and charismatic, and spoke in such eloquent ways that left audiences enraptured and clinging to every word. He was bringing peace and prosperity to a war-torn, troubled world – a monumental task for any nation, and how much more for a single person!

But he wasn't sure about Medine being the Messiah. Why did they even need the Messiah now anyway? Israel and the rest of the world still had their problems, to be sure, but wouldn't the world go on as it always had? What more would the Messiah do for Israel now that she had her Temple and peace with her neighbors? In some ways, he felt as if he wanted to just go back to the old days that had been simpler and more predictable, even if they had been more dangerous.

Jacob continued to walk on the beach for another half-hour, before finally turning around and heading back to his car. The long walk and soothing environment of the ocean had helped him calm his thoughts and feelings. And while he hadn't completely solved the mystery of who Medine was and how he could be doing all those miracles, he did feel much better. He would have to continue to watch and listen before he could make a decision about Medine.

Hopefully tonight he would be able to get a good night's

sleep for a change.

*   *   *

With all the media attention focused on David Medine's funeral and resurrection, the Two Witnesses had faded to the background. They had evidently ceased most of their plagues after the shooting, but they had continued to preach louder and more intensely than ever. They weren't even harassing the reporters that spit in their direction any more. What used to bring a burst of fire from them didn't even cause them to look up now. But very few people were paying any attention to them. One or two reporters would cover them every day or two, but to the press, they were preaching the same old sermon they had been for the last thirty-six months: wrath, judgment, Yeshua, and all that nonsense.

But the Two had indeed changed their message, even if few noticed. They were preaching more woes upon the nation of Israel and the earth, and were declaring that David Medine, the "Beast of the Abyss", would soon usher in the time of Jacob's trouble. Everyone who followed him would eventually meet the same fate that he would: eternal torment in the lowest bowels of Hell.

The Two also said that their ministry was now over, and that they had done the task that Yeshua had given them. They had completed what had been left incomplete, and fulfilled what had been unfulfilled. But no one really cared about them or what they said. The god of the world had been raised from the dead, and the world would listen only to him.

They also prophesied that their own deaths would be approaching soon, and that they would be slain at the hand of David Medine, as a matter of fact. The great peacemaker would murder them in the very place where they now stood. That brought a response from some of the journalists, but it was full of jeering and scorn, and even some jubilation. But they only exuded what most of the world felt; the Two Witnesses had been a source of great torment to all the earth, and the day they died couldn't come soon enough. But the Two continued to preach their message, regardless of their audiences' response.

They pressed whoever would listen and begged them to not to believe Medine's lies or follow after him. They desperately begged and pleaded, which was much different than casting down fire and blood upon their audience as they had done previously. Do not believe the Imposter, the False Messiah, the Devouring Shepherd, they proclaimed; and they had many other similar names for David Medine and his companion, Franco Pontiffica. Do not take the "mark of the beast" they cried, or you would be lost forever. Accept the only provision for your sins that God has given and would ever give: Yeshua the Nazarene.

And now that their ministry was drawing to a close, the Two preached around the clock opposite one another on the Temple grounds, no longer taking turns praying and preaching. They no longer stopped to pray either, but continued to cry out against the Temple and what would soon happen there.

The Messiah that Israel had chosen was coming, but he was not the One that God had chosen. No one had listened.

*   *   *

If David Medine had been confident and charismatic before his death, now he was many times more so. He began proclaiming incredible things, and espoused to have divine knowledge of the future. He also now claimed that Yeshua the Nazarene and his disciples had fabricated the last resurrection two thousand years ago, which was why no one had seen it. But his had been visible for all the world to see.

Medine even produced video footage that the Anshar had taken during the time of the first resurrection, and it clearly showed a group of men stealing the corpse from the tomb three nights after the crucifixion, and then later burning the body so it could never be found.

Where he had been outwardly tolerant of Christianity before, now he openly derided it and its followers as thieves and liars, and he pointed to the aggressive, intolerant nature of the Gospel and how it had led to many of the evils, divisions, and inequalities on the earth.[51]

And now that he was resurrected, he claimed that he indeed was the Jewish Messiah, the 12th Imam of Islam, and the Promised One of many other religions. After all, wasn't the conquest of death the ultimate sign of godhood? Here was the first documented god-man of modern history, and he had come back to life before their very eyes! Some of even the Orthodox Jews began to worship him as God in the flesh, and requested that he enter the Temple and immediately take his rightful place in the Holy of Holies.

David Medine met with the JTA, who had now completely changed their minds about him and nearly begged him to come to the Temple. And he was all too happy to honor their request. He was quickly ordained as a priest, and they discovered that he already knew all the ceremonies and rituals that accompanied the priesthood. The Sanhedrin also authorized him to perform the Temple duties during the time of the Passover (which had been delayed earlier due to his death), and they made all the necessary arrangements for him to perform them later that week.

The next day, David Medine arrived at the Temple with great pomp and celebration. The king of Israel – no, the king of the world – had come to his Temple! The Golden Age was now beginning. There were no radical Jews to bar his way between his motorcade and the Temple entrance this time. In fact, many Orthodox Jews were all lined up to honor him as he passed by. The Messiah had finally come! And after thousands of years of persecution and turmoil, they would now have everlasting peace.

Everyone seemed to be rejoicing at Medine's arrival – everyone except the two strange old men who were dressed in sackcloth. Medine glared at them and then confidently walked over to where they were sitting. When Medine had entered the Temple grounds, they had suddenly stopped speaking and sat down.

---

[51] Revelation 13:5-7

For the first time in three and a half years, they had stopped preaching. They were now silent in his presence.

He stopped where the Two Witnesses were sitting quietly, and demanded that they stand up. Recognizing his authority, the Two Witnesses obediently rose to their feet. The mood of the people and priests quickly turned from rejoicing to intense anger at the Two. They had long been a nuisance to everyone in the world, with their insulting speeches, their supernatural ability to protect themselves, and their capability to call down plagues and other forms of torment at will. There still had been no rain in Israel since they had proclaimed a drought upon the entire nation over forty-two months before. The Two Witnesses were the most hated men in all of Israel, if not the entire world.

David Medine smirked confidently at them, and then proclaimed that their days of torment were over. He raised his right hand towards the sky, and immediately the entire sky filled with deep, ominous storm clouds.

And when he raised his left hand, rain began to pour down all over Israel, but not upon him or any part of the Temple grounds. Everywhere in Israel, people ran outside to see the rain and began celebrating – the long drought was over! And people everywhere in Israel began praising David Medine and praising God for sending their long-awaited Messiah to them. At the Temple, the observers were even more incredulous, because they realized that Medine could completely control the weather, causing it to rain everywhere in Israel except at the Temple.

Then David Medine turned his gaze towards the Two Witnesses. He was still smiling and then he shouted at them in sheer rage and hatred, "As you have done unto others, so shall be done unto you!" And then a huge stream of fire shot out of his mouth and engulfed them where they stood.

Their dry, thick clothing instantly caught fire and they began burning alive – but even as they fell to the ground in flames, they did not cry out or make any sounds of agony.

The Two Prophets were quickly consumed, and though many people nearby rushed over, no one moved to help them or put out the flames. The spectators mercilessly watched them burn and be consumed by the fire. Their Messiah had slain the tormentors of Israel with just the words of his mouth and his fiery wrath. As the flames died down, Medine mocked them again and spit on their smoldering corpses. [52]

And all over the earth, people began calling and emailing one another to share the good news. Many even began sending gifts to one another to celebrate the demise of the Two Witnesses and the end of all the plagues on the earth.

* * *

Jacob and Naomi sat in front of their television, watching the events unfold at the Temple.

David Medine had been in his finest form as he had finally put down the two worst tormentors of the earth. Jacob thought what he had done was completely justified, given all the problems they had caused, but he didn't really care for how Medine had done it. Why did he have to make a gruesome spectacle of them, even though they had deserved it?

But Naomi was watching all the events with apprehension. She had been leafing through a magazine every once in a while, but tucked inside were several printouts of Daniel 9, Matthew 24, and Revelation 11-13. She had studied them carefully, and had written notes all over the margins, along with the dates of all the prophetic events that had been fulfilled over the last few years. The Two Witnesses had just been murdered, and would be left where they had fallen for three days, for the entire world to see their demise and celebrate over their deaths.

She felt as if she had at last come to a "fork in the road", so to speak, and that the time had arrived for her to make a decision. Would she go to the left and follow Medine and his world system, or would she turn to the right and accept what the Bible declared: that Yeshua was the true Messiah.

Soon she would either become a believer in David Medine as the Messiah, or she would accept Yeshua as the Messiah. One

---

[52] Revelation 11:7

path would lead to eternal death, and other path would lead to eternal life. She had a strange feeling that she had to make the decision that day, lest it be made for her in the near future. Today she was safe and could make the decision by her own free will. But who knew how long that would last?

As they watched Medine victoriously approach the entrance to the Temple, she suddenly felt nauseous. She had read the Daniel and Matthew passages over and over the last few days. She had counted the exact number of days that had been foretold in the Scriptures, from the time the Two Witnesses had begun their ministry until the day they were to die: 1260 days. Now it was the 1261st day, and they had just been slain.

Upon conducting a careful study, she had found that the prophecies had been precise to the very day they had started preaching. They had been murdered exactly as the Scriptures had predicted thousands of years before, and the people were reacting just as the Bible said they would.

But there was another important event foretold in the Scriptures, which would also happen that day. It had also been 1260 days since David Medine had signed the peace treaty with Israel. And she knew what was to happen.

It was clear from the Scriptures: the Jewish Temple was to be desecrated in the most abhorrent way by the Beast. And then he would set up his image in the Holy of Holies in the Temple and demand that every person in the world worship him or suffer death. No one other than the Christians or serious Bible students would be expecting this to happen that day, but it would. With the murder of the Two Witnesses, she was certain of it.

Naomi read the relevant passages in Matthew and Daniel yet again, concerning the desecration of the Temple. With Medine and Pontiffica in their midst, the priests were now starting the sacrifices just outside the Temple. Jacob was still watching the television and not paying attention to much else.

She felt her eyes filling with tears and quietly stood up and left the room. She had to get out – she had to be alone when it happened. She didn't want to watch it or see it – at least not yet.

Naomi hurried to their bedroom and closed the door, quietly

locking it behind her, and then fell to her knees, still holding the magazine with the printouts. And there she poured out her heart to God, begging Him to forgive her for her foolishness and complacency. She accepted Yeshua as her Savior – as her Messiah – on the very day that the Temple would be desecrated. The very day that Israel's time of trouble would begin.

As her tears subsided, she thought about Medine and the Temple. No one would stop him from what he was about to do – it had been foretold and would transpire exactly as it had been written long before. Not even God Himself would stop Medine from his evil deed. She knew it, and considered the decision she had just made. No matter what happened during the rest of her time on earth, her eternal future was now secure.

She prayed for a short time longer, and thanked the Lord for preserving her until she could make that decision.

And then she turned on the small television in their bedroom. Medine had just finished the ritual washings and was approaching the High Priest.

Naomi looked down again at her printouts, even though she now knew the passage by heart.

Daniel 9:27 - And he shall confirm the covenant with many for one week: and in the midst of the week he shall cause the sacrifice and the oblation to cease, and for the overspreading of abominations he shall make it desolate, even until the consummation, and that determined shall be poured upon the desolate.

Matthew 24:15-20 - Therefore when you see the 'abomination of desolation,' spoken of by Daniel the prophet, standing in the holy place, then let those who are in Judea flee to the mountains. Let him who is on the housetop not go down to take anything out of his house. And let him who is in the field not go back to get his clothes. But woe to those who are pregnant and to those who are nursing babies in those days! And pray that your flight may not be in winter or on the Sabbath. For then there will be great tribulation...

* * *

After the slaughter of the Two Witnesses, David Medine and his prophet walked up to the Temple, and then boldly entered the Temple's Inner Courts. In honor of their Messiah's arrival and his first pilgrimage to the Temple, the JTA and Sanhedrin had also approved the use of video cameras inside the Inner Courts (but not inside either the Holy Place or the Most Holy Place). Now the entire world could see that their promised Messiah had come and would be offering the incense inside the Holy Place. To relieve some of the world pressure after the assassination, they wanted to be more open about Medine's visit this time.

David Medine and Franco Pontiffica had evidently practiced the sacrificial rituals well beforehand, and were nearly indistinguishable from the other priests performing the sacrifices and offerings. They washed their hands and feet in the Bronze Lavers and then approached the Brazen Altar where the lambs were then sacrificed. Following the priests ahead of them, Medine and Pontiffica were then immersed in the Molten Sea between the Temple and the Brazen Altar. Their security detail closely watched nearby along both walls of the Inner Court.

After they were cleansed, Medine left the group of priests and took the Golden Censer and filled it with the fiery coals from the Brazen Altar. He then solemnly turned and walked towards the entrance of the Holy Place. The priests and cameras watched his every step, and the entire Temple area was silent with reverence. As he approached the Holy Place, the two Temple guardsmen opened the great doors of the Temple, and he passed through with the censer full of smoldering coals. Once he had fully entered the Temple, the doors were closed behind him and the guardsmen returned to their posts.

Less than five minutes later, David Medine emerged from the Holy Place with a strange smile on his face, which puzzled several of the more attentive priests in the Inner Court. As he strode back to the High Priest, he casually nodded to Franco Pontiffica without saying a word. The High Priest and the others around them saw the slight gesture, but just as quickly, Pontiffica pulled out a small phone and spoke into it.

Within moments, they heard a commotion in the Outer

THE TIME OF JACOB'S TROUBLE

Courts and another group of priests was rolling in a large cart with a covered box on it. Some heard what sounded like snorts and grunts coming from within the box, but no one moved. The new priests rolled the cart up to Medine and Pontiffica, who were now both grinning wildly. Pontiffica reached down and swept the covering off the box with a flourishing motion.

The box was revealed to actually be a large animal cage, and inside was a filthy, enormous pig. The priests around them gasped and rushed forward to remove the creature. But the security forces had been prepared beforehand – they drew their weapons and immediately shot the astonished priests. The High Priest was speechless and was so shocked at what was happening that he could not move.

Then with Medine watching in approval, Pontiffica led the pig to the Brazen Altar and heaved it up on top, knocking the burnt corpse of the lamb onto the ground. It was at that moment that the High Priest gathered his courage and intervened.

But as he rushed forward to stop the desecration, Medine grabbed the back of his head and held him fast. Pontiffica quickly turned away from the struggling pig and with one quick, smooth stroke, slit his throat with the knife. And the High Priest collapsed to the ground in a pool of his own blood.

Pontiffica turned back to the pig and slaughtered it on top of the Brazen Altar, haphazardly gutting it so the entrails all spilled out. The other priests around them were surrounded by the armed security officers, and were too stunned to move. The blood of the pig drained steadily onto the body of the High Priest lying directly in front of the Brazen Altar.

Medine and Pontiffica turned to the cameras for the entire world to see. Then with Pontiffica still holding the bloody knife, he proclaimed, "This is what will happen to any who will not worship the Sarrim as their god!"

From the huge number of security forces, it was obvious that Medine and Pontiffica had prepared for this special day. Many of the Jewish priests and Temple workers were going to die very, very soon.

CHRIS HAMBLETON

*　*　*

Naomi turned off the television in bedroom, drew a deep breath, and then went back out to the living room to watch the news with her husband. The desecration evidently had not happened yet, but it would soon. She knew from the Scriptures what would transpire that day; perhaps not the precise details of the events of course, but it was clear that the Temple would be defiled in one of the most vile ways possible.

Naomi walked back into the living room and sat down where she had been before. Medine had just entered the Holy Place carrying the censer of burning coals and incense. Jacob was still watching the news off and on, but not as intensely as before. He almost hadn't noticed what was happening, but he looked up just in time to see the video footage change from showing what was happening outside the Temple to what appeared to be from a much smaller, personal camera displaying the inside of the Holy Place.

The camera seemed to have been placed in along the southern wall to provide a wide-angle view of the front room near the Golden Incense Altar. And then David Medine stepped directly in front of the camera holding the Golden Censer of smoldering coals. But instead of pouring the coals on the altar, he kicked it over and then ripped open the thick veil of the Most Holy Place. He dumped the hot coals onto the floor and tossed the incense on top of it, and then proceeded to enter the Most Holy Place, the Holy of Holies.

He jumped up on the small platform that was reserved for the Ark of the Covenant, and then proclaimed that he was the Most Holy One – God of the entire universe. He reached down on the floor and picked up several of the hot coals, and squeezed them tightly. The coals should have burned his flesh, but they did not, and he held his hand up to the camera to show that the burning coals had not even left a mark on his skin.

He smiled again for the camera and then picked up the Golden Censer and the camera, and strode out of the Holy Place. Moments later, the scene erupted even further – Pontiffica was heaving a huge pig onto the altar.

That caught Jacob's full attention, and he saw that his wife was watching as intensely as he was. He watched as Medine grabbed the High Priest and held him fast. His heart was pounding, yet his mind had not yet processed what Pontiffica was about to do.

Pontiffica slit his throat and Medine let him collapse in front of the Brazen Altar. There was murder and chaos in what should have been the most holy, peaceful place on earth. Almost before anyone could react, Pontiffica slaughtered the pig also and dumped its guts all over the High Priest! Not only had they desecrated the Holy of Holies, but they had also murdered the High Priest!

Jacob jumped from his chair in anger. Even though he had not been very serious about his religion and had more national pride than love for the new Temple, he was still Jewish, and that was still his Temple.

He couldn't believe what he was seeing! He suddenly felt like the world had been turned upside down once again, and that all of his hopes in Medine had been completely dashed to pieces.

He felt like he was going to throw up – how could Medine do this to them? Many had been calling him the Messiah even before his resurrection, and now to see him do this – it was almost beyond comprehension.

Jacob shook his head and began to pace about the room, trembling in shock. Israel's most important ally had not only turned out to be a traitor, but had betrayed them in the worst possible way. It was almost like Medine was intent upon deliberately provoking them – for what purpose?

His mind instantly jumped to the Holocaust, and the many events that had led up to it. He had never believed that another one could take place, yet there was the king of the world in essence declaring war upon them.

What had they done? Why was Medine doing this? Could there be a greater purpose in what he was doing, in that they would one day be able to look back on and somehow understand?

CHRIS HAMBLETON

And then on the television – in front of the entire world – Pontiffica set up a golden idol of what appeared to be a lifelike statue of David Medine himself directly on top of the carcass of the pig on the Brazen Altar. Pontiffica turned to Medine and called him the "god of the universe" and declared that everyone on earth should bow before him immediately. There would be no more sacrifices anywhere except to Medine and his image.

And then gesturing to the image on the altar Pontiffica exclaimed, "I said, 'Now you shall worship David Medine – the god among men – and his image forever!'"[53] No one moved again, and Pontiffica reiterated his demands that they worship the Sarrim and his image.

Many of the worshippers in the Inner and Outer Courts began to run towards the exits, and upon reaching the outer gates were met with a barrage of gunfire from the security forces. The rest were too terrified to move.

But they would meet their fate soon enough.

The new Holocaust had begun at the very heart of Jerusalem. And this time, there would be no savior of the Jews to interfere with this Final Solution.

---

[53] Matthew 24:15; Revelation 13:14-15

CHAPTER 11
THE FLIGHT INTO THE WILDERNESS

The priests and other attendants standing outside the Holy Place had no knowledge of what had happened inside the Holy of Holies.

But everyone outside the Temple grounds had seen the entire incident on television and the Internet as it had unfolded. Even after Medine had emerged with the empty censer, the priests didn't know they were in danger until the High Priest had been murdered and Pontiffica proclaimed the immediate ceasing of the Temple ceremonies.

Franco Pontiffica's phone call was apparently the signal that the security forces had been waiting for, and they had quietly entered the Outer Courts and sealed off all the exits. But it wasn't until the idol was placed on the Brazen Altar did the worshippers comprehend that they were trapped. They had been so completely focused on what Medine and Pontiffica were doing at the Brazen Altar that they had not seen the guards seal the exits.

When the people finally scattered and began running for the gates, they were met with soldiers holding semi-automatic weapons that barred them from leaving. A few brave men attempted to break through, but they were quickly cut down in a barrage of gunfire.

Those who huddled near the Temple sought whatever cover they could find, but within minutes, everyone was forcibly gathered in the large area directly in front of the Temple porch. The security forces remained at all the gates and the exits, and it was clear that there would be no escape from whatever fate Medine had decreed for them.

Then Pontiffica proclaimed that any religions that did not acknowledge the supremacy of the Ankida religion were no longer tolerated, and that the traditional Temple sacrifices would be immediately stopped. Any unauthorized worship at the Temple was now considered illegal.

The same would later hold true for all religious schools, teachings, books and all materials that were not expressly approved by the World Union's Department of Education. And then Pontiffica went on to proclaim that the Ankida religion was the one, true religion described by the Anshar, of which all the other religious systems had been merely shadows. And anyone who proclaimed otherwise would be severely punished. When he had said 'severely punished', he indicated the type of punishment by kicking the fallen High Priest.

Pontiffica raised his hands in a mocking gesture and beckoned all those at the Temple to put aside their petty religious differences and join the Ankida religion. Both he and Medine knew the worshippers would refuse, but that was what they had hoped for all along. Pontiffica turned and pointed to the image and cried out, "Israel, behold your God! You shall worship him and him alone! Now show your devotion to your God!" But no one moved.

He smiled wickedly, raised his head, and began to chant quietly under his breath. But as the chanting grew louder, the image itself began to shake and tremble, and then wobble on its base. As Pontiffica's rhythmic chanting grew louder and louder, the image violently shook and then suddenly began to move on its own. The image raised one arm and then the other, and then appeared to looked down on the crowd. And then the image began to speak in a low, terrible voice.[54]

"Bow low with your faces on the ground," it demanded. "All who fall within my gaze shall worship me!" And still no one budged. Pontiffica snuck a quick glance over to Medine,

---

[54] Revelation 13:15

who replied with a silent nod. That was all he needed to teach those imbeciles a lesson in who their god really was.

Franco Pontiffica's eyes blazed with anger, and revealed an inner fury he had never displayed before. Medine still stood next to him, clearly empowering him to deal with the defiant crowd. Pontiffica raised his arms to the sky, and then quickly snapped one of his arms down in a striking motion towards a group of priests standing nearby.

A bolt of blazing lightning shot out of the sky and engulfed a group of huddling priests and instantly consumed them. People began screaming and scattering, and suddenly huge streams of fire poured from the sky and burned up the fleeing people. Any who came within a few meters of the gates were slaughtered by the security forces, and the rest quickly found they had nowhere to flee.

With a small camera crew following him, Medine confidently walked back into the Most Holy Place and sat down directly on the platform, showing the world that he was now the god of the Temple, and that he was to be worshipped directly. [55]

For the Jewish worshippers that remained, Pontiffica had something worse than death in mind. [56]

* * *

Jacob felt numb – he didn't speak, and didn't look up from the television for a long time.

Naomi had been watching him and his reactions almost more than she had been watching what was happening at the Temple. She knew enough from the Scriptures that they would soon need to go somewhere safe before Medine turned Israel into a huge concentration camp. He would not waste any time, and they could not afford to either.

"It's really happening," she said, breaking the silence. "Just like the Bible says – it's all happening."

---

[55] Daniel 9:27; Matthew 24:15; 2 Thessalonians 2:3-4
[56] Revelation 13:12-13

"What are you talking about?" he said, looking over at her.

She stared directly at him and repeated it, but with even more confidence than before.

"All these things that have been going on the past few years – they're all happening just like the Bible said they would." She paused. "Medine is going to come down hard on Israel, and we'd better leave here soon. He's going to re-create the Holocaust, but this time he'll kill many more of us than Hitler did."

"How do you know that?" said Jacob.

He was scared now – Medine had definitely turned on them, but even then he couldn't comprehend how deadly serious it was. He could understand Medine and Pontiffica being upset with the Orthodox and Ultra-Orthodox Jews, but with all of Israel? Why? Much of Israel stood by the World Union and was still quite secular in many ways.

But another Holocaust? He found that too much to imagine.

"I've been reading the Bible the last few weeks, and what happened at the Temple just now was predicted thousands of years ago. It also says that after the Temple would be desecrated, the world leader would slaughter the Jews and then attempt to destroy all of Israel. Two out of every three Jews will die in the next three and a half years."

"Two out of every three?" he asked. The Holocaust had only taken one out of three. "Where do you get that?" he said.

"It's in the Bible. I'll show you later – first, we need to find out where to go. We won't be safe here for long, but longer than if we were in Jerusalem. Look!" she exclaimed.

On the television, they could see the World Union troops storming the exterior Temple grounds and quickly sealing off the streets nearby. Then there came breaking news that several brigades of World Union troops were already approaching Jerusalem, and would reach the city limits within the hour.

"We need to call Saul and find out where we'll be safe," she said.

"Why would he know?" he asked.

"Because he's been studying the Bible and all the prophecies for much longer than I have, and he'll know what to do.

I've heard some say that it's in Petra, but we need to find out for sure."

She picked up the phone and dialed Saul's cell-phone number. It rang and rang, and eventually went to his voice-mail. She knew enough about technology to know that any message she left would be monitored, so she would have to be careful. She would mention none of what was going on at the Temple, or what she needed to know.

"Hi Saul, it's Mom," she started. "We just wanted to see how you're doing – I just decided to accept the 'good news' and wanted to tell you about it, so call me back as soon as you can." She hoped he would pick up on the "good news" phrase and call her back right away. She hung up the phone and turned to Jacob.

"What 'good news'?" Jacob said.

"Nothing – I just want him to call back," she said, avoiding the question, at least for now.

"We should call Ahban and see if he's heard what happened," he said, not really thinking about it. Ahban was a news junkie like himself and with news this big, he was certain to have heard, if he wasn't watching it now.

"Okay – maybe he knows where Saul is," she said. She picked up the phone to call Ahban.

Ahban answered right away, but of course he was at work. Jacob wasn't happy about that, but he quickly remembered that Ahban was no longer in Israel where Shabbat was still observed. Even though Jacob worked long hours, at least he had always tried to keep the Shabbat.

They talked with Ahban for only a short time, since he was quite busy. He told them he hadn't seen Saul lately, and also that his brother was no longer living at his condo. Naomi wanted to press him on what had happened, but he changed the subject before she had the chance. But he reassured them that Saul was fine and that if he ran into him, he would have him call them right away.

After the conversation with Ahban ended, Naomi began to pack some essentials and make preparations for when they had to leave. Jacob still didn't know what to think. Everything was happening so fast, and he wanted to see more of what was going on in Jerusalem. He wasn't about to run from something he didn't believe was going to happen again. In the least, he wanted to wait until Saul called and he could get a second opinion on all this prophecy stuff.

"Another Holocaust?" he said to himself. He just couldn't believe it. For decades, one of Israel's mottos (directed toward the Holocaust) had been "Never again!"

Surely the world would not allow that to occur again!

* * *

The phone rang just after dinner, and Naomi knew it was Saul even before she looked at the Caller ID. As she answered and heard him say his cheerful "Hi Mom," she instantly felt a wave of relief. Just from his brief greeting and tone, she could tell that he was safe.

"Hi! Are you all right?" she asked with urgent concern.

"Yeah – you? I just caught up on the news," he said.

"We're pretty surprised – we're just waiting to see what happens next," she said. "Actually, part of the reason why I called you was to see what we should do and where we should go when it's time. That and how you can know for sure."

Saul could tell that she knew their conversation was probably being monitored, which explained her caution and ambiguity. Those talking explicitly about the Temple and Jerusalem would be among the first to be rounded up and imprisoned (if not worse).

"Okay – remember the vacation we took twelve years ago in the spring? It's the same place, but it should soon be much busier now. Daniel has all the info you need. Do you want me to call him for you?"

"That's would be nice – it's no trouble for him, is it?" she asked.

"Not at all. He'd be happy to talk to you or even drop by. He has your address," he said. "It sounds like you've been doing your reading, Mom," he said. She could almost see him smiling.

"You're right – I have been. Thank you for leaving those books here, and those links on the web."

"Sure – is the 'good news' what I think it is?" he asked.

"Yes. Your father doesn't know yet, and I'm waiting for the right time to surprise him with the news."

"Congratulations, Mom! That will be something else for him to deal with," he replied.

He felt a pang of sympathy for his father, considering that nearly his entire family had converted to Christianity. He remembered how he had reacted when he and Ruth had told him about their own conversions. Now his wife had become a Christian also. He wondered how he would take the news.

"It sure will," she acknowledged. "Well, I have to go – your father stepped out for a while but he'll be back soon. I'll tell him that you're all right," she said.

"Cool. Talk to you later, Mom!" Saul said.

"Okay – thanks for calling me back so soon. I'm glad to hear you're okay."

"Same here – oh, and Mom?" he said. "Happy Birthday!"

She smiled and gave him a short laugh, understanding the quick joke he had made. It was indeed her birthday – but her spiritual birthday, not her physical birthday.

"Thanks – we'll celebrate the next time you're in town," she said, and then she said goodbye and hung up the phone.

She continued to smile as she thought about what he had said. And then she began packing more of the items that she and Jacob would need when they left.

She would be surprised if they would be at home for the next Shabbat.

*　*　*

Many Jews who had seen or heard what had happened at the Temple did not immediately panic, but everyone felt something ominous beginning to set in.

The World Union had quickly sealed off Jerusalem after the Temple incident, and everyone in Israel hoped the quarantine would be lifted soon. As the Israelis realized that no one could go in or out of one of their own cities, they collectively began to get the sinking feeling that their nation would be turned into a huge ghetto. The only thing they could do was to quickly buy food, weapons, and supplies, and then hunker down as best they could.

As a nation, the Jews had survived thousands of years of tremendous, brutal persecution, and they were confident that they would survive whatever the World Union threw at them. But with the full weight and power of the world against them, they were afraid like they had not been since the Coalition for Peace had gathered.

For the three days that had followed the desecration of the Temple, nearly everyone on earth was glued to their televisions and computers, to watch what was happening in Israel. Another huge golden image of David Medine had been set up on top of the Temple, and the rest of the Jews who had survived the initial firestorm from Pontiffica were rounded up by the security forces.

There were hundreds of survivors, but one by one they were marched up to the Brazen Altar, where Pontiffica forced them to eat the raw flesh of the butchered pig. Those who refused were struck by lightning or consumed by fire, and even those that partook of the meat soon met the same fate. Others were brought forward to the image of Medine and shot regardless of whether they bowed down to it or not.

While the Israelis were still reeling from the horrific actions of Medine and Pontiffica at the Temple, thousands upon thousands of people were rushing to join the Ankida religion, if for nothing else than shelter from persecution. But many were joining because they were very convinced of the sheer power and authority of the Sarrim and his High Priest. Another factor in many peoples' decisions was because Medine had finally killed the Two Witnesses, the most hated men on the entire earth.

The Two were so despised that they had been denied any form of a burial, or even removal from where they had been murdered. Their bodies had been left where they had fallen and were steadily showing signs of decomposing. Flies, birds, and other creatures could be seen picking at the burnt bodies as they laid in the open air. Cameras had been set up for everyone in the world to see that the Two were indeed dead. People were still even exchanging gifts days afterwards, in celebration of the end of all the plagues and curses. [57]

But exactly seventy-two hours after David Medine had slaughtered the Two Witnesses, the cameras captured a sight that caused all the celebrations to suddenly cease. It all started with a strange, strong breeze that began blowing over the bodies. Many of the flies, rats, and birds flew away or scurried off, and an eerie silence followed. Then the bodies themselves began to morph, appearing to spontaneously heal themselves.

The flesh that had been burnt black, rotted, or chewed open began to close up and appear normal. And then soon after their flesh had been made whole, the Two Witnesses suddenly opened their eyes and clamored to their feet, in front of all the cameras. The shocked security guards maintaining the perimeter ran over to see what was happening, but the sight of the Two alive once again stopped them dead in their tracks, and several even ran away.[58]

As the Two Witnesses stood up, they slowly turned to each camera, as if to show the entire world that they were indeed completely alive and whole. And as they turned to the last set of cameras, a great voice from the sky shook the entire earth and every person and creature on it, and commanded the Two Witnesses to come up to Heaven. The Two slowly began rising from off the earth and ascending into the sky. The cameras followed them until they were engulfed in the clouds. [59]

Less than ten minutes after the Two Witnesses had disappeared into the clouds, a great earthquake struck Jerusalem, and a tenth of the buildings and homes in the city collapsed into rubble. All over the city, people scurried for cover from the falling debris. Thousands of men and women in Jerusalem died in the earthquake.

---

[57] Revelation 11:7-10
[58] Revelation 11:11
[59] Revelation 11:12

CHRIS HAMBLETON

After seeing the supernatural resurrection of the Two Witnesses and hearing the voice from the sky, many in Jerusalem and throughout Israel immediately worshipped the Lord God in great fear. And a number of the Jews realized that the Two Witnesses had indeed been sent from God Himself to chastise and awaken His people. And now that David Medine had betrayed them and desecrated their Temple, many realized they should have listened to them from the beginning.[60]

And then a long, deafening trumpet blast rang out from the sky – the seventh of such blast that had occurred – and a loud voice proclaimed, "The kingdoms of this world have become the kingdoms of our Lord, and of His Anointed; and he shall reign for ever and ever." [61]

*   *   *

As much as he was growing accustomed to unbelievable events happening everyday, what Jacob saw still caused him to tremble. When he had turned on the news at the office, he saw the latest news update from the Temple Mount. And what transpired as he watched made him turn white and sit down. The Two Witnesses had been raised from the dead. At first, he thought the scene was a movie clip – perhaps computer-generated or with special effects.

But the reactions of the newscasters and observers on the scene immediately nullified that possibility. The incredible resurrection of the Two Witnesses had been very real indeed, and all the eyewitnesses were very afraid. And they had every right to be; if these Two had wrecked utter havoc on the earth before they had been killed, what would they do now that they had been resurrected? Not even the horrible death they had suffered had been able to stop them, at least not for more than a few days. And then the terrible, thunderous voice followed that beckoned them up into the sky. And up, up, up they flew,

---

[60] Revelation 11:13
[61] Revelation 11:15

straight through the atmosphere into space, where they then vanished. The satellite cameras tried to track them, but they appeared to instantly vanish once the satellites were in range.

As he was watching the news, suddenly the cameras began shaking and fall to the ground. Jacob realized there was a huge earthquake occurring in Jerusalem. A moment later, the windows in his office began shaking, and Jacob jumped up and ran for the door, to stand directly under the frame. He managed to shout out "Earthquake!" just seconds before it struck, and most of the people in the office scurried under their desks and covered their heads. For over thirty seconds, the whole building shook and rattled.

Later when they watched the news again, they found that the entire land of Israel had been shaken by the earthquake. But all the land outside the borders had not shaken at all; even a few meters outside the borders had not been affected.

And then a booming voice rang out, proclaiming the overthrow of the kingdoms of the world. Some of the pictures on the walls rattled when the voice sounded, and it felt like the voice boomed all the way through him. His fillings even hurt, and he found he was trembling. His assistant stood up from under her desk and asked if he was all right, and he left to see if anyone was hurt and then if there was any damage to the building.

Aside from some broken glass and wall pictures, there was no damage or injuries. He called Naomi and made sure she was safe. And then after spending another hour or two in his office without doing very much, he decided to just go home (and he told everyone else still there to do likewise).

As he drove home, he thought about little else other than what he had witnessed earlier that day. The voice had really shaken him up, and the recent events were now starting to make him question what he really believed. Did he really buy into David Medine's propaganda about world peace and evolution? After the massacre and the desecration at the Temple, his faith in them had been deeply shaken.

He didn't know who to believe or who to trust any more. He had never liked the Two Witnesses because of their manners, message, and their wrath, but at least they hadn't acted as disgusting and power-hungry as Medine and Pontiffica. What if the Two Witnesses had been true in who they said Medine was – some terrible Beast who would bring all the world against Israel to destroy the Jews?

Another Holocaust was almost too much for him to comprehend; he was still trying to understand how the Two could have been resurrected. Their bodies had been burnt, trampled, and even starting to rot – and then they had just become whole again and stood up for all to see.

And then the voice that followed – that was what had really shaken him up. What if Yeshua was the true Messiah of Israel, and that He would be coming back to establish His rule? But the years of wariness towards religion continued to keep that possibility at bay. Any type of messianic faith ran counter to much of what he had been taught and believed.

He felt tired and broken – he didn't want to fight those he loved any longer. He just didn't know what to believe or who to trust any more.

* * *

When he got home, he found that Naomi was already there too. She hadn't been going to the flower shop as much as she had before, usually just a few hours a day now, and she seemed somewhat tired of it.

He could understand how she felt – business everywhere had been slow ever since the plagues had begun, but especially for the floral industry. No one had the money to spend on gifts and flowers when they were simply trying to survive. He thought about encouraging her to sell it, but he doubted that anyone would buy it until life returned to normal. As he walked into the kitchen, he put his briefcase on one of the chairs and went to find her.

She was sitting in the living room watching the news, which was replaying the resurrection and the voice. He also saw that she had what looked to be a Bible on her lap. As he sat down in his chair, he said hello and asked if there had been any additional news from Jerusalem yet. It was estimated that thousands had died from earthquake earlier, but the emergency crews were working on getting a more accurate count. A significant fraction of the city had been leveled, and more had been badly damaged.

"Yes. I had the news on when it happened. You?" she asked.

He nodded. "I had the TV on in the office and saw the whole thing. Pretty awful, huh?" he said. "Was there any damage here?"

"No, just some fallen pictures and rattled dishes." She looked up from her Bible and looked at him. "Did you hear the voice too?" He nodded that he had, and then she asked, "What do you think about it?"

"I don't know – it's kind of confusing. Medine and the Anshar say one thing, and then those Two and that voice say another. I'm not sure what to think now –" She nodded again and gestured to her Bible.

"I've been reading some of this lately, and it's helping me understand what's going on." She hesitated, as if waiting for him to react, but he didn't. "I know how you feel about the Bible, but maybe you should give it another look. Everything that's been happening over the last few days is in here – nearly word for word."

"How's that?" he asked. And for the first time since the Anshar had come to earth, he sounded genuinely interested in the Bible, or at least without outright skepticism.

She looked down and began reading.

"Revelation 11:3-6 - And I will give power unto my two witnesses, and they shall prophesy a thousand two hundred and sixty days, clothed in sackcloth. These are the two olive trees, and the two candlesticks standing before the God of the earth. And if any man will hurt them, fire proceeds out of their mouth, and devours their enemies: and if any man will hurt them, he must in this manner be killed. These have power to shut heaven, that it rain not in the days of their prophecy: and have power over waters to turn them to blood, and to smite the earth with all plagues, as often as they will."

She paused and looked up at him. "That's exactly what the Two Witnesses did up until last week."

He nodded and motioned for her to continue. He was still uncomfortable with the Bible and prophecy in general, but he finally wanted some answers as to what was happening in these days and hopefully what was coming next.

She began reading the next section.

"Revelation 11:7-12 - And when they shall have finished their testimony, the beast that ascends out of the bottomless pit shall make war against them, and shall overcome them, and kill them. And their dead bodies shall lie in the street of the great city, which spiritually is called Sodom and Egypt, where also our Lord was crucified. And they of the people and kindreds and tongues and nations shall see their dead bodies three days and a half, and shall not suffer their dead bodies to be put in graves. And they that dwell upon the earth shall rejoice over them, and make merry, and shall send gifts one to another; because these two prophets tormented them that dwelt on the earth. And after three days and a half the spirit of life from God entered into them, and they stood upon their feet; and great fear fell upon them which saw them. And they heard a great voice from heaven saying unto them, 'Come up hither.' And they ascended up to heaven in a cloud; and their enemies beheld them."

She could see from his reaction that he was surprised at how precisely the passage had described the astounding events of that very day.

And then she went on to finish her reading.

"Revelation 11:13-15 - And the same hour was there a great earthquake, and the tenth part of the city fell, and in the earthquake were slain of men seven thousand: and the remnant were afraid, and gave glory to the God of heaven. The second woe is past; and behold, the third woe cometh quickly. And the seventh angel sounded; and there were great voices in heaven, saying, 'The kingdoms of this world are become the kingdoms of our Lord, and of his Anointed; and he shall reign for ever and ever.'"

"Wow – that's fascinating," he said. "How could they know

that all those things would happen?"

"I don't know – but there's more," she added.

"Like what?"

"The next chapter of Revelation describes a war in heaven that comes to the earth. There's also the story of a woman who flees into the wilderness, and a dragon pursues her and tries to destroy her. When he fails, he goes after her children that are all over the rest of the earth. The woman described is Israel, and she stays in the wilderness for 1260 days (or about three and a half years)."

"What happens after that?" he asked.

"Well, then comes what's referred to as 'the Beast' who has been healed from a head wound and who blasphemes God and the saints. He's given the authority to persecute and destroy the believers all over the earth, and kill everyone who won't worship him or take the mark," she said.

"The mark? Do you mean like 666 and all that?"

He shook his head, almost in disbelief that those prophecies that people had mocked for centuries were now coming to pass all at once in his lifetime. Yet here he was – one of his children had been taken from the earth and another had become a street preacher. All that had been written in the Bible thousands of years before was clearly happening over these last few years.

"Yes – and from what I've been reading, it sounds like the only place we'll be safe from this beast or his servants is in the wilderness. When I talked to Saul yesterday, he told me that we should go to Petra as soon as possible – before it's too late. They've already shut down the ports and the outgoing air traffic, so we can't leave the country, at least not very easily," she said.

"I saw that too – I thought it was just to keep extremists from escaping or and causing more problems. But it could also be to keep us bottled up, I suppose," he acknowledged.

Something on the television caused him to look up and he turned up the volume. It was the death count from the earthquake in Jerusalem.

"How many people did you say were supposed to die in the quake?"

She looked down and found the verse. "It says seven thousand men."

He shook his head. "The report here says they're estimating that over ten thousand died. Maybe closer to fifteen once they're finished digging everyone out."

"Well, that's probably about right – most likely half will be women," she stated.

"True – I hadn't thought of that," he said.

He watched the news for a moment and shook his head in disbelief at what he saw. She reached over and turned off the news, and he turned and gave her a questioning look. Her hands were folded on her Bible.

"Jacob, with all that's happened, I wanted to tell you that I've become a Christian too. I've been thinking about it more and more over the last few months, and three days ago, I made the decision."

He looked down at her Bible, but didn't say anything. Part of him couldn't believe it, but it just added to the other shocks of the day. He could almost understand it though. After all, two of his children had become convinced of its message – why did he think she would be any different, given the times they were living in?

Jacob suddenly felt like everyone else in his family had more of the answers than he did. He felt alone and excluded now more than ever.

"What does that mean?" he asked.

She shook her head again. "I don't know yet, but from talking to Saul, it was clear that we need to leave here right away, before they quarantine us in our own cities. If we don't go to Petra quickly, it may soon be too late."

"Alright – I need to think about it awhile. Everything is happening so fast!" he exclaimed in frustration. "I need to get some air," he said, and he quickly rose from the couch and headed for the backdoor.

If only the world would slow down for a few days to let him figure things out. He took a long walk, but it didn't help him much at all that night. He thought about going to the beach, but it was getting close to dinnertime and he didn't want to be rude.

THE TIME OF JACOB'S TROUBLE

After he returned home, they didn't talk any more about it that night, even though he could tell that she wanted to.

* * *

As David Medine and Franco Pontiffica watched the scene at the Temple Mount, their reactions were profoundly different; Pontiffica was visibly shaken at seeing the Two Witnesses be resurrected, but Medine was furious, cursing and hurling many blasphemies against them. The media and cameras hid the worst of Medine's tirade, but the redness of his face betrayed his true feelings. It was clear that he had had enough of all the problems that had come upon him while he was in Jerusalem. And it had only been a week!

But instead of going before the media and explaining the resurrection of the Two Witnesses away, he began condemning the entire religious environment of Israel, particularly Jerusalem. He blamed the Jewish extremists who had yearned to have the Temple rebuilt as belonging to the same group as the man who had assassinated him. And then he went further, and proclaimed that Israel would be the first nation in which the Ankida religion would not only be initiated, but enforced in order to begin ridding the entire region of its extremist religious views.

No one could deny that the Middle East had been the hotbed of religious problems for centuries, but it had calmed down over the last few years. Also, he threatened a myriad of political, military, and economic sanctions against Israel if it did not immediately comply with his demands. And from his threats, he made it clear that if Israel did not change, they would not have just a coalition of nations against them, but the power of the entire world would be gathered against them to enforce his mandates.

Yet the Sanhedrin in Israel and the general population refused to be cowed by the demands of Medine and Pontiffica. They had been appalled by what had happened at the Temple, and it was quickly sinking in that Medine and Pontiffica were no longer on friendly terms with them. The Israeli people were nearly unified in their reaction to the demands, and utterly refused to give in to the World Union. The Jewish people had witnessed firsthand the shock and glee at Medine's desecration of the Temple, and the murder of the High Priest inside the Temple courts had made them very wary of him.

Medine threatened to turn his full wrath upon Israel and make an example of them for all the world to see. He first ordered that every Jew be immediately fired from any form of public office (outside of Israel, of course), and then he moved to declare that the Sanhedrin would no longer be recognized as the ruling body of the nation. The tiny nation was immediately isolated from the rest of the world, and its membership in the Middle Eastern Union was revoked. Medine then ordered the rest of the Israeli government to disband and cede its power and authority over to the World Union, which they promptly refused. In order for Israel to rejoin the World Union, they would have to agree to all of Medine's demands, namely turn over their government and recognize the Ankida religion instead of Judaism.

Israel again refused, and since Medine and Pontiffica were still in complete control of the Temple grounds, Medine commanded Pontiffica to continue forcing the Jews to worship him, just like he had done during the massacre. Pontiffica was all too pleased to carry out his orders, and had the security forces regularly round up dissidents. Any Jews going near the Temple or the Wailing Wall were caught and immediately taken to the Temple and then forced to worship the image of Medine. And any who refused were beheaded where they stood.

As Israel dug in her heels, the disposition of the world fully turned against her. The majority of nations had always been anti-Semitic to some degree or another, but as the sentiment grew and spread in a matter of weeks, Israel found herself increasingly alone and hated as never before in history. Long-time friends and allies were now siding with the World Union, out of fear that the World Union would turn against them as it had against Israel.

Perhaps Israel would be the sacrificial lamb that would bear the brunt of Medine's wrath.[62]

---

[62] Revelation 12:13-17

THE TIME OF JACOB'S TROUBLE

* * *

Saul was thrown onto the floor of the cell and suddenly regained consciousness, once again feeling the many wounds that had been inflicted upon him over the last several hours.

He was disoriented for the first ten minutes, but then began to remember what had happened. His left eye was terribly swollen and there were several cuts on his face and chin. His nose had finally stopped bleeding, but it didn't feel broken. His back was no longer bleeding, and his shirt was soaked in his own blood. He was surprised that he had escaped the beatings with no broken bones. With a small measure of comfort, he remembered that they didn't have the power to break his body, only hurt it – and it hurt terribly.

He had been arrested less than six hours before. Medine, Pontiffica, or some other power in the World Union had given the order to arrest any public proselytizers. He had been one of the first, he and others of his group: those of the 144,000. He was severely interrogated, and for the last hour, they had used a taser, a club, a thick chain, and even a strip of barbed wire on his back for a time.

But he had told them nothing, because there was nothing to tell. All he had done was continue to preach the Gospel and the news of the coming Kingdom. No matter what they did to him, he didn't change his story. The interrogation had continued until he had passed out, and they finally took him to his cell. He was surprised that they hadn't forced him awake so they could continue the questioning, but he was glad they hadn't. His first experience under torture had been worse than he had expected, but he was proud that he hadn't been broken.

The Iraqi police still retained much of their brutality from the days of Saddam Hussein, even though they had been somewhat civilized by the Americans during the rebuilding of the nation. But many Iraqis remembered the interrogation stories, and these were now used upon the enemies of the state. Medine was their king – no, he was the world's king – and no one should speak against him and go unpunished. Not only that, but Saul was both a Christian and a Jew: the worst of the infidels in their eyes.

Saul stayed on the floor for a long time. He could feel every cut, every bruise, and every wound. But in spite of his condition, he began to pray, thanking his Lord that he had been granted his life and that he had been given the courage to be beaten and yet not deny his King.

As he prayed, he began feeling something else aside from the pain. A pleasant, warming sensation began moving over his body, and he found that the acute pains he had felt only moments earlier were becoming dulled, until he no longer felt any pain at all. His face was still puffy and swollen, but his back, legs, and arms were no longer aching and sore either.

He got up and looked over his body in surprise – the swelling, bruises, and wounds were still there, but he felt as good as he had hours before. Even his back which had been flayed by the barbed wire was not stinging any longer.

He looked up to the ceiling, gave thanks, and then knelt down to continue praying.

* * *

Daniel browsed the news on the Internet after the eventful day, and suddenly came across a headline from one of his RSS feeds that caught his eye: "Proselytizers arrested in Babylon". And after a quick scan through the article, he found the names of those arrested, and it was as he had feared – Saul was among them. The persecutions of the Beast had begun, and David Medine had apparently started with the 144,000.

He printed the news page and then quickly browsed around and found that public proselytizers had been arrested in many other cities as well, such as Chicago, London, Paris, Beijing, Hong Kong, and dozens of others. From the number of arrests made, it was obvious that the World Union and the smaller governments had been tracking them for quite some time. When the order to seize them had been given, the police had known exactly where to find them. None of them had apparently given the authorities any problems, and Daniel figured that most would be detained indefinitely.

THE TIME OF JACOB'S TROUBLE

His first impulse was to call Saul's parents to tell them what he had found, but then he realized that the World Union was monitoring all electronic traffic, which meant he would not be able to call or email them without it being detected. But he could drive over to their house and tell them in person. The satellites and traffic cameras would also be watching of course, but no one cared about his movements – at least not yet. The time had come for him to close up the ministry and go underground, as many others soon would.

Daniel put down the printout and considered what he should do immediately – there were a number of resources such as books, CDs, DVDs, and pamphlets that would surely be confiscated and destroyed when the World Union began cracking down. He knew he should go to Petra soon, and that he would probably be arrested over the next week or two if he did not move quickly.

He got back on the Internet and looked up rental storage facilities in his neighborhood, and called to reserve a unit. He would stow as many of the materials in the unit as he could and then come back for them later, if he was lucky. At least they might not be confiscated as quickly as if he left them in his home or at the office.

He checked his watch – it was just after 8 o'clock. He decided to go to Saul's parents' home before it was too late.

* * *

When Daniel knocked on the door, a middle-aged, attractive woman answered the door. She had a look of what seemed to be partial-surprise and partial-suspicion, but also a look of fear.

"May I help you?" Naomi asked as she opened the door.

"Hello. My name is Daniel Hershel – I'm a friend of Saul's. We used to be partners at the ministry," he said.

She looked down at what he was holding – it was just a printout or something. After the last few days, she was increasingly suspicious of strangers, and especially anyone who came to the door.

He continued, "I have some news about Saul."

"Okay – please come in," she said, and looked out toward the street as he entered.

"If you're wondering, I wasn't followed or anything. It's still a little too soon for that," he reassured her. But it didn't make either of them feel much safer.

She led him back to the living room where Jacob was watching the news, and he stood up and shook the stranger's hand. Daniel introduced himself again and sat down, still holding the piece of paper. Naomi offered him a beverage, but he declined, wanting to get straight to the information he had brought.

"What is this news you've heard of Saul?" she asked. "We talked to him yesterday and he seemed to be doing fine."

He handed her the sheet of paper. "I was catching up on the latest news earlier this evening on the Internet, and discovered that the World Union began rounding up missionaries and other proselytizers. Saul is among those who have been arrested."

"Are you sure?" Jacob asked. "There could be others with that same name, especially in the United States."

"I'm sure it was him – he was arrested in Babylon, and in more or less the same district he had been working in before. There were likely others with him who have been arrested too," he said. "I'm sure that the World Union and other agencies have had him in their databases for a long time. He mentioned to me several times before that he knew he was being watched."

Naomi quickly skimmed the paper. He was right, most likely it was Saul, but she wanted to be sure. She called his cell-phone, but no one answered.

"It went to his voice-mail," she said. "I'll call Ahban and let him know. Maybe he can go look for him or something." She quickly stood up and went into another room to call Ahban.

Daniel and Jacob were left alone in the living room, and neither felt very talkative. Jacob turned up the volume on the television so they could both watch the latest news. There had been a large number of arrests all over Israel during the past few hours, just as in the rest of the world. The media was painting all proselytizers as dangerous extremists who had belonged to the same group as the man who had assassinated David Medine.

With the events of the last week, most of the public was sick of all the fanatical monotheists in the news and just wanted them to go away.

*　*　*

Naomi came back into the room and spoke up. "I just talked to Ahban and told him that Saul is in jail. He promised to go find him and bail him out if possible. He said he knows some people in the city government and might be able to call in a favor."

"That's great!" Jacob said, looking somewhat relieved. "I'm sure all this will be cleared up soon. Saul has never committed a crime in his life!" he exclaimed.

Daniel and Naomi both nodded, but without as much confidence as Jacob had. From the Scriptures, they had a better understanding of what was in store for Saul, and eventually many others. The law was no longer a keeper of rights and justice, but a tool to be used to accomplish David Medine's goals.

Daniel cleared his throat and gave Jacob and Naomi a very serious look. He hadn't been sure of how to bring up the subject, but it had to be done. And now was as good of a time as any.

"How long are you going to stay here?" he asked pointedly. "Sooner or later, they're going to start arresting the friends and families of those they've arrested today, especially their immediate families. The World Union will not be merciful."

"What do you mean?" Jacob asked. "This is our home – I don't think we need to be worried about that, do we?"

Daniel leaned forward, his voice low and very serious. "I beg to differ. They will give no warning and bring no warrants. When the purge begins, they will strike hard and fast. They won't bother with ghettos like before – all of Israel will be the ghetto. If I were you, I would go as soon as possible. In fact, I'm leaving tomorrow morning."

"Where will you go?" Jacob said. "This is the World Union we're talking about – they control everything! Where can you go that you'll be safe?"

285

"Petra – there are some people that have already begun fleeing there, especially from Jerusalem. Some groups have even
been preparing for this time and are taking tons of supplies
there," he said.

"Why Petra? There's nothing there except some ruins and
ancient buildings," Jacob said.

"That's true, but they're going there because that's one of
the only places that will be protected during the next three and a
half years from the Beast and his forces," Daniel said. "There are
several places in the Bible that describe how a remnant of Israel
will escape any harm by fleeing there. Also, when Yeshua comes
back, He goes to Petra (or Bozrah) first. Then He goes to Jerusalem to make His grand appearance."

Naomi nodded. "In the Gospels and Revelation, is Petra the
wilderness that is spoken of?" she asked.

"Yes. There will be other places, like caves and such, that
people will find shelter in too, but Petra is the main refuge. It's
easily defensible, and its tiny entrance will prevent any military
forces from easily overrunning the area." He smiled – Saul had
mentioned before that he had been speaking to his mother about
Yeshua and the New Testament, and evidently she had been
studying it well.

She looked over at Jacob, who she could tell did not want to
leave their home at all. "What time are you leaving tomorrow
morning?" she asked.

"During rush-hour, about 8 o'clock. I figure that it's much
less likely that the police will stop anyone when it's so busy and
crowded, as opposed to the middle of the night. It would look
much less suspicious. Besides, I still need to pack tonight." He
paused, "Do you still need some more time to think about it or
talk it over?"

"A little," she said. "I've been packing for the last week, but
we can be ready by tomorrow morning," she said. Jacob jerked
his head toward her in surprise.

"What are you talking about? We're not leaving tomorrow
with him! We can't just go and leave our house and our jobs on a
whim!" he exclaimed.

286

"Why not?" she replied. "I packed for you too. Just think of it as a long vacation. If nothing happens over the next two weeks, we'll come back, okay?"

"Fine!" he answered gruffly. "Two weeks – if nothing happens, I'm coming back!"

Daniel knew it was time to leave, and looked down at his watch. "I have to go finish packing. I'll be back at 7:30 tomorrow morning, if that's okay?" She nodded, and Jacob just looked back at the television with irritation. Daniel felt a pang of sympathy for her – Jacob was exactly as he had pictured him: full of pride and as stubborn as a mule.

He stood up and thanked them for their hospitality, and again expressed his regret about Saul's arrest. She thanked him and then walked him to the door. After she opened it, she stepped out with him quietly, and apologized for her husband's behavior. Daniel waved his hand nonchalantly, and then she told him that she had become a Christian only a few days before. Jacob was still irritated about that more than Daniel's visit.

Daniel smiled and congratulated her on her decision for Yeshua, and told her they could talk more about everything on the way down to Petra tomorrow.

And with that, he said goodnight and drove back to the office to finish packing.

*   *   *

Daniel spent the next few hours making trips back and forth from the office to the storage unit. By about three o'clock in the morning, he was finished. Then he went back to his house and gathered the essentials he would need: clothing, toiletries, important personal papers, his laptop, and his Bible. He finished just in time to get two hours of sleep before he went back to the Rosenberg's to pick them up.

He found them tired also, and Jacob was still grumbling about having to leave their home. Both had called their businesses and told them they were leaving for a few weeks, and that they could take the time off also if they wanted to. She had apparently been able to placate him, and several times he reiterated the agreement he had made with her: if nothing major happened in Israel during the next two weeks, he would go back home, with or without her.

As they loaded Daniel's van, Naomi thanked Jacob for agreeing to come with them to Petra in spite of how he felt about it. He grimaced in response and helped Daniel load the last suitcases and boxes of food and toiletries that Naomi had packed for them.

For the most part, the drive to Petra was quiet and uneventful. They saw several police roadblocks set up, but they weren't stopped even once. When they finally arrived at the outskirts of Petra, they found most of the visitor parking lots already full, and people were beginning to arrive from all over Israel. The word was spreading: "flee to the wilderness of Petra".

The gathering of the remnant of Israel had begun.

CHAPTER 12
THE MARK OF MAN

Two guards came to the door of his cell and ordered him to back away from the entrance. Saul immediately obeyed, and they roughly handcuffed his wrists behind his back and pulled him out of his cell.

He didn't obey out of fear of additional beatings, at least not entirely. The "mark" had not come yet, so there was still a hope that everyone he had contact with could be saved – including his guards.

"How are you today?" he asked. It was a stupid question, he supposed, but at least it was a start.

"Shut up! Jewish vermin!" the guard who was holding him by the arm spat.

The other guard turned his head slightly and said, "You're being released. You must have powerful friends to be let go after all your hate speech."

Saul grew quiet – who could it be, he wondered. Everyone he knew in Babylon was poor, someone else in the ministry, or someone off the street.

But as they rounded the last corner and passed through the thick doors, his question was quickly answered. It was Ahban! As soon as he saw his brother, a huge smile crossed his swollen face; but it appeared that his brother wasn't quite as amused as he was.

"Is this him?" one of the guards asked Ahban, who promptly nodded. They pushed Saul forward, so he was closer to his brother, but directly in front of the clerk's desk. Saul was quickly processed and released into his brother's custody.

As he was being signed out, the guard who had been most hostile to him said with a growl, "Next time, you won't be as fortunate as you were today – no one will be able to bail you out, if you even make it here at all."

He could tell the not-so-veiled threat unnerved his brother, who sneered back at the guard. But Saul was more amused at the threat itself than anything else. Since he had become one of the 144,000, he knew that there was no force on earth that could end his life. He would remain alive until the Messiah came to the earth to take back what was His.

Ahban looked over at him as they were leaving the prison and shook his head, but didn't say anything. Saul knew he looked terrible, but he felt normal for the most part. When he looked down at his arms, he was a little surprised at how bruised and marked up they were, yet how little pain he felt now.

Once they were out of prison and safely in Ahban's car, his brother finally spoke up, "You look terrible! Do you want to go to the hospital or something?"

Saul smiled, and felt his still-swollen cheeks and eye. "No, I'm okay. It looks a lot worse than it feels. Thanks for bailing me out – do Mom and Dad know?" he asked.

"Yeah, they called me last night – I think one of your Jesus friends found out on the web that you had been arrested, and told them. Do you want to give them a call?" He handed Saul his cell-phone as they left the parking lot and quickly got onto one of the expressways. Saul could tell his brother was irritated at him for having been thrown into jail, but now was not the time to talk about it. He was sure there would be time for that later.

"Sure – I know they'll be worried." He dialed their number and his mother answered. She was thrilled to hear his voice and that he was safe. He told her he was fine and that they had just held him for questioning; she didn't need any more to worry about. More worries would be coming her way very soon.

As they talked, he got the impression that she was keeping something from him, but he didn't press her on it. He figured she knew they were now being monitored all the time, and he didn't want to put her or his father in danger.

By just being related to him, they would soon be considered enemies of the state.

*   *   *

The unification of mankind was faltering. While millions of people across the world had joined the Ankida religion, it was simply not taking root as it should have.

The people still joining in vast numbers, but they were mixing it with their own traditional religious practices, instead of abandoning them altogether. The fear was that the religious pillar of the World Union could collapse at any moment, especially if more natural (and unnatural) disasters struck. Medine knew Franco Pontiffica was frustrated – he lacked the widespread appeal needed to coalesce the masses behind the movement.

But he had all the charisma Pontiffica lacked. He was a man of power, not religion, and was finding the whole venture of the Ankida religion to be an utter failure. If he was to unify mankind quickly, using religion was not the tool he had hoped it would be. Fortunately, he had other plans that would be much more likely to succeed. The centuries of secularism in Europe and much of the modern world had left most people somewhat incapable of faith in the miraculous. Their faith and beliefs could no longer be simply redirected from one god to another.

Perhaps there would still be a place for the Ankida religion in the future, but possibly as only a stabilizing force to prevent dissention, rather than a progressive force. Medine had been pleasantly surprised with the progress of the unification of the currencies and financial markets, and he understood that using economics rather than religion to unify the masses would produce the results he desired. And rather than attempting to change the hearts and minds of millions of people over a long period of time, Medine realized that he could accomplish the same goals of unification in a matter of months by using the economic tools at his disposal.

His attitude toward Pontiffica and the Ankida religion was

souring quickly, but he kept his feelings largely to himself. With all the disasters that had occurred over the last few years and the continuing advance of technology, the counterfeiting of even the new currencies was becoming more of a problem. While every government had to worry about the counterfeiting of its currency, it had never been on a scale that it was now. The problem needed a permanent solution, and Medine saw a great opportunity to solve both the massive counterfeiting problem and also more speedily unite the peoples of the world.

The grand solution that David Medine had chosen involved RFID tattoos that would be inked into either the right hand or the forehead of the wearer, symbolic of where he had been wounded. It would have both a practical purpose and also serve as a mark of loyalty to him and the World Union. The RFID tattoos could be visible or invisible, depending on which option the wearer chose.

In order to conduct any personal financial transaction, the RFID tattoo in the wearer's hand or forehead would be detected and they would be instantly identified by the system. This would then grant them access to their World Bank account in order to be debited or credited. Every individual would be assigned a unique, secure World Bank account that only they could access. All financial transfers would be made with those accounts, and companies would automatically debit the individuals' accounts, and employers would perform direct deposits for all their employees. Every business would be assigned an identification number and ordered to display the World Union seal on all financial documents.[63]

He considered how to best promote the RFID tattoo and his economic reforms to the world populace at large. The term "RFID tattoo" was too ugly and cumbersome. He wanted people to be excited about taking and wearing them. They had to be more than just a tattoo, but a symbol – a seal they could proudly display to show their allegiance to the new world order. He thought back to the times of the Sumerians, and how they had

---

[63] Revelation 13:16-18

loved and adored Enki, the Lord of the Earth. All the people united in their great cause would soon be lords of the earth.

That was it, he decided. These tattoos would be known as "Enki Seals", to show that the wearer was committed to their collective vision to becoming gods of the earth.

Once the new personal financial technology was in place, all forms of currency would be quickly replaced with the World Bank credits, and the problem of exchange rates, counterfeiting, and economic disunity would vanish. In addition to the incredible simplification of financial transactions, other personal information could be quickly accessed and updated. In time, other services and benefits could be easily added, such as insurance, legal documents, and medical information. And loyalty credits.

The possibilities were nearly endless.

*　*　*

Ahban came home from work and found Saul reading the Bible.

It had been a few days since he had been released from the city jail, and Saul was looking remarkably better. Some of his wounds were still quite visible though, but many of his bruises and other marks appeared to be healing very quickly.

He had been staying mostly in his room, probably reading his Bible and praying, and today was the first day he had seen him out when he came home. He had been feeling increasingly uneasy about Saul staying with him, even though he was his brother. The brother of a criminal was viewed by many as a criminal too. The state took precedence over the family.

"How are you feeling today?" Ahban asked, putting his keys and his briefcase on the counter. He began flipping through the mail and sorting it.

"Fine – how was the office?" replied Saul, looking up.

"We were busy today – the city officials are doing inspections of one of the bigger projects tomorrow, so we've been preparing for those. I'll be busy with that tonight, so I'll probably be on the phone a lot," he said. He finished the mail and walked over to where Saul was sitting.

"So, let me ask you, little brother," he said with a pause, as he sat down on the sofa. Saul looked up and gestured for him to continue. "Was it worth it?"

"Going to jail?" Saul asked.

"Yeah – after all they put you through, why are you still reading that stuff?" Ahban said. "Don't you know what they might do to you next time?"

"What? Beat me again?"

"No, next time they will kill you!" Ahban exclaimed. "Didn't you hear what that guard said when we were leaving?"

"Yeah, I heard him. But so what? I know where I'm going after I die. Besides –" he said, pointing to his Bible, "I don't think they'll be able to kill me. In Revelation, it says that everyone like me will still be here when Yeshua comes back."

"What are you talking about: 'everyone like you'? What's different about you than everyone else?" Ahban said.

"I'm one of the 144,000 Hebrews set apart by Yeshua to be His special witnesses until He returns."

At the mere mention of Yeshua, Ahban bristled. But Saul continued, "In the Tanakh, the entire nation of Israel was to be a witness for God to the nations. When they failed and turned from their purpose, God clarified that a remnant would be His witnesses during the latter days, but after the Messiah comes, the entire nation will carry out that mission like they were supposed to."

Ahban shook his head in amazement.

"So, you really think you can't die? That's silly!" he exclaimed.

"Well, that's what it says," Saul replied. "And that's probably also the reason I've recovered so quickly."

Saul could tell how the conversation was going, and he knew he would be leaving tonight. He did not want to be the instrument that pushed Ahban further away from the Lord.

Sometimes the last person that could reach others was from within their own family. It saddened him, but he would continue until it was clear the conversation was over.

THE TIME OF JACOB'S TROUBLE

"Why do you need to do that? The preaching and Bible-thumping and everything! Why can't you just be normal like you used to be?" Ahban's face was hot and red, and his temper was rising.

But instead of matching his brother's tone, Saul responded by speaking softer.

"Because I'm different now. I've been given a new life and a new purpose." He paused and thought for a moment, thinking of a verse from Jeremiah. "To me, preaching is like a fire that can't be held back – if I don't speak out, it grows inside me until I can't hold it back. It's like a fountain whose pressure must be released, and I have to let it out – I can't hold back the words that He gives me to speak."

Ahban shook his head again. He couldn't understand, but he was already sick of talking about God and especially Yeshua. He turned away from Saul, going back to the counter.

Saul was silent, but soon knew it was time to speak once again. He had read over and over what was coming next upon the world, and soon there might never be another opportunity to even speak to him, let alone bring him into the light.

Since distribution would most likely start in Babylon, Ahban would be among the first to take the mark. Unless he turned to the Lord, he would be lost forever – and how could he if no one spoke to him? Saul drew up his courage; he could talk to complete strangers about the Lord Yeshua so easily, yet he hesitated to even mention Him to his own brother!

"Why do you hate Him so much – Yeshua, I mean. What do you have against Him?" he asked his brother directly.

Ahban looked up, and started with an angry tone. "He's a fraud – he always was. And all his followers are murderers of our people. You know what they have done to us ever since that religion started! And now you're one of them! I should be asking you: how you can possibly even be in the same room with those people?"

"I understand how you feel, but those people who persecuted us were not following what Yeshua taught. They persecuted us because their leaders told them to, and they obeyed. Most people

295

in the church often weren't really true Christians, because they weren't following Yeshua," he said. "Also, those same Christians who persecuted us were even worse to their fellow Christians who refused to follow them."

"So what?" Ahban said. "Those Christians have always persecuted everyone! And now with the Anshar and Medine here, we are finally going to be free from all that and have peace."

"But what if you're wrong? What if all this stuff that's happening is a deception to keep people from coming to Yeshua the Messiah? What if you're wrong about Him?" Saul said.

"Who cares? You're wasting your entire life on someone who may not even be real!" Ahban shook his head – he had said enough. "I can't talk about this stuff anymore. I have to get back to work. I'll be in the den if you need anything," he muttered, and then took his briefcase to the back room.

Saul felt his heart sink as Ahban walked briskly away. He had to accept that only the Lord Himself would be able to break through to him. He had said all he could, and Ahban just would not listen. Time was running out – if he took the mark, there would be no chance of salvation for him. The acceptance of the mark would be his brother's final answer as to where he was placing his allegiance. And his eternity.

He turned on the television and then wrote a short letter to his brother. He began the letter about how Yeshua had come to save everyone, with the Jews being His first audience, and then the rest of the world. He told him all about Yeshua's love and mercy, and how He offered eternal life to him instead of the unknown, or worse: eternal torment.

And lastly, he warned him directly to not take the mark of the beast, whatever that might be. Any type of personal identification used to buy or sell could be the mark. He told him he loved him and then closed the letter.

He would be sure to leave it in a place where Ahban was sure to find it after he left the next morning.

* * *

THE TIME OF JACOB'S TROUBLE

Saul rose from the floor of the guest room in Ahban's apartment and drew a deep breath.

Ever since he had been called to be one of the 144,000, he had prayed as often and as much as he could. He needed oneness with his Lord more than food and water. He ministered to people of every race, religion, and background during the day, and then at nighttime would read his Bible and pray until he fell asleep.

His relationship with the Lord was vibrant and growing, and even after a long day on the street he was soon refreshed after he spent some time with Him. When he was ministering, he yearned to read and pray, and when he prayed, he yearned to minister to others. "The time is short, and the workers of the harvest are few," he often told himself.

From the first day of his calling, he had felt directly connected with the Lord. He had a deeper understanding of His will than most others outside his group, and could hear His voice as clearly as if He was standing next to him. During the interrogation and subsequent beatings, he often saw Yeshua standing next to him (although invisibly to the guards), comforting him and reassuring him to be strong and courageous, telling him that they could only hurt his flesh but not his spirit unless he allowed them to. He helped Saul maintain his perspective and witness throughout the torture, and then He lessened the pain when it was over.

When Saul had fallen to his face in his room the night before (after writing the letter), He had been there to comfort him once again. When he had finished pouring out his heart, he was ready to begin his next task. Yeshua told him to leave Babylon, and that there were others who must be ministered to in nearby regions even darker than this one. He and the others like him had planted many seeds in Babylon, and though still buried, they would soon begin to sprout and grow. It was time for him to go northward into another of the enemy's strongholds, where the Gospel had not been preached for many centuries.

Saul was thankful for the new assignment and began making the mental preparations for it – he would wait until after Ahban left for work, and then pack quickly and leave. He left the letter on the counter where Ahban always placed and sorted his daily mail, and then he packed his meager belongings. He didn't have much more than a backpack of very basic necessities and his Bible, but that was all he now needed. The Lord provided for all his needs, and any necessities he had were often given away to others who needed them more than he did anyway.

A few minutes later, Saul locked the front door of Ahban's apartment and was soon walking down the streets of Babylon once again. He headed for one of the bus terminals and bought a one-way ticket to his destination, and boarded in less than an hour.

As the great towers and city of Babylon faded behind him, he smiled and looked out the window. He grinned at the Lord's sense of humor when he opened his Bible – it had fallen open directly to the book of Jonah. And then he thought about that angry, stubborn prophet who had prophesied to very region that he was now going: Assyria.

But whereas Jonah had brought a message of coming judgment to the people, Saul would be bringing one of salvation and mercy.

*　*　*

The first step in establishing the new world economy was to convert all the banks in the world over to Enki Seal Administration Centers (ESACs).

All their banking customers were immediately told they must get an Enki Seal in order to access their bank accounts. The customers' financial and personal information among the governments and banks was quickly aggregated into personal World Bank accounts. Those with existing bank accounts had no choice but to take the Enki Seals, or all their financial assets were confiscated. Once all their customers had taken the seals, the banks were closed or be converted into other government service providers.

In the industrialized countries, most banks, government agencies, and grocery stores began distributing the Enki Seals. The widespread distribution was immediately met with great success, but many of the poorer countries and regions had a difficult time, so incentives were quickly devised and offered. Food, water, medical supplies, and even bonus World Bank credits were granted when an individual accepted the Enki Seal. From the pilot programs and cities, it was estimated that over ninety percent of all the world population would have Enki Seals in only three months. David Medine and his associates were very pleased at the initial success, and moved quickly to fully distribute the Enki Seals all over the world. [64]

But just as the first widespread distribution of the Enki Seals began, a strange creature appeared in the sky and began flying throughout the earth with a great booming voice. The creature looked like a man clothed in a radiant white garment that made him appear to glow brightly, but was clearly not human. Some said it was an angel, while others said it was one of the Anshar's enemies come to subvert their work and mankind's divine future.

The creature flew swiftly and purposefully, as if he were attempting to broadcast his message to every single person on the earth. He began delivering his message over Israel and flew in great, ever-widening circles outwards toward the poles of the earth. Once he reached the poles, he then began flying in smaller circles until he ended in the middle of the South Pacific, precisely on the other side of the world from Jerusalem.

Wherever the creature flew, every person within range of his booming voice heard him in their own language, saying "Fear God, and give glory to Him; for the hour of His judgment is come, and worship Him that made heaven, and the earth, and the sea, and the fountains of the waters."

People stared up in wonder as he flew, but most ignored his message and went about their daily activities. Some tried to shoot him down with guns, but the bullets passed right through him. Several rockets and missiles were launched at him also, but they did not explode. For the most part, his message fell upon

---

[64] Revelation 20:4

ears that had long-since grown deaf towards God. [65]

After the first creature had reached the borders of Israel, another supernatural creature that looked much like the first appeared and began following him in his circling pattern. But this one had a different message, and his voice was even louder and more penetrating than the first. Those inside buildings, underground, and inside their cars or homes heard the voice as if he were standing next to them. And his great, fierce voice rang out saying, "Babylon is fallen, is fallen, that great city, because she made all nations drink of the wine of the wrath of her fornication." [66]

And yet another creature followed the second one, with his specific message also, but his voice boomed over the earth for hundreds of kilometers at a time. And he repeated his message over and over, saying "If any man worships the beast and his image, and receives his mark in his forehead, or in his hand, the same shall drink of the wine of the wrath of God, which is poured out into the cup of his indignation; and he shall be tormented with fire and brimstone in the presence of the holy angels, and in the presence of the Lamb. And the smoke of their torment will ascend up for ever and ever: and they have no rest day nor night, who worship the beast and his image, and whosoever receives the mark of his name." [67]

*　*　*

Ahban re-read the meeting appointment that had just come into his email inbox and thought about what Saul had written in the letter to him only days earlier. "Do not take the 'mark'!" he had adamantly warned him. He had wondered what was this 'mark' Saul was referring to, but now he knew. And even now, he still thought his brother's warning was quite foolish.

Suddenly he heard the voices of two men, as if they were standing the same room with him, and he looked around the

---

[65] Revelation 14:6-7
[66] Revelation 14:8
[67] Revelation 14:9-11

room to see where they were coming from. A small tremor rushed through him when he heard the explicit warning not to take the mark. He suddenly felt angry, but not at his company or the World Union or even David Medine, but at his brother. He didn't know why, and he found that he didn't even care. He simply hated what Saul stood for and his foolish notion of God and the Messiah.

The contents of the company-wide email detailed the new payroll system that was immediately being implemented as part of the pilot program for the World Union. Many corporations in Babylon were also undergoing the pilot program, and the email said that the company was very honored to be included in the initial rollout. Every employee would be required to partake in the rollout, or they would not be able to collect their paychecks until they took the Enki Seal. Ahban rolled his eyes at the sternness of the policy, but knew he would participate in whatever was required. He still liked his job and the money in Babylon was still too good to pass up.

The email described how the secure, invisible Enki Seals would be immediately issued to all the employees to access their payroll and bank accounts. The tattoos guaranteed nearly a 99% drop in identity theft, many forms of fraud, counterfeiting, confusing taxation laws, and even many types of terrorism. Soon all the businesses, companies, and banks would be working in conjunction with the World Union to ensure that as many people as possible signed up to take the tattoos.

All the employees at his company would be tattooed a few days from now and then were even free to have the rest of the day off. Not only that, but the memo stated that a small cash bonus from the World Union had been added to each of their paychecks since they had participated in the pilot program. Ahban doubted he would take the offer for time off though; he was just too busy. But the extra money would be nice and well worth the price of such a minor inconvenience.

He sat back and took a moment to think about the memo. The tattoos sounded like they would solve many of problems that were holding back the world economy. Terrorism, theft, and

301

smuggling had plagued the world for the last century, but especially during the recent years. But at least it sounded like they had come up with a simple solution, so he was all for it. What was the big deal about this Enki Seal anyway? Maybe Saul had just been in one of his crazy moods or something when he had written that note. Sometimes he wondered if Saul had gotten hooked on drugs or something, with the fanatical ways he acted at times.

There had to be a reasonable explanation for everything, and he was sure that in time all that was happening would be revealed and explained logically. And his brother and sister would be shown for the religious lunatics they were. He looked around for the source of the voices again, and then accepted the meeting appointment.

* * *

Two days later, Ahban lined up with the other employees in the company cafeteria to take the seals. It took less than a minute to have the Enki Seal placed on them, and it looked like no one was feeling any pain or discomfort from it.

He noted that nearly everyone was taking them on their right hand, yet when they walked by, he couldn't see any indication of the seal at all – they really were painless and invisible. Everyone who took the Enki Seal was smiling and talking about the bonus money and the time off. His brother had been foolish, and had been making a big deal out of nothing.

When it came his turn to take the Enki Seal, Ahban didn't even hesitate for a moment. As he held out his right hand, he briefly thought about the letter and the supernatural warnings, but didn't pull his hand back. Within seconds, the seal had been stamped on his hand and then quickly tested under the scanner. He was surprised when he saw his personal information instantly displayed on the LCD screen in front of him, and he nodded to the clerk that all the information was correct. He was also given a small piece of plastic the size of a credit card that he could hold over his hand to see the Enki Seal.

Back at his desk, he took the plastic sheet from his pocket and held it over his fresh Enki Seal. In the middle of it was the picture of a proud David Medine and the Great Seal of the World Union, along with a long number, which he assumed was his personal identification number. With it, he could transact any type of sale or purchase online as soon as the online vendors updated their software.

He tested it on his computer with his company's payroll site and sure enough, it worked perfectly. He also noticed that the bonus had already been deposited in his bank account.

Yeah, he smirked. He had been all wrong to take the Enki Seal and get more money. Maybe the next time he saw Saul, he would buy him dinner with it or something. Or maybe even a new Bible to replace that tattered old one he always had his face buried in.

* * *

At first, many heeded the voices of the flying creatures and the number of people lining up to take the marks dramatically decreased, but the numbers quickly returned to their previous levels within a matter of days. People wanted full access to their money, and the widespread infrastructure and incentives that David Medine had enacted guaranteed that most people would quickly take the Enki Seals voluntarily. For those who did not do so, additional incentives would be offered for a short time. If that failed, then other procedures would be enacted that would compel any holdouts to take the Enki Seals.

After three months of widespread distribution, it was clear that not only were there millions of people not voluntarily taking the seals, but their numbers were at much higher rates than the World Union had expected. David Medine was furious at the stubbornness of the world population at large, even in the industrial, richer nations. Even though the majority of the population had taken them, millions still had not.

He was increasingly becoming more and more short-tempered, and he decided that the penalty for refusing to take the

Enki Seal must be swift and harsh. He had been merciful long enough. Every individual on the earth must take the seal, and that was all there was to it. There would be no exceptions. And if it took a small amount of bloodshed and suffering to accomplish his goals for the betterment of all mankind, so be it.

The punishment for refusal must be swift, permanent, and very persuasive to both the individuals refusing the marks and those who had not quite made up their minds. After exploring a number of options, Medine decided that public beheadings at the ESACs would be the most compelling way to force people to take them. Was it brutal? Of course. Would it work? Certainly.

To counter the massive underground resistance that was bound to arise, incentives to report the holdouts would also be offered. The amount of World Bank credits that would be given for each holdout would be sure to quell any feelings of guilt or conscience. Medine understood that he could later use these same incentives to put down any other forms of rebellion and terrorism, and control any group or individual he desired.

But for now, the fate of the world and its future unity hinged upon everyone taking the Enki Seals.

* * *

"Hello?" Ahban answered, speaking into his cell-phone's wireless headset.

He was busy putting the finishing touches on the designs for the latest building contract for the city. It had taken him the last month to put it together, even though many parts of the design had come from previous projects.

"Hi – it's Saul. How's it going?" his brother said. He sounded happy, and that was irritating. Saul had been gone a week, and Ahban had been somewhat relieved last week to find he had left unexpectedly.

"Good. Busy!" he stated dryly. Saul was the last person he wanted to talk to at that moment. He was annoyed at just the sound of his brother's voice.

"Cool – hey, I'm sorry about the way we left things last

week. I got called away and had to leave without much of a goodbye."

"Thanks – no big deal." His answers were short and curt, and he resumed his typing away on the computer keyboard. Maybe the sound of it would help his brother get the hint that he really was quite busy.

"Hey, uh, did they start distributing the Enki Seals there yet?" asked Saul.

"Yes – just a few days ago," Ahban said.

"Wow! You didn't take one, did you?" he asked. He knew Saul was hoping he had taken the letter to heart and refused.

"Actually, since the company works with the city government, we were one of the first to get them. I like it – it's pretty slick, and they gave us a nice big bonus too," he said, just to figuratively twist the knife a bit.

"Oh," he heard Saul say. From his tone, he could tell his brother was deeply upset by it. Good. Saul and his stupid religious garbage.

"Did they force you?" Saul asked.

"Not at all – they made some announcement about not getting paid until you got one, but everyone I know couldn't pass that up or the bonus. I bought a new cell-phone with mine. There were a couple of nuts who refused and then quit the next day. Kind of stupid if you ask me," he stated.

"Oh," Saul said again. "Well, anyway – I'm up in Mosul now. So that's where I'll be from now on, if anyone comes looking for me. I'll let you know if I change locations again."

"Okay. Hey, I have to get back to work now," he said.

"Alright – goodbye, Ahban," replied Saul.

"Goodbye," Ahban said, tapping his earpiece to close the connection.

He wasn't feeling as irritated now – maybe it was from knowing that he had struck a big nerve with his younger brother. So what? He didn't care for him much more these days anyway.

Ahban smiled as he looked down at the small gold statue next to his laptop screen. It was a tiny replica of the image of David Medine that Franco Pontiffica had set up in the Temple back in Jerusalem. They were all the latest craze in Babylon, and it seemed like everyone was rushing out to get one. Rather than having the employees all go out and get them, the company had just ordered a large quantity all at once and handed them out as part of the bonus for taking the Enki Seals.

Was it a bit sacrilegious? Sure. Did anyone there care? Not at all!

What a great company he worked for, he said to himself. They thought of everything!

* * *

Saul awoke and slowly opened his eyes. The walls of his tent billowed in the cool desert morning breeze, and the ground was stiff and hard under his back.

He looked around and remembered where he was: Mosul. He rubbed his eyes and stretched, and shook the sleepiness from his limbs. He remembered the events of yesterday and a deep sadness swept over him once again. And then he knelt and began his morning prayers, almost from the very place he had left off the night before.

Since he had last talked to Ahban the day before, he had been hours in prayer. It had started off with a sense of desperation and pleading, as if somehow God could reverse or undo the decision that Ahban had made. But the Scriptures were clear: once some-one had taken the mark, there was no more hope for them. Their eternity had been sealed the moment the mark of the beast was placed on their skin. They were Medine's property now – his and his "father's". And once someone had forever chosen death over life, how could their fate be changed?

To add to his grief, he knew that Ahban had been under very little compulsion, and yet he had taken it anyway. He had chosen it willingly. The time was coming soon when people would be of-fered a clear choice: take the mark and live, or refuse the mark and die. Many would be beheaded, and thus quickly end their earthly suffering, but he knew the cruelty of the beast would soon make the methods of death much more painful and inhumane.

THE TIME OF JACOB'S TROUBLE

Public torture would soon become commonplace.

Even those who somehow managed to escape the compulsory mark would have a very difficult time trying to survive in a world where it was required to buy or sell anything. An underground economy was already beginning to rise against the World Union, and there had always been a black market for drugs, prostitution, weapons, and other contraband. But soon the black market would be primarily used for buying and selling food, water, and other basic necessities rather than illegal items.

The Lord spoke to him as he silently cried out again. Ahban had chosen his fate, and He reminded Saul that few chose the road of Life that He alone offered. The path to life was very narrow and lonely at times, but the road to death was wide and crowded. He should not allow himself to be overwhelmed with grief at a decision that his brother alone had made.

There were many more people who had not made a decision yet, and they must be reached. He could grieve when he was alone, but not in public. In Babylon, the city had been rich and the people had been concerned with mainly money and pleasure, and they had little use for God or faith of any sort, other than faith in Medine and the world economy. But in Mosul it was much different: many of the people were still poor; the incredible economic progress that had overtaken Babylon and its outlying regions had not made its way up to the north yet. The people had much more money from the oil revenues than they had years before, but they were still relatively poor compared to those living in Babylon.

When Saul was finished praying, he arose and rolled up his tent, and cleaned up his small campsite. He felt lonely as he walked into the city – he was the only one of his kind there in Mosul, but that wasn't the reason for his sad feelings. It was because he knew he had lost his brother – forever. At least in a normal death there was still some remnant of hope that remained, that the person who had lived their entire life in rebellion to God might possibly repent in the last few moments of their life, and find their way into Heaven.

But with Ahban, no hope remained whatsoever. He had unabashedly taken the mark of the beast, even after he had been clearly warned by Saul and the heavenly messenger. He had always despised religion and faith, especially the Judeo-Christian beliefs. Some of it had come from his years in the university, and some from their own father and secular home-life. But the inner rebellion – the intense hatred of God had come from deep inside him. And it was that rebellion against God and the hatred of faith that had driven his brother to take the mark, even against any hope of a better judgment.

After several more minutes of grieving over his brother, Saul felt an air of comfort sweep over him, and as he walked his intense grief over Ahban lifted. He thanked the Lord and then began praying over the people he would meet that day, and that He would give him the words to speak to them.

He prayed for a plentiful harvest among these people, whose ancestors had destroyed his own nation thousands of years before. The ancient Assyrians had been among the most brutal people on earth, and even in recent times, they had not been much better. Much of the violence after the fall of Saddam Hussein had taken place in Mosul and the central provinces of Iraq, and Mosul was renowned for its barbarism.

Many of the Assyrian Christians had left Iraq years before, and there were very few left. Likewise with the Assyrian Jews, who had been largely driven out over the last few decades with the rise of radical Islam. But unlike Babylon, Assyria had not quickly turned secular after Saddam's fall and their newfound wealth, and still remained largely Islamic. Even democracy had been resisted there until it had been forced upon them by the United States. But after they had gotten a taste of true freedom, it bloomed and flourished throughout the area, and they were very resistant to giving up their independence to anyone.

Yet in spite of the cruelty and barbarism of those people, there he was, much like the prophet Jonah who had been sent to this same region many centuries before, called by the Lord to be His witness. He felt his hope rising when he thought of how Jonah's ministry had so profoundly affected the ancient Ninevites: hundreds of thousands of people had repented and begged the

Lord for mercy at the order of their great king, after only a few days of Jonah's outcry against the city.

Perhaps he could use the story of Jonah to similarly affect these people, the very descendants of the ancient Ninevites.

* * *

Saul had been ministering on the streets of Mosul for two days, and already dozens more people had been saved than in his months in Babylon. The contrast between the people of Mosul and Babylon still amazed him. They were hungry to hear about God and His Anointed One. There were the usual hecklers and naysayers (and even stone-throwers at times), but they didn't cause as many problems as those in Babylon had. Many of the citizens were loyal to Medine and the World Union, but their own independence from tyranny was still fresh in their minds.

On his first day there, he had bought a map of the city and its outlying villages, and started in the most populated section first, and then moved outward from there. The markets were where he preached during the day, and he spent several hours a day at the same market, and then moved to a different one. After a week or two, he would change his schedule to reach a different audience. At night, he would find another place to preach where there were large groups of people, and continue until either everyone had gone home or until he was too exhausted to continue.

During his first few days in Mosul, he had quickly learned to not preach against Islam or criticize their beliefs (at least not outright), but keep his message simple: preach Yeshua and the message of the cross and the Resurrection. The apostle Paul had used the same tactic when he preached to the Corinthians after having a meager harvest among the Athenians.

Keep the message Christ-centered, and let the Holy Spirit do the work, he often told himself. His task was to preach the Gospel and speak against the evil kingdom of the beast – nothing else. Time was running out, and soon he might be forced to flee underground, not only for his safety but for the safety of those he had reached.

The spreading of the mark had started; it was already sweeping through Babylon, and would soon be coming to Mosul. He warned everyone who would listen not to take it, no matter what the bribe or the cost. What was their present life worth compared to eternity? Why take the image of a mere man on your hand or forehead when you could have the seal of the Holy Spirit on your heart? Don't let yourself be owned as a slave or controlled as a puppet by Medine, he proclaimed. Remember the judgments of the Lord that had just recently passed; remember the angels who had warned them not to take the mark; remember their ancestors, who had heard the witness of Jonah the Prophet and immediately taken God at His Word.

But today was Friday, and many of the citizens were attending services in the nearby mosques. They had been attending the Friday services their entire lives and most of them still did, at least for social and ritual reasons. He did not attend of course, so he had an hour or two in which he could have some personal time. He was still grieved over Ahban, but the pain wasn't as sharp as it had been, and the groups of people coming to hear him everyday had lifted his spirits.

Saul thought of his parents and chided himself for not praying for them more often and calling them sooner with the news about Ahban. His mother had sounded worried the last time he had spoken to her – maybe it would be safer to talk now. He pulled his cell-phone out of his back pocket and dialed his parents' home phone number. There was no answer, so he tried her cell-phone.

"Hello?" she answered.

"Mom! It's Saul – it is okay to talk?" he asked.

"Yes – are you alright?" He could hear voices and heavy rustling in the background, like she was standing outside in the wind or something.

"Yeah, I'm not in Babylon with Ahban anymore. I'm in Mosul now – Mom, I have to tell you something. Are you sure it's okay to talk?" he repeated. She confirmed that it was again, and he continued.

"It's Ahban," he said. "He's taken the mark!" he exclaimed.

"The mark? You mean the Enki Seal?" she asked, with a worried tone. "How do you know?"

"He told me the day after he took it. I told him not to, but he didn't listen. He was one of the first. It was with his company, as part of the city's pilot program or something. He didn't seem concerned in the least!" he said emotionally. He hadn't shared what had happened to his brother with anyone else except the Lord yet, and he felt like just pouring out his grief to her.

She was silent, letting the news sink in.

"Are you at home?" he asked.

"No, your friend Daniel helped us get to Petra a few days ago. You won't believe how many people who are already here. When we first arrived, there were over a thousand, but now there's at least ten times that!"

"That's great, Mom. Dad's there too, right?" She replied that he was, at least for now. She explained the two-week vacation agreement they had made to get him to go to Petra with her, and how they had traveled down there with Daniel in his van.

"Are you coming here soon?" she asked. From her tone, he knew that she was making more of a request than asking a question. He paused slightly before answering her.

"No – I don't think I'll be going to Petra at all. When the End comes, I'll be in Jerusalem. Besides, I have a lot of work to do here, at least while there's still time," he replied firmly.

She tried to convince him otherwise, but could not change his mind. He had a different calling than she did, and each of them had others they needed to bring into the coming Kingdom.

*   *   *

The first Enki Seal Administration Center had been put in the prisons during the pilot period, and only a handful of prisoners refused to take the marks, and were then promptly beheaded.

At each ESAC, there were several large, imposing guillotines set up in such a way that those in the lines got a side view of the devices, and what would happen to them if they refused. Those in the lines would see the rebel's entire body from the side and watch as the blade swiftly dropped and separated the victim's head from their shoulders. The heads would then be stacked in large, clearly visible containers throughout the day, and then disposed of every several hours. The corpse in front of the guillotine would be left where it lay, and would only be removed when the next person who refused to take the Enki Seal was due for punishment. Later, the bodies and heads would be disposed of in the incinerators outside. [68]

Most of the smaller ESACs were soon closed and larger ones were constructed, which were better capable of enforcing the new procedures and disposing of those who refused. Police and World Union security forces were ordered to monitor as many ESACs as possible. Most were fully armed with stun guns, rifles, handguns, and even semi-automatic weapons.

Medine assured the public that once everyone had taken the tattoos, the harsh procedures would cease and they could all move forward together. However, everyone must work together to accomplish the magnificent goal of a united world economy and currency. The days of personal freedom and independence must be temporarily suspended until the people were united, and then all the freedoms would be restored. The people had nothing to fear if they simply obeyed the law and took the Enki Seals.

When the first public ESACs were opened, only a tiny number of people refused to take the marks. But as the incentives and rewards to report rebels and holdouts increased, a startling phenomenon began to occur – a growing number of people began to actively refuse the seals, regardless of the punishment for their refusal. The security forces were surprised at first, and when they reported the growing numbers of beheadings to their superiors, the World Union began to grow concerned.

The number of bodies that the enforcers were tasked with disposing of was becoming unmanageable, and they showed no sign of decreasing. And when the phenomenon was more closely investigated, it was discovered that the people choosing death were mostly Christians and observant Jews, along with a much

---

[68]   Revelation 20:4

smaller number of Muslims, Buddhists, and others.

Reports by the ESACs' guards and workers revealed that the majority of those refusing to take the tattoos were Christians. As the number of Christians that refused the marks increased, more people began to admire their bravery and courage. Some would even leave their lines to accept death rather than take the Enki Seals. Due to the self-sacrifice of the Christians, their stories of courage and bravery began sweeping across the Internet, and the number of people that began converting to Christianity dramatically increased, and along with them the numbers of those refusing to take the seals.

In some places, the lines for beheading became longer than those for the marks. When overwhelmed, the enforcers simply began shooting them and at other times just throwing them alive into the incinerators. Suicides by those who had already accepted the marks began to surge, and some even tried to surgically remove the Enki Seals themselves by cutting out large chunks of their skin.

But regardless of the brutality used to administer them, the Enki Seals continued to be distributed around the world. Everyone would either take a mark or be dead.

*   *   *

David Medine and the rest of the World Union leaders continued to grow frustrated at the outright rebellion and stubbornness of the people refusing the marks. It was even more alarming at how their numbers were growing instead of diminishing.

Medine had reached the point where the widespread shedding of blood no longer concerned him. In his eyes, everyone on the earth had a choice: take the marks and live, or refuse them and die. The world would soon be rid of the divisions, dissenters, and the rebels throughout the earth, and the mandatory Enki Seals were quickly making that a reality. And as their frustration grew, Medine and the World Union decided to actually increase the incentives for reporting holdouts and others they had deemed undesirable to remain alive in the new world.

The financial incentives offered to the masses were altered such that not only was a specific amount of World Bank credits given for each rebel turned in, but the amount of credits given was doubled for Christians and Jews, and tripled for any in leadership positions in the underground movements. Incentives were also added such that the more rebels an individual would turn in, the more credits they would receive per person they reported.

In this way, Medine and the World Union turned the populace even further against the Christians and Jews, causing the slaughter of millions who simply did not want to go along with their plans and goals. Neighbor turned against neighbor, brother against brother, sister against sister, and parents against their offspring. The world would indeed be united soon, but by the decree and power of the state, rather than by individual choice.

Medine and the administrators of the ESAC bureaucracy decided to allow the "good neighbor" policy to continue for a few months before they would become more forceful. Those months would give them the time they needed to prepare for the next phase of Enki Seal enforcement, which would involve very aggressive measures to force compliance. The enforcement teams would monitor all electronic communications, Internet traffic, use satellite thermal imaging, and even go door-to-door in specific areas to root out rebels and subvert the underground economy. And any who were found to be hiding rebels or ignoring the law would be severely punished as well.

Regardless of the persecutions and the slaughter, the number of martyrs throughout the earth grew exponentially. Yet the Sarrim and the World Union remained firm: every person who refused the Enki Seal must be removed from the face of the earth.

CHAPTER 13
THE CLEFT IN THE ROCK

D uring the first few days after David Medine had desecrated the Temple, most of the people in Israel had
not fully understood the significance of what had happened. Medine's public condemnation against the Jews was
equally startling to them, and the majority of the public assumed
that he was speaking primarily of the more-zealous priests and
Temple workers. And he was for the most part – at least at first.

The majority of Israel had been upset by what had happened
at the Temple, and supported their leaders who had finally stood
up for them. But as the days turned into weeks, Israel saw the
World Union completely turn against them. Their ports were
threatened with blockades and nearly all the foreign embassies
had been closed in Israel. Anti-Semitic violence skyrocketed
worldwide, and many of the persecuted fled to Israel as fast as
they could by boat, plane, or car. Even in the more tolerant nations such as the United States, the Jews found they were no
longer as safe and comfortable as they had been for centuries.
And soon Jewish refugees began to stream into Israel from all
corners of the earth.

The global rise in anti-Semitism continued to increase until
the vast majority of Jews had been driven out of the lands all
over the earth where they had lived for hundreds of years. David
Medine and the World Union let the immigrants gather into Israel freely, but refused to let anyone leave. Several popular
statesmen in Israel began expressing the concern that Israel was
being turned into a huge ghetto.

But this time, instead of being forced into crowded concentration camps and districts, they were being driven into an-already crowded Israel. Some of them felt as if a great noose would soon surround their tiny nation, and then quickly tightened to strangle them. And if the noose were drawn, there would be no place left on earth for them to escape. [69]

*   *   *

Jacob wandered back to their tent and found Naomi still asleep. It was just after daybreak, and he had been getting increasingly restless the last few days.

Most of the camp was still asleep too, but they would begin rising within the next two hours. Everyone was still getting used to their new lives in the camp, and with more and more refugees coming every day, the camp leaders had their hands full. He was surprised when he had walked around earlier that there were already a number of people in the Treasury, listening to the daily Scripture readings and praying together. He backed out and closed the tent flap and strode down the path to the main trail, and then continued walking.

The camp leadership (the Council) was a loose co-operative comprised of a number of Jewish and Christian organizations. One or two leaders represented each group in the camp, and it appeared they were working quite well together. They had their specific theological and religious differences, but they had a common purpose: to provide refuge for as many Jews as possible. Most of the people who had first arrived in Petra were Christian or Messianic Jews, but the number of Orthodox Jews was beginning to increase also. A small number of Muslims and Arabs had trickled in, and they were welcomed immediately. No one seeking refuge would be turned away, but any troublemakers would be quickly forced out of the camp.

Many of the Jewish newcomers were in the same state of mind as Naomi was: the desecration of the Temple by Medine

---

[69] Zechariah 12:2-3; Revelation 12:13

and his state-religion had frightened them, and as the World Union turned against them, they wanted to escape to a safe place.

The rest were much like him, he supposed: wary and unsure of what Medine was up to. The desecration of the Temple had showed a sinister side of him. The memories of the Holocaust were still too real to many Jews, and they would take no chances.

Jacob had to admit that the Tanakh was quite clear that God would protect His Jewish remnant in Petra (also known as Bozrah in a number of other Scriptures). In the New Testament, Yeshua had instructed both Jewish and Christian followers to flee to the wilderness, which had always been to the far south and east of Jerusalem, around the Dead Sea area. Much of the south had been irrigated and turned into farmland, but the mountainous region was still arid wasteland. And the most inhabitable and defensible area there just happened to be in the ruins of Petra.

The Council was basically in charge of the camp facilities and services at Petra. They had already completed a significant amount of planning and preparing for this time of refuge in the desert. An entrance fee had been immediately implemented in order to pay for water, sanitation, and supplies, and that was working rather well. Of course, the Council encouraged those who could give more to do so, and they would not turn anyone away if they were unable to meet the entrance fee. The camp was entirely non-profit, and had nothing to gain from setting up and maintaining the refuge. Their primary purpose was to save lives if and when the World Union's policies towards Israel took a turn for the worse.[70]

Most refugees still had a decent amount of food that they had brought with them, and a new supply of water had just been trucked in. Jacob had seen drilling equipment and large water pumps at one end of the valley a few days ago when he had taken a long walk to the outskirts of the camp. Presumably, they were already drilling for, purifying, and storing water in preparation for the growing population.

Three and a half years were how long some were saying they

---

[70] Revelation 12:14

would be at the camp, but he felt skeptical. That was a long time to be away from home, but if another Holocaust was imminent (as many in the camp believed), then a long tenure in Petra would be worth a few years of inconvenience. Many in the camp believed the Messiah would come, but he was still unconvinced and hoped they would be able to return home much, much sooner.

Sometimes tempers flared in the camp, especially in the heat of the day and when there were long lines for water or the sanitation facilities. But other than an occasional raised voice, everyone was getting along exceptionally well for having been thrown into the huge melting pot of Petra.

The Council understood the danger of having a large number of people confined to a small space with little or nothing to do, and so upon entry, each person was required to volunteer for one or more daily or weekly tasks that would benefit the camp or their neighbors. Some would carry water, others would help with the infants and elderly, and others performed a myriad of other duties. Tents and other forms of shelter needed to be set up, in preparation for the thousands who would be coming as the international pressure on Israel increased. The registrars had briefly asked each new entrant their background and then tried to match their skills to their duties as closely as possible.

Their first week in Petra had gone by like a whirlwind, with them getting an understanding about what was happening there and getting settled in. Because of his background, Daniel had been pulled into the leadership of the Council, while Jacob and Naomi were assigned other duties.

They would be starting their new jobs today, as a matter of fact, and he was looking forward to that. He was tasked with inspecting many of the ruins and caverns, and coming up with ways that they could be utilized or converted into living facilities. He had been told to expect the camp to be constantly growing over the next six months to a year, and to plan accordingly. The walls and ruins of Petra had been standing for centuries, and were hopefully able to support thousands of people. He figured that most of what was going to fall or collapse had already done so in the recent earthquakes, but it was part of his job to be sure.

He had promised Naomi that he would stay two full weeks, and if nothing significant had happened in Israel, then he would go home. But she had made it clear that she would remain, which still irritated him. They had been married a long time, and Naomi was fairly compliable most of the time, but when she set her mind on something, she could be quite stubborn about it.

He mostly just wanted to go home, but some of the reports coming from the Internet and the radio were not very promising. Medine and the World Union had all but sealed off Jerusalem and had closed all the outgoing borders of Israel. The urban centers would be targeted first by whatever policies the World Union implemented, and then progress to the less populated areas. Perhaps being in Petra for a time would be the safest place to be, at least until the World Union came to its senses.

As he walked by the numerous buildings and carvings made by Petra's former inhabitants, he marveled at their artistry and magnificence, even in decay. Many of the statues and buildings were still in excellent condition – he couldn't imagine how they had appeared at the height of Petra's glory thousands of years before. The climate had become incredibly arid and barren over the last two thousand years, and now few people other than the desert nomads and tourists ever visited the area. Various groups over the years had left their mark on Petra, such as the Crusaders and some of the Muslim conquerors, but never dwelt there for long. No large groups had settled there for centuries: until now.

As he was walking along the path, he looked up to see a building that had been apparently carved during the Crusades and he stopped to examine it. At the top, he saw a large cross on the front of the structure, and it initially startled him.

He knew there were such symbols in Petra, along with many other symbols from other religions, but he was still surprised to see it. It made him start thinking about Naomi again, and his reaction when she had told him that she had become a Christian. When Ruth and then Saul had converted, he had figured it was a phase they were going through, especially after the Magog Invasion. But it was Naomi's news that had really shaken him, because he knew her so well and yet had not known beforehand.

What had suddenly made her decide to become a Christian, he wondered? After all, she had been largely neutral on religion for most of the time they had been married. Even after she had just come from the United States, she had not been very religious at all. They had been more observant and attended synagogue on Shabbat for a time after the Magog Invasion, but after a while, their attendance had dropped off and then just attended it around the holidays, much as they had before.

The more he thought about her turn towards Christianity, the more curious (and uneasy) he became. He would have to ask her about it later. After all, now they were not nearly as busy or distracted as they always had been back home. And other than their duties in the camp, they didn't really have all that much to do.

He had been feeling somewhat depressed and lonely since they had arrived in Petra, even though they were surrounded by thousands of people. The sudden removal of much of his life's busyness was showing him a different perspective of what his life had become and how his relationship with his wife had changed over the years. And he didn't like what he saw.

As he turned to walk back to their tent, he admitted to himself that he had let his business and career increasingly isolate him from his wife and children. He was responsible for his family, and he felt a sharp twinge of shame at how far he had let his own interests and aspirations distract him. Besides, Petra wasn't so bad, and he would be bored and lonely at home by himself.

Now that he had nothing but time, perhaps he could start to make things right – the way they should have been all along.

* * *

Naomi opened her eyes and for a moment, wondered where she was. She still found waking up inside a tent somewhat disorienting after waking up in her own bedroom and her own house for so many years. They had never really camped out much, even back in America. There had been a few times when she was little when she had slept in a tent at a friends' house, but that was much different, of course. After living in Israel for decades, thinking back to her childhood in New York sometimes made her feel like she had lived two completely different lives.

She hadn't spoken to her parents or family back in the States for weeks, and wondered how they were. So far, they had been quite fortunate: only a few of her cousins had died from the events of the last four years. The cell tower just outside Petra had been destroyed long before, but fortunately, they had satellite access, at least for the time being. The satellite bandwidth from Petra was very limited, and was frequently restricted to off-hours for personal use.

Since the United States was nearly a day behind Israel, maybe she could try calling them in the middle of the night. News from the Western Hemisphere had been nearly non-existent recently, and in some sense that was a good thing. At times, she didn't want to know what had happened to her former country and her relatives. Much of what she had known had been destroyed in the nuclear exchange during the Magog Invasion.

She unzipped the sleeping bag and crawled out, and then stretched to help her wake up. She was used to her morning tea, and hadn't had one since they had arrived. She had been stiff and a bit sore the first few days, even though they slept on an air mattress. It wasn't as uncomfortable as it had been at first, and they were slowly adjusting to it. Jacob seemed more relaxed than he had been in years, and she attributed it to the lack of work emergencies and other issues that accompanied owning and running a growing, demanding business. He had needed a real vacation for a long time, but had never really left work behind even when he had taken a week or two off.

Jacob had surprised her over the last few days by not grumbling as much as he had when they had first arrived. Since Daniel was still more or less a stranger to them, Jacob had curbed his complaining on the way down, but once they were alone, he let most of his true feelings show.

It had improved somewhat once he had been given some work to do around the camp, and she figured that that was just the way he was. If he didn't have something to occupy his mind, he just wasn't happy. She had grown used to that part of his personality long before, and his complaining and grumbling had not really bothered her for a long time.

She wasn't thrilled with being away from their home either, but she also understood that they had no other choice. If they remained at home, who knows what would happen to them? She hadn't been aware of how much she had needed a break from her business herself until she had been forced to slow down even more. She had been feeling more relaxed the last few weeks too, and was looking forward to exploring Petra more in depth this week. The ruins were large and spread out, and their previous trips here had only given them the main tourist attractions. Since they would most likely be there a while, they might as well explore it as much as possible.

Naomi looked up one side of the path and then the other, but did not see Jacob in either direction. And then she looked down and thought she saw his set of fresh footprints that led off to the left, and began to follow them. It was nice to be outside, and she realized how much she had missed the outdoors. She hadn't kept a garden the last few years with everything that had been happening, and she often reminisced about that too.

She worried about Jacob and often prayed that he wouldn't leave her to return home. She didn't know anyone except Daniel (somewhat) and their new neighbors in the tents nearby. But even though her feelings were so strong, she hadn't brought up the matter up to him yet – she didn't want him to think she was nagging him to stay or anything. She wanted him to stay because he wanted to. And even though there were flocks of new people coming to Petra every day, she felt safe, away from the rule of Medine and the World Union.

The distribution of the Enki Seals was already starting in Babylon and would spread quickly to the other urban areas. The pressure to take the seals would probably increase just as quickly, and Petra and other refuge areas would swell in the next few months. The thought of Ahban voluntarily taking the mark made her spirits sink, and she tried not to dwell on it long.

"Naomi!" she heard a familiar voice call out, and she looked up in surprise. It was Jacob! She realized that she had been so focused on her thoughts that she hadn't seen him walking towards her on the dusty trail.

He had a big smile on his face, and that lifted her spirits, and he hugged her when they met. She had missed that too – they had allowed too many distractions to come between them. She was beginning to warm up to her husband again for the first time in what seemed like years, and she felt old feelings being rekindled.

"Good morning," she said. "Would you like to take a walk?" she asked him with a smile.

"Sure. I had gone back and found you were still sleeping, so I decided to go out for a while longer." He paused for a moment. "Actually, I've made a decision about going home." He wanted to tell her directly, but also wanted to bring in a little levity.

"Oh really? And what have you decided?" she said, as they began walking side by side.

"Well, you know what I said about staying here a few weeks and then going home if nothing happened? So far, nothing has," He watched her reaction carefully, and her face fell.

"But – I've decided to stay anyway," he said with a grin.

She stopped suddenly in surprise. "Really?"

"Really. I'm still thinking of it as a long vacation though, and we've needed one of those for a long time," he replied. He reached out and took her hands in his.

"That's wonderful!" she said, with her voice trembling. "I'm so glad you decided to stay," she whispered. They kissed and held each other, and then turned back to the trail.

And holding hands like they had years before, they walked back down the trail to their tent to find some breakfast.

*   *   *

Daniel looked over one of the numerous maps spread across the table. Petra was quite naturally defensible against any type of large land invasion, but an attack from the air was a much different story. Petra was situated in a long canyon, and many buildings, caves, and tunnels had been carved throughout the canyon over the centuries. Medine would most likely just bomb them first, and then send in ground troops to wipe out any survivors.

There wasn't much point in trying to protect themselves from an invasion army, he supposed. The refugees were in no condition to fight or even put up much of a resistance. They had no weapons other than rocks, and even at that there were very few men of fighting age there. Most of those who were coming were in their middle ages, and few had ever seen real combat.

If the World Union forces did invade Petra, it would be an absolute slaughter, and there wasn't much that he or the Council leaders could do. But they did have God's explicit promise to protect them, and that was all that really mattered, he supposed.

On his second day there, the Council leaders had asked to meet with him, and after few short interviews, invited him to join their leadership team. He had immediately accepted their offer and began learning about the camp. Hundreds of thousands of refugees would be coming soon, and the Council had prepared as much as possible beforehand. From the Scriptures, he knew the Remnant that would gather there in the wilderness would be huge. And yet it wouldn't be nearly as many as they were all praying would come. Those who didn't flee to the wilderness would be bottled up in the cities and then systematically slaughtered, starved out, or hunted down like animals.

The Council was very well-organized, as far as he could tell. They had been buying and storing as many tents, air mattresses, first aid kits, and other basic camping supplies for over a year. Most of their supplies had been donated, and were repaired as needed. They also had a decent supply of water and even large water filtration and pumping equipment. A crew had begun drilling for water only days before the first refugees had arrived, and had yet to strike water. The water was down there of course, but it would be most likely very deep – after all, they were in one of the most arid places in the world.

Earlier that week, hourly services had begun in the Theater – the huge outdoor amphitheatre built during the Roman times, easily capable of seating thousands of people. Even after nearly two thousand years, it was still in remarkably good condition. The sight of the Treasury when he had first glimpsed it from the cavern had taken his breath away!

Petra was just as the last inhabitants had left it, except for where an army or another group had defaced various carvings and statues and such. But Petra still remained an incredible testament to the ingenuity and persistence of man, spending years carving a city and monuments out of solid rock and sandstone.

Daniel smiled when he thought about some of the prophecies in the Bible about this place and this time. The prophets had proclaimed over and over that Edom's proud capital would be laid waste and be uninhabited when God's people flocked there to take refuge from the Beast. The ancient Edomites had constantly warred with Israel and Judah until the Babylonians had all but wiped them out as a nation. And while Petra had fallen to Nebuchadnezzar, the ancient king of Babylon, the modern king of Babylon would not be nearly as successful.

Another ancient name for Petra in the Scriptures had been Bozrah, meaning the "sheepfold" or the "sheep pen". How fitting it was that God had reserved this place to be the location for the gathering of His faithful Remnant during the Last Days. Over and over in the Scriptures, Yeshua had referred to Himself as the Good Shepherd and His people as the Flock, and now it was literally the case. It was here that Yeshua would first come back to the earth, to save His people from annihilation by the Beast. From there, He would turn northward to Jerusalem to the Mount of Olives, and destroy the great armies there. Daniel hoped he would live long enough to see that great day, but that was up to the Lord and His purposes for him during the time that remained.

Daniel continued looking over the map, which was now becoming more and more heavily marked with little pictures and notes in felt-tipped pen. The food and water stations were in one color, the portable restrooms and sanitation areas in another, the tents and camping supplies in yet another, and so on. The Council had spread the supply areas out over the entire area of Petra, so the refugees would not have to walk very far to the necessities, and also to keep the lines as short as possible. They also had a good supply of Bibles and other books, but not nearly as many supplies as he'd had back at the ministry.

He thought about all the books, materials, and other supplies he had hurriedly stored away less than two weeks before. He wanted to leave Petra to go get all those materials so the Council could use them there, but it would be too dangerous for him soon, if it wasn't already.

Suddenly he realized what he could do – what he had to do while they still had the chance. He had some money from the ministry left, and he estimated that would be enough for his immediate purposes. He asked to borrow a laptop with an Internet connection and quickly looked up some moving companies that covered all of Israel, and that serviced the Dead Sea area.

After several calls, he finally found a moving company that was still in business. Fortunately, they still accepted Israeli currency, and he offered to pay them more than double the normal rate if they made it their top priority. It would use up nearly all the money he had left, but it would be worth it. And considering that such ministries were now all but outlawed, he might as well use the money while he could.

He breathed a sigh of relief when the order was finished – the moving truck would be leaving later that night, if all went well. With some prayer and luck, the shipment would be there in Petra late the next day.

* * *

The observant Christians and messianic Jews all across the earth had recognized who David Medine was soon after he was introduced to the public, especially after he had confirmed the seven-year treaty with Israel. But many had ignored their warnings and had often ridiculed them publicly. But after Medine desecrated the Temple, more of the Jews began to awaken to what was happening, and finally began to listen to what the Bible – even if just the Tanakh – had to say about what would soon happen to them.

THE TIME OF JACOB'S TROUBLE

Most of the believers in Yeshua throughout Israel obeyed the words of their Lord in the Gospels immediately after the Temple had been desecrated, and fled to the ancient ruins of Petra. There they began making preparations for the great remnant of their people who would soon be joining them as they became aware of the fate that Medine and the World Union had in store for their nation. They gathered as many resources as possible and put them towards preparing the city for a massive influx of people. And thus the Council had been born.

As the noose of the World Union began to tighten around Israel, more of the observant Jews saw what was happening, and fled to Petra. They had heard of the ancient city being prepared for the faithful remnant of their people, and it was the only escape from the trap that was being set around Israel. They too had read the ancient prophecies from the Tanakh and understood that their nation would be overrun by the Gentile armies that had just started to gather against them. There would be no escape for those who remained in Israel, and especially in Jerusalem.

The non-messianic Jews had expected to be refused and turned away from Petra, but they were immediately welcomed with open arms. There were regular worship times, prayer groups, and regular teaching from the Tanakh as well as the New Testament, and the spiritual eyes of the Jews began to open for the first time in over two thousand years. The veil that the Lord had placed over them in order to stay His Hand of judgment had been removed. And they now read and heard their own Scriptures with new eyes and new ears.

The Orthodox Jews slowly began to turn to Yeshua, and after being converted, they often wept bitterly at how they had warred against Him for so many years. And all throughout Petra there was repenting, fasting, and a growing spiritual hunger to know their Lord they had been separated from for so long.

But according to the Book of Hosea, the Messiah could not return until the Sanhedrin specifically asked Him to come and save them – the same leadership body that had condemned Him to death during His first visitation two thousand years before.

The Scriptures were clear that some day the Sanhedrin

would join them in Petra, and then all would repent and beg for Yeshua to save them in their darkest hour.

* * *

Daniel found himself growing more and more restless every day. He had been in Petra nearly two months, and had watched with excitement as thousands upon thousands of refugees came through the checkpoints. The books, Bibles, and other materials from the ministry had run out within three weeks, and the Council had asked the people to return the materials to their makeshift library or pass them around after they were done reading them. The camp had plenty of Bibles though, and a huge shipment of Bibles in Hebrew, Arabic, Russian, English, and several other languages had come into the camp by way of the black market.

At first, he didn't know why he was fidgety and impatient, but after talking with some of the pastors and rabbis there and some quiet prayer time, he understood why he was feeling the way he was. He almost felt like he was bored at times, but he was still as busy as the rest of the leadership team. He regularly spoke at the Theater or one of the other meeting places, but he increasingly perceived that he wasn't doing what God had intended, almost as if he wasn't fulfilling God's purposes for him any more. He was helping his people and reaching them for Yeshua, but he still wasn't feeling complete somehow.

When a small group of frightened Jewish refugees came in from Ethiopia and told what was happening in their country, he finally figured out why he was restless. He wanted to be out there helping the rest of the Remnant find their way to Petra, or wherever else they could find safety. The Ethiopians had reminded him of something he had read about on the Internet concerning the American Civil War: the Underground Railroad. As he began thinking more about how the Americans had put together the vast slave smuggling operation, he considered how a similar network could be put into action against the growing tyranny of the World Union.

As he thought about it, he realized that the Underground

Railroad model could still work in modern times. Rather than clustering and gathering in large groups like they were at Petra, many small "stations" could be set up to move "passengers" along the "route", where they would eventually end up in Petra or other safe locations. They could also transfer food and supplies along the routes and then redistribute the goods from the stations. Though heavily monitored, the Internet still provided many ways for people to communicate without being discovered, but at least not as easily as being out in the open. As he mentally worked out the details, he began to grow more excited about the idea, though it would be very dangerous and difficult.

Daniel felt a sense of urgency about putting together the Underground Railroad – the World Union would be clamping down on everyone very soon. Even if the Underground Railroad never expanded outside Israel, at least it was better than doing nothing.

The ESACs were spreading all over the world, and soon taking the mark would be compulsory everywhere. After most of the population had taken the mark, the World Union might even go so far as to go from door to door, hunting down any holdouts. At first, common sense told him that no government would be so intrusive as that, but then he considered the authority Medine had been given and the choice that would be put before every person on the earth. And then he realized that the World Union would be that aggressive, and probably much worse. He could see a day coming when any holdouts would be simply killed instead of being offered a choice.

He thought about it further and brought his idea for the new Underground Railroad to the Council. They listened carefully to his plan and then endorsed it. The only critical part he couldn't quite work out was the secure communications between the stations, groups, and other individuals. He could really use Saul's expertise with computers and networking, but he was still in Iraq and unavailable. The Council brought the technology issue before some that had marked as having computer and networking knowledge on their registration forms, and they quickly showed him what he needed for secure communications over the Internet. The leaders also mentioned that they and others had left behind many of their homes when they had fled, and many could be used for the stations and safe-houses.

Daniel continued working out the details of his plan and sought the advice of many in the Council. After a week, he felt comfortable enough about it to get started. And with that, he said farewell to the Council and the Rosenbergs, and then took his van and drove north towards Amman, Jordan's capital. It would be easier to start the network in Jordan, which wasn't being monitored as closely as Israel yet.

As he left the camp, he smiled when he thought of Jacob and Naomi. They had seemed strangely happier than he had seen them before, especially Jacob.

* * *

The huge gathering of the Jewish remnant in Petra had not gone unnoticed by David Medine. In his view, these were the worst of the religious extremists and some of his greatest enemies. They must be destroyed lest they spread their foolishness again over the rest of the earth.

He would use his supernatural powers to compel them to surrender, or he would destroy them in the process. More and more, he simply wanted to kill them all regardless of who they were or even how loyal they had been to him before. In most of the world's opinion, the Jews had been causing everyone problems since the beginning of history. Hitler and Stalin had come close to solving the problem, but he would be the one to succeed where all others had failed.

At first, Medine saw that the refugees there had very limited supplies of food, so he moved to ensure that no additional supplies of food and water could be delivered or airdropped to them. They would soon run out of food and be forced to flee, and his forces would be there to catch them when they finally dispersed.

But after three months, they had not run out of food even though thousands more empty-handed refugees had joined them. He ordered that the satellites begin monitoring them, and to his dismay, he discovered that each morning the refugees would go out to the grounds of Petra soon after dawn and gather something from the ground in baskets.

As for water, a spring of fresh water had opened from what appeared to be a huge rock just outside the Treasury. He was furious when he realized what was happening: Yahweh or the Elohim was feeding them just like the old stories of the Jews when they were wandering in the desert after escaping from Egypt.

So Medine and Pontiffica decided to send various plagues down to Petra upon those gathering there: locusts, fleas, frogs, lice, and vermin. But the camp of Petra was somehow supernaturally protected. After two weeks of failure, Medine and Pontiffica began sending harsher forms of terror, such as great scores of lightning strikes, fireballs from the sky, earthquakes, sandstorms, and even several tornados.

But still the camp was protected, so Medine resorted to sending a massive bombardment of nuclear weapons upon Petra. The remnant in Petra would surely be wiped out – he had been certain of it, but they were supernaturally protected from that too. [71]

He then turned his wrath upon the Temple – he would level it to the ground and pollute it with the most vile forms of desecration possible. But when he attempted to destroy it, he was dismayed to find that it was supernaturally protected also. They had continued to desecrate it with their images, idols, and bloodshed, but the Temple itself could not be destroyed.

David Medine could barely control his frustration – if he could not destroy the Temple or the religious extremists at Petra, he would destroy everyone they cared about, along with any of their brethren who had not joined them.

Every Jew and Christian was now marked for the slaughter, and slaughter them he would.

* * *

---

[71]   Matthew 24:22-27

CHRIS HAMBLETON

Jacob heard the roar of fighter jets far overhead as he sat next to Naomi in the crowded Theater. And then he could hear a louder, lower-pitched sound of a larger aircraft following the fighters.

He instinctively looked up, along with everyone else in the huge outdoor amphitheater. As the missiles streamed down and the bombs dropped towards them, they cringed out of old habits, knowing what the bombs could do. And even though they knew the outcome, they still couldn't help ducking for cover.

When the bombs and missiles were less than fifty meters above the Theater, they suddenly vanished in mid-air.

Only a small percentage had grown used to the frequent occurrence over the last few weeks, and some quietly believed that one day they would be hit by the weapons and obliterated. But they were completely safe in Petra, and the only injuries during any of the bombings so far had come from people scurrying to take cover and then slipping or falling down. Yet not even a shred of shrapnel had penetrated the invisible shield above them, regardless of what weapon had been used.

The first attack by the World Union air forces had driven everyone in Petra to immediate prayer and cover among the buildings, caves, and rocks. They all knew the shelter would be insufficient to protect them, but perhaps some would survive and be able to escape. After the first wave did not strike, the people sheepishly looked out from their hiding places and heard the jets and bombers coming back for the second wave. And once again, they heard the bombs and missiles scream down towards them, but nothing happened.

But that time, some had dared to look up as the bombs were nearly upon them, and were shocked to see that they would simply vanish into the air. The bombs weren't simply detonated or rendered inoperable, they just disappeared from above them. Those who had been brave enough to watch them started telling everyone nearby what they had seen. By the fourth and fifth wave of bombing, nearly everyone in Petra was standing out in the open staring at the sky (although most still stood close to their shelters).

THE TIME OF JACOB'S TROUBLE

Nearly every day that had followed was met with jets, bombers, armed helicopters, and any other terrible weapon that could be used against the camp at Petra. Chemical sprays, biological weapons, napalm, and guided missiles all failed to even weaken the shield above them. Some of the people swore that even nuclear bombs had been dropped on them, especially when some had struck outside the perimeter and the huge mushroom clouds had risen all around.

The effect on the people in Petra was nearly as incredible as their supernatural protection. Though the squabbles and complaints had never really been very pervasive, some had begun taking place, and the miraculous protection quickly extinguished their trivial grievances. They knew that none other than God Himself was protecting them, and suddenly their problems weren't even worth talking about. They all knew they were fortunate to be alive after the first bombing. And as the bombings had increased in their intensity, any discord that remained in the camp was promptly purged.

The ministers, rabbis, and other leaders recognized what was happening from the Scriptures – specifically from the typology in Revelation 12:13-17. This passage portrayed the faithful Remnant as a woman fleeing into the wilderness from the dragon, who tried to destroy her with a flood. God had surely covered them with His protection, and even though the dragon was failing in all his attempts to annihilate them, he would continue trying different ways. And sure enough, though all the air strikes had failed, Medine refused to give up.

A few days later, Medine surrounded Petra with several divisions of tanks and heavy artillery, but as they approached the main entrance to the camp, an earthquake struck all around Petra. Outside, the ground underneath the armada suddenly opened up, and then several moments later closed shut again.

The shaking all around Petra had been enormous, but those inside the camp barely felt it. They could hear the deep rumbling and shrieking of metal and men, but they were not shaken inside the canyon. It was as if Medine's flood of men and weapons had been swallowed up by the earth itself, and had then closed its mouth over them. The land where the soldiers and tanks had been was easily identified because of all the tortured earth, with no plants or shrubs on it any longer.[72]

After the first day of the supernatural protection of Petra, Jacob had become quiet and aloof. He could not deny it or push it away any longer: God had His hand on the camp and was directly protecting them. Over and over, he had heard the verses from Revelation that spoke so clearly about the woman who portrayed Israel – the wife of God – fleeing into the desert and being protected from the dragon and his evil forces. The plagues, judgments, the mark of the beast – all of it had been detailed thousands of years before, and it had been accurate as to what was happening in these days. And the latest miracle in Petra had driven him to prayer.

The food shipments to the camp had ceased just before the air strikes had begun, and everyone assumed the World Union had finally cut off the supply lines to Petra. Three days after the leaders had beckoned everyone to pray to the Lord for help, they awoke to find the ground covered with a pale-colored film. Many picked up pieces from the ground and smelled them, but only the bravest had dared to taste and eat them.

They found it to be sweet like honey and have a texture like small wafers. But somehow everyone knew what it was before anyone had said it outright: it was manna. Just as God had fed His flock in the desert after coming out of Egypt, so God was feeding His new flock in the sheepfold of Petra.

Jacob was sure that Naomi had noticed his recent changes in behavior, but he didn't want to talk to her about them yet. He wanted to find his own path, and figure out for himself what it all meant. He decided he would read the New Testament and try to look at it with fresh eyes, and put his negative feelings aside. He usually rose very early to pray and read the Bible before gathering his manna for the day. Sometimes he would be praying and find the manna had appeared by the time he had finished.

---

[72] Revelation 12:15-16

THE TIME OF JACOB'S TROUBLE

When he was ready, he would ask her (or others) questions about the New Testament, but he wanted to read it for himself first. Revelation was so clear and precise as to what was going on – only a fool could deny it. And he was tired of being a fool.

* * *

David Medine also had become a man of prayer, but prayer of a different sort. He rose from the floor where he had been kneeling. He detested doing it every morning and evening, but he knew where his incredible power came from, and was therefore compelled to worship him. His master took note of his allegiance and dismissed him with a wave of his hand.

He dreaded his dark master, who had been revealed in his true form when he had died months earlier. His master was nearly all-powerful (or so he said) and he definitely had more power than Medine could ever imagine himself having. Yet he wanted it – all of it – all of his master's power. It was a hunger he couldn't explain. It was a hunger he had not really known until the moment of his resurrection.

Lucifer usually resided in the pinnacle of the Tower of Illumination, directly above his own residence. He didn't know what his master did there most of the time, but every so often he would hear thunder and other sounds of anger and vengeance coming from above him. Someone was being punished for disobedience or other failure or infraction. Frequently he left and went to Jerusalem to sit in the Most Holy Place, reveling in the accomplishments of himself and his lieutenants. Medine had not gone back there though – that was now his master's place.

As Medine slowly walked down the huge marble staircase that descended from the pinnacle, he glanced down at his right hand, and raised it to his face to more closely examine it. He shut his eyes and concentrated, but he could still not make it close by his own thoughts, nor open it for that matter. His master now controlled his right hand, and only sometimes relinquished control over it to him.

He considered the dark power that animated his lifeless

335

hand, and how much a part of him was now under his master's control. His right eye was useless also, but it had been replaced with a life-like glass eye before his entombment. Sometimes he could feel it moving back and forth in its socket, and it always enraged him when Lucifer invaded his person unannounced. [73]

But soon after his resurrection from the dead, David Medine had discovered he possessed many more miraculous qualities than he'd had before, similar to Franco Pontiffica. He could not only call down streams of fire and lightning bolts from the sky, but could also replicate many of the supernatural plagues and phenomena that the Two Witnesses had wrought. Together they turned any water they wanted to blood (and then back), they took the lives of any they wished, and they caused bizarre weather over specific areas whenever they desired. He reveled in his own godlike power and relished every moment of it. [74]

Most of the destructive miracles they performed were on the various groups that opposed them, and most frequently throughout the land of Israel. Both Pontiffica and Medine destroyed a number of the larger buildings, and caused earthquakes and winds to terrify the millions of Jews gathered in the tiny nation. But something they apparently did not have the authority to do was to destroy the Temple, even though they had tried numerous times. Over and over they sent rainstorms of blood, fire, lightning and even earthquakes against the Temple Mount, but somehow it still stood unaffected.

His master demanded to only be referred to by his original name: Lucifer. He hated the others he had been given, even though they more accurately described him: Satan, the Adversary, the Evil One, the Dragon.

Lucifer opposed and hated everything his Enemy stood for. And since he could not destroy Him (at least not yet), nor trap Him in a lie, he had grown more and more crazed with hatred, jealousy, and anger. He had long pondered what would happen to Him if He ever did lie – would He self-destruct, or would He

---

[73] Zechariah 11:17
[74] Matthew 24:22-27; Revelation 13:11-15

quietly slink away and relinquish His all-powerful hold on the universe?

Or (and even this thought made him shudder with fear) would He simply think a Thought as He had long ago and undo everything and everyone He had created by the very power of His mind, including him. But to trap the Ever Truthful One in a lie – the thought filled him with glee.

But Medine, to his great relief, knew that Lucifer could not read his mind, or at least if he could, he was keeping that knowledge to himself. The thought of that scared him, but as he had sometimes imagined the most rebellious thoughts against his master, he couldn't see how Lucifer could contain his wrath, if he was in fact able to read his mind.

Medine definitely knew that Lucifer was not all-powerful, and that he was also subject to his Enemy. He hated Him nearly as much as his master did. Yet – and he still hadn't worked out how this could be achieved – perhaps he could find a way to overthrow his master. Perhaps a temporary allegiance with the Enemy could be used to suddenly overthrow Lucifer so he could take his rightful place – along with all his authority and power. The thought of having his master's power and hatred made him tremble with lust and jealousy.

But taking the chance of allying himself with Enemy was nearly out of the question. For one thing, he was sure that his offer would be spurned and rejected, but worse than that, he could be destroyed when his own master discovered the treachery. His master had even more spies than the Enemy did! The only way that subversion could even remotely be a possibility would be if his master were so pre-occupied that he could be thrown down before taking vengeance on him.

He meditated on his master's weaknesses, and found them to be many, and some very exploitable. But his master knew them also, and was constantly monitoring his servants for signs of betrayal and treason. Lucifer trusted no one, not even his most loyal, strongest angels – not even those who had stood up with him at the moment of his first rebellion against the Enemy.

David Medine had been given the complete authority to

cause all people on the earth to worship him, with the agreement that one day soon he would turn this into the worship of his master. Lucifer still had a bad reputation by the centuries of Christians, Jews, and even Muslims speaking directly against him, even though they had often unknowingly served his purposes. Therefore he could not be worshiped directly, at least not yet.

That infuriated his master, but as long as they weren't worshipping his Enemy, he could settle for indirect worship of any kind. This could work to Medine's advantage: all the people were worshipping him directly and were pledging their loyalty to him, thousands upon thousands more every day. He reveled in it, relished it, and wanted as many aligned with him as possible.

But Medine knew he must ensure that as many people as possible were marked as his own before attempting his ultimate act of treason. He perceived his master's power and authority was quickly diminishing – for millennia since his rebellion he had been allowed to stand before his Enemy and come and go as he pleased throughout the universe. But he had recently been soundly defeated by the Enemy's cohorts, and had been shamefully cast out of Heaven. He had been furious and had unleashed his wrath on his lieutenants for failing him. Medine was happy he had been dead when all that had transpired.

Perhaps as his time on earth dragged on, Lucifer would continue to lose his power and cunning. He was, after all, the Prince of the Air. But he would never willingly allow anyone to capitalize on his loss, at least not if he could help it. His master's main weakness was his insatiable lust for power and his boundless pride in his own abilities. He would continue to compliment Lucifer and laud him and puff him up, much like Pontiffica did to Medine himself. But he wouldn't be as foolish as his master.

Pontiffica was an imbecile, but possibly he too could be a valuable instrument in stirring his master's pride. Perhaps when Lucifer's wrath arose, Pontiffica could shoulder more of the blame and therefore, more of the punishment. He smiled silently to himself: suddenly Pontiffica might be an invaluable asset that could be helpful in his own rise to supremacy. Medine licked his lips in anticipation of that future glorious day.

He then began considering how Pontiffica could further be used for his purposes. Pontiffica must be given more power – if only for a short time. Just as Medine controlled all the physical aspects, resources, and people of the world, so must Pontiffica control the spiritual realm. Pontiffica was a coward, and worshipped both him and his master with absolute devotion. He would be easy to control; once he had finished his task of unifying the world under Medine's authority, he could be destroyed. But first, he would have to remain and be given even more power in order to accomplish his purposes (and his master's, of course).

Medine was loath to even think about relinquishing power to Pontiffica, even temporarily. Yet power that could be given was power that could later be taken away, and authority that could be granted one day could be denied the next. He and Pontiffica must remove the foolish wall between religion and the state and unite them as they had always meant to be. Many religions and governments had done this since the first civilizations, and many had achieved the very control that was now desired. He must control the hearts of men, and not only their outward behavior. He would be the new Nimrod – the hunter of the souls of men.[75]

He needed more beings under his control – and not just any normal people, but supermen like himself. The Anshar must mate with more women and produce offspring in the millions – no, in the billions. But their offspring would take too much time to grow. Perhaps technology could be used to augment and speed up their growth. He would implement this program immediately – it would be an easy sell to his master and all the people.

The War of Wars was coming soon, and they needed as many soldiers as possible. And besides, who wouldn't want to become one with and give birth to gods?

* * *

---

[75] Micah 5:5-6

Since his resurrection, David Medine had been given much more authority over the Anshar and they were now subject to him. His proposal to create an army of super humans had been immediately accepted and put into motion.

His master understood that the time was short, and had sent as many of his underlings as possible to mate with the women of the earth. His minions had failed him countless times in the past, and since he had been cast to the earth, he might as well use them to their utmost. He had always hated mankind, but more than ever since he was now forced to live among them. He would make all of them suffer soon.

Along with the thousands more Anshar that had come, another breed of Lucifer's servants had been sent to earth too. These creatures seemed to fall somewhere in between the typical Anshar and Lucifer, at least in terms of power, authority, and brilliance. They were called the Luciferim, the "light-bearing ones."

They were his master's personal guards – the elite of the elite. Their duty was to support David Medine and ensure his orders were executed properly. They were also tasked with ensuring that both the Anshar and the armies of men were prepared for their coming war against Yahweh and the Elohim. But they only answered to his master, and not him. They would also need to be turned against him when the time came.

The lesser Anshar had also been given orders to root out and lure Jews and Christians from their hiding places for slaughter. The Anshar were given additional power from their master to accomplish this purpose. They would often surround themselves with blinding light and appear to the refugees hiding in caves, proclaiming that the Messiah had come. When the refugees would emerge, they would slay them or cause the caves or shelters to cave in and crush them. Other times they would work in conjunction with the police forces to entice the holdouts out of hiding so they could be bombed, shot, or captured.

Both the Anshar and their Luciferim counterparts had changed their forms to become even more handsome and breathtaking, and the women (and even many of the men) could not resist their will. And sometimes they were taken against their will. The supernatural creatures cared nothing for the humans, and used them for their own amusement and gratification as often as they wanted.

Medine had proclaimed that all gender and sexual barriers of every society be immediately eliminated in order to further mankind's evolution to godhood, and pushed the policy that in order for the people to become gods, they must behave like gods.

Frequent, unrestricted copulation was encouraged between the Anshar, the Luciferim, the humans, and even many of the animals of every sort. [76]

Any hindrances or barriers that society might have had to the abhorrent and bizarre were removed, and evil greatly increased on the earth.

---

[76] Genesis 6:1-4; Daniel 2:43

CHAPTER 14
THE GATHERING STORM

Nearly three and a half years had passed since David Medine's miraculous resurrection and his desecration of the Jewish Temple. Most of the world was still in a shambles compared to how it had been before the World Union had been granted authority.

David Medine sat behind his grand desk and glanced over the latest round of reports that had been delivered to him. His master would be pleased, at least once he reinterpreted the reports spread out before him.

The financial markets had stabilized, but even with the widespread use of the Enki Seals, theft was still widespread in the underground communities. People everywhere had grown desperate and unspeakably wicked as the moral conditions on the earth descended. Murder and burglary were rampant, and law enforcement rarely pursued any personal crimes, other than religious infractions against the state.

Some would either steal the Enki Seals of others who had died, or even kill them for their seals. In the underground, a market of hacked and stolen marks quickly arose, and many used them without actually needing to have the marks on their own bodies. But while the world appeared as if it was recovering to some extent, few individual freedoms remained. The World Union controlled nearly every aspect of each individual's lives on the planet, and those who wished to be free (and expressed it) were quickly removed from society.

For over four years, David Medine had exercised authority

over nearly all the world's military, economic, and environmental resources, but had lost much of his widespread appeal. Over the last few years, he had moved from being a reasonable, brilliant leader to one filled with cunning and ruthlessness, and he no longer hesitated to use whatever force it took to accomplish his goals.

The World Union security forces had killed millions, and entire nations were now little more than prison camps in which the people were simply waiting to die. Starvation and disease had wiped out millions upon millions of people on the earth, and the policies of the World Union had turned the once-powerful, democratic nations into poverty-stricken lands. Even nations that had never known hunger before were starving, such as Canada, the United Kingdom, and even large portions of the United States.[77]

Sorcery, drug-use, prostitution, and other former crimes of every sort had been legalized. Whatever the people wanted to do, the Ankida religion allowed as long as it did not interfere with the goal of world unification and elevation of the state. Morality and any sense of moral duty or right and wrong no longer existed, or even came to mind in most cases. And while many forms of other crime were tolerated, religious persecution had taken on a new meaning.

Those who outright refused to worship Medine were quickly tortured and then killed, usually in a very public manner. Violence was rampant on every level of society. Public killings and torture had become the new form of entertainment on television and the Internet, and incredibly painful and gruesome means of torment were invented and put to widespread use. [78]

The city of Babylon in Iraq was by far still the greatest, most beautiful city upon the face of the earth. It gleamed like a brilliant jewel in the desert, and was covered in lush, rich gardens and magnificent buildings. Nearly everyone in the city was a multi-millionaire (aside from the thousands of servants and

---

[77] Revelation 13:7-10
[78] Revelation 9:20-21

slaves), and the wealth of the nations flowed into Babylon as it once had to New York, Tokyo, London, and Paris.

But Babylon had far surpassed those great cities in only a few years, and the high concentration of vital oil production and the location of the world capital ensured its top place among the other cities of the world. It was the city truly fit for the greatest king, to which all the power, authority, and wealth of the earth belonged. [79]

Yet as absolute power corrupts absolutely, so it breeds jealousy, subversion, disloyalty, and rebellion. Small pockets of resistance high in the large bureaucracy of the World Union began to form, and careful plans were implemented to wrest control of significant portions of power away from Medine. And while he knew of some of the conspirators, he recognized he would not be able to stop them without causing a global civil war. But he could still heavily control and bend them to his will.

The World Union was still composed of eight primary districts, and each still operated under his control. Perhaps if he loosened his hold on them a bit, it would flush out more of the conspirators and he could more easily set them against one other. But he also needed a scapegoat on which to focus and redirect the anger of those who were coalescing against him.

As David Medine turned his eyes from the reports and looked at the huge globe near his desk, his eyes fell upon the tiny city of Jerusalem – the home of his greatest Enemy – and he immediately knew how he would continue to keep what was rightfully his. [80]

* * *

Daniel stole a quick glance into his rearview mirror and then jerked the wheel hard to the left. Too hard, he realized, and his car began to slip sideways off the road.

From the posts along the side of the road, there once was a

---

[79] Revelation 17-18
[80] Daniel 11:41

guardrail there, but it had not been replaced for years. And the posts wouldn't be enough to stop his car now.

The back of the driver's side struck first and spun even further away from the road. The flashing lights were still behind him; they had been gaining for the last few minutes. He closed his eyes and pressed his back hard against the seat as the car spun.

Suddenly he felt the front tip forward, and he realized what was happening: he was going over the cliff.

But he was prepared for death if it came – he had been ready since the beginning of the Tribulation. As the ground slipped from beneath his car, an odd smile crossed his face. Yes, he was ready to meet his Maker. He had been looking forward to this day for a long time.

He had run the race that had been set before him, and he had finished well. He wanted to be free of this terrible world and all its wickedness. The world had become the closest thing to Hell he ever wanted to see.

He kept his eyes closed all the way down the cliff. He didn't want to open them until he woke up in Heaven. He could still faintly hear the sirens, but they were far above him now. He hoped he wouldn't be hearing them for long.

The car was diving headfirst directly into the sea. It wouldn't be long now. He felt it begin to flip upside down, and he clenched his teeth and waited for the impact.

As the car struck the water, Daniel was slammed into the steering wheel and then was flung sideways onto the seat as the car tipped onto its side and began to sink.

He must have briefly lost consciousness because when he finally opened his eyes, the car was already filling with the cold waters of the Mediterranean. As he gathered his bearings, he realized that he was alive and still on the earth, and with that realization, he was disappointed. But his King evidently still had a purpose for him in keeping him alive. He would obey and continue following Him wherever he was asked to go.

He painfully lifted his legs off the seat – he didn't have any broken bones, at least as far as he could tell. He struggled to roll down the passenger-side window and then took a deep breath before squirming out the window.

He made a conscious effort to keep as much of his body under the water as he could, and quickly found his way to the shore. He wouldn't dare look up until he was safely hidden among the rocks. His ears were still ringing from the impact, but he didn't think he heard the sirens any longer.

When he was finally safe, he glanced up to the cliff from where he had fallen, and to his surprise he didn't see any police at all. Regardless, he decided to get comfortable in his hiding place and would stay there for at least an hour. He needed time to stop and think, and more importantly, to pray and give thanks.

He looked back towards his car – it had already disappeared into the sea. He lowered his head and closed his eyes, and thanked God for keeping him alive, and giving him another opportunity to serve Him. But he was honest and also expressed his disappointment at having remained on the earth, but he didn't complain nor grumble. He said his peace and left it at that.

He continued praying over an hour before the Lord answered him. "Go to Jerusalem and wait for Me there," He said.

Daniel rose and looked back up the cliff, and realized that yet another miracle had taken place in his life. He should have died from that fall, and it had not been the first time.

He decided to walk up the coast for a few kilometers and then find a road. He thought back to all that had happened to him over the last seven years. He could have been proud of all he had done since leaving the safety and security of Petra, but he was very modest. He simply had done what the Lord has asked of him, and tried to help others as much as he could.

If there was something he was proud of, it was that he was very high up on the World Union's Most Wanted list, at least in Israel. But then again, the World Union was more concerned with religious "extremists" than murderers, kidnappers, rapists, and thieves. Besides, the religious extremists like Christians and Jews rarely fought back. The World Union hadn't exactly picked formidable adversaries upon which to unleash their wrath.

Soon after leaving Petra, he had gathered what meager resources he had remaining and began recruiting churches, synagogues, and individuals to become stations along the Underground Railroad. He had been arrested and even beaten several times, but the police in Israel were much more sympathetic to their own kind as opposed to their World Union counterparts.

Once he had nearly been forced to take the mark, but he had been able to escape before being taken to the processing room. Often he wondered what would happen if someone received the mark against their will, without being given the choice between taking the mark and death. Surely the Lord would not condemn one of His own if they received the mark against their will!

After three years, the Underground Railroad was a thriving combination of a black market/underground economy and a system of safe-houses that funneled political prisoners, ministers, rabbis, and other individuals from all races, faiths, and backgrounds into safer areas, sometimes all the way south into Petra.

On the Internet, it was always referred to as "Ur", which had caused teams of World Union security forces to be sent to the ancient ruins in southern Iraq a number of times. He had always found that quite amusing. The Underground Railroad had saved thousands upon thousands of people who would have been killed (or at least tortured and imprisoned) by the World Union. The underground system he had started had kept tens of thousands more from having to take the mark in order to survive.

The Underground Railroad was made up of people of many different faiths and backgrounds. In fact, their only real commonality was their dislike of Medine and their disloyalty to the World Union and its policies. But that was enough. Sometimes a station or a safe-house was discovered by the World Union and immediately shut down permanently, with all the people in the station slaughtered or imprisoned. Fortunately, few ever talked.

He had narrowly escaped detection and raids several times, and the recent car chase and fall from the cliff had been his latest escape. The Underground Railroad kept nothing on their computers or in writing; all of their information was highly encrypted and stored all over the Internet. He had adopted the "cell" mentality for the Underground Railroad much like the Islamic terror-

ist cells of the past. Each station only knew of a few others immediately in their vicinity, and none knew (except for probably
himself and a few of the other organizers) just how extensive the
network was.

As he turned from the coast and headed up the rocky cliffs to
find the nearest road, he hoped that some of the recent pressure
from the World Union would be lifted. They were relentless!
Perhaps they would consider him dead now that he had driven
over a cliff. One could only hope, he thought.

He trudged along the road until he found a safe place to rest
for the night. He was hungry, but his discomfort would have to
wait until the next day. He was a mess, and would have no problem passing himself off as one of the many homeless until he
found his way to another station.

* * *

After nearly three and a half years of relative relief from the
plagues, the first of the next set of plagues struck the earth, and
these were much more terrible in comparison.

The people who first noticed the new plague were those in
the World Union government offices in Babylon. Huge, bloody
boils began breaking out all over their bodies, and their doctors
were baffled. And then the plague struck the doctors also.

Everyone who had taken the Enki Seals all over the earth
suddenly found themselves lying on the ground screaming and
writhing in pain, nearly incapacitated. The world economy
screeched to a halt, and the doctors worked feverishly for an an-
tidote to the disease, or at least a remedy to decrease the pain.
But they suffered just as much as their patients. [81]

Strangely, the boils would dramatically increase in size and
pain whenever the individual accessed their accounts, and then
would ease somewhat when they did not use the mark. The boils
did not completely clear up nor the pain vanish, but they became
slightly less painful whenever they hadn't used their mark for

---

[81] Revelation 16:2

several days.

Few drugs could diminish the pain – not even the strongest painkillers. Drug-use of every sort skyrocketed, at least to help them sleep through the torment. The medical teams and research labs of the World Union immediately inspected the Enki Seals to see if they were creating some form of allergic reaction in their wearers, but they found nothing. Yet the plague was strictly confined to only those who had taken the seals.

Even stranger, whenever an Enki Seal was removed from its wearer, the person would go into traumatic shock and often die within a matter of minutes. The doctors had no explanation for that reaction either. So the people were forced to continue wearing the seals, even though some with a lower tolerance for pain removed the seals themselves, just to end their suffering. But the boils on the mark wearers were only the beginning of the new plagues and torments that would soon befall the earth.

Two weeks after the boils had appeared, all the oceans and seas of the earth suddenly changed from saltwater to deep red, stinking blood. All the fish, sea creatures, and other marine life died within minutes, choking from the contaminated water. Billions of their carcasses floated to the surface and only added to the reeking stench. Nearly all the fishing and merchant sea vessels were also stopped dead in the water when their engines clogged and overheated from the blood. A number of ships sank, but most just sat idle, unable to head for land. Their stores of freshwater had not been touched by the plague, and most of the ships had days or even weeks of adequate freshwater supplies from which to draw upon. [82]

But the day after the oceans had all been turned to blood, all the freshwater lakes, ponds, rivers, and streams over the face of the earth also turned to blood, and a great voice could be heard throughout the skies, saying "Righteous are You, O Lord, the One who is and who was and who is to be, because You have judged these things; for they poured out the blood of saints and prophets, and You have given them blood to drink, for it is their

---

[82] Revelation 16:3

due." And all the earth-dwellers trembled at the voice, and began hunting for whatever water they could find. They momentarily forgot the terrible pain of the sores and the boils, and scurried to horde all the water they could find. [83]

As in the previous plague, all the fish and creatures in the freshwater sources died within a matter of minutes. Freshwater was no longer available except from bottled sources and tanks, and that would soon run out from the hoarding and stealing. The price of water skyrocketed overnight, and many stores were destroyed just for their supplies of water and other beverages. Tap water in homes across the earth had also been turned to blood since it was typically from the reservoirs or other freshwater supplies.

But for those in hiding who had refused the marks and were faithful to Lord, the blood was turned back to water for them so they could drink freely. Everyone else who eventually was forced to drink the bloody water immediately choked and died.

After seven days, the waters of the sea and all the freshwater sources turned back to their former state, except that the water in the oceans was no longer saltwater, but freshwater. But there were no fish or other sea creatures that remained; even most of their eggs and such had been poisoned, and the seas were utterly empty and lifeless for the first time since the Creation.

But even though the water supplies had been restored, the plague of the boils on those who had taken the Enki Seals still remained. And those who had sworn allegiance to Medine continued to suffer terribly.

* * *

Ahban awoke again in the middle of the night, writhing in pain. He grabbed at the back of his hand and felt the huge boils nearly bursting from his skin.

He screamed in agony and rushed into the bathroom to run

---

[83] Revelation 16:4

cold water over the boils. He was having another outbreak, and he immediately knew this one would be terrible. How he regretted ever taking the mark! The pain was overwhelming, and he cursed and screamed and wept. The running water did little to ease his pain, but at least it cooled the skin around the boils.

He took some aspirin with vodka, both of which was becoming increasingly rare even in Babylon, especially ever since the boils had come. He couldn't believe the magnitude of pain he was in. At first, he had thought he was having an allergic reaction, but it seemed that everyone else was too. Numerous people had attempted to remove them but had quickly died in the attempt. As soon as the mark had been cut out of their skin, they had died sudden deaths. Sometimes at the height of an outbreak, the pain was so horrible that he had seriously contemplated taking his own life, just to stop the pain.

He felt the growing, burning pain all over his back flare up again and screamed. He turned around and looked into the mirror behind him so he could see his back. The outbreak was happening so fast that he could literally see his skin reddening and bubbling with boils. He frantically reached back to the sink and felt around as tears filled his eyes. Before he knew it, his back was oozing with puss from the red sores.

There it was – a thick leather belt – and he quickly picked it up and pushed it into his mouth before he fell to the floor. He bit down as hard as he could until the episode passed, at times pounding on the walls and the cabinet when the pain overwhelmed him.

Minutes later, Ahban was exhausted, and didn't bother to get off the floor or even remove the belt. He had to sleep while he could, which was more or less only between outbreaks. He hadn't been to work since the plague had started, but he had worked from his apartment whenever he could. The company understood of course – after all, everyone there was suffering exactly like he was. Everyone in Babylon and all the rest of the world was too. The news was often taped or just read, instead of showing the live newscasters who looked as awful as he did.

An hour later, he awoke and found the belt still partially in his mouth, dripping with saliva. He spat it out and then washed his face and rinsed off the belt. Deep bite marks covered it all over – some had almost gone all the way through the tough leather. His jaw and all the rest of his body was tired and sore. He checked his back again, and it was just pink and irritated, with no red blistering boils. He dabbed his face with the towel again and went back to bed.

It was still dark, and that was good; hopefully he could get a few hours of sleep before the next outbreak.

*　*　*

Hundreds of miles to the north in Mosul, Saul tried to hold back his trademark smirk, but it was too late. The guard caught the look on face and punched him again, this time on the side of his mouth.

That one hurt, and he shook his head and spat out some blood. He was almost getting used to these daily beatings. Oddly, he almost felt sorry for his captors, and not just for the fact that they were unsaved and doomed. How frustrated they must be at their inability to break him, he often thought.

He had been captured nearly a month before, just before the first outbreak of boils. Over and over the "doctors" of the prison and several of the guards had tried to stamp the Enki Seal on his skin, and all had miserably failed. Even a few others, who he still couldn't figure out what position they held in the prison, had tried but with no success.

They had tried the standard Enki Seals at first, but they simply weren't able to enter his skin. Then they tried various injections, but the needles kept breaking instead of his skin.

But it was his laughing that really infuriated his captors, making their frustration all the worse. He just couldn't help it. He thought of all the different surgical instruments, clubs, knives, and tasers that had been used on him, and for a while he had even tried to maintain a count.

Sometimes his interrogators were struck with an outbreak during the middle of a session, and it was always a relief to get a temporary recess from the torture. Sometimes he would let go and would sing or praise the Lord during a session, and that always nearly drove the guards mad. Other times he quoted Scripture to them. The first time he had done that, they repeatedly clubbed his mouth with a thick metal pipe, but hadn't been able to knock out any teeth, no matter how hard they tried.

He still felt the pain, of course, but his body was becoming so broken and bruised from the continual beatings that he was growing numb to it. He was very sleep-deprived, and couldn't remember the last time he had slept more than two hours straight. They were trying everything they could to break him, and several times he was certain that he had died.

But he had been sealed by the Lord and was unable to be permanently harmed or killed. So for now he was simply the object of their anger and torture. He remembered being shot all over his head and chest, and even feeling the guillotine blade on his neck, yet they had no effect on him – other than terrible pain.

He knew he would survive anything they came up with – that was for sure. His King would be coming soon, and he would be meeting Him in Jerusalem before long. He didn't know how he would make it back there, but he knew he would. He had memorized the entire Book of Revelation months before when he had been free, and mentally recited it at least once a day, even on the bad days.

Soon they would take him back to his freezing cell and blast deafening sounds at him until he would pass out from exhaustion. Sometimes he would talk to them and tell them about Yeshua, but more often he would just remain quiet and continue praying. During the worst of the beatings, he was able to focus so closely on the Lord that he felt entirely disconnected with what was being done to his body. But when he took his mind off the Lord, even for a moment, the pain was nearly overwhelming. So he had learned to stay focused on his Lord.

Thinking back for a brief moment, Saul had been surprised it had taken them so long to arrest him. After all, he was sure that most of Mosul had heard about him. He was the strange

Jewish young man who often, openly spoke out against Medine and preached of repentance and salvation that could only come from Yeshua the Messiah.

He had been there nearly three years, and had been arrested numerous times before, but it wasn't until this last time that he knew he would not be released after only a few days. The converts from his street preaching had rapidly diminished after most of those who had refused the mark had been beheaded. He had gone into hiding several times when he knew they were coming for him, but the last time he had just let them take him – his Lord had told him to.

He couldn't imagine going through a worse time than what he was currently experiencing, yet even that was bearable to some degree. He had rejoiced with loud singing in his cell when he had realized he had finally reached the point at which he had learned to be content in whatever state he found himself in, like the apostle Paul.

That had brought an onslaught of torture for the next hour, until the guards had tired of pounding him with their fists and clubs. But he still felt content.

He clung to his Master and his Friend, and often saw only Him in the midst of his torture, and only heard the calm, soothing voice of His Shepherd over the wail of the mind-numbing sound blasted into his cell.

He would stay until He called for him, and would continue to grow closer to his King.

* * *

David Medine took credit for stopping the plagues of blood upon the waters, and declared that the boils and sores would soon be coming to an end also.

And within days after the plague of the Bloody Waters had passed, as it was called, the people of the earth quickly found that their boils were beginning to clear up. They were still sore and painful, but they no longer broke out as frequently as before, and they were able to somewhat subdue the remaining pain by various creams, lotions, and ointments.

But they refused to change their evil ways and continued to practice all forms of wickedness, and they worshipped Medine more than ever. Now that trade and business had resumed, small statues and idols made in Medine's image were once again distributed all over the earth and everyone in the Ankida religion bowed down to him and his idol.

Since Medine had never been much of a religious person, he had grown increasingly tired of the Ankida religion. But he had found that since ever his resurrection, he craved the worship, respect, adoration, and the praise of others under him. He had noticed other changes in himself, in addition to the power to manipulate matter and perform miraculous deeds, such as the ability to see the many spirit-beings that moved throughout the earth (who were also under his control).

He also had regular interaction with his master Lucifer, the king of the spirits, who was both beautiful and terrifying. He admired and loved his power, and worshipped him openly, and Lucifer continued to give him secrets and power that he could only dream of. And yet he also hated him for the very power he himself craved.

Medine decided to stop toying around with the Ankida religion, and ordered Pontiffica to have the religion begin worshipping him and his master Lucifer directly. There would be no more worship of whatever the people felt like, no more tolerance, and no more mixing of other religions into the Ankida religion. Everyone would worship David Medine directly, and revere Pontiffica as his prophet. Those who refused would be tortured and then slain under the most brutal conditions. Everyone would revere them and worship them, or they would suffer severely – no exceptions.

* * *

Two weeks after the boils of the mark-wearers had cleared up, the sun abruptly became much brighter in the sky, and much hotter.

355

The moon lit up the entire sky at night as if it were morning, and darkness across the face of the earth was nowhere to be found. The scientists and the astronomers were baffled – it was as if the entire surface of the sun had suddenly erupted in tremendous solar flares and an incredible amount of solar radiation was blasting outward from the sun.

Any person unfortunate enough to be caught outdoors found themselves becoming scorched and burnt with third-degree burns within seconds. Inside their shelters, buildings, and homes, the sun was so hot that often the roofs would melt or even catch fire, and the heat trapped inside was so unbearable that many people sweltered and died. [84]

As the sun's heat had suddenly been increased, so had temperatures all across the earth; most of the temperatures increased by over seventy degrees. Those in the coldest of climates found the temperatures to be nearly sweltering and tropical, while those in the formerly warmer climates suffocated and died in the extreme temperatures. Only those who fled into caves or underground had any real chance of survival, and the people cried out from their misery.

At the north and south poles, the great ice sheets and polar ice caps quickly began melting and breaking up. All over the oceans a foggy, thick mist covered the surface of the water. The oceans were heating quickly and evaporating in unbelievable amounts, but there was no rain because the temperatures were too high. It frequently rained at the poles, but that only caused the ice caps to melt faster. It was worse than the global warming advocates could have ever imagined.

In the great city of Babylon, the people were suffering just as much as the rest of the world. But they had the financial and technological resources to dampen the effects of the scorching heat. The World Union put all its available resources into preserving itself through the plague. Everywhere on earth, people cursed Yahweh and the Elohim, and cried out to Medine and the Anshar to save them, but no relief came. And then just as sud-

---

[84] Revelation 16:8-9

denly as the scorching heat had come upon the earth, a great Darkness fell upon the city of Babylon and all its surrounding areas.

The Darkness was not just the absence of sunlight, but a thick, suffocating, terrifying darkness that blacked out all light from every natural and artificial source. No light sources could penetrate it, not even candles, headlights, streetlights, or flashlights. From the images pulled from the satellite cameras above the earth, it appeared that the entire area had been turned into a black hole, in which no light could enter nor escape. The Darkness was so terrifying that people intermittently screamed and gnawed on their tongues because of their fear and anguish.

The citizens of Babylon continued to beg Medine to relieve them of their suffering, yet all the while still cursing their Enemy. But no help ever came. [85]

* * *

Ahban bumped his head against the overhanging cabinet in the kitchen and swore furiously. Sometimes when he closed his eyes, he moved around better than when they were open. Besides, it wasn't nearly as frightening when his eyes were closed – at least then he had some sense of control over the Darkness. At times, he even wore a blindfold whenever he had to walk around. Nothing was more unnerving that looking around with open eyes and seeing nothing but penetrating blackness.

This might be the end of the company, or at least the end of the office in Babylon. Most of their contracts had been completed, but the optimism that had flourished in Babylon had left with the arrival of the Darkness. Perhaps it would return after the plague had been lifted. But Ahban was tired of Babylon – it just didn't feel the same as it had before. It was still incredibly wealthy and full of nightlife and entertainments, and compared to the other cities on the earth, it was still the grandest and most beautiful. But inside, it felt like Babylon was rapidly was burn-

---

[85] Revelation 16:10-11

ing out as quickly as she had risen.

Since the Darkness had come, he had begun having wistful thoughts and memories of his native land of Israel. He found himself missing the familiar little things that he had known most of his life, like the sea, the beaches, the Saturday night celebrations after Shabbat ended, and even small things like the quaint cafés and newspapers. Especially in the unending hours of Darkness, going back home to Israel seemed more and more like what he should do.

He felt old and tired, almost as if he was burning out like Babylon. Yet he was still young and had many years left, but he just no longer felt it.

How could he move back to Israel at this time, though? The entire nation was more or less bottled up and quarantined. He couldn't leave everything behind in Babylon and simply fly back home – what would he do with all his expensive belongings and furniture?

He thought about it for a long time. He still had some seniority left in the company, and had worked hard for them a long time. Perhaps he could put in for a transfer back to Israel, or at least take an extended vacation. He had done everything they had asked of him in Babylon, and more. But over half the people he had worked with years ago were either dead or no longer with the company.

Where were his parents now? He hadn't spoken to them in ages – were they even still alive? Suddenly going back to his homeland was the first and foremost thought in his mind. And what of Saul? He hadn't spoken to him since he had left his apartment over three years before. He doubted his brother was still alive – how could he be? The World Union had slaughtered as many religious Christians and Jews as they could over the last three years. If he did try to find Saul, he might be imprisoned himself (or worse). But they were still brothers, and he at least owed it to his parents to find out what had become of him.

Ahban was very disenchanted with Medine and the whole World Union – they had failed miserably and had lied to everyone time and time again. Now they were worse than any of the other governments and societies that had ever existed, at least those he had studied in school.

Even he as a humanist blanched at the immorality they encouraged throughout the world. Yes, he decided, it was time to go back to Israel.

* * *

While the Darkness covered the region of Babylon, the intense heat and radiation from the sun continued.

Sea levels across the earth had already dropped over ten meters, and no rain had fallen on the earth except over the extreme poles. Many of the rivers had dried up, as their sources had all evaporated, and even some of the largest rivers in the earth stopped flowing completely. The Amazon River in South America was turned into little more than a muddy canyon, as did the Yellow River in China. In the Middle East, both the Tigris and the Euphrates rivers dried up, along with the Jordan River in Israel. And more people began to die of thirst because of the scorching heat and lack of water. [86]

After one full month had passed, the sun suddenly dimmed back to its former intensity. The solar radiation returned to its normal levels, and the inhabitants of the earth found it safe to go outside again. The skies were filled with a thick mist that also made the sun not as bright as before, even before the last two plagues. Surprisingly, the climate was now mostly uniform and tropical across the earth, and plants began to even bud in the deserts that had long been too hot to sustain them. The temperature extremes across the earth had been greatly reduced, and now much larger portions of the earth were habitable, even at the extreme poles.

When the climatologists studied the changes in the earth's temperatures, climate zones, and the atmosphere, they were astounded to discover that another atmospheric layer had been added above the earth, made up mostly of the evaporated water

---

[86] Revelation 16:12

vapor. The new atmospheric layer was also now shielding the earth from many of the sun's harmful rays. [87]

David Medine used those discoveries to reassure the citizens of the world that this had been the earth's way of protecting herself from destruction by the sun, and that it was preparing to evolve into her next phase of fruitfulness and prosperity. But the message was not received with as much acceptance as before.

As the people emerged from their shelters and caves across the face of the earth, the sky that they had just grown accustomed to changed yet again, and was now filled with dark, immense storm clouds. At first, the onlookers smiled at the thought of rain providing them with some needed water and relief.

But their hopes of relief were soon dashed as the first hailstones began falling from the sky. The first several seconds of the hailstorm were met with wonder at the small pea-sized balls of ice, which many people on the earth had never seen before, especially in the tropical regions. But suddenly the size of the hail grew much larger until they were the size of golf-balls, then baseball-sized, and then bowling ball-sized. It was then that the people realized the next plague was upon them. They were going to be stoned to death if they didn't find shelter quickly. [88]

The great hailstorm increased in ferocity until the hailstones were the size of large beach balls, weighing nearly thirty kilograms each. Any person or animal left unsheltered did not survive. The hailstorm continued pounding the earth for three days.

Houses, huts, buildings, cars, roads, and every other mark of civilization was crushed and torn apart by the massive bombardment of ice-stones. When the storm had finally ceased, the survivors emerged from their shelters to find most of the land was covered with huge balls of ice. But at the north and south poles, there were no more ice caps or glaciers, and polar soils that had not seen sunlight for thousands of years began to

---

[87] Many creation scientists surmise that the atmosphere had a 7th layer of water vapor or small ice crystals that blocked much of the harmful solar radiation, enabling the earth's inhabitants to live much longer life spans.

[88] Revelation 16:21, Job 38:22-23

awaken and put forth buds of new life. [89]

The Luciferim and the other Anshar had used their powers over the air, land, water, and other elements to protect Babylon from the terrible hailstorm. At times, Lucifer himself had to intercede to shield the city from the judgment that had been decreed upon the entire earth. But in the end, Babylon escaped much of the damage that had trampled the other cities of the earth.

* * *

Saul felt something warm on his cheek, and for the first time in weeks, he knew the sensation of something other than pain.

It was pleasant, and he had nearly forgotten what that was like. Also, his cell seemed brighter than normal, and he cautiously opened his eyes. The light was intense, and he instinctively closed them, but then started blinking rapidly. It wasn't the searing beams that had been shined into his eyes repeatedly as before, but it was still very bright.

He looked up to see daylight and then smiled as big as he could – even if he was beaten again for showing happiness, it would be worth it. He could still feel the hard floor beneath him, but it seemed like it was tilted and even not as uniformly flat as it had been before. He sniffed the air carefully, and realized that even though it was dusty and smoky, it was somewhat fresh.

Saul glanced around him and saw he was still wearing his familiar tattered, filthy prison clothes, and he was still sore and bruised all over. But he could indeed see sunlight coming down upon him from above and from one of the nearby walls of his prison cell. He knew he should get up or at least move and investigate what was going on, but the light was so comforting that he wanted to just lay there for a long time.

He tried to recollect what had happened while he had been unconscious. During the last week, the guards had been particularly brutal – apparently the air conditioning in the prison had

---

[89] Revelation 16:21

finally given out, and they were nearly as miserable as the prisoners were. But he had found the intense heat in his cell to be somewhat comforting instead of the freezing temperatures they had typically kept it at. He had finally been able to sleep better and under the torture he had endured for months, those hours of rest were precious.

As Saul finally rose to his feet, he could see that a huge earthquake or something had destroyed the entire prison. He looked around and realized he could see through many of the concrete walls. Wires and insulation were exposed and sticking out all over the place, and more surprisingly, there didn't appear to be any guards in sight. He could see large holes and craters on some of the walls, and that puzzled him further. He heard some quiet voices, but they seemed to have tones of excitement rather than fear or anger. And that realization brought a big smile to his face once again.

He began picking his way through the rubble in the direction of some of the voices, and soon found that they were from some of his fellow inmates. One of them, a middle-aged man, appeared to be in as nearly as bad of a condition as he was. A few of the others gasped when they first saw him, and Saul realized that perhaps his injuries were worse than he thought. He had been in solitary confinement since he had been brought into the prison, and the only other humans he'd seen had been his guards and interrogators.

Saul told them who he was and asked what had happened at the prison. He apparently had been either asleep or unconscious when the events that had destroyed the prison had transpired.

There had been an enormous earthquake one said, which had badly cracked the walls. The guards had fled during the earthquake, and had all left the prisoners to die when the roof had begun to collapse. But it never fully did, and though the prisoners had all been tempted to flee, some of them were familiar with the Book of Revelation and knew what would happen next, and convinced the others to stay put in their cells. Some of the prisoners had ignored them anyway, and had foolishly fled into the open.

That explained the most of the rubble and the massive interior damage to the prison, but what they told him next surprised him even more. At first, everyone had heard a faint clattering sound that steadily grew louder until it was a deafening pounding all above them.

Many had taken cover in the corners or under the larger sections of the walls and ceilings that were still intact. A huge hailstorm had struck just after the earthquake, and many of the pieces of hail were the size of large balls. Many had furiously exploded when they struck the earth or the concrete of the prison. Whatever remained of the hailstones had quickly melted in the desert heat when the storm was over.

Saul thought carefully and seemed to remember having intense dreams of a rumbling and shaking, and even some loud hammering going on all around him. He thought it had just been a dream, but evidently it had not. The hailstorm at the prison had lasted for hours, according to one who had seen a clock in the rubble.

He asked what they should do next – where would they go? Where could they escape to that would be safe from being captured again? And that was what they had been discussing when Saul had first heard their voices.

Some said they were going underground again in safehouses nearby, while others said they were going to scatter elsewhere. There was about fifteen prisoners all together, and two said they were heading down the Euphrates River to the coast. Saul thought for a moment, and remembered what would be coming next on the prophetic timeline, and then asked to accompany them. They readily agreed, and after they picked themselves out of the rubble of the prison, they bid the others farewell, and then set out on their separate ways.

As the prisoners emerged from the debris, what they saw shocked them to silence. The area all around the prison had been completely pummeled and devastated. There was rubble from buildings everywhere, along with ruined vehicles, and even bodies strewn about. Many of the cars and trucks had huge holes in their roofs, hoods, and trunks.

Often, they could see the drivers still in their vehicles where they had been struck down from the great hail. Huge pockmarks and craters covered the land as far as their eyes could see, making the wilderness around them look like the ravaged surface of the moon.

* * *

Saul and his two companions had been following the Euphrates River southeast for two days, or at least what was left of it. They had expected to encounter the familiar sights, sounds, and smells of the great river, but what they found was a dried up riverbed, pocked with great holes and craters just like the desert sands they had recently left.

The riverbed stunk terribly from the carcasses of thousands upon thousands of dead fish of all types and sizes. They held their noses at first and began to move away from the riverbed, and then realized that they would encounter far fewer people if they stayed close to it. So they stuffed small pieces of their clothing into their nostrils and covered the lower part of their faces as tightly as they could, and set off down the Euphrates.

When they finally came to the outskirts of Babylon, Saul headed into the city while the others tried to find food. They would meet at a place back near the river later that evening, and then would go their separate ways from there. Saul (and hopefully Ahban) would go north, while they would head south and reach the coast in the next week or so, if they were not captured.

As Saul walked through the city, he marveled out how little it had been damaged in the last plague of the hail, though the rest of the countryside was pocked with craters. With the sparing of the city from the last judgment, perhaps the people would be more open to the warning of the further wrath ahead. Yet Babylon had never been a city of repentance or humility, and from what he remembered from the Scriptures, there would be little hope for those who lived in Babylon.

He went up to Ahban's apartment and found the door unlocked. Was he dead or injured? Saul felt a pang of fear and rushed in. He found Ahban sitting inside his apartment, watching the news with a drink nearby. From his dazed look, he was quite drunk, or was well on his way.

Saul was relieved when he saw his older brother, who hadn't really noticed him yet. A brief memory of their previous fights and disagreements fleeted across his mind, but he pushed them away. He felt nothing but love and compassion for his brother, and he wanted to comfort him and help him get out of the city while there was still time.

"Ahban!" Saul called out, now just a few meters away from him. "Ahban, it's me – Saul!"

He was relieved again when Ahban finally looked up and recognized him. A big smile came over his face, but then somewhat diminished, as if he was ashamed or something.

"Hey, little brother!" he replied in his familiar way. "What are you doing here?" he asked. His speech was slow and slurry. As he looked Saul over, he grimaced and said, "What happened to you? You look about as bad as I feel!"

"That's an understatement. Listen, we need to get out of the city. Some friends of mine are waiting for us by the river. Let's go!"

At first, Ahban hesitated and looked around at his apartment, still filled with all his belongings and furniture. He thought of staying, but what was left for him there? Nothing. He could always hire someone to pack and ship everything back to Israel. He just didn't care anymore. He was worn out from everything that was happening, and just wanted to be free again.

He looked around again and nodded, and then replied, "Well, seeing as how I don't have anything better to do at the moment, why not?" He stood up and shook himself off. "Where are we going, little brother?" he asked.

"Back to Israel! Back home!" Saul replied, and he slapped him on the arm.

And those were the best words that Ahban had heard in a very long time. He grinned and downed the rest of his drink.

*   *   *

After three weeks, Daniel had mostly recovered from the crash. He had been fortunate to make it to one of the better-equipped safe-houses outside Haifa. A doctor who had also gone underground examined him, and he was found to have some deep bruising and a minor concussion. His neck and back were still sore, but nothing had been broken or dislocated.

The recovery time had forced him to prayerfully consider what he was to do next. The Underground Railroad was now running quite well without him and besides, it would only be needed for one more month. One month! He almost couldn't believe it – mere weeks until the return of the King (as many involved in the Underground Railroad referred to it).

He had always liked reading those old J.R.R. Tolkien novels, but now that the time of the final battle was approaching, he cherished it even more. Like the book, the true heir would soon be revealed and take His place as the King of the earth.

Perhaps his race was not yet finished, and he was determined to finish well and finish strong. He studied the Scriptures while he recovered and saw another opportunity to do good and save lives, even among the lost. He listened to the rumors and read the reports from his sources, and knew that the armies of the world were mobilizing and would soon be moving towards Israel. Soon Babylon would be destroyed and then Jerusalem would be besieged. After that, the Messiah would return just before the massive thrust towards Jerusalem to destroy it for the final time.

Daniel considered what Medine and the World Union forces would attempt to do to Jerusalem. They could drop nuclear bombs on it for sure, but that didn't seem to be his style. He was convinced that Medine wanted the last Jewish holdouts to suffer tremendously, as evidenced by the dozens of concentration camps throughout Israel.

Also, Medine would want to plow Jerusalem under just like his Roman predecessors had done long ago. No buildings had remained after they had leveled it, except for some of the poorer homes and walls that they didn't bother to completely tear down. The Scriptures were clear that Jerusalem would be besieged and then fall to the Beast, but not leveled.

What could he do to further help his people and the captives in Jerusalem? Even though food and medical supplies were a huge part of the black market after the mark of the beast, weapons of all kinds still made up a significant share of the black market transactions. He could cultivate his contacts and associates in the underground and perhaps purchase or trade for weapons to help his people defend themselves during the final battle of Jerusalem. And even though he knew the city would ultimately fall, at least he could help delay it and save some lives.

He began studying detailed maps of Jerusalem – where it was most defensible and where it was the least. The topography maps and detailed street-level maps proved to be invaluable, and he spent hours pouring over them, marking them up, and making plans. When he was finished several days later, he rescanned the maps and uploaded them to one of the secure sites. He then told a few of his closest contacts in the Underground Railroad, in the event that he was caught or something happened to him.

After his planning had been finished, he began contacting some of the shadier figures in the black market and began procuring weapons, bullets, and other munitions the holdouts would need. Shipping and storage would not be as nearly as big of a problem as it would be shipping them into the city before it was fully under siege. The only real option was to have all the weapons and munitions shipped directly into the city itself, and as deep inside the city as possible.

He had a good number of contacts, stations, and safe-houses in and around Jerusalem, and they would need to be brought on board with his plans immediately. He was reasonably sure that they would agree to them, even though it meant a much higher risk on their part. He had a feeling that once the city came under siege, many of the Israeli and Jerusalem police would turn and side with their fellow Jews than stay loyal to the invading World Union forces. Eventually, Medine would certainly have them slaughtered also.

After two more days, all the remaining details of the plan had been finished and the munitions began to flow along the

Underground Railroad into Jerusalem. Daniel disguised himself and then took it into the city as well. As he entered the city, he could already feel an unspoken fear growing among the people. They knew what was coming, and they would prepare for the worst.

* * *

David Medine and Franco Pontiffica were summoned to appear before their master, the god of the earth: Lucifer, the brilliant, shining figure they feared and obeyed. He had been commanding them and directing their every move since before Medine's resurrection. The time had come to finish what he had started thousands of years before: the destruction of his enemies.

And as the two men knelt before the shining creature of light, strange spirits that had the appearance of frogs suddenly began streaming from each of their mouths. They choked and fell over, but the spirits continued to emerge from within them. A few moments later, the spirits coalesced in front of Lucifer and the two men returned to their kneeling position, rubbing their sore throats.

The frog-like spirits morphed and solidified, and took the forms of the Luciferim, and then swept out of the Tower. They sought out all the rulers of the earth, and began counseling them to gather their armies for the final war of the earth.

And so they did – the rulers and leaders of the earth gathered all men and women who could fight. The great Enemy of the Anshar was coming to destroy the earth and all who were in it. The Anshar also came to the earth in even greater numbers, and pressured the nations to gather their forces against the Elohim. [90]

The armies of men mustered themselves for the war of wars, and would soon began moving towards the tiny land of Israel, the nation that sat in the center of the three great continents.

For it was in the land of Israel that Yahweh and the Elohim would launch their final assault on the earth.

---

[90] Revelation 16:13-16

CHAPTER 15
THE FALL OF TWO CITIES

The World Union as a working government was in shambles. The last series of plagues had destroyed nearly all its infrastructure that did not reside in Babylon. The very top levels of the World Union government remained intact, along with the military arm which was based mostly in and around the world capital.

But the World Union army itself was no longer the superpower it had once been, but that had been by design. Months before, David Medine had loosened his iron grip on the national and multi-national military forces and let them grow, giving the impression that the World Union's might was weak and faltering. In reality, the World Union forces were growing stronger.

Medine knew the other armies from the north, east, west, and south would be coming towards Israel soon. But they were walking into a trap – into their own destruction. His goal was to draw them into Megiddo, a huge plain in Israel, and have them finally slaughter every living Jew in the nation. And then he would use his power and influence to cause them to vanquish one another.

In the end, he and his loyal army would be the only ones left, and then he would begin rebuilding the earth. The population of the earth was now less than half a billion people. But that was fine with Medine – the fewer people there were, the better he would be able to control, shape, and mold them.

The remains of the great armies of the earth were being gathered quickly, most even faster than he had anticipated. The sooner the better, he supposed. He would leave it to the other armies to engage the rebels in Jerusalem, while he moved his main divisions southward to destroy the rock city of Petra and slaughter all who were in its havens.

But he had to move quickly – his master was furious that the rebels (and any of the Jews, for that matter) were still alive. Lucifer was insistent that if those in Petra were destroyed, the Enemy would not return. Then there would be nothing to stand in their way of their subjugation of the world. After he was finished in Petra, he would turn back to Jerusalem and finish off whatever armies of his enemies that remained.

Both the Luciferim and the Anshar were now very much in the public eye, and they continually warned of the great battle with Yahweh and the Elohim that was approaching. They reiterated that mankind had almost finished their progression to the next stage of evolution. What lay ahead would be the worst battle in all of human history, but if they fought hard and stayed true to Medine and their destiny, mankind would emerge from these days of war into the promised golden age of peace.

Though the world would be pushed to the absolute brink of destruction, they would emerge into an eternal paradise.

* * *

"Get down! Get down! If they see you, we're all dead!" Ahban hissed at his brother, who quickly ducked as low as he could and pulled a cover over his head.

Saul and Ahban, along with several others, were crowded into the rear of an open-backed truck. They were stopped by security at the northern border of Iraq, and they could see the bright searchlights shining in front of the truck, and smaller lights flashing behind them from the approaching security agents. Only one of the stowaways had a gun, aside from the driver, who had presumably hidden his within easy reach.

All of them doubted they would fire their guns though; otherwise the better-equipped border security would overpower them within seconds. Besides, the truck was much too slow for a getaway, and they would be quickly overtaken if they attempted any type of escape. It just wasn't worth the risk – at least not yet.

Everyone in the truck stopped moving and made no sound. The driver was talking rapidly, explaining that he had to leave the truck running, otherwise it might not start up again. And judging from how the truck rattled and shook most of the time, it probably wasn't far from the truth.

They heard one of the soldiers reluctantly agree, but ordered him to keep both his hands on the wheel. The rumbling of the truck disguised all of the sounds of breathing and slight movements in the back. The lights flashed over the boxes and covers from one side of the truck to the other. One of the guards briefly lifted a cover or two near the tailgate, but they didn't search any deeper. After several minutes, they heard the driver thank the border guards, and felt the truck shift into gear, and then it rumbled on its way across the Iraqi border. No one in the back moved, but everyone quietly breathed a sigh of relief.

When they had first met up with Saul's companions outside Babylon, one of them mentioned the Underground Railroad, and then explained what it was and how it worked. It sounded exactly like what Saul and Ahban were looking for. The others were heading back to either their homelands or for safer regions away from the Middle East, but Saul and Ahban were not.

Their companions were heading away from the war zone, but Saul and Ahban wanted to go directly into the heart of it. And not only did they want to go into Israel, but to Jerusalem! One of their companions gave them the address of a hidden Underground Railroad station in a village north of Babylon. He also gave them the protocol (a simple password and answer to a strange Bible question) that would help the station's "conductor" know that they were safe to trust.

Saul and Ahban knew they wouldn't be able to go directly to Israel, since the entire nation was sealed off. They would get as close as they could and then have to sneak their way in by whatever means possible. Syria bordered both Iraq and Israel at the Golan Heights, and that would be the quickest route. But the security at the Golan would be tighter than ever, so they would have to go south into Jordan first. From there, it wouldn't be too difficult (or so they hoped) to get back into Israel, especially close to Jerusalem. From what they had learned, the Underground Railroad was much more active in and around Israel and its immediate neighbors than in Iraq and the other Middle Eastern countries.

They stayed hidden in the truck until the driver banged on the back of his cab, signaling that it was safe. The northern lands of Iraq had been little more than wilderness for many years, and it was even worse now after six years of destruction and neglect. Refueling stations would be scarce in northern Iraq and Syria, and probably even in Israel now. So they had stowed several large containers of gasoline in the back, along with food and water. On the Underground Railroad in Iraq, the volunteers were no longer trying to move people into Israel as much as moving them out of Babylon and its vicinity. They had carefully studied the Scriptures about what John, Isaiah, and Jeremiah had written about the final days of Babylon, and her deadline with destiny was rapidly approaching.

Over an hour later, the driver pulled off onto an empty dirt road and stopped, and turned off the truck. Everyone slowly emerged from the back and took a traveling break. But they couldn't rest for long – five minutes was about all they could afford, and soon they were off again. They changed drivers and settled back into their hiding places, just in case the truck was suddenly stopped by a border patrol. The journey was long and boring, but no one complained of their discomfort. They all knew that there things much worse than long, uncomfortable rides through the desert.

The next morning, they were stopped at the border of Syria and Jordan, and promptly ushered through. Jordan was one of the few countries still allowing visitors to enter, mostly because they typically brought in money from Iraq. Everyone breathed a collective sigh of relief to finally be in Jordan.

Saul and Ahban would stay with the others until they arrived at their destination in Amman. From there, the two brothers would head south and then sneak across the eastern border of Israel near the Jordan River. The others had tried to convince them to go all the way to Petra, but neither wanted to. Their homeland was under siege, and Saul and Ahban wanted to stand with their country in her darkest hour.

Later that day, the two brothers found another safe-house and both slept well that night, finally out of immediate danger and no longer sitting in a bouncing, rumbling truck.

*   *   *

Daniel turned up the volume of his small pocket radio and drew a long breath. The end was near – they could all feel it – he and all the leaders of the militias in Jerusalem. The others were gathered around a table covered with laptops, cords, and phones. One of the IT personnel leaned over a computer, checking the connections and cables. On the empty wall opposite the table, a clear image suddenly appeared and came into focus. The technician looked up and then made some minor adjustments before sitting down in front.

The room quickly became quiet and everyone gazed intently at the makeshift projector screen. It was streaming video footage from an Israeli satellite that had eluded the World Union's attention. They could clearly make out the familiar shapes of the lands and rivers and deserts of the Middle East, with Israel being at the center of the screen. Most of the map was quite clear, except for some blurry lines that looked like they were being drawn together from the east and the south, and even some faint streams from the north. As they watched, some of the lines seemed to be converging towards Israel, and they could make out faint black spots all over the faded lines.

Just east of Babylon, they could make out much thicker, but blurrier lines with numerous pin-sized dark spots in it. But that line seemed directed towards Babylon, and not Israel. They all knew what they were seeing on the screen, and what all the blurry lines were: they were the enormous clouds of dust, smoke, and exhaust coming from the vehicles of the remaining armies of the world. All the armies appeared to be heading for the Middle East. And more than half of them were moving rapidly in the direction of Israel.

One of the militia leaders walked over to stand near the image, and turned to face the crowded room. "May I have your attention please!" he called out. "Thank you. As you can see from the screen, the military forces from all over the world are all moving towards Israel. The blurred sections you see here are the mobile units, tanks, supply trucks, and other vehicles," he said, pointing to the lines all inching towards central Israel.

"To the east of Babylon, we have the armies of the Near East, India and Central Asia, and the Far East converging. The large mass here is the Chinese."

That announcement drew gasps from the room; no nation had ever roused the great Chinese army in over eighty years. As a nation, the Chinese still had more people than any other on earth. Even after the last seven years of devastation, they could still field an army of well over five million men. And from the clouds on the screen, it looked like they were all on the move.

"Sir, where is their staging area? Lebanon?" one of the other leaders called out.

"Part of it may be in Lebanon," he replied. "But we presume that most of it will be here in our own backyard: the Valley of Megiddo, near the Sea of Galilee. Most of you may know that as 'Armageddon'." And that statement drew even more gasps from those in the room, and then everyone was silent.

"I don't need to tell any of you what they're coming here for – you all know it. These forces mean to stage the next war here in our land. Of course, all of them will attempt to take Jerusalem first and then use the Jordan as the main front. Whoever controls Jerusalem controls Israel, and whoever controls Israel will end up controlling much of the Middle East," he stated solemnly.

Daniel could have quibbled at the commander's reasoning for the approaching armies, but he didn't want to debate Scripture with them right now. Most of the militia and their leaders were either secular or Orthodox – he was one of the few Christians among them, and he preferred to not ruffle any feathers among his own, at least not yet.

THE TIME OF JACOB'S TROUBLE

But what he had said was probably true, at least for most of the people in the room. All the armies of the world had been roused, and were rushing towards Israel for the Final Battle – the War to End All Wars. All the military forces in the world had been awakened all at once, and were in a mad dash to Israel.

The ragtag militia in Jerusalem still had much to do to prepare for the siege; it was despairing to watch the hordes steadily roll westward, northward, and southward through the deserts. Every so often, the projection switched from the satellite view to live coverage of the forces streaming towards the Middle East.

Most of the Jerusalem militia was made up of former IDF soldiers and reserves, and the rest were residents of Jerusalem and many others who had gathered to help them. They were adequately supplied with weapons and ammunition, thanks to Daniel and the others involved in the Underground Railroad and the black market. If anything, the World Union had made the black market economy flourish because of their harsh economic policies and the mandatory use of the mark.

The militia leaders were desperate, and many of them had even resorted to studying what the Tanakh said would happen to Jerusalem during the final battle. They had recently taken a number of steps to use those prophecies to their advantage, such as making sure the eastern portion of the city was clear for the people to flee through when the Mount of Olives split and broke through the city. Another strategy involved bulldozing large portions of the city that were just inside the walls, blocking the streets and roads. The rubble would not keep the invaders out even after they broke through the walls, but it would slow them down and prevent them from immediately bringing in their tanks and other heavy artillery.

The strategy meeting continued for the next hour, as they reviewed the status of the city's defenses, their military resources, the civilian leaders, and the other miscellaneous reports. Most of the civilians were scared, yet determined. The people of Jerusalem were conducting themselves exceptionally well, knowing that if they didn't work together, very few of them would survive the siege.

From the Scriptures, Daniel knew that Jerusalem would indeed fall and be taken, and many of its inhabitants raped, killed, and taken captive. But soon after the city was overrun, Yeshua would return to the summit of the Mount of Olives. The mountain would then split in two, with half moving to the north and half to the south, creating a great valley from just inside the eastern wall all the way to the other side of the mountain range for the survivors in Jerusalem to flee through.

Later that day, one of the leaders he had seen earlier in the briefing came up to him in a cautious manner. He told him that Daniel had to come with him immediately, and that it was extremely important. Daniel's guard instantly went up, but he followed the officer anyway. For days, there had been rumors floating throughout the city that spies from Medine and the World Union had infiltrated them, and were monitoring and reporting all their activities. They had discussed this several times in their strategic meetings, and had decided to just be on guard, but not hold hearings with any suspects unless it was absolutely necessary. The leaders were quietly guarded, at least the more senior members were, and several undercover units were planted among the citizenry in an attempt to quietly track down Medine's spies, if they existed.

Daniel followed the officer back to the building where the meeting had been held earlier and they walked down into one of the secure areas. They entered into another large room that was crowded with older men that he had never seen before. All of them looked uneasy and very afraid.

The officer began introducing him to the new faces – they were all who were left of the Sanhedrin! They were no longer dressed in nice suits and robes, but normal street clothes so they would not attract much attention. They had been in hiding for over a year, and had not shown their faces in public for months. Rumors had frequently circulated that all the Sanhedrin had been arrested or taken to one of the many concentration camps.

The leader of the Sanhedrin, the High Priest who had replaced the one who David Medine had murdered, approached

Daniel and introduced himself.

There was little time for idle talk, and the High Priest immediately stated his request: he wanted Daniel to smuggle the rest of the Sanhedrin to Petra before it was too late. They had seen and heard of the miracles that were happening there, and how it had been supernaturally protected against the World Union's numerous attacks. They needed to be moved immediately, perhaps even that night before Medine's forces could fully prevent their escape.

Daniel immediately agreed, and came up with a plan among the other militia leaders in the room. Supply trucks were still allowed in and out of Jerusalem through the southern gate, and they quickly arranged to put the Sanhedrin into one of the trucks that would not be likely to be stopped. The eastern border of Israel with Jordan near Petra was virtually non-existent, and Daniel contacted several of the Underground Railroad stations near Petra and arranged for them to be smuggled into Petra.

The plans were solidified and put into action, and later that night the Sanhedrin were smuggled out of Jerusalem and were quickly on their way south into the wilderness.

* * *

Jacob carried the two small water containers to the Spoken Spring. He could have just gone down to the river that flowed out from it, but then they would have to filter the water or let it settle out for an hour or so.

Going directly to the source meant the freshest, coldest water, and he needed his morning walk anyway. He frequently brought his Bible with him when he got their daily water, and then would find a quiet place just off the path where he could read, pray, and think. After he finished, he would go to the spring and get their daily water supply.

As he approached the great spring, several others were already there, and he smiled and nodded to them in a quiet greeting. He was a little late that morning; he had spent extra time reading the Bible and praying.

He had been studying the Book of Hebrews for the last two weeks – it was one of the New Testament books he still had difficulty with. Most of the others he understood, but Romans, Galatians, and especially Hebrews he still didn't fully comprehend (or agree with at times). Some referred to those three as the Trilogy of Faith, because the main point of all three was "The just shall live by faith". He understood the faith part, but he still couldn't understand how God could simply replace the "old covenant" of the Law with the "new covenant" of the Spirit. Perhaps he was still blinded to it or something.

He went to the other side of the spring and began filling the containers. The water was ice-cold and crystal-clear. It had been that way since it had first appeared. Soon after the camp had been settled, the pumps failed and all their water supplies had finally run out, and the people had begun to talk of leaving the camp. At that time, the leaders of the Council had gathered and told the entire camp to begin praying and fasting, and to do so for three days. The people obeyed and everyone abstained from food and their normal activities, and focused on praying to the Lord concerning their problem with the water supply.

At the end of the three days, the leaders called all the people together and led them to a large rock near the east side of their camp, which appeared to be alongside a river that had dried up many centuries before. The riverbed ran down toward a large basin in the ground, evidently a pool or reservoir used in the ancient times of Petra's history. The leaders stood before the great rock and read the story from Exodus 17, the passage in which Moses and the ancient Israelites had the same problem (lack of water) in the wilderness. Moses had prayed to the Lord and then struck the rock to make the waters flow out, and it appeared that was what the leaders of the Council were attempting to do.

The Council leaders prayed and then all struck the rock in unison, and immediately they heard a great rumbling sound coming from deep inside the rock. And then it split in two, right down the center. From the inside of the rock, water began pouring out in a great torrent on either side. Several of the leaders became drenched when they had not stepped back quickly enough.

THE TIME OF JACOB'S TROUBLE

All the people fell on their faces and gave thanks to the Lord. And then the leaders began directing them in an orderly fashion to go fill their water containers from the new river.

Seven days later the Stricken Spring, as the leaders had named it, stopped flowing nearly as quickly as it had begun. Some had even seen it cease as they had been filling their containers, and ran back to tell the leaders. Fortunately, most of the people had already obtained their water for the day and shared with any who were still thirsty. Understanding the Scriptures and the model that God had provided in the Tanakh about Yeshua's life, they told the people that they would wait three days, and then gather again. Until then, the people should again pray and fast, but this time with much grief and mourning, as if their firstborn son had died.

Early in the morning three days later, the leaders called all the people together at a large rock further down the riverbed from the Stricken Spring. And there they once again prayed with all the people, and then read Numbers 20, in which God had told Moses to speak to the rock in order to produce water from it. But Moses had disobeyed and had stricken the rock as he had done before, and then God punished him by preventing him from entering the Promised Land. But the Council leaders had understood Moses' error, and they would not repeat his mistake.

After they finished reading the passage, they prayed again, and then the leaders began speaking to the rock. They didn't pray to it, of course, but fervently asked God to forgive their unbelief and to produce water from it. And just after they had begun speaking, they heard a rumbling sound like what had happened before, and the new rock split apart and produced an even greater flow of water than the Stricken Spring. Once again, the people prayed and thanked God for His Providence.

And so they named the new one the Spoken Spring, since the waters had been spoken from the rock. And unlike the Stricken Spring, the Spoken Spring did not dry up after a week, and had continued flowing as strong as it had the first moment it had been opened from within the rock.

Jacob's water containers were quickly filled, and he thanked the Lord as he always did. He began the long walk back, and greeted others as they passed by with their own containers and jugs. He didn't mind carrying the water for him and Naomi; she took care of their living quarters and he brought them water and other supplies. But both had to gather their own manna every morning, and they usually did that after he returned with the water. If they waited too long in the day before gathering it, the sun would make it melt and they would go hungry that day. So far, it had only happened once to him, and after that he had never missed their Daily Bread, as many called it.

He and Naomi frequently talked about their children, especially Saul and Ahban. It had been over two years since they had spoken to either of them. They often wondered if they were even still alive, especially Ahban since they assumed he was still living in Babylon. Every day, they prayed for the well-being of their two sons, and that God would protect them and watch over them during this time.

He had not become a Christian like Naomi, even after reading through the New Testament several times and attending many sermons about Yeshua being the Messiah and about His Second Coming. He was no longer hostile to it, but had not converted either.

Most of the rest of the camp had converted to Christianity over the last three years, but there were still a number of Jews that held to their orthodoxy. Even a number of the leaders of the Jewish organizations had converted, but they didn't press it on their people. In fact, there was surprisingly little pressure by either side to convert others, and they tried their best to keep together as a people, even though their beliefs were different. But the foundations of both beliefs were essentially the same: the God of the Bible and the ancient Scriptures. Sometimes there were heated exchanges and arguments between individual Jews and Christians, but they never became violent or overly divisive.

Jacob looked up and saw the familiar sights of the landscape around their tent, and breathed a short sigh of relief – he was almost there. He quietly carried the containers up to the shady side of their tent, careful to not wake his wife. After he set them down, he straightened up and stretched.

He was about to go into their tent when he heard her quietly praying, and he turned away to give her privacy. But as he turned to leave, he heard her quietly speak his name as she prayed, and he stopped to listen out of curiosity. He felt a little guilty about eavesdropping, and he would apologize later if need-be.

As he listened, he could hear her pouring out her heart to Yeshua, pleading with Him to bring her husband in to His Family. Tears suddenly came to his eyes, as he was moved at how much she still loved him and how concerned she was for him. She also prayed for Saul and Ahban and their camp, but she soon came back to praying for him. She continued to intercede for him, asking God to remove whatever blindness, walls, or other obstacles that were preventing him from choosing Yeshua as his Messiah and Savior.

He wiped his eyes, picked up his Bible, and silently backed away from their tent, and began walking back down the path, towards the Stricken Spring.

Why was he really still holding out? Christianity was not the anti-Jewish, hate-filled religion he had always thought it was. Aside from the Trinity, he could not see how the New Testament was contrary to the Tanakh. And even with that, he could see how having a Triune God explained some of the textual oddities in the Tanakh.

He decided to try to finish the Book of Hebrews and better understand it once he reached the Stricken Spring. Perhaps the Lord would help him understand and answer his questions.

* * *

David Medine had studied and mastered many of history's greatest military maneuvers. He was a military genius on the level of Alexander the Great, Napoleon, and Cyrus the Great.

But like his predecessors, he too suffered from an overabundance of arrogance and pride that blinded him to the intentions and fortitude of his enemies. He left Babylon with nearly all of his military forces and moved up into Syria and then rapidly south into Israel.

The miniscule IDF border forces that remained were quickly overrun in the north and defeated. Medine had ordered his troops to take no prisoners and leave none alive. With his path to Jerusalem unobstructed, he would quickly isolate the city and then head to Petra with the main bulk of his forces.

But he underestimated the resolve of the feeble remnant of Israel. Part of their military leadership was still intact and had gone underground over two years before, waiting for Medine to either lessen his pressure on their nation or make his final strike. While underground, they were able to cobble together enough nuclear weapons to be able to launch a crude (though still deadly) version of the Samson Option when the need arose.

As they watched Medine and the World Union approach their borders, the IDF leaders warned him to halt his invasion. They informed him that they had a significant nuclear arsenal and that they would use it upon their oil-rich neighbors if he crossed their borders. But Medine had scorned them and only drove his troops faster towards Israel. When Medine finally entered the northern border, the IDF decided to use the Samson Option while they still could. They could not remain hidden for long once he was in their midst. They notified the Sanhedrin of their decision, and then launched nearly all the nuclear weapons in their possession.

The nuclear missiles had been set to target the cities of all Israel's neighbors months before and could not be changed to strike at only the armies coming from the north – the invasion forces were too mobile. Even their relatively peaceful neighbors like Jordan and Egypt were targeted, not because they were at war with Israel, but because the invading armies would have to go through them to reach Israel. This would not only hamper their enemies but force them into only invading from the north. Then they would try to reduce the size of the northern front down to less than twenty kilometers.

It was a similar strategy as Leonidus had used at the Battle of Thermopylae, when the Greeks were up against a huge invasion force and had only a small handful of troops. But this was on a much larger scale. The invaders would be funneled into a small space and be prevented from using their overwhelming numbers. The IDF would force them into the plains of Megiddo, where the more-agile Israeli tanks would be most effective.

When it was clear the Medine had crossed their borders and had no intention of ceasing the invasion, the leaders of the IDF gave the order to launch the Sampson Option. Within minutes, over twenty cities in the Middle East were completely destroyed by her nuclear weapons. Israel would not go down without bringing her enemies down with her.

Not only had the IDF targeted their immediate neighbors, but they also attacked the ports, cities, and major oil producing centers of Yemen, Saudi Arabia, and the Arab Emirates. They had also attacked Iraq, but Iraq's missile shield rendered their missiles useless. Regardless of whether Israel and the Jews survived, there were now far fewer of their enemies left. [91]

When Medine had pulled his forces out of Syria and into Israel, the armies of India and the remnants of the Islamic republics swept in to surround Babylon. Medine's enemies had been waiting for this opportunity for the last two years. They quickly sealed off the city and then sent the bulk of their armies northwest to follow after Medine and attack him from behind when he was bottled up in Israel.

They didn't want to destroy Babylon, but merely capture it and hold it hostage. But less than five hundred kilometers east of the city, another army was steadily rolling westward: the great and terrible armies of China and the Far Eastern nations. [92]

As the city was surrounded, a great earthquake suddenly struck, with its very epicenter at Babylon. Every city, island, mountain, and every tall building on the earth collapsed from the terrible shaking. Even the great city of Babylon was nearly leveled, and it split into three sections centered on the Tower of Illumination, which now lay in ruins. The cities of all the nations

---

[91] Zechariah 12:6
[92] Jeremiah 51:44-49

were brought down to the ground, and few mountains and islands remained higher than several hundred meters. [93]

* * *

The security forces of Babylon had been on full alert for a week as they watched the great armies from the Near East and the Far East roll westward. But the armies of the East had assured Medine that they would not lift a finger against Babylon, and that they were merely passing by the great city to re-supply and re-fuel on their way to Israel. Medine did not trust them, but their forces were too huge for him to even consider opposing. He quietly put the security forces on alert in Babylon, and waited to see what they did next. If they attacked his city, his wrath against them would be swift and terrible.

As the armies of the East gathered near Babylon, another great army suddenly swept down from the north. It was the remnants of the once great Russian army, combined with many of the former-Soviet-bloc nations from the Cold War. Russia and her satellite republics had been nearly silent since their humiliating defeat at the Magog Invasion, but they had been secretly, steadily rebuilding their forces and vast weapons stores.

Their ambitions had not changed in thousands of years: the conquest of the entire continent of Asia. Since the times of their ancestors, the Scythians, had subdued the vast lands of the north all the way to the East, the Russians had never given up their goal of conquering the largest landmass on earth. This time, they had not wasted their resources on slow-moving tanks, trucks, and manpower, but had put all their resources into their air forces. Just as their Scythian ancestors had relied upon the speed and stealth of their horses and lightning-like strikes, so they would rely upon their jetfighters.

After the destruction of their armies in Israel over seven years earlier, the Russian bear had licked its wounds and went into hibernation. At the highest levels, her government and military

---

[93] Revelation 16:18-20

leaders began studying Bible prophecy. But it wasn't for the purpose of repentance or salvation, but to gain an understanding of what would happen in the future. Their supernatural defeat in Israel had humiliated them. Many argued that they would not have sided with the Muslims to invade Israel if they had taken Bible prophecy seriously.

When the Anshar and David Medine arrived on the scene of world politics and power, the Russians presented them and the rest of the world with the image of a destroyed, defeated people. But just as during the decades after the Cold War, she quietly rebuilt and reorganized, and waited for the opportunity to strike again and regain her reputation.

From the intense, systematic study of Bible prophecy, the Russians understood that the best time to overthrow Medine and the World Union would be when they moved against Jerusalem. The Russians had never felt any great love for Israel, or any nation other than their own, for that matter. They saw Medine's extreme, irrational anti-Semitism as a weakness – and an opportunity to recapture control of much of the world's oil supply. All the armies of the world were streaming towards Israel, and Babylon would be left nearly defenseless. If they could seize control of Babylon, they could cut out the heart of the World Union and then finally have the upper hand against Medine.

The Russians had also been discreetly cultivating secret alliances with China and many of the other Eastern nations, who despised Medine nearly as much as the Russians did. They agreed to join forces and would keep Medine distracted so the Russians could attack suddenly and swiftly. In exchange for their cooperation, Russia offered the Chinese all of Africa (rich in natural resources) and India (rich in intellectual resources), along with half of the oil reserves in the Middle East. The Russians would then take much of Asia, Europe, and the rest of the Middle East. When they were finished, there would be no more World Union, but a world ruled by the two largest nations in the world: Russia and China.

As Medine and his forces surrounded Jerusalem and began their siege, the armies of the East were in place just to the east of Babylon. A great black cloud suddenly appeared in the sky and covered the entire city and all its outlying regions, much like the plague of Darkness had before. Then brilliant lightning began falling from the cloud in tremendous bursts and streams, lighting up the whole sky over Babylon, even though it was the middle of the day.

Without warning, countless jets and bombers descended upon Iraq from the far north, all the way from Russia and the southern republics. Russia's new air forces were incredibly stealth and fast, and moved deep into Iraq so quickly that Medine himself was caught off-guard. He furiously ordered that the Russians remove themselves at once from Iraqi airspace and come to Israel, but the Russians ignored him.

By the time Medine gave the orders to send a portion of his own air forces back to Iraq to fend off the threat, the Russian air forces attacked and dropped dozens of neutron bombs on Babylon and its suburbs. They wanted to destroy the city yet leave its oil resources intact, but early on they had realized that would be very difficult. The oil deposits were just too close to the surface to leave them completely unaffected. Perhaps they could detonate the bombs just above the city enough to destroy it, yet not damage the oil deposits. The Russian planners had made their calculations carefully and were confident their scheme would work.

As the nuclear bombs hit their specific targets just above Babylon, another great earthquake struck. The huge natural gas deposits underneath her caught fire and exploded with fury. The armies of the East had already moved to the south before the Russians had begun their attack. The Russians were unnerved at the destruction of the oil resources – they had been certain there would be no earthquake from the altitude of their bombardment. They had known the city surface would burn from their military actions, but they had hoped the oil fields beneath it would not catch fire also.

In less than an hour after the first bombs struck, the entire city of Babylon had been destroyed. Thick, black smoke from the oil fields under the city scorched her from below, and the bombs had obliterated her from above. The great oil deposits on which Babylon sat also erupted with a terrible vengeance, and the smoke of her burning was so black that it turned much of the outlying areas as dark as night, blotting out the sun for dozens of kilometers around her.

The Russians were angry and frustrated at the turn of events, but no matter. They would finish what they had started. Medine was bottled up in Israel, and they would move to attack him from the north and the east immediately. There would be nowhere left for him to turn, since the armies of the south, the desert wilderness of the Sinai Peninsula, and the Mediterranean were blocking any other possible escape routes from him and his forces.[94]

All over the world, the financial markets collapsed and the merchants panicked as word of Babylon's destruction spread. The world capital and their entire economy had been destroyed in less than an hour, along with all the systems that controlled the financial institutions throughout the world. [95]

* * *

The army led by David Medine had rushed swiftly south from his positions in Lebanon to surround Jerusalem. They rolled through villages and towns with their tanks and cut a great path towards the capital. They controlled all the roads and most of the infrastructure. So little remained of the once mighty IDF that most of them just surrendered, only to be shot or blown up before they could lay down their weapons. David Medine had ordered that the armies of the World Union show the Jews no mercy, and they readily (and gladly) obeyed his orders.

With the city of Jerusalem completely surrounded, Medine ordered his armies to begin bombarding the city, but to not destroy it until he returned. They would demolish as much of the walls and the city as possible and do whatever they wanted with

---

[94] Jeremiah 51:44-49
[95] Isaiah 13,14; Jeremiah 50,51; Revelation 17-18

CHRIS HAMBLETON

it and its people until he arrived to claim the city as his. Jerusalem would be his trophy, and he would scrape it clean to show the world what would happen to any who stood against him.

With those orders firmly in place, Medine began moving a significant portion of his forces south along the Jordan, heading directly towards the other rebels and holdouts in Petra.

He was emboldened to hear that the other armies of the world were quickly converging upon Israel in the north at Megiddo. It was a magnificent battlefield, and large enough for all their forces to gather in. It was an enormous valley with steep mountains all around. Once they were fully gathered, he would meet them as he headed north and put the next phase of his plan into action. Jerusalem, the city he had hated for as long as he could remember, would soon be destroyed forever. But first, he had another critical matter to bring to a conclusion: the slaughter of the Jewish remnant.

But his comforting thoughts were disrupted soon after he left Jerusalem. His beloved city of Babylon was under attack, and there was little he could do to stop it! He became more enraged than he'd ever been before and vowed to kill every last person within Petra and the borders of Israel. And after the final destruction, he would ensure that nothing would ever be built in Israel, and no Jew would ever set foot in this land ever again.

The entire nation would be a desolate, ever-burning wasteland, and he would make sure it stayed that way for thousands of years. And then he would do the same against all his enemies. [96]

*   *   *

The Sanhedrin had made the arduous journey to Petra safely in less than day and were immediately welcomed by all the Council leaders. To their surprise, miracles were indeed happening all around them, from the incredible fountain of waters streaming from the great rock, to the healings of all sorts of diseases and ailments. And they were astounded to learn that their

---

[96] Zechariah 12:2-8;14:1-2

388

Jewish brothers and the Christians were united and worshiping the Lord God as one body. Some of them even wept when they heard of the manna that everyone gathered each morning, as in the days of their forefathers.

They met with the Council leaders and spoke with them in depth about the Scriptures and the prophecies of what was to come. The Jewish leaders who had converted to Christianity showed them how Yeshua was indeed the Messiah, but that it was up to the Sanhedrin to save their people. From Hosea it was quite clear: the Messiah would not return until the Sanhedrin – the very group that had rejected and condemned Him two thousand years before – repented of their unbelief and asked Him to return.[97] The time was approaching quickly for them to decide – once Medine and his forces began moving towards Petra, they would not have much time to save their people or their nation.

Soon after the Sanhedrin arrived, word swept throughout the camp that Babylon had been destroyed and all the oil fields on which it stood were burning with a tremendous fury. As they looked to the east in Babylon's general direction, they could see the darkened sky from hundreds of kilometers away.

And then they received the news that Medine's armies were already moving southeast towards Jerusalem. But they also heard that nearly a third of them had broken off from the main branch and were heading south along the Jordan, presumably towards Petra. South of Jerusalem there was little left except wilderness and abandoned fields. Thousands upon thousands of soldiers, tanks, and heavy artillery were on their way to wipe them out.[98]

When Jacob heard of the incredible destruction of Babylon and also of the Sanhedrin's arrival in Petra, he finally stopped holding out against what he knew in his heart to be true. He re-read the accounts in Isaiah and Jeremiah, and also in Revelation of Babylon's final judgment.

It had happened just as the Scriptures had foretold thousands of years before. The New Testament had been as accurate as the

---

[97] Hosea 5:15
[98] Micah 2:12-13

Tanakh, and was divinely inspired for certain. There could be no other logical explanation – no matter how hard he tried to believe otherwise – that the entire Bible was the revelation of God given to mankind. And now that he had accepted that the entire Scriptures were indeed from Him, he came to the vital conclusion that Yeshua was who the Bible said He was: God embodied in the form of a Man.

And with that acceptance, the book of Hebrews with which he had been struggling with for months – he now finally understood. It was written to convince those Jews who had come to Yeshua and were later falling back into Judaism, and also to demonstrate why the Old Covenant was incomplete and a New Covenant was necessary.

He could no longer deny it – the New Testament really was the new covenant that God had given to Israel and the rest of the world through Yeshua the Messiah. The New Covenant had forever put away the laws of the flesh and had replaced them with the laws of the Spirit.

As Jacob was sitting near the Stricken Spring, another thought came to him: in a sense, he was personally modeling his own land and people of Israel. Over and over in the Scriptures, God had referred to his people or nation as "Israel" when they were walking in obedience or faith, but as "Jacob" when they were being stubborn, disobedient, rebellious, or faithless. The very name "Israel" meant "struggles with God".

In many ways, he felt worn out and trampled on in his heart, much like his own nation. He was tired of being stubborn in the face of such overwhelming evidence and denying what he knew deep down to be true. He was tired of struggling with God.

Jacob bowed his head and closed his eyes, and made a final decision. He begged Yeshua to forgive him and to make him a new man, and cast away his unbelief and lack of faith. He wanted to start over with his wife and sons and friends, whoever was still alive. He vowed to follow Him wherever He led him, and that he would no longer doubt and be faithless like his beloved nation had been. He wept as he never had before and began mourning and praying as the rest of the camp was doing.

THE TIME OF JACOB'S TROUBLE

He stayed there a long time, until he was spent. He knew Naomi would be worried about him, and he rose and dusted himself off. His cheeks were filthy and streaked from his tears and the dust, but he didn't care.

He wiped his face and looked up to Heaven for the first time without shame or guilt. He thanked the Lord Yeshua for being so merciful to such a foolish, stubborn man as he, and for being so patient with him and his nation. Inside, he immediately began to feel a peace that he had never known before. He smiled – a true, genuine smile that he had not had for many years.

And with that, Jacob began hurrying along the well-worn path back to his tent, to tell his wife the good news: that he was finally saved.

* * *

Daniel was anxious at the morning briefing, along with everyone else in the room. They could hear the bombardments of the city, and frequently had to duck under the tables when a mortar struck too close to them. Everything in the room was covered with dust and rubble from the constant shelling. The morning report was dire, but not as bad as he had feared. Their enemies had not entered the city yet, nor had they broken through the walls, and that was better than he had hoped.

The city of Jerusalem had been surrounded for over a week without a shot being fired, and then all at once the shelling had begun on all sides of the city. The outer walls were weakening, but even after they were broken through, the thousands of tons of rubble from the bulldozed buildings and homes would slow them down. The demolition crews had continued to work around the clock, and had left small openings frequently in the rubble, through which the foot-soldiers and smaller vehicles of the World Union forces would pass. But they would then be faced with another inner ring of debris, with Israeli militia hidden in the rubble and firing upon them when they moved through the small openings. The holdouts had created a huge labyrinth of rubble.

The militia leaders in Jerusalem knew they could not win against the sheer might and number of the forces set before them. But they could bog them down in a guerrilla war. It could be days or weeks before they took the city, but the leaders hoped that the coalition against them would fall apart before then. The recent news of the Russian air forces attacking Babylon had given them a remote hope, and they had no other alternative but to slow down their enemies and try to survive.

The briefing did not last long that day – it was more of the same as the previous week: continue to bulldoze as much as possible and set up the militias and mines in the gaps. When the walls of the city were finally breached, Medine's forces would find themselves behind walls of rubble and buildings that they couldn't just plow their way through. Hopefully this would be the last war for a long time, and Jerusalem could finally live up to her name: the City of Peace.

As Daniel walked out of the building, he spotted a familiar face on the other side of the street. But since it had been nearly four years since he had last seen him, he had to look twice to be sure. He felt the heaviness of heart that he had grown used to over the last few weeks suddenly lift, and a big smile stretched across his face. The man he saw on the other side of the street was none other than his best friend and old ministry partner! It was Saul!

Daniel shouted Saul's name and rushed across the street to meet him. Saul was nearly as happy to see him as he was, and he quickly made the introductions between Daniel and his brother Ahban. When Daniel saw it was Ahban, he felt himself instinctively withdraw, because he knew Ahban had been among the first to have taken the mark. But he quickly overcame his initial hesitation and then smiled and shook his hand anyway.

"What are you two doing here?" Daniel asked them with a big grin. "This isn't exactly a vacation spot."

They smiled and then Saul replied, "Are you sure? We heard this was where all the excitement was. How can we help?"

Daniel thought for a moment and then replied, "You both

have experience in the IDF, right?" Both men nodded. "Great – come with me. Let's go find out where we can put both of you when the fun starts – maybe today, as a matter-of-fact. Is that okay?" he asked.

Both Saul and Ahban glanced quickly at one another and then looked back to Daniel and nodded. He began walking back from where he had come, with them keeping up beside him.

They all knew exactly what they had come to Jerusalem for, and were ready to help defend the city in any way they could.

* * *

Six days after the intense shelling of the city had begun, the northern outer wall of Jerusalem was broken through. The invaders immediately demanded the unconditional surrender of the city. But the defenders of Jerusalem knew what was in store for them if they did. Most of the fighting men would be slaughtered or worse, not to mention what would happen to the women and the rest.

After initial breach of the wall, the invaders did not immediately rush in, but widened the gap with high-capacity explosives, and then continued to destroy other sections of the wall. They knew if they poured through just a single narrow place in the city, they would be easily cut down by a tiny number of the rebels and therefore lose their advantage of vastly superior size and firepower. No, they would continue demolishing the wall until they could invade the city from all sides, except for the eastern side just above the Kidron Valley. No army had ever successfully broken into Jerusalem from the east, not even the mighty Romans who had besieged the city for nearly three years.

The World Union forces continued tearing and fracturing the wall in dozens of places, but still no one entered. Then early at dawn on the eighteenth day after the siege had begun, the World Union troops rushed in all at once, and were met with silence.

Tons upon tons of rubble were in front of them. They swept the gaps between the wall and the row of demolished buildings for mines, and then sent in the huge earthmovers and bulldozers to begin clearing the rubble. As the heavy equipment moved in, the invading security forces kept watch and began roving between the wall and the rubble, looking for guerilla forces.

But still there was no sign of the rebels. They had blanketed the city with infrared scans and satellite images, and knew that most of the people were in the center sections, but still spread out. Within an hour after the earthmovers and bulldozers began clearing paths for their troops, most of the city was filled with thick, blowing dust.

It was then that the holdouts attacked from their hiding places in the debris. The tremendous dust from the demolishing of the city wall had provided them with ample cover to get into position, and there they had waited for the World Union troops to invade.

The Israelis were clever and used the dust, noise, and confusion of the heavy equipment to their advantage. The Israelis attacked the earthmovers and the bulldozers first, taking out many of the troops guarding them and then the equipment operators themselves. Then they entrenched themselves among the equipment, and even turned the equipment against the invading troops themselves. When the firefight around the Israeli guerillas scattered among the equipment became too heavy, the Israelis blew up the equipment's controls and then retreated for the rubble.

The guerilla tactics used by the Israelis worked very well for the first few days, until the World Union forces figured out how to systematically uproot them. As the heavy equipment would move in, they would launch grenades and missiles at the nearby rubble, thereby trapping or killing the Israelis hiding inside.

They also utilized their superior satellite and infrared information on much smaller areas, and then sent in troops to gas or burn out the guerillas. When progress moved too slowly in clearing the debris, the World Union forces resorted to using their superior numbers to take more and more area from the holdouts, even though it cost them many of their soldiers.

But the World Union forces cared little for how many troops they would lose in their taking of Jerusalem, and the Israelis killed as many of them as they could. The new strategy finally proved to gain ground against the guerillas, but cost the World Union thousands of soldiers. They sent in scores of storm troopers and small vehicles through the gaps, and the Israelis would shoot them, briefly revealing their positions. Then as more troops poured in, they killed the guerrillas and the hiding snipers. As they began to increase their territory, the Israeli resistance weakened and retreated further into the labyrinth.

Days later, the World Union forces finally broke through the last ring of rubble and surrounded the thousands of Israelis holed up in the central and eastern portions of the city. Those who had been unable to find adequate refuge and cover were slaughtered.

When the World Union forces were confident they had broken the will of the resistance fighters, they suddenly stopped. They were under strict orders: David Medine himself would be the commander of the armies who would finally destroy the rebels in Jerusalem.

The siege of Jerusalem was over and the city was under their complete control. All it would take to destroy the city forever was one more push through the section of the Old City in Jerusalem, where little more than the Temple remained.

But first, Medine had another band of rebels to deal with: the pitiful remnant in Petra. They had infuriated him for years, and Medine wanted to personally exterminate them all. [99]

---

[99] Zechariah 14:1-2

CHAPTER 16
THE RETURN OF THE KING

Soon after the Sanhedrin had taken refuge in Petra, the Council began to notice a divide between them and the rest of the camp. In the days that followed, a number of the Jews that had not converted to Christianity began to side with the Sanhedrin, and the Council began to sense that the Sanhedrin would start exerting whatever authority they could.

But the Sanhedrin had no more real authority in the camp than any other small group of people did, unless other people began choosing them over the Council. And it appeared that some in the camp were now doing just that.

Many in the Council grew concerned and reiterated to the Sanhedrin that they were guests there like everyone else. Others wanted to wait and not cause any divisions in the camp. From the Scriptures, the Council leaders knew that it was necessary for the Sanhedrin to stay with them, since it was they who would need to personally, corporately ask the Messiah to return.

The present circumstances almost called for the Council to give the Sanhedrin more power and authority, but many wanted the situation to remain as it was. From the prophesies of Daniel, there were only a few days left before the Messiah should return, and they had to be patient, cautious, and trust in their King.

But all their concerns over the Sanhedrin and their authority vanished when the news came that outer wall of Jerusalem had been broken through. The news shocked everyone in the camp, even though they had known what would happen to the city in the days before Yeshua's return. They knew the city would be taken and thousands would be murdered, raped, and enslaved. But they also knew that when He returned, there would still be many left in the city that would flee through the valley when the Mount of Olives split apart. They were just days away from the end, and that realization humbled everyone in the camp.

Days later, news of Jerusalem's fall reached the camp, and the faith of everyone was shaken again. The latest reports clearly showed that a huge army led by David Medine himself was moving swiftly toward Petra. The realization that all of Israel was now destined for extermination shook the Sanhedrin, and they finally began to waver. If the Jews were wiped out, it would be their fault for not accepting Yeshua as the Messiah.

The Jews had been in tight spots many times before in their history, but God had always preserved them. But this time was different, and many in the Sanhedrin felt it; there would be no salvation for the Jews if not from their faith alone.

And not just faith in Yahweh, which they had always had, but faith in Yeshua, the Messiah they had rejected. Several of the older members of the Sanhedrin refused to hear of it, while most of the rest continued to listen to the rabbis who demonstrated from their own Scriptures that Yeshua – and only Yeshua of Nazareth – was the Messiah of Israel.

The Sanhedrin was now thoroughly divided into thirds. A third of them believed that Yeshua was their Messiah, another third refused to believe, and the last third had not decided yet. The Council leaders and the rest of the camp were growing concerned. If the Sanhedrin did not repent quickly, all their people would die.

The Council leaders intervened and counseled the Sanhedrin to stop debating the issue and simply fast and pray about it with all their might. If God answered them that Yeshua was His Son, then they should immediately repent and ask Him for forgiveness. But if He did not answer them or told them that Yeshua was indeed not the Messiah, then they should not repent.

The members of the Sanhedrin unanimously agreed, and spent the rest of the day praying and fasting. For many of them, they truly prayed to God and sought Him with all their hearts for the first time in their lives. They were afraid and had been thoroughly humbled by everything that had happened to them.

And then the Lord spoke to each of them privately and audibly, and told them clearly that Yeshua was indeed His Son, and told them that the time was short. They must turn and repent, and ask forgiveness for the long stubbornness and sin of themselves and all of Israel. The last days were upon them, and that fact finally pierced them through.

By the time they had finished praying and met the next day, their eyes were opened similar to how many of the former Orthodox Jews' had been. The veil of blindness had been removed, and now they understood what was expected of them.

Medine and his armies were coming to destroy them first, then the rest of the Jews in Jerusalem, and then all of Israel. There would be no savior or escape for them but the One they had rejected. They needed their Messiah now more than ever, and they wept at all the pain and misery that they and their forefathers had wrought by their rejection of Him two thousand years before. They tore their robes and garments and begged for Yeshua – the Yeshua of the Gentiles – to come and save them.

The Sanhedrin and the Council leaders proclaimed a three-day fast of prayer and mourning. The Scriptures were clear: three days after they would repent and beg the Messiah to save them, He would return to earth in power and glory. He would come to Petra first, and then go to Jerusalem where He would provide an escape for the survivors of Jerusalem.

And then finally, He would destroy all the armies of the world that were now gathered at Megiddo – the Valley of Armageddon.[100]

* * *

The two men crouched silently in the brush near the western entrance of Petra, awaiting further instruction. Minutes later their earpieces hummed softly and the voice of their commanding of-

---

[100] Hosea 5:15, 6:1-3

ficer confirmed their orders and gave them additional details. They were to infiltrate the camp and perform reconnaissance, gathering as much information as possible. Who were the leaders? Who was in charge? What were their defenses like? What were their armaments? How much resistance would they put up when they were finally attacked?

They were dressed in dusty, worn-out civilian clothes, but both were heavily armed with knives and handguns hidden under their clothes. They were not to engage anyone in the camp, but were authorized to kill any of the leaders or the Sanhedrin, if possible. The main forces of Medine's army were not far behind, and they would be highly rewarded for their important mission. There were two armed guards at the western entrance watching the horizon carefully, and those would need to be neutralized before they could enter.

Just after daybreak, they watched as the guards were relieved, waited another fifteen minutes, and then made their move. The scout-leader motioned for his partner to take the one on the left and he would take the other. Within moments both guards were sprawled on the ground, both shot silently in the head. The scouts swiftly approached the entrance and moved the bodies behind a rocky enclave, and then kicked dust over their blood. They brushed themselves off and checked over each other – they would fit in perfectly.

Both scouts had several tiny wireless microphones and cameras embedded in their clothing, which they had activated just after their last orders had been given. Even if they didn't make it out of the camp alive, the information they were gathering would not be lost. They had four hours before the next shift came on duty, so they had until then to make a sweep of the camp. And after three and a half hours passed, they were authorized to kill as many of the Sanhedrin and other camp leaders as possible.

They moved quickly down the path, their cameras capturing and transmitting everything around them. The camp was strewn about with thousands of tents and other makeshift shelters, as they had expected. Except for a handful of people walking toward the main water source of the camp, everyone was still asleep, which was what they had been counting on. But some of the leaders would most likely be meeting early in the morning, and perhaps they could even infiltrate the main structure where they met.

They walked through the center of the camp and easily found the leaders' meeting place, but it was empty except for three younger men watching the news on their laptops. The scouts continued down the path to the other end of the camp.

But as often happens to the best-laid plans, the unexpected occurred. The wife of one of the guards that morning was bringing breakfast for her husband and his partner standing watch. But when she found that they were not at their post, she became concerned and began searching the area nearby. She quickly discovered their bodies, but had the sense to maintain her composure; otherwise, the assassins might escape, if they were still in the camp. From the tracks around the bodies, she could tell that the spy (or spies) had headed into the camp from outside. But she didn't want others killed either, so she quickly went back to the main building and told what she had found.

The leaders were initially surprised that their defenses had been breached. They had assumed that God was still supernaturally protecting them, but evidently He had removed His protection. The World Union had not dropped any bombs or missiles on their camp in a long time, and they had not visibly noticed the change. They prayed for the woman and admonished her not to tell anyone in order to prevent confusion that the infiltrators could use to their advantage. The leaders made the assumption that the spies were still in their midst, and that they were merely the scouts sent to spy out their camp. Also, they understood that since the camp had been infiltrated, David Medine and his lieutenants would know that the camp was now vulnerable as well.

The leaders debated what to do next: should they start a camp-wide manhunt and try to track them down, or should all the guards just be alerted and quietly search for them? They might even be able to apprehend them, but most likely it would cost even more innocent lives.

In the end, they decided to alert the rest of the guards and have them quietly begin searching the camp. They would also hide additional guards at each entrance to see if the infiltrators would leave.

But by the time the orders went out and the guards sent to the entrances, they discovered the bodies of the guards on the eastern entrance, but they had not been hidden. They had been shot in the back of the head, completely unaware that anyone had been behind them. The spies were nowhere to be found, but they had left faint footprints leading into the wilderness, and then vanished. The guards sadly notified their commanders and a group of men was sent out to the entrances to collect the bodies. They would tell their families and then find a place to bury them.

When the bodies were carried back into the outskirts of the camp, word of what had happened began to spread, and before long all the camp was talking about it. Everyone knew the armies would be coming soon. The people were afraid, and the leadership was divided as to what to do: should they immediately flee the confined area of Petra and spread out in the wilderness, or should they stay put and trust in Yeshua's imminent return to save them?

Both sides had valid arguments, but both paths would end in certain death if Yeshua did not appear. If they stayed in Petra and the Lord did not return, they would be slaughtered all throughout the camp. But if they left the fortress for the desert wilderness, they would die of thirst or exhaustion, and their enemies would simply hunt them down and exterminate them.

Then one of the older Jewish rabbis who had accepted Yeshua spoke up. Where were the sheep best protected when danger was about, especially when their Shepherd was absent? The sheep-fold. The sheep should stay and not scatter, especially when the wolves were outside. Their Shepherd had provided supernatural protection over them the entire time they had been in the Petra, and He had promised to return. They must trust Him – it would be the most important test for the Remnant, which had already trusted Him every step of the way. Why should they turn at the last moment, at the very time of His return?

One by one, the other leaders saw the wisdom in his advice and changed their minds. They would stay and then admonished all the people to stay in the camp for their own safety and trust in the Lord. Anyone who left the camp would most likely die. But if any of the World Union forces set foot in the camp, they would be ready to defend themselves. The leaders had planned for the day when Petra was surrounded and perhaps even invaded, and they heavily armed all the guards and many other volunteers, and put them on immediate alert.

As for the rest of the camp, the Council leaders admonished everyone to pray for the immediate return of their Savior. And then everyone throughout the camp obeyed, from the least to the greatest, and earnestly sought the Lord.

This would indeed be their final, greatest test.

* * *

David Medine and his terrible army rolled steadily toward the ancient rock city of Petra. The armed forces were immense, and after several days of steady, constant travel, they were nearly at their target. Medine had already tried every form of missile, bombardment, and supernatural catastrophe at his disposal, and all had failed. But the hour was late, and the news of the infiltration of his scouts filled him with hope – sheer manpower would conquer them now.

As the tanks and infantry neared the entrance of Petra, Medine ordered the bombers to drop their payloads, and the tanks to begin shelling the rock city. The infantry would soon roll in and then the entire army would storm the city simultaneously.

But as the bombers roared overhead to begin their drop, the sky changed to an eerie, sickening color of red, like the color of blood. The sky was deep-red and dark, and the moon shown black behind it. The sun at its fullest height in the sky was suddenly also the color of scarlet. No stars were shining, but growing streaks of flaming meteors could be clearly seen in the heavens overhead. The great day of Yeshua's fury, wrath, and vengeance had come at last.

THE TIME OF JACOB'S TROUBLE

All of a sudden, the entire sky lit up as if from a great blinding spotlight, and the murky clouds seemed to split apart and flee before the brilliant light.

In the midst of the light, there was an awesome human-like shape. As the figure of light descended, it appeared to be a man clothed in shining white robes and surrounded by pure white light, riding on a spotless white horse.

He too had an innumerable army behind Him, but far back in the distance. They filled the skies above just as the armies of men filled the land below, and gazed down at Him with awe and reverence as His horse touched the ground at the entrance of Petra, directly in front of the army.

Without warning, terrible streams of lightning began to fall from the skies and all around Him, blinding bolts of lightning flashed. Many of them seemed to come from the Man Himself. And then He gave a deafening roar like a mighty lion that caused everyone below Him to tremble and fall. He drew a huge flaming sword from His side and launched His steed forward to battle the hordes before Him. The time of His vengeance had come, and none could endure Him.

Medine shouted for his forces to stand their ground and destroy the shining horseman who was rushing directly towards them. The tanks, helicopters, and bombers launched their weapons directly at Him, but they struck with no result.

The soldiers, though terrified, rushed forward with their guns firing, but they too had no effect upon Him. He began cutting a great swath through their midst with his long sword of fire. As He struck, even those outside His reach disintegrated into heaps of tattered clothes and bloody flesh and bone, as if their bodies had been turned inside out. The great swath of red remains grew outward from Him as He pressed into the midst of the armies.

The refugees in the camp of Petra cheered and wept at His arrival – their Messiah had finally come. He had kept His promises and was trampling their enemies. The heavenly armies that had followed Him were clothed in gleaming white and were also riding on horses, but none as great and glorious as the one He was on.

His armies floated in the midst of the sky, silently watching their Master avenge Himself upon His enemies, after thousands of years of restraint. They were the Church – the Bride of Christ – every believer from the moment of His resurrection to the last person had been saved the instant before the Rapture.

As Medine saw there would be no stopping Him, he hurriedly called for a helicopter to rush him back to the bulk of his forces surrounding Jerusalem. If he could not destroy those in Petra, perhaps he could wipe out the rest in Jerusalem first. He would not go down without fighting to the death with all the forces at his command. Today was the terrible day of slaughter he had warned of, and all men must fight behind him if they were to survive.

Medine jumped into the helicopter and ordered it back to Jerusalem as quickly as possible. If he were to make his last stand, it would be with all the armies of the world united behind him.

With the legs of His great horse and His white robes covered in the blood of His enemies, Yeshua steadily, methodically destroyed all the remaining brigades of Medine's forces in Petra.

And then He turned and rode away to the northwest, towards the besieged city of Jerusalem. His army followed a short distance behind, praising Him and glorifying Him at the saving of His people. [101]

* * *

Jacob and Naomi had been face down on the ground ever since the rumbling outside the camp had begun. They could feel the earth underneath them vibrating from the huge military forces surrounding the canyon. The walls and rocks in Petra only amplified the noise from the multitudes of vehicles nearby and the aircraft overhead.

Like everyone else in the camp, they had been praying throughout most of the last three days, but in the last hour, their prayers had become increasingly fervent and desperate. How

---

[101] Isaiah 63:1-6

long would it be until the armies invaded them?

Suddenly the desert landscape around them changed, and many who had noticed it immediately opened their eyes and looked around. All the sky had turned to the reddish-orange color of dusk, but it was only late-morning and there were few clouds in the sky.

Some of the people began shouting that the time had come, and that they should all look up to the skies – there were only minutes left before the end! But no one had needed to say anything – everyone in the camp knew that the great Day of the Lord had finally come.

Jacob and Naomi rose to their feet and stood watching and praying. She reached for his hand as the roar of the aircraft overhead grew to a deafening pitch. He put his arm around her to reassure her – they would live to see tomorrow, since He was sure to be coming soon. But he could feel her trembling and he closed his eyes, pleading with the Lord to hasten His arrival.

And then a blinding light appeared above them, many times brighter than the sun overhead. Everyone covered their eyes from the light, but they could clearly see the figure of a Man standing in the midst of the light, hovering in mid-air hundreds of meters above them.

He quickly descended from the sky and stopped between the camp and the invading armies. Everyone who saw Him – both those inside the camp and those outside the camp – knew who it was. It was Him who was known by many names: Yeshua, Jesus Christ, the Lord God Almighty, the Messiah, the Avenger, the Destroyer, and the Savior. [102]

His kinsmen in Petra gasped at the awesome sight and cheered His arrival. Behind Him was an innumerable army of the Church, all glorified and waiting for Him to save the Remnant. There were millions upon millions of them, riding on brilliant white horses like their King, all the while praising Him. Lightning began to pour outward from all around Him, and pounded the earth below.

---

[102] Revelation 1:7

He roared with a sound that shook all the ground like an earthquake, and then spurred His horse toward His enemies.

Yeshua quickly disappeared from the sight of all the onlookers in Petra, but they could still see His glory, the blinding-white aura that surrounded Him, moving among the enemies. All the soldiers were firing their weapons and launching their missiles as quickly as they could, at both the King and also at those who had come with Him.

But the bullets and the artillery did nothing to any of them, and as the horrible screams began, the slaughter of His enemies commenced, even though they could not see it from inside the canyon. They could hear the screeching sounds of metal and the tearing of flesh and the crunching of bones by the thousands. There would be no mercy for anyone outside. This was not a day for mercy, but one only reserved for unrestrained wrath, slaughter, and judgment.

For several minutes, the screams and the sounds of slaughter continued in the desert wilderness, and then there was silence once again. But every few seconds, a fuel tank or other piece of equipment of the vanquished armies exploded, and the only sounds they could hear outside Petra were the flames of the burning equipment and the wind blowing all around them.

There were no more screams or cursing or shooting – not a single one of His enemies had been left alive. And as He rose again into the air on His mighty horse, everyone in Petra could see that the brilliant white of His clothes were drenched in the blood of His enemies.

He proclaimed that the Kingdom had now come, and that they were free and should not fear any longer. He would return to take them to Jerusalem in three days. And then He turned and rode away to the northwest, towards the besieged city of Jerusalem.

The Church, who had stayed behind Him during the slaughter, quickly followed on their steeds towards the holy city and the salvation of the rest of His people.

As He rushed northward, a huge trail of fire and destruction followed in His wake – even the sands of the wastelands were scorched black. And though the skies remained flaming-red in color, those in Petra could still see His brilliant light far off in the distance, and the trail where He had been only moments earlier.

Everyone in the camp was ecstatic at the return of their King for hours after He had left. Some bravely stepped outside the safe confines of Petra to survey the vanquished enemies, but what they saw overwhelmed them.

Thousands more hiked to higher ground to see the slaughter, but did not leave the canyon. The air all around them was filled with acrid smoke and the stench of burning metal, plastic, clothing, and also of charred flesh and blood. Many gagged when the smells blew in too close, and most felt nauseous at the thought of so much terrible destruction.

For those brave enough to look, the sounds they had heard outside the camp were nothing compared to the scene outside. In every direction as far off into the horizon as they could see, the land was covered with wrecked military vehicles, equipment, and crushed, mangled bodies. There was so much blood from the enemies that it was already gathering in thousands of small pools, and slowly draining towards the lower-lying areas in widening streams. It was a horrific sight, sickening to behold. [103]

Those in the camp who had wanted to leave earlier, changed their minds upon seeing the carnage. That night after sunset, the ground was covered with manna as it had been earlier that day in the morning. There was much rejoicing, praising, and praying throughout all the camp that night, and then they rested.

They would all wait there in Petra for their King to come and bring them to Jerusalem in three days, just as He had promised.

*   *   *

Saul, Daniel, and Ahban stood sweating with their weapons ready, along with thousands of others who had sworn to defend Jerusalem to the end.

The thundering sounds of the explosives and the heavy

---

[103] Isaiah 63:1-6

equipment tearing through the last barriers between them and their enemies made the thought of the next few hours even more terrifying than they already were.

The holdouts were completely surrounded, and evidently the order had been given to finish them off. Their enemies had been waiting for Medine to arrive before taking the last strongholds, and now they were making their final push into the Old City.

A huge array of explosives tore away the last walls of rubble between the World Union forces and the Jerusalem militia, and the tanks began to roll in. Many of the militia were hiding in and among the remaining buildings of the Old City, but the tanks quickly blasted them and slowly rolled on through the streets. Behind and among the tanks were other military vehicles full of soldiers, and thousands more soldiers followed them. The tanks destroyed the buildings while the other vehicles cleared the streets, and the myriad of troopers began hunting down any resistance fighters still alive.

The three men heard the whine of an incoming mortar round, and quickly dove away in separate directions as the building they were taking cover in was shelled. They hastily hid in the rubble, concealing themselves as best they could. They knew the invaders were heavily-armed and merciless. Wounding them was not an option, especially since the troops they had encountered earlier were all wearing thick body armor. The head-shot was the only way to bring them down, but that meant smaller targets.

The strategy of the holdouts had not changed for days: slow the enemy down and hamper their surges. The holdouts would attack furiously, and then immediately retreat when overwhelmed, and then they would repeat it. But this strategy could only work so long, and given their present conditions and location, not much longer. They were less than half a kilometer from the Temple compound, and they were losing ground fast. More troops swarmed the area, and they could not hold their positions longer than a few more minutes.

Ahban suddenly popped his head up from where he had been hiding and fired his gun three times in rapid succession. They heard a cry followed by shouts and curses, and several troopers began firing upon his location and surrounding him. Saul and Daniel had been behind him and stayed low, shooting the soldiers as they closed in.

Ahban shot the last one when he turned to find his comrades, and then he fell back to where Saul and Daniel had regrouped. More soldiers were coming to their position and the three retreated deeper into the Old City to find new hiding places.

The battle continued for several hours, with the militia attacking and slowing down the invaders, but then being overwhelmed and subsequently retreating. Finally, the only place left to flee was the Temple grounds, and that would only provide refuge for a few more hours at the pace the enemy was keeping.

In and around the Temple, their fellow holdouts were firing furiously at the approaching troops and keeping them back, at least for the time being. They were able to provide enough fire-cover until the bulk of those retreating to the Temple had come through the outer gates.

Daniel was the first to reach the Temple, and he yelled at Ahban and Saul to hurry. But both were pinned down from enemy fire and could not move. One of the Temple guards threw two of his grenades towards the source of most of the gunfire, and the two brothers made a frantic dash for the gate.

Once inside, all three took up positions alongside the others, and helped provide cover for the rest of the militia who were trying to get to safety also. The World Union troopers seemed to slow as they approached the Temple – perhaps Medine or their commanders had told them to wait once again and not push through into the Temple compound.

The pause gave all those inside the Temple area time to rest and fortify their positions. In front of the Temple were strewn numerous cars and trucks that had been driven in to provide cover once the forces would breach their last defenses.

Most of the civilians were massed near the back of the Temple structure itself, and the militia was positioned in front of them. They would be the last to fall, but they would not surrender those under their protection. Everyone in Jerusalem had known from the start that surrender was not an option, and not once had the matter of surrender ever been brought up. If they failed, they would be the sacrifices that David Medine, the god of the earth, demanded.

As Daniel caught his breath, he suddenly noticed thousands more people than he had been expecting at the Temple. He was confused – they had accurate counts of how many people had been left in the city, and that had been less than five thousand. But now in the Temple there were many times that number, and many of them were dressed in clothing that was much different from the typical style of dress seen in Jerusalem. He recognized American, Asian, European, Indian, and even some Chinese clothing, and then he became even more puzzled.

Many were dirty and holding weapons – apparently, they had been fighting alongside them earlier from inside the Temple grounds. But whereas many of the Jews who had been holed up in the city for weeks looked terrified and exhausted, these new-comers looked fresh and almost calm. They had a certain air of self-assurance about them, a confidence that he had not felt for weeks. Saul noticed Daniel's look of confusion at the tens of thousands more men present in the area and smiled at him.

They were the rest of the 144,000, Saul told him, and they had all been called by their King to return to Jerusalem to help the last of His kinsmen. They would keep the refugees safe in the Temple until the Mount of Olives split and then help them escape into the great valley. The 144,000 had been called from all over the earth to await the arrival of their King.

Later, it was discovered that many who had been unable to find transportation to Jerusalem had been instantly transported there by their Master, and had found themselves in the middle of the firefight raging through the Old City.

Daniel felt some measure of relief and hope at the news – just knowing that the King's return was imminent gave him re-newed strength and courage. But new, tremendous rumbling sounds coming from just outside the walls of the Temple compound didn't help his courage last long.

The enemy had regrouped, and was preparing for the final surge into Old City.

THE TIME OF JACOB'S TROUBLE

* * *

Blasts and explosions erupted from outside the Temple grounds, and the outer wall shuddered and buckled. It would not last much longer. The Temple wall had not been designed to withstand any type of siege or battle, much less the magnitude of the forces arrayed against it. Inside, those who were armed checked and re-checked their weapons. Those who were unarmed but could fight had made small piles of stones and rocks in front of them to throw when the invaders stormed the complex. And those who could not fight crouched at the back of the Temple, furthest from the walls. But everyone there was praying and hoping this would not be the end.

Minutes later, the Temple wall was broken through, and the soldiers poured onto the Temple grounds. The rebels were prepared for them though, and cut down many in the first wave. Before the second wave struck, tear gas and grenades were thrown to drive the rebels back, and then the next wave of troops rushed in. They too were cut down, but took a number of the rebels with them, and the fighting from the second wave lasted nearly twice as long as the first. The next wave would be much larger, and many knew the rebels would not be able to hold out long after that.

The rebels were exhausted after days of fighting, and their ammunition was quickly running out. The next wave would force them to retreat again, and many had already selected where they would take cover next.

Daniel, Saul, and Ahban were still close together and had chosen a location near one of the trucks that had been driven into the compound earlier. Small explosives had been set under many of the vehicles, which would be detonated once the invading forces reached them in the compound. It wasn't much, but it would add to the confusion and provide cover to retreat again. The rebels were no longer fighting to win the battle for Jerusalem – they were fighting to survive.

The next surge began with intense fury, and this time the rebels were pushed back far enough into the complex for those armed only with stones and rocks to help them hold off the invaders. The IEDs had all been detonated and stopped the last wave of troops long enough for them to retreat for the last time.

But most of the rebels had run out of ammunition. The end was only minutes away, and it would be furious and brutal. Many were praying and crying, and the militia had dug in again as best they could. Over half their numbers had been decimated in the last wave, and their corpses littered the Temple grounds.

Suddenly several shells screamed through the air and struck the Temple behind them, and debris rained down on everyone. The final surge had begun, and they waited for the ground forces to storm through the smoke. The rebels would not begin their attack until the enemy was close enough to be sure targets.

But they never came – then the rebels heard numerous popping sounds and looked up to see hundreds of grenades falling from the sky. They shouted and scattered, but many were killed and dozens more wounded from the shrapnel.

Saul heard Daniel scream and turned to see him fall and roll in the dirt, writhing in pain. He shouted for Ahban, who was firing upon the troops storming the complex. He rushed over and helped Saul drag him over to the north side of the Temple, and then he went back to the front.

Saul stayed with Daniel and frantically looked over his wounds. They didn't appear to be too deep, but his arms and torso were bleeding badly. He could see chunks of shrapnel sticking out all over him. He tried to stop the bleeding, but applying pressure only made him scream in pain.

If their salvation didn't come soon, Daniel would be lost.

* * *

In Jerusalem, the officers and soldiers of the greatest army in history received word that David Medine was coming to personally oversee the destruction of Jerusalem.

They had already conquered much of the city, and many of its inhabitants had been taken captive or killed. Medine had told them to be unrestrained and as brutal as possible, and they had gladly followed his orders. They had given their troops free rein, and let them rape, torture, and murder as many as they desired. Any survivors they had taken prisoner would be later made slaves or objects of torture – whatever suited their master.

As Medine arrived at the main command center of his forces, he discovered that the armies to the north, east, and west had all converged in the great Valley of Megiddo as he had planned, but there was also another huge army approaching from the south. He was completely surrounded and boxed in, and he was furious with rage at being cut off.

He must turn them against the Man at Petra and then he must turn them against one another without being caught in the middle. But the Man and His armies were coming quickly – perhaps he could convince his enemies in Megiddo to attack Him instead, and then he would mop up the mess afterwards.

The skies over all of the earth suddenly changed, and people everywhere stopped what they were doing and looked up at the bizarre sight. Lightning and other flashes lit up the reddened sky, but no rain or hail accompanied it. The officers and soldiers of all the armies gathered at Megiddo hesitated for a moment as their gazes were drawn to the distant, brilliant light in the midst of the south, and watched as it seemed to grow larger and larger on the horizon.

And then the orders rapidly streamed down from Medine and the rest of their commanders: the light was from Yahweh and the Elohim, and their terrible armies were with them. They must be destroyed no matter what the cost. Every soldier and commander frantically readied their weapons and took aim at the growing light in the distance. [104]

Suddenly as the light grew closer, the soldiers began turning against their officers and shooting them in an insane frenzy. Some were on horses and donkeys, and their own animals attacked them and each other in a furious rage and terror. [105]

The brigades gathering to the south of Jerusalem saw Him

---

[104] Joel 3:15; Acts 2:20-21
[105] Zechariah 12:4

first, and they burst into heaps of tortured, smoldering flesh before His blazing wrath.

Yeshua came into Jerusalem from the southeast, heading towards the ancient Mount of Olives, from where He had ascended nearly two thousand years before. His gleaming white stallion descended to the top of the mountain, and as soon as He set foot on the ground, a tremendous earthquake shattered the land. The Mount of Olives shook with terrible fury and split in half, opening a great crevice that ran from west to east that started from the Golden Gate of Jerusalem and ran all the way east to the Jordan River. [106]

The multitudes trapped in the eastern side of the city near the Temple saw their chance to escape the invading hordes of soldiers streaming in from the other three sides of the city, and ran out through the crevice as fast as they could.

Yeshua mounted His horse once again and rode through the air to the Golden Gate of the city, which had been sealed for thousands of years. It had been reserved for Him and only Him to pass through, and now that time had finally come. [107]

As He approached the Golden Gate, another tremendous earthquake struck and the ancient seal of the gate was ripped apart, and He rode through triumphantly as the Great King coming to save His people.

And the fear of all the people in Jerusalem who had been fleeing for their lives turned to joy and shouted out cries of thanksgiving and victory at His arrival. [108]

*   *   *

Saul had been so focused on Daniel's condition that he almost hadn't noticed the skies change above him. The scenery grew dim and reddish-colored without warning.

When he finally perceived the change and looked up, the skies had taken on a fiery red hue and the sun seemed to be

---

[106] Zechariah 14:3-4
[107] Zechariah 14:5
[108] Amos 1:2; Joel 3:16; Zechariah 14:3-4, 12:8

much darker than it had been only moments before. As he looked through the smoke and dust, the shadows around him on the ground seemed to shift and then suddenly became darker. At first, he was confused by the shifting shadows and then he realized they were coming from a light source other than the sun.

The strange shadows grew sharper and darker, and the light was now blazing, even though he couldn't directly see it from the north side of the Temple. A huge spotlight was quickly moving towards them, making everything else grow faint.

A huge smile burst across his face and tears filled his eyes – the King had arrived! The fighting had been so intense all around him that no one seemed to notice until the light was nearly blinding. And then the shadows began to change again as the light shifted and moved nearby to the east instead of continuing to come directly from the south.

Daniel wouldn't want to miss this, Saul thought, and he turned his friend around so they could both look to the east, and Saul shook him awake.

And there on the Mount of Olives, the brilliant light grew brighter and brighter, until its source dropped from the air and seemed to descend onto the mountain. And as the King of Kings landed on the Mount, the entire mountain range shook violently and split apart from the top down. When the shaking finally stopped, He was no longer standing on one side or the other, but was floating in mid-air next to His great white horse.

The crevice that had been created by His arrival ran through the Kidron Valley all the way to the Jordan River, many kilometers to the east of Jerusalem. Also, a great fissure was created at the western end of the new valley that had torn the Eastern Gate of the city of Jerusalem in two, all the way up to the Temple Mount.

The people cowering in the eastern side of the Temple Mount were no longer trapped, and they quickly poured through the opening into the valley. The soldiers, still shaken from the earthquake and the blinding light in front of them, began to regain their footing and pressed forward, and the captives fled even faster into the valley.

Ahban used the confusion of the earthquake to fall back and rejoin Saul and Daniel, and he began shouting at them. The noise was so loud that at first they didn't hear him at all. So he shouted again and told them to leave the Temple. He would cover them while they made their escape. But they had to hurry, and he fired some shots in front of them to keep the invaders back, at least for a few more moments.

He bent down and helped Saul get Daniel to his feet. He wobbled but stayed standing with one arm around Saul's shoulders and leaning heavily against him. Saul turned him around and began moving slowly, and then stole a look back at his brother. He had already turned away from them and was crouching low to shoot anyone who came too close to their side of the Temple.

Ahban shot a quick glance back at them standing there and shouted for them to hurry. Saul complied and began dragging Daniel as fast as he could down into the new valley.

As they descended, they saw thousands of others streaming down into it fast as they could. People flooded the sides downward from the top to the bottom. Many of the 144,000 were carrying people or helping them along as best as they could, and then left them for others to take further east into the valley.

None of the 144,000 would be lost – they had been promised as much – and therefore were using that to their advantage, helping as many of their brothers and sisters escape the invasion as they could. [109]

* * *

Saul and Daniel safely made it into the crevice and merged with the thousands of refugees scurrying through the valley. Many were helping others and tending to the wounded.

He took Daniel over to one of the sides and set him down on a rock. He was breathing rapidly, and was bleeding profusely from many of the shrapnel wounds in his chest, torso and limbs.

---

[109] Revelation 14:1

If he didn't get more blood soon, he would die.

Saul called out for help and several people quickly came over to them. He took off his shirt and tried to use it as a bandage, but it did little to stop the bleeding. Someone else brought over a medical kit and began looking over him.

Suddenly he remembered Ahban and ran back to the edge of the crevice. He felt a chill sweep over him as he rushed back up the west side towards the Temple. He needed to get to Ahban before it was too late – before he was killed. Perhaps if his brother was still alive at the Judgment, he could throw himself upon the mercy of the Court, and beg Yeshua for forgiveness and for taking the mark. Maybe seeing Yeshua with his own eyes would turn him and cause him to repent.

He scaled the rugged slope faster than he thought possible and ran over to where Ahban had been before, but he wasn't there. Now he felt even more afraid for his brother, and rushed forward, heading straight toward the northwest corner of the Temple.

It was only then that he noticed how badly it had been damaged. There were bullet holes all over its walls and numerous gaping cracks ran up and down the sides, and part of the roof was even burning. But this Temple had never been meant to last, for it was the Temple of Man, not the Temple of God. Yeshua would build His Temple in a completely different place soon anyway.

As he was halfway to the northwest corner, the shadows changed around him like they had moments before the Mount of Olives had split apart, and he knew Yeshua was moving again. The King was coming to the Temple to destroy His enemies, now that His flock had been taken to safety.

Saul couldn't help but stop and look up, and he saw Him roar overhead and then land in front of the Eastern Gate with such ferocity that the entire city shook. He was no longer on His white stallion, but was standing alone. The King calmly strode through the broken gate in the midst of tremendous gunfire, and continued onward to the front of the Temple.

He watched Yeshua begin speaking as the thousands of soldiers in front of him were frantically firing their weapons as fast as they could. And as He spoke, they began melting away where they stood and turned into small mounds of blood-soaked clothes, full of their mangled flesh and bones.

Saul was speechless at what he saw. Every soldier within hearing range of His voice would simply collapse into lifeless, disgusting heaps of flesh on the ground. And as He stepped forward and began moving outward from the Temple, countless more melted away as soon as they heard His terrible voice.

A few moments later, Saul recovered and remembered what he still needed to do. He rushed toward the Temple, frantic to find his brother.

Was he still alive? Had he been killed in the final, furious attack that had come just before Yeshua had landed in front of the Temple? Had he been among those who had fallen lifeless when they heard Yeshua's voice?

*   *   *

The adrenaline flowing through him was all that was keeping him going. He was exhausted and nearly ready to give up. He didn't even care any more if he made it through that day. His brother and his friend were now safe, and he had done all he could to serve his country. He felt like just throwing down his weapon and letting the enemy take his life; it would hurt, but only for a brief moment. But something inside compelled him to keep fighting – maybe it was because that was all he had left.

Ahban moved closer to the corner of the Temple and quickly saw the foolishness of staying there and trying to fight on two sides. He pressed himself up against the wall and then swiftly moved around the corner so he would be at the very front wall of the Temple.

He found at least twenty others in front of the Temple fighting with everything they had left. Many more of their fellow fighters had fallen in front of them, and they wouldn't hold out for long. The next surge of the troops was already rushing towards them and was now less than fifty meters away. And from their furious expressions, they clearly intended to finally put an end to the rebellion.

But when the enemy was less than twenty meters away, they suddenly stopped and looked up with terrible fear. The light that everyone had seen before seemed like it was coming from behind the Temple, but he dared not take his eyes off the enemy. For a few moments, the light vanished, and then it burst out all around him.

Ahban could clearly see that there was a great Man in the center of the light with His back to them, facing the enemy all by Himself. And Ahban trembled even more than he had when he had seen the last surge coming; he knew who the Man was, and he was terrified as he beheld Him in His glory.

And then Ahban heard Him begin speaking to His enemies, and he and his fellow countrymen were shocked to see them melt away in His Presence. He didn't strike at them or even draw His sword. He just spoke to them and proclaimed that His Kingdom had now come, and that there was no place for them on the earth any longer. And then He began walking away from the Temple, with countless more troops and equipment before him melting into heaps of metal and raw flesh.

Ahban felt a mixture of different emotions simultaneously, and found himself still clenching his gun, but he wasn't ready to put it down yet. He felt gratitude and relief at being saved from the invasion, but a terrible fear ran deep in his soul because of who the Man was. He was Yeshua, the very One who Saul had told him about time and time again, and the One he had always mocked and rejected.

He looked down at the invisible Enki Seal on his hand and remembered what the flying creature had said years before: there would be no salvation for those who took the mark. Not for any who swore allegiance to the Beast by taking his image.

At that moment, Saul came up beside him and called out his name. He turned and saw his brother, and they both grabbed and hugged each other hard. The battle was over and they were still alive. But for one the future held peace and promise – for the other it meant uncertainty and judgment.

CHRIS HAMBLETON

* * *

Once outside the Temple walls, Yeshua roared as He had in Petra and began destroying the invading armies with His shouts of battle and His long flaming sword. Every enemy in His path was immediately slain by His glory and His terrible presence. And after all the enemies in and around Jerusalem had been wiped out, He headed north to attack the multitudes gathered north of Jerusalem, flooding the entire land. His land.

As He lit up the entire sky with His blinding glory, all the soldiers who were still alive were dumbstruck with fear and terror and began firing all their weapons at Him as fast as they could. But they had no effect on Him – even the nuclear warheads that struck Him did nothing. And as He passed through their midst, they were turned inside out and collapsed in heaps as had all the others who had stood against Him.[110]

The Messiah continued to sweep through the millions upon millions in His path until He reached the back of the forces, from where David Medine had been commanding them. He seized Medine by his throat and threw him to the ground.

Pontiffica, who had been by Medine's side during the entire battle, fell upon his face and begged for mercy. Medine scoffed at his cowardice and looked around for a weapon or someone to intervene on his behalf, but he discovered that everyone around him had melted into bubbling pools of flesh and blood.

Two shimmering men from Yeshua's army in the skies above them came to His side – the same Two Witnesses that Medine had killed years earlier. They grabbed him and Pontiffica by the scruff of their necks and put them in heavy, glowing chains.

Medine writhed and whimpered in His presence and then erupted into a vile stream of cursing and rage, but with a mere glance Yeshua silenced him and he made no more sound, regardless of how hard he tried.

As He finished the slaughter of the armies near Jerusalem,

---

[110] Joel 3:12-15; Zechariah 12:9

THE TIME OF JACOB'S TROUBLE

He pressed north towards the plain of Megiddo – to Armageddon. The Church saints who remained behind Him quickly separated and spread out all over the land of Israel, slaying all who had taken any Jews or Christians prisoner.

They rushed through concrete walls, prison cells, homes, buildings, bunkers and bomb shelters, with nothing able to prevent their invasion and wrath. They freed those chained in the dungeons and the slave camps, and lifted others out of the pits and cisterns where they had been cast. [111]

The eerie red sky suddenly grew dim over the land of Israel, and the cries of millions of squawking birds of all shapes and sizes rang through the air. Birds of prey filled the sky as far as the eye could see, and the sheer number of their multitude darkened the horizon as they flew to Megiddo and Petra. As they swooped over the areas where all the bleeding, fresh corpses of the armies of men lay, their cries became silent.

They plunged to the earth and began feasting on the carrion in a frenzy, and continued until they were full. The multitudes remained there for the next several days, until little remained of the corpses.

* * *

After all His enemies had been destroyed, Yeshua flew back to land in front of the Golden Gate and looked over the thousands of people who had sought refuge in the valley. The crowd before Him fell on their faces and worshipped Him. Soon He bid them to rise, and they began to cheer and praise Him.

He smiled and then blessed the crowd, raising His hands and proclaiming peace to them. And then He began walking through the valley, from the west side all the way to the east to the other side of the Kidron Valley. And as He did so, the wounded, maimed, crippled, and dying, received new life.

Even those who had died after His return were brought back to life, much to the shock of everyone around them. And those

---

[111] Joel 2:3-11

with old injuries that had long mended and even those with other common diseases found themselves healed and renewed.

In addition to their restored bodies, He healed their spirits by removing the last of the spiritual blindness that had been placed over them. And the Jews finally saw Him for Who He was: their Kinsman-Redeemer, their Savior, their Messiah.

At that moment, the unsaved in the valley began to weep bitterly and wail over Him, and many tore their clothes in mourning.[112] They separated into families or by themselves and sobbed over what they and their ancestors had done to Him before, and how they had rejected Him over and over again. [113]

As they mourned over Him, He was moved with compassion and pronounced forgiveness upon them for all their sins and their unbelief. But when they saw His pierced hands and feet, they continued to sob and mourn.

And then He once again moved back through the crowded valley, blessing each of His brothers and sisters again.

---

[112] Zechariah 12:9-11
[113] Zechariah 12:12-14

CHAPTER 17
THE GREAT JUDGMENT

An eerie calm swept over the earth, as the thousands of years of war and bloodshed were finally brought to a close. The world was in ruins, shattered by man's sin and greed and evil. It had also been shattered by God – by His need for Justice and Judgment. The time for renewal and rebuilding was coming soon, but not until the last remnants of the old world were sentenced and swept away.

The land of Israel was littered with the rotting flesh of Medine's armies and the rest of the military might of the world. The bodies and equipment filled the land from Petra north to Jerusalem and then even all the way up into Galilee. The great river of bodies was wide and rancid, and there was so much blood from the corpses that it ran like streams from the hills of Jerusalem and the high country.

Billions of carrion birds had been drawn to the carnage and devoured the raw flesh, and soon the insects and worms would have their turn. The stench of the bodies was overwhelming, but it would grow much worse in the weeks ahead. The land was completely contaminated with death and disease, and it would take nothing less than a miracle to make it habitable again. [114]

In most nations, little more than the minimum police forces were left to maintain basic law and order. When Yeshua had returned, the prisons, jails, and dungeons all over the world had been instantly flung open, and all the prisoners set free. Some in the prisons were criminals, but many more were innocent, being

---

[114] Isaiah 63:1-6; Revelation 14:20, 19:17-18

imprisoned only because of their religion, politics, or opinions.

There had been widespread looting in the final hours leading up to the End, but immediately after Yeshua's return, all crime suddenly ceased. Everyone seemed to know that the true King had come to earth, and that they would be punished for whatever crimes they committed.

The world was like a huge house of rebellious children whose parents had suddenly come home unannounced, and soon it would be time to pay for their disobedience. But in this case, not only had the King returned to His rightful place of authority on the earth, but it was the God of the entire universe. And everyone instinctively knew that He saw, heard, and knew every deed they had ever done – whether good or bad.

Far to the east of Jerusalem, the former capital of the world – the great city of Babylon – was a burning heap of rubble. The vast oil deposits beneath the city and the surrounding areas were still on fire, and tremendous billows of thick black smoke rose from the land.

Along with the destruction of the world economy, most of the media outlets had been silenced as well. Nearly all computers, electronics, and electrical systems had been wiped out upon Yeshua's arrival, and the people were forced to interact with those around them, without the distractions of television, radio, and the Internet to occupy the bulk of their time.

As far as the basic necessities, Yeshua provided immediate relief for everyone on earth, whether they believed in Him or not. The day after His return, it began raining all over the earth for at least several minutes every day to provide fresh water for drinking and washing. He also announced that they would have no more need for food until after the Great Judgment, when the world would be returned to the condition in which He had originally created it. He would sustain all the people by His Word, and to everyone's astonishment, they found they were no longer hungry, and had no need for food.

Everyone on the earth had seen His return with their own eyes – even the blind – and those who were sleeping or unconscious. Later that Day, everyone once again saw Him and His voice rang through out all the earth. He declared that the World Union and all the governments of the world were no more, and that the government now rested on His shoulders.

The world that everyone had always known was passing away and would soon be remade. No violence, wickedness, nor injustice would be tolerated any longer. Of what few of these evils would take place, their perpetrators would be swiftly and justly dealt with. Law, order, and justice would rule the earth from the highest person down to the lowest.

Yeshua then declared that the two greatest commandments were in immediate effect, and He said them clearly for everyone to hear: "You shall love the Lord your God with all your heart, with all your soul, with all your heart, and with all your strength. And you shall love your neighbor as yourself."

He also put the Ten Commandments into effect and read them to all the inhabitants of the earth also. And then He reiterated the two greatest commandments again. Everyone was now expected to care for their neighbors, whoever they might be. Give and you will be given to, serve and you will be served. Bless and you will be blessed. Curse and you will be cursed. Help one another, give without fear or worry, and bind up the broken and the broken-hearted.

After He had finished speaking, He caused a cool, refreshing wind to blow over all the continents, providing comfort and fresh air to everyone on the earth. In Israel, where there was mass devastation, Yeshua made the great East wind blow once again, and the gorged birds were carried away to the Mediterranean Sea in the west. The overwhelming stench of death and the billions of insects and airborne contaminants were blown out to sea as well.

Many were excited about the arrival of His Kingdom and the hope and promise of the new life and new world He brought with Him. But millions more were terrified at His arrival, and many knew they would be punished. The most fearful were those who had taken the Enki Seals on their foreheads or on their right hands. With the arrival of the King of Justice, many feared that judgment would soon be served without leniency or mercy.

CHRIS HAMBLETON

*   *   *

Three days after His return, a huge crowd of people instantly appeared in the flat, wide valley on the east side of Jerusalem. As they readjusted to the different scenes around them, they began to understand what had occurred.

During their morning prayers, everyone in Petra had been praying and thanking God for hearing their pleas and for saving them. Suddenly they had seen a brilliant light before them and felt the ground shift beneath their feet. But when they quickly looked around, they found they were no longer in Petra but just outside the Old City of Jerusalem.

At first, they didn't quite comprehend what had happened, but when they saw where they were, they suddenly knew: they had been taken from Petra to Jerusalem in the blink of an eye. They looked up and saw Yeshua standing above them at the entrance of the Golden Gate. They cheered and praised him again, with their shouts ringing all throughout Jerusalem.

Yeshua welcomed them to His City and beckoned them to come up from the valley, but gave instructions that they should stay in the city until the Great Judgment was over.

"Come and be reunited with your brothers and sisters, sons and daughters, and fathers and mothers," He said to them. "Help those in need, and comfort the broken-hearted."

All the people of the world, good and evil, saved and unsaved, had suffered tremendously and the Remnant was to show compassion to everyone as best they could. They were to walk carefully in His steps and to be sure to obey all of His commandments, for it was they who would repopulate the land of Israel, which would be a beacon and a light to all the world.

Jacob and Naomi, along with the rest of the people from Petra, made their way up from the new valley and began looking for familiar faces. They didn't have too many expectations, but they at least hoped to find someone they remembered either from their old lives or from Petra.

They walked through the city for several hours and surveyed the damage that had been wrought by the World Union forces when they had laid siege to Jerusalem. The entire city was in ruins, and they watched as numerous people picked their way through the rubble, looking for anything that could be salvaged. Most of Jerusalem outside the Old City district had been completely leveled, aside from the remains of some of the larger piles of rubble used to slow down the invasion. There were many bodies of both the World Union soldiers and the Jewish fighters intermingled amid the debris.

As they were heading back towards the Temple, Jacob and Naomi saw someone who looked vaguely familiar. But it had been a long time since they had last seen him, and so many people had died that it probably wasn't who they thought it was. Yet as they came closer to him, he recognized them and when his face brightened, they knew it was him.

"Daniel!" Naomi called out, waving him over.

"Jacob – Naomi! How are you? I wasn't sure you were here or not!" he said, greeting Jacob with a handshake and Naomi with a hug.

He noticed that they were still together and standing close to one another at that, and that was a good sign. Upon first glance, Jacob seemed different somehow, like he wasn't quite the same as he had been the last time he had seen them in Petra. Daniel realized he had been saved – otherwise he probably wouldn't have been there, and he definitely wouldn't have been smiling.

"We're fine – you know, still adjusting to what's been going on the last few days, but good. And you?"

"Very well – now. I was wounded near the end of the battle, but He healed me," he said. "Saul had helped me escape into the valley, and —"

"Saul?" Jacob interrupted. "Do you mean he's still alive? You were with him?" Both Jacob and Naomi looked at each other, and Naomi began to weep with joy at the possibility.

"Oh yes – both of them were with me. We were over there at the corner of the Temple, and his brother stayed behind to help us get to safety."

"Ahban – Ahban's alive too? And he's here?" Naomi asked.

She shook her head and bit her lip, trying to hold back even more tears. Hearing that one of their sons was alive was enough of a shock, but that both had survived was more than they could have ever dreamed possible. They hadn't heard from either of them since they had fled to Petra over three years before.

"Are they still here?" said Jacob. "Can you take us to them?"

"Of course! They're just a couple blocks up the street near the Temple. They're helping clean up around there and set up tents and shelters." He motioned for them to follow him and then turned around and began walking up towards the Temple.

They quickly followed alongside him up the street. They asked him about where he had gone after he had left Petra and what had happened to him. He gave them the short version, telling them briefly about the Underground Railroad and how he had helped in Jerusalem during the siege. He didn't mention the car accident and his other narrow escapes – he didn't like to think about it much, since it still frightened him at times.

Daniel smiled as they walked along, about how kind and merciful the Lord had been to this particular family. They had all been unbelievers when the Tribulation had begun, and now they were all saved and alive, except for one. And to think that now the entire family was in the same city at the same time, after all that had happened to them, was even more to be thankful about.

The reunion would be simply wonderful, and he was grateful he'd be able to see it for himself.

* * *

Saul saw his parents and Daniel first, and a wave of emotion swept over him. He recognized them right away, but he knew he would probably look much different to them. His clothes were filthy and it had been days (or was it weeks?) since he had showered, but he hadn't really cared about his appearance until now. He smoothed down his hair and then he nudged his older brother.

"Ahban – look!" he exclaimed. "It's Mom and Dad!" he said, pointing to a small group of people walking up the street.

Ahban turned and squinted. His eyesight had been getting worse over the last year or two, but he was able to see that they were indeed his parents. He smiled and grabbed Saul's arm, and they immediately ran towards them.

Daniel looked up to see two men running towards them and he slowed. Jacob and Naomi saw his reaction and followed his gaze. The two men were their own sons!

All three of them stopped, and huge grin crossed Daniel's face as he stepped aside to watch their reaction. Naomi was already crying at the sight of them, and Jacob was trying to hold back his own tears, but then he finally gave into them.

Saul reached Naomi first and nearly knocked her off her feet when he hugged her, while Ahban nearly did the same to his father. And then they switched and all wept together.

They looked one another over to see how they had changed or if they were hurt. None of them could believe it, yet there they were – years after they had gone their separate ways. The terrible arguments and fights were forgotten as if they had never happened. They were a family once again.

"Saul, Ahban, thank God you're all right!" Naomi exclaimed. "Were you hurt?" she asked Saul, looking him over closely to see if there were any scars or marks.

"Yeah, but that's all over now. I had some souvenirs of my prison stays, but it looks like they're all gone now," he said with his trademark grin.

Ahban chimed in, "You should have seen him the first time he was thrown in jail. You would've never let him go outside again!"

They all laughed and then Saul asked about their time in Petra. It was a camping trip with no end, Jacob replied with a smile. They told all about how they had lived in a small tent, with hundreds of thousands of other people doing the same. It had been strange at first, but after a few weeks they had gotten used to it.

They told about what had happened near the End in Petra, and about how the Sanhedrin had come to believe that Yeshua was the promised Messiah, and that three days later after they had begun praying, He had returned. So much had happened in such a short time, it was surprising that it had been only a week ago that they had been surrounded in the rock city by Medine's forces, preparing for the worst.

Both Ahban and Saul noticed that their parents were standing much closer to each other than they used to, and they seemed much more kind and affectionate towards one another. It was the first time in years they had seen their parents together like that, and it was a welcome change. Their years in Petra must have rekindled their marriage, and given them both a new outlook on life. Seeing them together now, Saul hoped they would never return to their old lives of coldness and isolation.

"So, what happens to us now?" Ahban asked, and then he remembered. He glanced down at his right hand, where he still had the mark on his skin. Everyone became quiet and somber, and Naomi became teary-eyed again, but this time not out of joy.

"Oh – right," he said, looking ashamed and humiliated.

They all knew what would happen next: the Great Judgment. Ahban had not really thought much about it since Yeshua had destroyed the armies surrounding Jerusalem. But now he would have to. Ahban wanted to start over and live a new life in this new world. Was it too late? Could he throw himself upon the mercy of the King and beg for forgiveness?

Daniel broke the uncomfortable silence by asking how Saul and Ahban had been able to get to Jerusalem from Iraq. That helped everyone elude the subject of Ahban's future, and they spent the rest of the day together, catching up on what had happened to each of them over the last four years.

* * *

She had been watching them for the past seven years. She had seen each of them moment by moment from the time she had left, and she could still see them as clearly as she ever had.

In fact, she could see them all no matter where they were or what they were doing – she simply needed to focus on one of them and it was like she was standing right next to them. And now, she was watching them be reunited as a family, and she longed to be with them once again. But it was not time yet.

THE TIME OF JACOB'S TROUBLE

So much had changed in their lives over the last decade. The world had been tormented, ruined, and destroyed. Billions had died in the wars and judgments. Many like her parents had come to Yeshua and had been reborn. They had been saved, but her other brother had remained as he always had been: lost.

She was most thankful for the many changes she had watched take place in her parents' lives over the last three years. She had seen them settle in at Petra when they had first arrived, and had been certain that her father would leave. She had prayed that he would stay and open up to the Spirit and to seriously consider what the Scriptures said.

But the change hadn't take place as soon as she had hoped, yet he had remained in Petra. She had rejoiced when Saul had been called to be one of the 144,000, and had been broken-hearted when Ahban had defiantly taken the mark. He had indeed chosen his fate and his future, and he would have to live with that decision for eternity. Her King did not violate the sovereignty of His masterpiece – everyone had their own free will.

While her parents had been with their new family in Petra, she had been with her new one in Heaven. At the moment of the Rapture, she had been given her new eternal body – one that was no longer limited to space, time, or to the other confines of matter. She had immediately discovered that she could overcome matter and space by only her thoughts, just as Yeshua could.

All of His brothers and sisters could as well: the Saved, the Raptured, the Church. Her new body was one that could not be hurt, damaged, become sick, feel pain, or die. She no longer experienced aging and would never again suffer. She was immortal, eternal, and timeless.

She could remember everything that had ever happened in her old life like it was yesterday, fresh and new. She found that she even had clear memories of things she had never remembered while on earth, such as her early childhood, her birth, and even before her birth. Her new memories started with clarity from the moment of her conception all the way to the present, and would continue on into eternity.

And the clarity of every memory had been heightened dramatically across all of her senses, and she found she was now able to much better interpret the thoughts, words, and body language of all those in her memories. Everything and everyone she remembered was clear and distinct.

All those who had been called to be part of His Church were the same as she. And someday, all the believers in the One True God who had accepted the new life He offered would be as one – from Adam to the last one before the Final Judgment at the end of time – united forever.

From the instant she had been transformed, she immediately knew everyone else who had been called with her by name. All the Church had been raptured at the same moment, from those first followers of Yeshua at the Day of Shavuot to the last one who had accepted Yeshua as his Savior before the Rapture.

In that instant, the lives of millions of believers had been joined and intertwined, and they all shared common memories of when they had been worshiping, serving, and following the Lord. They all now knew the impact of their individual contributions to the Body, and how they had helped in ways they themselves did not know until that final moment of the Church Age.

The moment after the last one in the Church had raised his head from his prayer, he found himself alongside millions upon millions of others standing directly in front of the King, sitting on His Throne in Heaven. The transformation into Eternity and journey to Heaven had been instantaneous, and it felt as if they were seeing, hearing, smelling, touching, and feeling for the first time in their lives. The fog of their sin and flesh had once and for all been removed from their consciousness. Instead of seeing and hearing everything through a filthy, darkened window from far away, they saw and heard everything as it truly was.

The instant when they realized what had happened and where they were, the Church fell on their faces and worshipped the King and His Father. A long time later – even in the timelessness of Heaven – He beckoned them to celebrate with Him.

THE TIME OF JACOB'S TROUBLE

After the reunion between the Groom and His Bride the Church, He once again took His Throne and began the Bema Seat Judgment – the Judgment of Rewards. And there He rewarded every individual believer for their service while on the earth. He also judged the individual groups and churches and denominations.

Many received very little, being either saved in the last moments of their lives or having been saved a long time but never serving the Body. Others received moderate rewards, and a few were greatly rewarded. But few had accurately estimated their crown: those who had thought themselves great often received little, and those who had thought little of themselves and their service often received much.

After the Judgment of Rewards, they worshipped Him again and then they were ushered into a huge room where there was a single, massive white Table that stretched as far as the eye could see. A great company of others in clean linen suddenly appeared next to them, and they led the Bride to their places at the Table and seated them.

And then Yeshua stood at the head of the Table and welcomed them to the Marriage Supper of the Lamb. He blessed them and sat down, and the servants next to everyone began to set huge plates of food before them. And all the saints feasted with their Lord and King and celebrated with one another.[115]

When the celebration concluded, He beckoned them to His side to watch what was happening on the earth. As they looked down from Heaven, only a brief moment had passed from the time they had been raptured to the moment in time they were watching.

Only their immediate friends and family appeared to miss them, but most of the rest of the world barely gave them a passing thought. The great delusion of the Enemy had begun, and for the next seven years on the earth – barely a moment in Eternity – they watched as the Great Dragon and his servants (the Anshar, the Luciferim, David Medine, and Franco Pontiffica) deceived

---

[115] Revelation 19:7-9

the peoples and slaughtered others by the billions, condemning many of them to his own fate in Hell.

And then came the moment when He declared it was time to take possession of Their Inheritance: the world and the rest of His Creation.

But the Church was only the First Fruits of the Body of Christ – the very beginning of a huge harvest of souls that would be gathered to Him and united as One, with Him as the Head of the entire Body. Those who had died from Abel, the first of the martyrs, to the last person who had died at the moment of Yeshua's death were among those would be resurrected and transformed at the end of the Millennium. Those believers who died during the Millennium would be transformed with them, and then they would go through the Great White Throne Judgment with all the rest. And after the remainder of the harvest was brought into the Body, they would know them too, and there would be perfect unity among the entire Body.

And now that the King and the Church had returned to the earth, they would be given authority and rulership over those who remained. After the coming judgment had been completed, only the believers would be left among the survivors of the Great Tribulation. And they would begin replenishing the earth for the third and final time under ideal conditions and under the ideal Government.

There would be perfect law, order, and justice. Prosperity and peace and contentment would flow throughout the earth, from the least to the greatest. There would be no more famines, disasters, or destruction. And everyone would live in harmony with one another, until the very end of the Millennium.

Her own rewards from the Bema Seat Judgment had been much more than she had expected, and she was tremendously thankful to her Lord. Like the rest of the Church, she would be given authority in the new Kingdom, and would rule with Him and His Church.

She did not know yet exactly what her new position would be, but she trusted Him to provide the right one for her. Yeshua had kept the Body together with Him until the last of the armies were destroyed, and just today He had told them to go to their friends and families who were still alive and then return to His side when the Great Judgment began.

And now, for the first time since she had been transformed, she felt nervous and even a bit afraid. Who should she meet first? Would it be too much to see her entire family again at the same time? And then looking once again to her King, she asked Him what His will was, and He instantly answered her. She thanked Him and waited for the precise time He had told her.

Saul had been the first and one of the few people she had brought into His Family, so he would be the first she would introduce herself to in this new age.

Ruth smiled and waited patiently for her brother to be alone.

*   *   *

The end of another long day came, and Saul wandered away from the others and hiked up the north ridge of the small mountain that had formerly been the Mount of Olives.

After seeing so much destruction and debris all day, it was relaxing to see trees and grass again, even if most of them were just small shoots and sprouts. He tried to focus on all the sights, sounds, and smells he could, and after he had put the day's events out of his immediate thoughts, he stopped to kneel behind a large scorched rock and began to pray quietly.

While he was praying, he heard footsteps nearby, and he opened his eyes and saw that the scene around him was lit slightly, as if there a glowing light coming from behind him. He turned around slowly and saw a woman clothed in brilliant white linen, and it appeared as if her body itself was shining underneath her garments.

He squinted and held his hand up to his eyes to block out some of the light to identify the woman. After his eyes had adjusted a moment later, he could see her clearly.

At first, he feared that it was one of the Anshar, but the King had imprisoned them all after the last battle at Megiddo had ended. From the form, he realized it was a female. She wasn't a ghost, but was one of the Church who had returned with Him.

"Hello, Saul. Do you remember me?" she asked.

Saul blinked for a moment, trying to associate the voice with a face. And then it struck him – the voice was different, but the tone and the manner were of his sister.

"Ruth? Is that you?!" he exclaimed. She nodded and he instinctively stepped forward, but then stopped. Was she really there, or was he seeing things?

"It's okay – don't be afraid," she reassured him, and then she stepped towards him and gave him a sisterly hug.

It *was* his sister, and he remembered how long it had been since he had last seen her – just over seven years. After a moment, they let go and he stepped back, and looked at her more closely.

"You've changed – did you grow taller?" he joked, and she laughed the old familiar way he remembered, and then he was certain it was her.

"You look different too – a little older maybe, but more or less the same. Same mischievous smile! Are you up to trouble or something?" she joked.

"Nah, I've been too busy to be up to my old tricks. Maybe in a few weeks or something," he said with a laugh. "Have you appeared to Mom and Dad yet?" he asked, fluttering his fingers as if she was a ghost or something. That made her laugh again, and she shook her head.

"No, not yet, but I plan to tomorrow. I didn't want to frighten them or anything. I was hoping that you could prepare them. Could you talk to them for me?"

"Sure. You know, I had a feeling we would meet up sooner or later. I had been waiting for this disembodied voice to come in the middle of the night saying, "Saaauuul, Saaauuul," he said, imitating a ghost from one of the old movies.

"Yeah, that would've been funny. I should have thought of that," she chuckled.

They spent the next several hours together in the olive grove, talking about what had happened since the Rapture. He asked her many questions, mostly about what Heaven was like and all sorts of things about Eternity. She answered them as best she could, but most of her answers were inadequate, since those who had not been transformed could not even comprehend what Heaven was really like. No words could begin to describe the glory of Heaven, much less the Throne.

The next day, Saul told his parents and Ahban that he had met Ruth the night before while he was praying, and that she was coming to meet them later that day. When he asked when they would like to see her, they all said "right away" and a moment later, Ruth herself appeared within their midst. No longer bounded by time, space, or matter, she could appear, disappear, and even travel great distances with just a mere thought.

After they overcame their surprise at her sudden appearance, they all embraced her, and like Saul, they asked her many questions about where she had been, what had happened to her, and what Heaven was like. They all appeared to be more or less their usual selves, with the exception of Ahban. In most ways, he was the same, but below the surface, he wasn't able to hide his fears as well as he had been before Ruth had appeared.

Ruth spent the rest of the day with them, and then at sundown she bid them farewell. The Great Judgment was coming soon, and she would not see them again until after it was finished.

As she said goodbye, she looked briefly over at Ahban and looked him directly in the eyes. And he had the brief awareness that she knew of his decision to reject the One she treasured the most.

She gave him a solemn look, and he knew he had deeply grieved both her and her King.

* * *

Yeshua had returned exactly 1290 days after the Temple had been desecrated by David Medine and Franco Pontiffica, just as the angel had prophesied to Daniel the Prophet thousands of years before. [116]

---

[116] Daniel 12:11

CHRIS HAMBLETON

He had given all the people who had survived the Tribulation and His Second Coming – both the wicked and the righteous – five days of rest before the Great Judgment began. It would last for the next forty days, and when it was over there would be no more wicked or unbelieving people left on the earth.[117]

Yeshua the King took His place on the high throne that had been placed outside the ruined Temple in Jerusalem. A great pit of burning sulfur was to the left of His chair, and the pit reeked of molten, bubbling rock. His angels were ordered to quickly roam throughout the earth and gather every Gentile who had taken the mark of the beast and throw them into the pit. For what seemed like hours, thousands upon thousands of angels hunted down those who had taken the mark and dropped them into the molten pit. [118]

After the Gentiles who had taken his seal were destroyed, the last leader of men, David Medine and his prophet, Franco Pontiffica were brought forward to stand before Him. They were forced to bow with their faces buried in the dirt.

They were silent and did not struggle, at least not on the outside. Their souls screamed out cursings, pleadings, rantings, and rage, but their bodies no longer obeyed their minds. The One on the throne before them was in complete control, and He immediately condemned them to eternal torment in the Lake of Fire.

Two gleaming, powerful angels stepped forward and took hold of Medine and Pontiffica by the arms and cast them headfirst into the pit, and they screamed before vanishing into its fiery depths.

Those close enough to the pit could still hear their terrible cries, even though they were now in the Lake of Fire in the bowels of Hell, and no longer in the pit of molten lava on the earth. In the Lake of Fire, they would be ever-burning, but never consumed – ever-tormented, but never slain. And there they continued to scream hour after hour, day after day, month after month, and year after year. [119]

---

[117] Daniel 12:12
[118] Matthew 13:40-42
[119] Revelation 19:20

438

THE TIME OF JACOB'S TROUBLE

In front of the pit, a great angel clothed in white suddenly appeared with a multitude of other gruesome creatures bound in gleaming chains, all gathered to watch the judgment of the remnant of man and all the nations they had corrupted by their deception. Those bound were small and great, terrible and mild, but all trembled from what they knew was coming. Though they struggled against their chains and bonds, they could not budge them no matter how hard they tried. Some gave up after several minutes, while others continued to strive and thrash in vain.

Within the midst of the demonic crowd was an exceedingly great red dragon. He was filled with uncontrollable rage but could not move from the heavy silver chains wrapped around him. The hordes surrounding him were the dark angels who had chosen to follow him before the Great Flood, and their offspring they had wrought with the daughters of men. These unnatural offspring had later become the restless demons who had roamed the earth as spirits, ghosts, and apparitions for thousands of years.

Also among these fallen ones were all the Anshar and the Luciferim, who had recently deceived mankind and led them into rebellion and war against the King. They had ravaged the earth and tormented His people, but now they all stood silent before Yeshua, but not by their own will.

The great adversary of God and men, Satan the adversary, was now forever trapped in the form of a hideous red dragon. No longer would he clothe himself in light and beauty – he would be seen for what he was: the Beast of Beasts, Liar of Liars, the Murderer of Murderers, and the Blasphemer of Blasphemers. [120]

* * *

After the judgment of David Medine and Franco Pontiffica, all of the leaders, representatives, and officials of the World Union, and all the government officials of the nations were brought before Yeshua and His Church. In addition to this multitude, all the Jews of the world were brought forward, each according to

---

[120] Matthew 25:31-33; Revelation 20:4

their tribe, clan and family. Most of the Jews had no idea to which tribe they had belonged, but as soon as they were brought into His presence, they were immediately aware of their entire lineage, and separated themselves into groups under the direction of the 144,000 Witnesses. [121]

Immediately in front of the King, a row of twelve judgment thrones had been set up, similar to His own but smaller and less impressive. And there the Twelve Apostles clothed in glowing white linen garments stepped forward from among His Church and sat down in their judgment seats.

One by one, every person of each of the tribes in Israel stepped forward and received judgment according to their faith in Yeshua: those who believed in Him took their place to the right of the judgment seats, while those who had refused Him took their place on the left in front of the burning pit.

They were not asked about their deeds in life, either good or bad – only if they had accepted Yeshua or not. Those on the left watched the multitude of their brothers and sisters be judged as they had been, and wept at their fate. Those on the right also wept, but out of compassion for their brethren. And when all the tribes of Israel had been judged, those on the left were cast into the pit of burning sulfur and vanished from sight.

When the judgment of the tribes of Israel had finished, the Twelve Apostles stepped down from their thrones and many more thrones were set up, one for each of the hundreds of nations of the world. And then another group of His servants stepped forward from among the multitude behind Him and took their seats on the thrones. A great company of people suddenly appeared before Him – those who had been slaughtered during the Great Tribulation by the Beast. [122] Then the long process of judging all the nations and the peoples began.

For the Gentiles, not only were they judged on whether or not they had accepted Yeshua as their Savior, but also how they had treated the Jews during their lifetime. Many former Muslims and

---

[121] Revelation 19:19-20
[122] Revelation 20:4-6

even Christians who had later accepted Yeshua but had beaten, killed, or harmed the Jews, were separated out for punishment. They would not be condemned to the fiery pit, but they would be punished as they had mistreated the Jews. Those who had murdered a Jew were put to death, and the rest were beaten or scourged.

The remainder of those who had not accepted Yeshua nor taken the mark were thrown into the pit, but their degree of torment would be increased or decreased according to their own deeds, respect for their laws, and their treatment of the Jews. [123]

The nations that had been kind to Israel over the course of their history were granted their own lands and people, while those who had raged against Israel, terrorized her, or persecuted her people had their authority, land, and people taken away and given to others. Many of the nations of the Middle East, Africa, and Europe lost all their territory and had it given to their neighbors who had helped Israel or the Jews. Some groups and tribes who had no borders or lands of their own, but who had treated the Jews with kindness were given new lands of their own. And all the nations of the earth and their borders were redrawn according to the deeds they had done, and how they had treated the Jews and the Christians. [124]

After thousands of years, the Lord kept His promises to Abraham, Isaac, Jacob, and their offspring: "Those who bless you I will bless, and those who curse you I will curse." [125]

* * *

Ahban stood trembling and shaking more than he ever had before in his life. He stood in the line for the tribe of Naphtali, in front of one of the Apostles. He couldn't remember which one of the Twelve he was, but it didn't really matter anyway.

Within an hour or so, he would step into eternal torment, and he thought he would pass out from how afraid he was.

---

[123] Matthew 25:31-33
[124] Matthew 25:33-46
[125] Genesis 12:3

During the long days and now the even longer hours that had transpired between the return of the King and the Great Judgment, he had thought of little else other than what would happen to him. Was there any possibility of a reprieve? Could he beg for forgiveness, or was it truly too late?

Before today, he had thought there would be a remote chance of that, but as he watched the millions of people be judged and then either blessed or condemned, he had given up all hope. The time for choosing one's fate had ended the instant the King had set foot upon the earth, or in his case, the instant he had taken the mark.

He had contemplated trying to hide, but how could one run away from God? It was almost silly to even think about it. Nevertheless, many of those who already knew their fate (as he did) tried in vain anyway. When His voice had rang out through the earth, calling His Court to order, all those in hiding found themselves instantly transported from wherever they had fled to Jerusalem and grouped into their respective places in their nations and tribes.

There was no possibility of escape, and there was no faint glimmer of hope. He had acknowledged to himself over and over that he had chosen his path, whether for right or for wrong. He had had numerous chances to turn and repent – the rest of his family had, but why hadn't he?

He also considered suicide, but what was the point of that? He would only appear there before the King at the White Throne Judgment, and receive the same sentence. And since death was timeless, to him it would only appear as if he had delayed his fate for a brief instant.

No, it was best to just get it over with. He smirked for only a brief moment when he thought he should take it like a man, but this wasn't a brief punishment – it was eternal! He had heard that many tried that also – killing themselves in a variety of ways – but he had already decided that he would not go out like a coward.

He knew he was a fool, but he would not be a coward too.

There were only a handful of people in front of him – a couple of older men and a middle-aged woman. She looked some-what like his mother, but this woman had been broken. When it was her turn and she stood before the Apostle, she wept convulsively and tried to cover her hand with the mark on it, but its blackness showed through no matter what she did.

Others had even tried to cut the mark out of their hands or even amputate their own hands! But even when they tried to be rid of it and change their fate, the mark had supernaturally reappeared on their foreheads. There was no escaping the choice they had made when they had sworn their allegiance to David Medine, the former god-king of the world.

The Apostle asked the woman if she understood what fate she had chosen when she had taken the mark and she acknowledged that she had. Every person on the earth had been warned several times by the believers around them, by the angels, and also by the testimony of the millions of martyrs.

There was simply no excuse: she had chosen Death, and to Death she would be condemned. The Apostle gave her the sentence and she broke down, begging hysterically for mercy. But she was led to the edge of the pit by the one of the angels regardless, and was promptly cast into the pit, screaming as she fell.

Ahban gulped, and wept quietly to himself. Moments later, he found himself standing before the Apostle too. No one was in front of him – it was his turn, and he knew what would happen. He had seen it thousands upon thousands of times since the Great Judgment had begun.

From the pit of burning fire and sulfur, he could hear the condemned screaming and howling. What would it feel like? Was there ever any relief? Even for a moment?

How could the King be so cruel to those who had rejected Him? It wasn't fair, he screamed to himself. It wasn't fair!

He barely heard the Apostle when he began speaking to him. He repeated the same questions that he had asked the woman and all the others, and that brought him back to reality.

And like the others, Ahban acknowledged that he had known the consequences of taking the mark before it had been imprinted on him, and that he had not cared at the time. But he cared now, and he apologized over and over for taking it out of rebellion. He had been deceived by his pride, his intellect, and his education.

But the Apostle reminded him that he had consciously decided to reject the Creator Himself – the God of the universe – and there was no place left for him any longer. He read the sentence, but Ahban no longer heard him speaking.

Ahban closed his eyes and hung his head. He desperately wanted to look back at his family and his loved ones, but he didn't want his last memory of them to be one of their sadness and grief.

He wanted to remember only the good times in his life and the love he had known with them. He didn't want to see any more judgment, and he surely didn't want to see the pit of fire that he would soon be thrown into.

He felt someone take him firmly by the right arm, and from the feeling of the heatless, unbreakable grip, it could only be the angel. Ahban let himself be led along, until he was finally stopped. He didn't dare open his eyes, because he knew where he was. He could already feel the heat searing the skin on his face and arms. The stench of the molten, burning sulfur made him nauseous and turn his head.

Then he felt a mighty shove forward, and suddenly he had the unmistakable sensation of falling. It was like he was falling into the depths of the sun itself.

When he finally struck the boiling lava, he screamed as he felt his flesh and body instantly catch fire and burn away. He opened his eyes, expecting to see fire, but all was dark around him. He couldn't feel his body as before, but he found he could still move and feel terrible pain somehow. How could he move or feel pain when his body was destroyed?

Yet the burning and torment continued, and he screamed as loud as he could. But no one acknowledged his cries, and no one came to his aid. This was now his eternity, and there was only agony, torment, and suffering.

* * *

444

THE TIME OF JACOB'S TROUBLE

When the judgment of the nations and all the peoples of the earth finally concluded, the multitude of demonic creatures chained nearby were brought forward to Yeshua, and then condemned and sentenced. The majority of the demons and evil angels were thrown into the pit of fire, while their rulers and demon-kings – the former principalities of the nations – remained in their chains next to the dragon.

These were the ones who had corrupted man and pushed him to his natural vices and into the wars in the centuries after the Great Flood, and the ones who had ruled over the kingdoms of the earth through their human servants. They would be condemned to the lower prisons of Sheoul in the center of the earth, the Abyss, with their brethren who had corrupted and tormented mankind before the Flood.

Lastly, the great dragon was brought forward and condemned for all he had done to the creation, the earth, and its inhabitants. His punishment was that he would be sentenced to the lowest part of Sheoul for one thousand years. Next to the pit of burning sulfur, another large pit abruptly opened up in the earth, but this pit was bottomless – it went all the way down to the center of the earth, into the Abyss.

And a great six-winged angel flew down from the sky and seized the dragon by one of the many chains that bound him, and cast him screaming headfirst into the pit. The sides of the pit quickly closed behind him as he fell, sealing him deep inside the earth. Satan would be imprisoned in the Abyss for the next one thousand years, before he was loosed once again for a final opportunity to repent and turn from his evil, rebellious ways. [126]

And now, only the survivors who had not taken the mark and had believed in Yeshua as their Savior were left among all the former multitudes of the earth.

The nations that remained were the ones that had helped Israel and her people, even in seemingly minor ways throughout their history. Those who would govern the nations of the earth were the believers who comprised the Church.

---

[126] Revelation 20:1-3

CHRIS HAMBLETON

The world was in ruins, but it would be rebuilt in righteousness, inhabited by one body of believers, and governed by the perfect Governor: Yeshua, the King of Kings and Lord of Lords.

* * *

After Satan had been cast into the Abyss, the judges of the Gentiles stepped down from their thrones and seats, and everyone worshipped Him. Only a tiny fraction of the former population of the earth remained – less than two million people, from what had been nearly ten billion from less than ten long years before. They had come from everywhere on the earth, from the remote jungles to the desert wastelands to the frigid polar regions.

The Great Judgment had finally ended, and all the people watching were exhausted from mourning and weeping for those they had seen be judged and thrown into the pit of fire. They were emotionally numb, and many were just trying to come to terms with all the condemned who had been in their lives.

But none of them were angry, at least not at the King nor the judges, because the condemned were indeed guilty, and they had each chosen their fates. Justice had finally come to the earth, but even perfect, righteous justice felt harsh when it was meted out against those known and loved by others.

Ahban's family had watched him be judged and receive his sentence. They had wept and cried out when he had been thrown into the pit, but they knew he had chosen his destiny years before. The good he had done throughout his life and even at the end could not change the fact that he had spurned Yeshua and the salvation He had offered countless times.

He had consciously, consistently chosen his own way instead of the Way of Life, and now he was gone forever. They understood from the Scriptures that they would never see him again once they reached Eternity, and that he would be forever more as he was: a tormented, tortured soul.

Jacob, Naomi, and Saul had seen many of their other friends

and family be condemned similar to Ahban. The sight of all of them being sentenced made them weep and be filled with regret.

They had wasted so much precious time before they had been saved – time they could have been using to turn people they had known from their destiny of torment. But they had been unfaithful at that time too, and it was only by the grace of God that they had been called and then accepted that calling to Life.

Yet in these last days, months, and years, everyone on the earth had been called over and over, and yet these people had still refused Him, even though it had been abundantly clear what awaited them in the end. But they had not believed in either the Life He offered or the Death He had repeatedly warned them of.

The King and His judges had indeed been fair, just, and righteous. And those left on the earth would soon be able to truly start over for the first time in thousands of years. But they would always carry the sting and the sorrow of their many missed opportunities to save others. And they would grieve for those whom they had loved but lost forever.

Yeshua rose from His throne and declared that the Great Judgment had ended. He tried to comfort the people with His words, but He knew that they had lost many they had loved. He had lost many that day too – He had loved all of the condemned from eternity past, since the very beginning, and had prayed many, many times for each of them that they would turn from their path and seek Him.

He and His servants had beckoned and pleaded with them over and over to repent and choose Life, but they had always refused. And they continued to rebuff Him, no matter how many opportunities He had given them, especially in these last years.

What more could He have done? No, they had chosen Death, and because they were free to choose, He could not and would not force them to turn to Him.

And then He began to describe the new world that would be coming shortly, how justice and liberty and righteousness would now rule the earth. Everyone would learn the Law and follow it, and those who refused would be swiftly rebuked and punished.

The Wicked One was imprisoned for a thousand years, and

those who disobeyed Him or His servants or the Law would have no excuse any longer. The remnant of the people on the earth who had survived would replenish it, and He admonished them to teach their children, grandchildren, and the multitudes who were to come about Him, the Gospel, and the Law.

Judgment against the disobedient would be swift and just and harsh. The nations that would not follow Him or His people Israel would be cursed and have their rain withheld until they repented. And the same would be true for families and individuals.

The people gathered before Him listened humbly and carefully, but inside were all wondering what would happen next. Their homes were destroyed and their lands unusable.

But Yeshua knew their thoughts and their concerns, and He reassured them the world would be made anew, and that they would no longer have to worry about what they would eat, drink, or wear, or how they would find shelter.

And with these last words being said, another incredible miracle began to take place for everyone gathered before the King of Kings and Lord of Lords to see.

CHAPTER 18
THE MILLENNIUM

I f one were able to observe the earth from space, they would have watched one of the greatest miracles of all time: the renewing of the earth. The earth had been utterly ruined over the last several years, and even before that had been largely uninhabitable after the Great Flood, the Ice Age, and subsequent catastrophes over the many centuries that had followed.

Even before the Tribulation, desertification, deforestation, glaciation, and erosion had laid waste to much of the earth, and the saltwater oceans left from the Flood covered other huge sections of the globe. But in a matter of minutes, all that would be changed back to how He had first created the earth – a breathtaking paradise full of beautiful scenery, trees, plants, and creatures of every sort.

The first event that took place was the remaking of the earth's surface. Immediately, most of the ocean basins rose up, causing untold volumes of water to rush off, back into the chambers that had once held them under the continents, and they were sealed back in as they had been at first. The sounds of the rising basins filled the earth and made everyone shake and brace themselves, but there was very little fear in their eyes.

The ocean water that remained was then purified and desalinated, and instantly turned back into fresh, drinkable, usable water. The great oceans were quickly reduced to a single, much smaller ocean that occupied the bottom quarter of the globe in a matter of minutes. Antarctica still existed, but was now connected to the lower portion of Australia. The eastern and western hemispheres, and all their continents were now re-connected by the risen ocean basins. The rugged, torn lands across the face of the earth were then leveled and flattened, and where great mountains had been moments before, only smaller versions of them remained. All the remnants of the last age – all the technology and buildings and cities of man vanished and new, unblemished land took its place. [127]

Then the next great change began to overtake on the earth – the barren wasteland that now made up most of the earth's surface began to show faint shades of green against the dreary brown backdrop. Tiny buds of grass and other foliage of every sort at first began to just break forth out of the ground, but then they rapidly rose several centimeters and seconds later were mature plants.

Trees of various kinds sprang up even faster than the grasses, and began peppering the newly greened landscape. The redwoods, oaks, cedars, pines, maples, and palm trees stretched their tops and branches up to the sky, almost straining up as far as they could go. Entire orchards of fruit trees also arose all over the earth, often in places where no fruit trees had ever grown in the past.

All the grasses, plants, and trees were fully mature, and were covered with perfect green leaves, seeds, nuts, and fruits of every kind. Many of the species of plants and fruit trees that had been lost in the Great Flood reappeared in abundance, and began yielding their fruit as if they had never been destroyed.

Immediately following the explosion of mature foliage, the air became much thicker and heavier. All the people and creatures alive instantly noticed the change, and they were suddenly revived and full of a new energy they had never known before.

The air smelled no more of dryness, dirt, and death, but was rich with the fragrance of the grasses and trees. Fresh and bursting with life, the sweet air filled the lower skies and every living thing on the earth breathed anew. The few people who had been inside hyperbaric chambers felt as if they were receiving the

---

[127] Isaiah 65:18-19

same treatment, but so much better.

And the air had not only been filled with two or three times as much oxygen as before, but the amounts of carbon dioxide had also been dramatically increased, giving the plants new life also. The waters of the earth also received the increased amounts of oxygen and carbon dioxide, and the plants in the waters burst with new life.

* * *

"Jacob, look over there!" Naomi exclaimed, pointing towards the west side of Jerusalem. The city was still in ruins.

He turned his head and was dumbstruck at what he saw, and together they stood in awe at the transformation that had begun to occur. It had started out slowly, but the changes all around them seemed to be quickly increasing in size and scope.

The tons of debris, rubble, and buildings that remained after the last war began crumbling to dust, and flattened out across the surface of the ground, as if being leveled and pressed by a great invisible hand. Moments later, they saw the silt began turning a bright shade of green, and then fresh buds of grass sprang up and instantly grew to a comfortable height of several centimeters.

And then they watched as trees of every sort erupt from the ground and rise to their mature heights. But the trees weren't just springing out of the ground haphazardly or intermixed – there were complete groves of the same types of fruit trees in neat, organized plots and rows. Paths appeared along the rows of trees, and then sections of the ground in other places dipped and fresh water began to flow in quiet, gentle streams.

Parks and gardens filled with many other types of trees and shrubs appeared in other areas of the city. Perfectly constructed streets suddenly rose out of the surface of the ground, and the trees that lined them sprang up and blossomed, providing shade, beauty, and splendor to every street in the city.

Homes, mansions, and other buildings rose just as quickly from earth and their spotless windows and walls gleamed in the mid-day sunshine. Many looked like modern buildings, but they were more wondrous and much more pleasing to behold. The former city of Babylon, the Jewel of Kingdoms, could not compare at all to this new city that had risen faster than Babylon had sank.

Close to where they were standing on the Temple Mount, Jacob and Naomi suddenly felt the ground shift slightly, and immediately heard the sound of a large flowing river very nearby. They turned and saw that the valley that had been created from the Mount of Olives, had just been extended all the way through Jerusalem as far west as they could see. Not only that, but it had also been extended far to the east, all the way past the Jordan River and into the former desolate Arabian Desert.

And as they watched, they looked for the source of the water, and they saw it was coming from directly underneath the Temple Mount itself. The Gethsemane River (as it would soon be called) started out very shallow, but as it ran down either side of the Temple Mount into the two valleys, the river grew deeper and deeper, and just outside the city it was a mighty rushing river as wide as the Jordan.

Though Jacob and Naomi did not know it yet, the Jordan River, the Sea of Galilee, and also the Dead Sea were transformed at the same time the Gethsemane River had begun to flow from under the Temple Mount. The Jordan River was widened to its greatest width at flood stage and ran straight from the Sea of Galilee, crossed the new Gethsemane River, and went all the way to the Dead Sea in the south. The ancient Valley of Siddim surrounding the Dead Sea had been raised to sea level, and was no longer the lowest point on earth.

The south end of the Dead Sea was also opened with a wide mouth and flowing into the Sea of Arabah for the first time in over four thousand years. The fresh water flowing from far in the north began to cleanse the Dead Sea. Within hours the Valley of Siddim would return to its former glory, which it had not known since its destruction in Abraham's day. From the skies far above Israel, the intersection of these two rivers made up a huge cross that overlaid the center of Israel and most of the Jordan plain, with the foot of it being in the northern parts of Arabia. [128]

In Jerusalem, the mountain range on which the entire city sat was lifted above the rest of the land, and then the Temple Mount itself rose above the city. The plot of land on which the Temple stood had now become the highest point on the entire earth, with a great river that flowed from it down either side of the Temple Mount, through the city, and across the land.

Then the entire Temple Mount began to shake, and the ground under which the old Temple had stood broke open and a new Temple, gleaming, white, and new rose from the earth and continued to rise until its lower doors and steps emerged and were level with the ground.

All the people in Jerusalem shouted for joy when they saw the new Temple arise – it was similar to what many scholars had pictured Solomon's Temple to be like, but this Temple was much larger and more magnificent. And like the other buildings that had risen from the midst of Jerusalem, the Temple was spotless, new, and fully complete from the moment it had appeared.

It was comprised entirely of white, shining marble, with elegant cedar covering the inside. The altar and the other furniture and implements were also provided, so that the daily sacrifices that would commemorate the Messiah's life and return could be started immediately.

But in this new Temple, there were no walls of overlaid gold, silver, or other precious metals inside its chambers or on the outside, which had previously symbolized the Holy One's presence in and among the Temple. There was no longer any need for them, because now the Holy One Himself would be inside the Temple. And He was more precious than gold, silver, or any other precious metal or created thing could even begin to represent His Glory and His Presence.

*   *   *

---

[128] In the Millennium, the Dead Sea will be "healed" and will be filled with fish. (Ezekiel 47:8-12)

Only several minutes had passed from the renewing of the foliage, air, and the waters all over the earth, but there were few creatures on the land or fish in the waters, and the new world was devoid of the familiar sights and sounds of life. The creatures that had survived the plagues and judgments were feeble and tiny. But just as quickly as the grasses and trees had sprang out of the ground, mounds of all shapes and sizes began to form on the landscape, almost as if the ground itself was bubbling and shifting from underneath.

And then the tops of the mounds burst open, and animals of every size, shape, and kind crawled out. From the smallest of mice to the greatest of the mammoths and all the creatures in between, they arose and began looking for food and sniffing the fresh, life-giving air. They began to call to their Maker with all their strength: whooping, calling, howling, trumpeting, barking, and cooing, and the land was filled with the sounds of the new creatures of the earth.

Out of the seas, lakes, ponds, rivers, and streams sprang forth birds of every sort – flying straight up from or rising in the midst of the waters. Great multitudes of the birds flew away to find trees or other places to feed or roost, but many remained near the water. And then in the waters, fish and other marine life suddenly appeared, and began swimming around vigorously, discovering and inspecting their new environments.

Along with them in the waters, other sea creatures appeared also, roving and swimming about, some of them great and others tiny, but all of them fully grown and bursting with life and strength. Sharks, whales, dolphins, octopuses, and all the wondrous creatures of the seas had come back into existence, and with them multitudes of other creatures appeared and flourished in the waters. These creatures had been seen by only handfuls of men in the former world, and had always been described as monsters and fables in their ancient stories.

To the surprise of many people after they had spread out from Israel to their allotted lands, they discovered that numerous creatures they had previously only read about in books were once again living, breathing, and walking among them. Many of the creatures that had been known from only bone fragments and fossils were now alive and roaming about the earth. Since they were fully grown and mature, many of the larger creatures were great and terrible to behold.

The huge woolly mammoths, saber-toothed variations of the familiar land creatures, and the other large mammals that covered the earth during the Ice Age were once again wandering and grazing about the earth, also fully developed.

And along with the great mammals, the greatest of the reptiles and lizards were also once again alive and roving about in herds, bands, and pairs: the various kinds of dragons, or dinosaurs, as they had been called in modern times. And the land shook when the largest of them ran or trod along the ground.

But instead of the food chain that had governed the animal kingdom after the Fall of Man in the Garden of Eden, none of the animals were carnivorous. All of them ate grasses, fruits, vegetation, seeds, or nuts – whatever foods that their Creator had originally designed them to consume, and there was no violence among any of the creatures on the earth.

The animals were completely at rest and peaceful towards one another, and there was no longer any fear between the various species and kinds. The larger animals were careful not to hurt or crush the smaller creatures, and the smaller ones no longer gathered in herds for safety or protection.

All the creatures had a strange, almost elaborate awareness of one another, and could now sense clearly when others were around them and what type of creature they were. [129]

* * *

Jacob and Naomi were still awed by the incredible changes taking place around them when they began hearing loud fluttering sounds nearby.

They looked over to the river, and they could see the water appear to tremble, almost as if it were beginning to boil, or like

---

[129] Isaiah 11:6-9

raindrops were falling on it, but the skies were all clear. As they watched, birds of every kind and size leapt from the waters and flew into the air, furiously flapping their wings. Some flew into the trees nearby, while others flew towards the parks in search of food and nesting places. Still others took flight and left the city altogether and flew off towards the horizon.

Everyone watching the renewing of the earth gasped once again at what they saw happening – the King, the Creator was bringing to life all the different kinds of creatures that had once inhabited the earth before it had fallen into decay and destruction. The birds, fowls, and every other kind of flying creature – even those that had long been extinct from the earth like pterodactyls and other flying reptiles, and even types of flying mammals they had never seen before emerged from the flowing river.

As they continued to watch the waters bring forth the flying creatures, they also began to notice movement in and under the surface of the river, and realized that the fish and other marine life was being remade also. Soon dorsal fins broke the surface of the water and then fish poked through, trying to snatch insects.

If they had been near the ocean or the lakes, they would have observed the whales, dolphins, sharks, and other great sea creatures leaping about for joy. Their environment was new and fresh and perfect, and they quickly began seeking food. But the sea creatures no longer ate one another or even fought – all were as they were meant to be, and sought after vegetation, algae, and other non-living seafood.

All along the riverbank, more changes were taking place, and they saw some people side-step or even jump back in surprise. Suddenly everyone took their eyes off the river and began looking at their feet and around at the ground. It had started as many small bumps rising from the ground, and then larger ones began to appear, some the size of small boxes, and others that were larger, and then some even the size of small hills!

But it was the larger mounds that astonished the people the most. Then like the birds the people had watched emerge from the water, animals of every kind popped out of the ground and shook the dirt off their coats, fur, scales, and hides. And then all the creatures, almost without hesitating, began moving about and spreading. The mounds and craters from which they had emerged soon closed up and appeared as if they had never been disturbed at all.

Land animals, both large and small, fierce and meek rose and began crawling, hopping, galloping, and running. The land creatures moved around the people staring in awe at them. The great reptiles, dinosaurs, and mammoths left the larger mounds – these were among the last to emerge from the ground. They were huge to behold, and they quickly moved away from the crowds towards the large open places. The dinosaurs were immense to see for the first time, and they drew the most attention. The great reptiles lumbered along to the river, pausing to bow their huge necks to drink and some let out deafening bellows to their Maker, while others headed for the new forests.

Within minutes, many of the creatures had lumbered, ran, and scurried away and were now finding their own grazing and dwelling places. Even more astonishing to the people was how the creatures no longer feared one another – the lions had been walking alongside the antelopes, and the tigers with the deer. The predatory creatures no longer pursued nor attacked the prey, and the prey no longer fled from the predators.

Instead, they paid one another little attention, and would stoop to drink or even graze without any fear of one another. The people also quickly discovered that none of the creatures instinctively feared them any longer either, and the people did not fear the animals. But the people still had authority over them, and the animals – regardless of their size – would come towards them if called and would flee if ordered. Every creature was tame and was completely obedient to man, no matter how ferocious they had previously been in the old world.

As the people watched the wide variety of creatures moving about them, some pointed out that many had never been seen before. They almost felt like the old European explorers who discovered the different types of animals when they came to the New World, and had encountered opossums, raccoons, and other creatures. And those were just the basic kinds the people realized they had not known before, not to mention all the thousands of types and variations among each kind.

Once again, the world was filled with the sights, sounds, and smells of life. The small creatures busily chatted their calls and sounds to one another, while the larger ones ate and lazily laid down for drowsing or rest.

When the earth and waters had finally stopped bringing forth creatures, the people once again fell to their faces and worshipped Yeshua, the King and Creator. Within a matter of minutes, all the earth had been transformed by the mere power of His thoughts and word from a world of death, destruction, and wastelands to a world new and fresh and teeming with creatures of every imaginable sort.

*   *   *

After all the earth and its creatures had been renewed, the people were the last to be restored. All the people on the earth, still gathered at Jerusalem before His throne, began experiencing an incredible, reviving sensation throughout their bodies.

Many among them had already been healed, but this was something different – something greater and more pervasive. It was a feeling of newness, wholeness, and complete healing. To many, it was as if a fog was lifting from their minds and they could suddenly think clearer and remember everything better than ever before in their lives. The effects of aging disappeared from even among the oldest among them, and the elderly looked and felt as if they were in their early thirties, except much better and stronger.

As the people looked over their renewed bodies and began talking to one another, they found themselves speaking a language they had never known before, but nevertheless they could speak and understand it fluently. It was similar to Hebrew, but a much better, more complete form of it. They still remembered their own native languages, but they felt no desire to speak them.

Also, they found that they were entirely fluent in reading and writing the new language that had been instantly implanted in their minds, made up of not mere letters or characters but hiero-glyphic-like symbols that each had a specific meaning which could then be combined to construct the words and sentences they found themselves speaking and hearing. The proper names of all the creatures, plants, and features of the earth had also been made known to them again, and all the previous names and terms were spoken no more.

With the renewing of their minds and bodies, all the people of the earth found they could sense one another with an almost supernatural awareness of their presence, feelings and moods. And along with sensing others, they also could sense and iden-tify any creature they came near to, and some of the creatures were even able to communicate with people in what many de-scribed as a wondrous, miraculous fashion. Some animals and sea creatures could speak the restored language of man, while most just communicated by their own distinctive mannerisms, calls, and sounds.

Suddenly a great company of people appeared from behind the throne, and the King rose to introduce them. More than a bil-lion people stood among them, and they were all young men and women of about the same age. These were all the unborn, the stillborn, the aborted, the infants, and the young children who had died or been taken from the earth before they had made a firm decision to believe in the Lord or rebel against Him.

They had been given a new life in a perfect world under a perfect government, and they would now be able to decide with-out hindrance whether they would follow Him or not. They would also be given their own inheritance among the nations and tribes they had originally come from – a new start at life under ideal conditions.

*   *   *

When everything had been restored to its proper state, it was time to divide up the earth once again into nations, the nations into tribes, the tribes into clans, and the clans into families, with each receiving their proper inheritance of land. The King would decide how to partition and allocate every piece of the earth, and He would start in His land: the land of Israel.

Israel would no longer be confined to the narrow strip sandwiched between the Jordan River and the Mediterranean Sea. The Lord Himself had made a specific promise to Abraham over four thousand years before, and the time had come for Him to fulfill it. Even at its greatest extent under the reign of King Solomon, Israel had only controlled about one-third of the total land area promised to Abraham. Since the restoration of the nation in 1948, room for her bulging population had always been a problem, but it would be a hindrance no longer.

Yeshua decreed that the new land of Israel would have the Euphrates River as its northern and eastern borders, and her western borders would be the Mediterranean Sea and the Nile River in Egypt. The waters below the Sinai Peninsula would be her southern borders. Whereas most of the region east of the Jordan River had been inhospitable deserts and wastelands, now it was filled with well-watered plains, pastureland, and great forests. Every trace of Babylon on the Euphrates River had been wiped away, and there was not even the hint of burnt earth where she had formerly been.

One by one, Yeshua called out the twelve tribes of Israel to divide the land and give them their inheritance. The land would be divided according to Ezekiel 48, which described the land of Israel and the inheritance of the tribes in the Millennium. The land allotments would no longer be by land features such as cities, mountains, or rivers as it had been in the first land allocation during the time of Joshua. The new allotments would be long bands that were roughly equal between the tribes. The land was to be divided into twelve sections, each of which ran the entire width of the land from east to west. The widths of each band were basically the same, but the lengths varied because of the southeast direction of the Euphrates River on the eastern border.[130]

He started from the north with the tribe of Dan, which had

---

[130] Ezekiel 47-48

the fewest of its tribe remaining. The tribe of Dan had been one of the more troubled tribes since the beginning of its history. It had been through Dan in which idolatry had come into ancient Israel, and Dan had been the first tribe to be carried away into captivity by the Assyrians. During the times of the Judges, many of the Danites had forsaken their inheritance and had turned to a marine lifestyle, sailing to distant lands on ships with her famous pagan neighbors, the Phoenicians. Dan had no remnant among the 144,000 who had been set apart by the Messiah to spread His message during the Tribulation, yet a tiny remnant of his tribe had still survived the time of wrath.

Dan's inheritance was from the Mediterranean to the Euphrates in the east, with the region of Damascus as part of its northern border. The next tribe to inherit was Asher, with Dan as its northern border. After Asher came Naphtali, then Manasseh, then Ephraim, then Reuben, and then Judah near the center of the land. Below Judah was Benjamin, then Simeon, then Issachar, then Zebulon, and lastly Gad which inherited the southern-most portion. Between Judah and Benjamin was set aside a smaller portion for the Levites in their cities.

After all the people of the earth had been renewed and the inheritance of the nations decreed, Yeshua and His glorified servants called each person, and the head of the family forward and gave them great parcels of land. Some received a larger amount of land, while some received smaller portions, but all of them were granted ample amounts of rich, fertile, fruitful lands covered with creatures and beautiful trees and gardens and pastures. He also gave out great portions of flocks of sheep, goats, horses, donkeys, and other domestic animals, which would already be waiting for them on their allotted lands.

Yeshua stood up from His golden throne and raised His hands in a welcoming gesture to all that stood before Him. His voice rang out throughout the earth, for every creature and person to hear, saying, "Now have come the days of peace and blessing – let us build and in truth and righteousness! You shall love the Lord your God with all your heart, all your mind, and all your soul. And you shall love your neighbor as yourself. You are all of one house: My house! And you are all of one blood: My blood! And you are all of one family: My family! Go forth and subdue the earth, and live in peace!"

Each person was blessed, and all of them rejoiced and then went forth from Israel to their new lands and homes. [131]

The people would once again spread out and subdue the earth, and build homes, villages, and cities, and plant crops and gardens. The Curse upon all Creation since the fall of Adam and Eve had been lifted, and there were no more thorns, sickness, disease, or ravenous beasts. [132]

The earth was truly full of life now that the Giver of Life was finally reigning on the earth.

* * *

Saul carefully adorned the attire designated for the servants of the King. The garments still took his breath away just like the first time he had worn them.

He stood before the mirror and adjusted his robes again and smoothed the seamless white linen. His hair had been neatly trimmed the day before, as was the custom of all the King's servants before their annual time of service began. Today was special for him – it would be the second time he had been chosen to serve in the Throne Room.

As one of the 144,000 Jewish missionaries from the Tribulation, he had the special privilege of serving the King directly. They all served one month a year, with 12,000 serving in the Palace for one month at a time. Each of the 12,000 had their specific assigned duties in the Palace during their time of service, with some attending to the King's other servants, seeing to the King's property on the Palace grounds, and performing a myriad of other royal duties. The King Himself always chose by lot who would serve Him in the Throne Room, and this time the lot had fallen to him. Saul had always thought it somewhat ironic that

---

[131] Micah 4:2-5
[132] Isaiah 35:1-2, 55:12-13

THE TIME OF JACOB'S TROUBLE

He cast the lot for who would serve in the Throne Room during each course, since He already controlled all the probabilities and the outcomes.

He was nervous, and the thought of serving so near to the King sometimes overwhelmed him. It wasn't the King's wrath that scared him, but the thought of being in such a high, important position for the next several weeks. But the King loved him, as He did all His servants and was very slow to anger. He knew they were nervous, and was very patient and understanding with them. If this time was similar to his last experience, it would take a few days before he grew accustomed to awesomeness of the sights and sounds of the Throne Room and being in the direct presence of His Glory. At least this time he had an idea of what to expect – the first time he had encountered it, he had fallen on his face and had been unable to move for several minutes.

Saul checked the light outside – it was almost dawn, and he was due to start his duties at sunrise. He looked over his attire once more and made sure nothing was out of place. He bowed his head and prayed a short prayer to his King, and then left.

He hurried to the Preparation Room, just outside the Throne Room, where he met with the others in his course who would also be serving, and they waited for inspection. The inspection itself took several minutes, and was always done very thoroughly by one of the King's elder servants, whose task was to ensure that nothing improper or unclean entered the Throne Room. The servant was one of the Church Fathers who had originally been converted by Paul, and he had been inspecting all servants and visitors to the Throne Room since the Dedication of the Palace.

The Throne Room servant asked if Saul had defiled himself with a woman, unclean food, or with wine since his lot had been chosen the month before. He firmly answered "no" and allowed himself to be looked over and checked by the servant. His linen robe, hair, hands, face, and skin were inspected for sores, cuts, scabs, or any other blemish that would render him ineligible for service. He was meticulous and even checked to ensure Saul was wearing the proper undergarments, as required by the Torah.

Next he was given a short verbal examination, to ensure he

was not even slightly intoxicated, and then the servant pronounced him clean and fit for duty in the Throne Room. Saul inwardly breathed a sigh of relief and walked over to stand in line with the rest of his course, where he was handed another brilliant white linen robe to wear over his garments.

When the Throne Room servant finished inspecting all the young men who were to serve the King, he rang a small bell near the door, and then stepped back and bowed his head and closed his eyes. He was not allowed to look inside the Throne Room unless called, and also to show his reverence for the King's Presence. The large door that the new course of servants stood in front of was suddenly opened, and they immediately bowed their heads. Two of the Throne Room guards moved into the entrance, and ordered them to step through the doorway. Billowing smoke hid most of the inside of the Throne Room from them, but even with the smoke, the blinding light of the King's Glory blazed through into Preparation Room.

* * *

Saul and his fellow servants were led through the smoke and were then stopped a good distance inside the great chamber. Even with their eyes closed, they could see great flashes of lightning and other bright lights all around them. Once they were all inside, the door to the Preparation Room was slammed shut and sealed, and then the lights inside the room brightened even more. And then they heard great voices in front of the Throne shouting "Holy, Holy, Holy is the Lord God Almighty! The whole earth is full of His glory!" Saul and his course repeated the praise back to them, and then they opened their eyes to behold the Throne and the Great King who sat upon it.

Saul looked up and his breath caught in his chest, just like the last time he had been there. The room was filled with the smoke of burning incense, and streams of brilliant light of every color and brightness blazed throughout the gigantic room. In the center of the room against the far back wall, there was a huge Throne made of solid white marble.

THE TIME OF JACOB'S TROUBLE

Around the Throne there was an even larger rainbow that almost seemed like a bubble of colors, and the smoke that passed through it made it appear to have a greenish hue, like a huge snow-globe. Encircling the Throne just outside the sphere of the rainbow were twenty-four seats, shaped like miniature copies of the main throne, and there were twenty-four men clothed in white sitting upon them, and each one wore a small crown of pure gold. They were the Circle of the Elders of the Church.

To the left of the Circle of Elders along the wall sat the Ark of the Covenant, gleaming brilliantly and reflecting the light and lightning flashes that streamed from the Throne. The Ark was no longer central to the Holy of Holies or the Temple, now that Yeshua, the Keeper of the Covenant dwelt on the earth.

Soon after He had returned to the earth and judged the nations, the Ethiopians humbly brought forth the Ark of the Covenant, to the great joy of the Jews. The Ethiopian Jews and then later their Christian brothers had hidden and watched over the Ark for over two thousand years. [133]

In front of the Throne, behind the Circle of Elders and the rainbow, there were seven huge gold lampstands burning pure olive oil, which represented the seven Spirits of God. And then behind the lampstands and the Throne was a large pool of crystal clear water that also surrounded the Throne.

At the four corners of the Throne were four great beasts: a lion, a calf, a creature shaped like a man, and an eagle. And each of the creatures had six wings: with two they covered their feet, with two they covered their faces, and with the middle pair they flew about the Throne. And as they flew, they cried "Holy, holy, holy, Lord God Almighty, the Ruler of Heaven and Earth!"

And at that moment, everyone in the Throne Room fell on their faces and worshipped the Great King on the Throne. And then the twenty-four Elders replied in unison, "You are worthy, O Lord, to receive glory and honor and power, for you have created all things, and for your pleasure they are and were created."

After this, everyone in the Throne Room rose and began

---

[133] Isaiah 18:7

their duties. Saul and his fellow servants were to offer incense and attend to the lampstands before the Throne. One by one, each servant filled his censer with burning coals from the altar nearby and then placed the incense over the hot coals, and then moved forward to stand before the Throne, just outside the circle of the awesome rainbow.

The sweet smell of fresh-burning incense filled the entire Throne Room. The twenty-four Elders fell face down and worshipped the King again, while the other servants continued offering the incense. As they held their censers aloft, others within their course tended the lampstands and the other furniture and articles in the Throne Room.

Several hours later, their time of service for the day had ended, and the course was led out of the Throne Room in a similar fashion as they had been ushered inside earlier that day. They were exhausted, not from the mere duties but from being in the Throne Room, which was almost like being in the Throne Room of the Father in Heaven.

They were briefly inspected once again in the Preparation Room to ensure that they had taken nothing from the Throne Room, and then the linen outer garments with which they had been clothed when they had first entered the Preparation Room were removed, and left inside the room. Those garments were holy and never left the Preparation Room. After each course had served their allotted time, the garments were then burned and new ones were provided for the next course that would serve.

From there, Saul and his fellow servants were dismissed to their quarters, and they would stay there until early the next morning, when it was time for service once again.

* * *

After Saul went back to his quarters, he found he was still shaking from his experiences that day in the Throne Room. He was emotionally exhausted, as he always was after the day's service had ended.

He couldn't help it – he felt like he had been on an adrenaline rush for hours, and now the rush had finally ended and he was settling down. He lay on his bed and closed his eyes, but he couldn't sleep – at least not yet. It was mid-afternoon, and normally he was in the middle of his day. He expected to be tired every afternoon until his days of service at the Palace ended.

A typical day for Saul was working in the city of Joppa, helping to build up the port and the harbor. He had always lived near the sea growing up, but had never really noticed how much he loved it until after the Tribulation had begun and he'd been in the desert for months.

He worked at the port during the day with the construction crew, and then would spend the evenings working on his own sailboat. He had begun living in it soon after the hull and the bottom floor were finished, but it would be another year before the entire boat was completed. Of course, it didn't sail yet, but he loved being in and around it all the time anyway.

In his previous life, he had not given much thought about how he wanted to spend his time or plan for his future. And after the Millennium had come, there was little need for what he had been originally educated in at the university. He then discovered how much he liked the sea, and moved to Joppa to find a job there. There was always plenty of work on the fishing boats and at the port, and for the first year, he had worked on one of the fishing boats. Later, he found that his background in math and science would prove to be better used in working at the port, so he left the fishing job and obtained a construction position.

Money was still used in the Millennium, but all the financial mediums had all reverted back to silver and gold, instead of paper money or credits. Money was actually worth its true value again, instead of the paper money of IOUs and guarantees from governments. There was no need for banks or the complex banking systems of the past; everyone bought and sold their goods and services honestly and fairly, and no one wandered about for lack of work, food, clothing, or shelter.

The world was now the way the Lord had always intended for it to be: a place in which everyone looked out for their neighbor and sought to do good, and not to take advantage of one another. With much of the world being still new, fresh, and somewhat untamed from its re-creation, there was plenty of work to do in building ports, cities, villages, buildings, and homes.

Saul began to calm down from the day's events, and thought about his sister Ruth. She lived fairly close to him, being a Bible teacher in one of the smaller cities near Joppa. She hadn't been to the Palace yet or to the Throne Room, at least not that he knew of. He was sure that if she had she would have told him about it at least once. It was true, however, that the Throne Room on earth was very similar to the Great Throne Room in Heaven, except for the size and some of the other minor details. In Heaven, the angels attended to the Father while on earth, the Church saints attended to the Son.

He would see her a few days after his month of service had been completed. They usually visited one another every week or two and spent Shabbat and the following Sunday together. She liked her work and took it quite seriously, of course. She was one of the many in the Church who ruled and reigned with the Messiah, and part of their rewards was to go back to the nations they had come from and administer justice and the Law. They had instant communication with the King for the more difficult questions, and they instructed and ruled with complete justice and authority. No one questioned their decisions, because they were righteous and true, and while there was no formal appellate process, the people could bring their cases before the King if necessary. But few ever did.

Saul thought about his future and tried to guess what the coming decades and centuries would bring. Time was still relevant on the earth, and everyone knew that the age they were in would last for only a specific time period. Then the Adversary would be released from his prison in the Abyss to ferment rebellion once again among the nations, and then he and his insurrection would be quickly put down.

After that came the final judgment, known in the Scriptures as the Great White Throne Judgment, which would conclude the current age upon the earth. And then after the Great White Throne Judgment was over, all those who had ever put their faith in the Lord and His Anointed One would be given their new eternal bodies and be transformed to be like those in the Church. Lastly, the New Jerusalem would come to join the new heavens and the new earth together as one, and The Father Himself would finally dwell with man.

But the Millennium had barely begun – it was still early in the first century and the nations, cities, and even villages were still being rebuilt. He was getting used to the new earth and all its incredible wonders; when he looked at a globe or a map, he still expected to see the old continents, nations, and places, but sometimes it still caught him off guard.

The world was finally at peace and rest, and the people were flourishing and treating one another with honesty and decency. There were also growing numbers of new children all over the earth, as multitudes of men and women had married a few years before and settled down in their lands, homes, and families.

He hadn't realized how much innocence and energy children brought to the earth, not to mention the refreshing life they carried with them. During the Tribulation, there had been no children at all, and wickedness and selfishness had flourished because the adults had no reason to restrain their behavior. And now with the ideal conditions of the renewed earth, the children were able to live to their fullest without fear of famine, poverty, war, or abuse. He hadn't yet heard of a murder or even a robbery happening since the end of the Tribulation, and he wondered how long those days would last. The earth and its inhabitants needed a good long rest from the years of evil and horror that had just ended, and from the many long centuries of bloodshed that had filled the earth.

Ruth would never have children, and also would never marry Sometimes it made him sad for her when he thought about it. But it was part of her immortal nature, as it was with all those in the Church. She didn't seem to mind it though, and he found that somewhat peculiar. Perhaps those natural desires and needs had been removed as part of her new eternal body.

She was still basically herself as he had known her before the Rapture, but the bad aspects of her nature had been completely removed and were no longer present, and the good, noble aspects had been augmented and amplified. The same changes had happened to all believers after they were saved. Yet they still had their sin nature and flesh to hamper and battle their new spirit, whereas the resurrected ones had no more of that old sin nature and its harmful, decaying effects.

He wasn't sure about marriage or children for himself yet, but he wasn't adverse to the idea either. It wasn't forbidden to him or any of the 144,000 chosen during the Tribulation, and he knew of a few who had already married and had several children. Perhaps he would in the years to come, but for the time being he was content to enjoy the new earth and explore it with all its wonders. He was still getting used to having dinosaurs and the other great beasts around, and had already taken several safaris in the savannahs in the eastern parts of Israel.

His eyes began growing heavy, and he gladly let them sink closed. Tomorrow would be another full day in the Throne Room, and he needed his rest. And even though it was frightening at times to be in the presence of the King, there was no other place in the universe he would rather be.

* * *

Jacob wiped the sweat off his brow and continued nailing the slats into the roof. It was warm and humid out today, but not all that uncomfortable.

He had been working on the roof most of the day and had only taken a short break for the mid-day meal. In the old days, he would have only been able to do a few short hours of this type of heavy activity in the middle of summer. But the hyperbaric conditions of the new world had made it so people would rarely become exhausted, except when doing the most strenuous of work or other activities without food or water. He often found his concentration waning and his mind tiring long before his body did.

He glanced down at Naomi below, who was busy in her garden – and what a garden it was! In the former times, it would have been worthy to grace the grounds of a palace. It was filled with trees of every sort, interspersed with multitudes of flowers and other foliage. She worked in it nearly every day, and they both were rarely indoors now, except when it rained or late in the evenings. Even after several years in the new world, he still couldn't get over how quickly the vegetation grew. Every kind of plant and tree flourished in the new world, and not only that, but there were no weeds to hinder or choke their growth. Also, the insects tended to leave the fruits, vegetables, and other herbs alone and get their food from withered or dead plants.

Most plants such as herbs and vegetables seemed to sprout within a day or two after their seeds had been planted, and the faster growing plants like pumpkins, squash, and tomatoes could almost be observed growing during the day. And not only did they grow faster now, but much larger and more numerous than was almost imaginable. He had made the mistake of planting too many tomatoes their first season there, and they had quickly overrun much of the garden in a matter of weeks; now he only planted a single seed or two and that produced enough for the entire season.

In the early morning, just before sunrise when the birds began singing, sometimes he woke up early to watch the plants open their leaves and stemma, and spread out to take in the first rays of sunlight. In the evenings though, they closed up too slowly to see unless the evening was cooler than normal.

They lived in the land of Uz, or formerly Jordan, named after the first settler there during the Great Replenishing after the Flood. The land of Uz was still a part of Israel, which had been transformed from a desert wasteland into a well-watered plain filled with rivers, lakes, ponds, and even a forest on the northern side. The plains teemed with animals and creatures of every sort, from the small rodents to the large hippopotamus, rhinoceros, and the elephant.

Still new to everyone was the behaviors and tendencies of the enormous lizards. The larger ones often stayed near the lakes and marshes, while others roamed the grasslands and the outskirts of the forest. They were incredible to behold, and they could sometimes be heard bellowing far off in the distance early in the morning.

Jacob and Naomi were still in their middle age years, but since the Lord had returned, He had reversed many of the effects of aging on the planet and all its inhabitants. Not only that, but the renewed environment of the earth had minimized the aging process and now they felt better than they ever had before, even back in the prime of their lives. The wrinkles and all the aches and pains had vanished, and any injuries they had sustained before had been completely healed as if they had never happened in the first place.

In the new world, everyone healed much faster too. Jacob had cut himself badly last week while working with the saw, and was stunned when the deep cut had vanished by the next morning. In the old days, the cut would have required stitches and would have taken weeks to heal.

He looked over the rest of the roof, saw how much he had left to do, and decided to get started again. He wasn't concerned with how much work he had, because now he enjoyed it. Besides, now he had all the time in the world.

He picked up a handful of nails and his hammer, and resumed his nailing.

* * *

Naomi stood up from her gardening and stretched. Her mouth was dry and she looked up at the sun high over head.

It was approaching the warmest part of the day, and her stomach had been feeling strange all day. She decided it was a good time for a break and checked over her work. She moved the unplanted seedlings into the shade and gave them a short sprinkle of water to sustain them until she could finish.

She looked up at Jacob, who was still hard at work on the roof, and smiled. He was such a better man than he had been before his conversion years before. Since they had settled in Uz, he had been working mostly out of their house. For income, he worked as a homebuilder and carpenter for their friends and neighbors. Sometimes he didn't charge them for his work, since

THE TIME OF JACOB'S TROUBLE

he figured that someday he would need their help as well. Money just wasn't that important to them anymore.

She began walking towards their house, and then stopped next to the ladder and asked if he wanted something to drink. He replied that he would and thanked her with a big smile.

When she reached down for the water pitcher, her abdomen fluttered again and she stopped and put her hand to her belly and felt around it. It seemed different than normal – firmer and slightly larger.

Another wave of nausea swept over her, and her stomach fluttered furiously. An old memory came into her mind, and she immediately knew what it was.

But how could this be? She was far too old now, and she just finished going through menopause years ago. She suddenly remembered all those old emotions and memories that she hadn't had in many, many years.

She became excited – she still couldn't quite believe it, but she knew it was true. Tears came to her eyes as she tried to concentrate and feel her stomach. There it was, and it quivered again. She wiped away her tears and thanked the Lord for this latest gift, and then quickly went to tell her husband.

And upon reaching the ladder she called out, "Jacob! Jacob!" He raised his head and looked down at her, wondering what was wrong.

"I'm pregnant!" Naomi exclaimed.

* * *

Daniel whistled an old hymn as he opened the door to his small bait shop and set the large bucket of worms and dirt on the floor in the dark corner.

He opened the blinds and the bright sunlight streamed into the store. Then he flipped the "open" sign over and then braced the front door open to let in the breeze. Sometimes the smell of the bait became too strong even for him, and that was never good for business. He opened the lid to the small fish tank and fed them, and then replaced the cover and grimaced. Even in the

473

CHRIS HAMBLETON

new world, there were some smells that just couldn't be covered. Maybe he should ask Saul to invent something for him.

He sat down behind the counter, took out the money drawer, and began counting the coins. He glanced over them and within seconds he had finished. Nothing was missing, just as he had expected. At times he found the new world to be almost too perfect – not in a bad way of course, but just so much better that he couldn't realistically compare it to the old world. Here, he had never locked the door of his shop and had yet to find anything even slightly out of place, much less missing, when he opened up every morning.

His shop was on the eastern side of the Sea of Fish, formerly the Dead Sea. It was one of the many miraculous changes the King had brought about in the new world since His return. The former sea in which barely even algae could survive, was now filled with marine life of all shapes, sizes, and kinds.

Sometimes the catches by the fishermen were astounding. And already there were numerous fish stories popping up around the towns and villages that surrounded them, and there was even rumored to be several "sea monsters" that some of them had spotted early in the morning. Daniel had no doubt they existed, especially with all the dinosaurs that now roamed freely about the forests, marshes, and the grasslands.

Perhaps she would come again today, Daniel thought to himself, and he let his mind wander for a short time. A woman about his age had been coming into the shop with her brother and father the last few days. Yesterday he had found himself looking forward to seeing her, though he didn't even know her name.

But there was something special about her, and he vowed that he would introduce himself the next time he got the chance.

* * *

For the next thousand years following the Great Tribulation, the world would experience a time of peace and prosperity and tranquility it had never before known except for a short time after

474

Creation. People enjoyed the fruits of their labors and no one threatened their freedom and the work of their hands, their loved ones, or their property. Everyone was content and well-fed, and both the people and all the creatures reproduced abundantly and replenished the earth like never before. [134]

Justice, righteousness, and faith permeated the nations and peoples of the earth. Yeshua, along with His priests and administrators scattered over the earth, dealt with everyone in justice, truth, and liberty, and gave righteous rulings and judgments to disputes and any crimes that were committed. No longer were the guilty set free and the innocent castigated, but perfect justice prevailed throughout the earth. There was no more war or hunger or poverty, and nations that fell into disputes took them to the King of Kings, and He resolved the matters promptly and judiciously, and all agreed that His judgments were just. [135]

Long life spans were given to every person and creature on the earth as they had been before the Great Flood and the few centuries that had followed. Children were declared to be adults at one hundred years old, and the elderly did not die until nearly one thousand years, though they still appeared aged and weaker than in their earlier times. Children everywhere obeyed and revered their parents, grandparents, and elders. The rebellious among them were given the first one hundred years of their life to learn obedience and righteousness. And evil was not allowed to take root and flourish like before. [136]

The parents were careful to train their children in all the ways of the Lord, and were careful to keep His commandments. Justice was swift and harsh, but righteous, and everyone knew that the Law was good. The people chose the ways of life and liberty, rather than sin and death.

The nations and the people were also careful to keep all the appointed times and feasts of the Lord, and all the nations sent delegates up to Jerusalem at least once a year to honor the King as commanded. But it wasn't a difficult command to keep, since

---

[134] Micah 4:4-7
[135] Micah 4:2-3
[136] Isaiah 65:20

the feasts were a grand time for rejoicing and worship of the King.

Those who refused to make the annual pilgrimage (without excuse) received no rain on their lands until the next year they honored the King, and only a few missed their annual pilgrimage more than once. [137]

And the earth brought forth its fruit and potential to the full, and all the creatures and people lived in peace and contentment. There were no more wars, famine, hunger, or violence anywhere in the world.

All the earth was filled with the knowledge of the Lord and His Word, and it blossomed as God had always intended. [138]

---

[137] Micah 4:2-5
[138] Isaiah 35:1-2, 55:12-13

CHAPTER 19
THE FINAL REBELLION

J acob stepped out the back door of the grand house and stretched his arms high above his head, and then relaxed. His muscles and joints were still a little stiff that day, and he set off down the well-worn path.

The sun would be setting soon, and the time of the evening sacrifice was approaching. He started and ended every day with quiet personal time with the Lord, and sunrise and sunset were good markers to help him keep up the practice.

His many years on the earth were starting to catch up with him, he supposed. Sometimes the thought of aging again saddened him, but most of the time he had no strong feelings about it one way or another. The former age and his old life on the earth seemed so distant and meaningless, and even the good memories he had of that life had been nothing compared to this life during the Millennium.

The years of suffering all seemed like a distant, bad dream. He could barely remember the former wasteland that had been the earth, and even the earth before the Tribulation was nothing like the world he was used to now. Those who had been born into the new world would have been shocked at how deserted and barren the earth had been before the Days of the King.

As he strode past one of the apple orchards, he still marveled at how large the trees were: some were well over a hundred cubits tall. He remembered when they were just seedlings, and how he had watched them grow year-by-year, century-by-century. Some of the older trees were showing signs of their great age too, and he sometimes wondered if he would outlive them. He heard a rustling in the grass just outside the orchard, and stopped to find its source. It was their two pet lions, Mahlon and Orpah, waking from their late afternoon nap and beginning to graze. Sometimes the lions chased each other and often played with the other animals, but most of the time they just kept to themselves.

Jacob shook his head and smiled at them. Who would have ever thought he'd have magnificent creatures like these for pets, not to mention a snow tiger, an elephant, a wooly mammoth, a giraffe, and many of the smaller animals. He had jokingly referred to their home as the Zoo of Uz when his children first started bringing the beasts home and begging him to let them keep just one more pet.

He had finally drawn the line at the mammoths, especially when one of the boys had started sneaking some of the larger kinds of reptiles onto the property. Once a behemoth (formerly known in the old world as a brontosaurus) took up residence on one's land, it was very difficult to get them to leave. [139]

The last of his children were all grown up now and had left home over ten years before. Once again it was just he and Naomi, along with all the pets their children had collected over the years and left behind. Since they had left home, he had thought often about when all his first children had moved out – it had been just before the Tribulation. Ruth had been the last to move out then, and this time it was their youngest son Elijah.

He and Naomi had had twenty-three more children during the Millennium, and for years their own children and even some of their grandchildren and even great-grandchildren were having offspring of their own. How he kept track of all their names was a mystery at times, but he still managed to remember them all, and many of their birthdays and anniversaries too.

Naomi was starting to age too, and he had noticed that over the last several years she tired more quickly than she had before. She no longer worked in the garden or with the trees and flowers as much as in their earlier years. They both were nearly at the

---

[139] Isaiah 11:6-9

same biological age they had been at the end of the Tribulation. Their anniversary was coming soon, and it would be their five hundred and fifty-seventh year together. Their five hundredth anniversary had been an enormous celebration thrown by all their children, and many of their neighbors had visited to congratulate them and wish them well. Saul and Ruth had also come to celebrate with them, and it was wonderful to have their entire family together with them again.

The earth had now passed the halfway point of the Millennium, and was in its five hundred and twentieth year of the age. The population had been low for the first century or so, having only a billion at the start of the Millennium. But as the children grew and began having children and then the grandchildren and great-grandchildren began having children also at the same time, the population quickly boomed. Cities, towns, and villages sprang up almost overnight everywhere on the globe, and now they were flourishing and more were being built every day. The King had desired that the earth be replenished and everyone be fruitful and multiply, and He had not been disappointed.

He left the gardens and came to the large stream that ran along the edge of the property. It provided fresh water for most of the entire district, and eventually flowed into Southern Sea far away. He sat down on one of the large boulders near the edge of the stream and watched the sun dip below the horizon.

It would be time for the fall feasts in Jerusalem soon, and he always looked forward to them. He typically enjoyed being back in the western lands, especially the Holy City. He didn't want to live there, but it was nice to visit several times a year.

He closed his eyes and bowed his head, and began to pray, thanking the King for another day and for His blessings upon himself, his family, and all the earth.

* * *

Daniel and Rebecca watched three of their sons untie the smaller fishing boat from the dock and saw them sail out onto the Sea of Fish.

They wouldn't be back until evening unless they had problems; if they did, Daniel would have to go out after them. He wasn't worried, but his wife was – it was their first time out on the Sea by themselves. He had carefully trained them and knew they had been ready for months. But they had made an agreement, and that had given him more time to prepare them, taking them through the spring season when storms were more frequent.

He put his arm around Rebecca to reassure her and told her they would be fine. He had been sailing for hundreds of years, and their other children had done fine when they had been the same age as these three. But these boys were the last of their children, and it was unlikely that Rebecca would have any more. After their last son had been born years before, the delivery had been rough, and the doctor had to come to help her through the childbirth. After that, she had not been pregnant again. The thought of not having any more children depressed her from time to time, and often it took weeks to help her overcome it. Sometimes he had to stay home from work to comfort her, but he didn't mind.

Rebecca was still as beautiful as the day he had first seen her in his old bait shop. She had been one of the few Jews to survive the Tribulation outside Israel. While many of them had been holed up in Israel, the rest who had been spread across the earth had been hunted down with vengeance. She'd had nightmares and night-sweats for years afterwards, and it wasn't until after their first child was born that they fully went away. There were many people who had similar problems, but most of them had diminished during the first few years after the Millennium had begun. In a few more years, the last of their many children would leave home, and then it would be just them.

He owned and operated a small shipbuilding and repair shop just down the coast, and his business was continuing to thrive. He had always loved the sea and sailing, and had learned the art of shipbuilding during the first fifty years of the Millennium. He had sold his small bait shop to start shipbuilding soon after he and Rebecca had married, and then the children began coming.

They had had thirty-one children in all, and there were still five at home: three boys and two girls. Their youngest child was a fifteen year-old girl, and she had just lost her first tooth. In the previous age, children had started losing their teeth at six or seven years old, but now it was usually more than twice that. The children of the Millennium aged much slower to their adolescent years, and children were not considered adolescents until they were at least thirty years old.

Daniel and Naomi both had not been able to travel extensively in their previous lives before the Millennium, so they had made a point to see as much of the new world as they were able to. It was an interest they both shared, along with sailing and fishing, and they took some of their children with them at least two or three times a year. Sometimes even the older ones came along, some having families of their own with them, and they would all go to a different place on the earth together. They had been to nearly every nation in the world, and had seen a great variety of the world's wonders. Even after being used to the new world for centuries, some of the wildlife and scenery still left them speechless in awe and wonder.

The last trip as a family had been to the Southland, the former continent of Antarctica. From the end of the Ice Age to the end of the Tribulation – nearly five thousand years – most of the southern continent had been frozen over solid under more than a kilometer of ice. During the Tribulation judgment that had scorched the earth and its inhabitants, the polar ice caps had broken up and melted. When the Millennium began, Antarctica had been completely remade and attached to Australia. Now it was one of the greatest forests of the earth, covered with giant redwood trees and cedars that stretched far into the sky. The forest was home to billions of creatures, and the polar bears, mammoths, penguins, and other animals that preferred the cooler climates thrived from the forest's edge to the sea.

Their next trip would be back to the North Pole, in the middle of the winter. It still snowed at the poles, but it was much less frigid than in previous times. They had only skied a few times in their lives, and they hoped there would be enough snow for them to have a good ski vacation. Some of their younger children had never seen snow at all, and often asked what it was like. They had never known what real temperature extremes were like, and sometimes they had a hard time believing their parents when they were told that much of the earth had either been scorching deserts or covered in frozen, unusable tundra.

The fishing boat was out of sight now, and it was time to get back home. Daniel had a ship design to finish, and he didn't want to be at the shop past dinner. Their younger children were playing back at the house, and they needed their schooling for the day. Daniel turned back with Rebecca, and walked up the dock to the shore, and then went back home.

Their sons had been instructed to return by late in the evening, and he had no doubts they would. They seldom had any discipline problems with their children.

* * *

Nearly two hundred years passed, and it was halfway through the seventh century of the Millennium. Every corner of the world was filled with creatures of every sort and people in their cities, towns, and villages now.

The technology of most of the world was still somewhat simple compared to that of the previous age. There were no computers, no cars, very little machinery, and few large companies. But there was a great amount of sophisticated metalworking, intricate woodworking, masonry, construction of every sort, and many other skills, trades, and arts. The world had returned to the principles of simplified ingenuity, and had not needed to build huge machinery, factories, or industries to build and sell their products. The people were content and lived comfortably, and very few were stingy with their money and talents. [140]

Over the last century, the remnant that had survived the Tribulation long ago and replenished the earth had grown old and begun to die. It had been only a few at first, mere drops in the vast ocean of humanity, then it became a trickle, and now it

---

[140] Isaiah 35:1-2, 5-10

was like a rushing river.

More and more of the oldest people were dying off, and there were now funerals for them nearly every day. Their first children were aging too and were well into their middle age, and some were even entering their twilight years. Most who died were buried on their property or the property of one of their family members, usually in a quiet garden plot or an orchard. The elders of the earth had begun passing away, and their children and grandchildren were taking over many of the family duties.

Much of the earth was still governed by the Church saints in the nations and cities, but not as much in many of the smaller towns and villages. In the vast majority of the smaller areas, the elders would typically govern and represent the residents, who could appeal to the Church elders nearby if they felt an injustice had occurred. Everyone was very familiar with the Scriptures from an early age, and the parents grounded their children, grandchildren, and the rest in the Bible and its principles. Everyone knew and obeyed the Law, and even after over seven centuries, violent crimes were still virtually non-existent.

Sometimes there were those with incorrigible, rebellious natures that refused to listen to or obey their parents, the elders, or even the Church. Children were given one hundred years to learn to control their sin nature and submit to the Law, or they would perish. Sometimes the King Himself would call them before Him and admonish them to turn from their evil ways, or death would suddenly take them. Often, being in His Presence was enough to set them on the right path, usually when they were younger. But some would not turn and repent, and one day after reaching their first one hundredth birthday, they would simply die where they stood with little or no pain nor warning.

Whenever a young person would suddenly die, the entire town or village would burn the body and not bury nor mourn them, and then they would read the Law of Moses to all those under one hundred years old, especially those with a rebellious nature, and would warn them to turn or they would suffer the same fate. They would stay with the burning corpses until they were consumed, so they would not forget what future awaited the disobedient and the rebellious. Quite often, the stench of the burnings was enough to make them sick, and often a town or village would only have someone die from rebellion every several decades or so.

But as more and more of the old remnant died off and their descendants took their places of authority, the people began to no longer hold as tightly to the Spirit of the Law as they once had, and began keeping it out of obligation. They still celebrated the feasts and holy days, but no longer with the same tone and spirit that they had when their ancestors had kept them.

The excitement of the new world and its wonders began to grow stale, and the people increasingly took the blessings of the world for granted.

* * *

Naomi was lying in her bed, and she called out in a weak voice to her husband. He came to her side as quickly as he could, but since he too was now very old, it took him several moments to get there. She was fine, but she couldn't remember where she was again.

Jacob comforted her and stayed with her until she went back to sleep, caressing her long white hair and quietly talking to her. He came back an hour later for awhile, watching her rest and thinking about their earlier times together. They were passing through the twilight years of their lives into the shadow, and night would be upon them both soon.

It was early in the eighth century, and he couldn't see either of them living another fifty years. In his earlier years, he had hoped that they both would live all the way through to the end of the Millennium, but now it was obvious that they would not. They would both die, and it was more or less how he had always pictured it: growing old and dying together.

He was still fairly mobile but much slower, and had found himself forgetting the little normal things of day-to-day life over the last ten years. He had a harder time getting up and down the stairs now, and sometimes he became frustrated at how he could no longer do the simple, everyday things that he had done for so many years.

Naomi was bedridden most of the time, but she wasn't sick nor in much pain. But her memory and strength were failing, and her body was quickly wearing out. She slept on and off in spurts throughout the day, but usually all the way through the night. He still slept beside her every night, and would sooth her when she was restless. They were both nearly nine hundred years old now, and they had been rapidly declining over the last twenty years. They were among the last of the Remnant, and the rest would likely die off in the next fifty years.

He understood why Yeshua was letting the first generation fade away: once the elders were gone, the young would be given a choice whether to continue in their parents' ways of righteousness, or rebel and face death. And he knew from the Scriptures that many would choose to rebel and try to overthrow the King, His government, and attempt to take over the earth.

Jacob felt honored to wait on Naomi and help her during her final days – they had lived a very long life with each other – longer than nearly everyone else on the earth. He couldn't imagine what it would be like without her after she passed. They had been through so much together, and had been with one another so long that he didn't really know how he would respond. But he knew he would be following in her footsteps soon, and it would probably be more like she was away on a long trip than that she was really dead. Before long, they would be back together in Eternity, with bodies that would never wear out or fade away.

Their youngest daughter, Ariel, had moved back home with them two years ago to help them with the day-to-day chores that were becoming increasingly difficult for them to do. Naomi had been spending more time resting, and Ariel felt it was time to honor her parents as much as she could during their final years.

They had raised many children, and most of them had moved away and had long ago started families of their own. But she had stayed close by, and had evidently planned to care for her parents when they would need it from the time of her young adulthood. She believed it was her calling and she didn't mind it in the least.

All of their children loved them dearly, but Ariel had always felt closer to them, especially to her mother.

Saul had just recently moved in with them also. After all, they had plenty of room in the great house now that it was mostly empty. In all those years, he had never married and had no children. Saul was now well over eight hundred years old, but looked much younger than his parents. He was aging, yet not nearly as fast as all the others his age or those even younger. In fact, some of their children and even grandchildren looked much older than Saul. Perhaps it had something to do with him being part of the 144,000 who had lived in the last decade of the previous age. All of them were still alive, and less than half had married and had children. He and Saul took a short walk together every morning, and usually another one at night.

It was good to have Saul with them, and Jacob often found himself thinking of their early years, when their first children were with them in the old world. They saw Ruth more often recently, and she hadn't changed at all since she had come back in her new body with the Lord.

He thought of Ahban too, and that usually saddened him. He knew his son was suffering horribly in his eternity, and that there was still no hope for him. Why had his son been so foolish and stubborn? But then he would remember that he had been the same way before Petra. Naomi had been so gracious and patient with him in spite of his foolishness, and for that alone she deserved whatever comfort he could give her in her last days.

* * *

Three months later, Jacob awoke at his usual hour and felt a strange coolness next to him. He rolled over to see what it was, and saw nothing else except Naomi. He was puzzled, and then he quietly caressed her face – it was deathly cold.

A tremor ran through him, and he quickly bent over to check if she was still breathing and if she had a heartbeat. He felt and heard none – no breath, no sound, nothing. Her time had come, and she had died peacefully in her sleep.

THE TIME OF JACOB'S TROUBLE

He began crying and lay back down next to her, holding her tightly for the last time.

As he grieved over her, he noticed the lighting in the room grow brighter, but even in his grief, he looked up. There were two figures glowing with light standing on either side of him, with one much brighter than the other. He wiped away his tears, and realized that it was Yeshua on one side of him and Ruth on the other. She knelt down beside him and put her arms around him, while Yeshua gently placed His hand on his shoulder and both began to grieve with him. After a time, He slowly faded from the room, but Ruth remained next to him, comforting him as he wept.

A few hours later when Jacob had not come downstairs at his normal time for their walk, Saul realized that something was wrong. He went upstairs to his parents' room and softly knocked. He could hear Jacob weeping inside, and he knew immediately what had happened. He slowly opened the door and saw Ruth next to him, and then quietly went to his father's side by the bed. He knelt next to them and was suddenly overcome with grief also – his mother was gone. A few minutes later, Saul rose to tell Ariel what happened, who was just starting to make breakfast. And there around the bed, all four gathered and mourned for their mother.

The funeral service was held two days later, and all their family (except for a few children and grandchildren) and many of their friends and neighbors gathered to pay their respects to her. Saul had dug her grave the day she had died, and Jacob had selected the plot in one of her favorite flower gardens. He had chosen one of the larger ones, and had instructed Saul to leave enough space for his grave also. Both men had tears streaming down their faces while Saul dug the grave, and sometimes he had to stop when Jacob became overwhelmed with grief.

At the funeral, many of their children spoke and told about some of the memories they had of Naomi when they were growing up. Some of their stories made everyone laugh, while others made them cry. Near the end of the service, Jacob rose and told about how they had met and some of his fondest memories of her. And then, breaking into tears, he went to her casket and told her that he would see her soon.

When the service ended, they moved the casket to gravesite, said another prayer, and slowly lowered it in. All those gathered at the funeral cast in a handful of dirt and said a few short words of farewell to her. Lastly, with Saul by his side, Jacob threw in a handful and stepped aside. Saul and some of the other men then filled the grave with the rest of the dirt and finished burying her.

Later back at the house, Jacob rose to speak to everyone before they began leaving for their homes. He thanked them all for coming, and for honoring him and Naomi. And then he told them about his and Naomi's first son, Ahban, which he had seldom mentioned to any of them before. Most were surprised and gave him their full attention, and he told them all about Ahban's life, and the final choice that he had made. He told them about what had happened to Ahban after the Lord's return, and his punishment. Ahban was in Hell – they had both watched him be cast into the pit – and would be suffering for eternity.

Jacob admonished them to not follow in the path of their oldest brother and to not turn from the Way. They must not take part in the rebellion that was to come, or they would suffer the same fate. He told them his own life's story and how he was saved in Petra, and how fortunate he was to have lived in this age of wonder and peace. Soon he would be following after his wife, and he would no longer be with them. They must keep themselves and their children obeying the Lord and following Him in whatever they did.

He spoke with the greatest strength, emotion, and authority he could muster. Everyone was very quiet while he admonished them. When he had finished speaking, he was exhausted and sat down, saying little the rest of the night. Many of his children and family began leaving a few hours later, and within three days the household was back to just him, Saul, and Ariel.

* * *

Four years after Naomi had passed away, Jacob fell sick and

was confined to his bed. Sickness usually happened only to the older people, as their bodies aged and weakened.

At first, it seemed to be just a bad case of the flu, but it grew worse and he came down with a high fever. But no matter what Ariel and Saul and the doctor tried, they could not get the fever to break. They prayed over him and by next day, he no longer appeared to be in any pain. The fever and the sickness was still there, but at least he was not suffering. Later that evening, they noticed that he was sleeping soundly, but could not be woken up.

Three days later, Jacob died early in the morning, about the time he would have taken his daily morning walk. Soon after Naomi had died, he had told Saul and Ariel that when his time came, he didn't want a big funeral. Just bury his body quietly next to his wife's and tell everyone after it was over. He didn't want any of the fuss over him that they had done for Naomi. He wanted everyone to remember her funeral instead of his. Those were his wishes, and he wanted them to respect them.

Later the day Jacob died, Saul went out to the garden plot where his mother's body had been laid a few years before, and he marked out the grave for his father. When the first stroke of the shovel struck, fresh tears came to his eyes and he began to weep again. He wanted to stop and put the shovel down, but he forced himself to continue. He had known for many years that sooner or later this day would come.

As he was digging, he abruptly heard the sound of another shovel striking the earth, and he saw that Yeshua was next to him, helping him dig his father's grave. Ruth was with Him again too and had tears streaming down her cheeks.

Saul greeted them and thanked Him for coming, and after awhile Ruth excused herself to comfort Ariel. Together Saul and Yeshua finished digging the small pit, both grieving the rest of the time while they worked. When they were finished, the King bid him farewell and gradually faded from sight.

In the evening at sundown, Saul, Ruth and Ariel said goodbye to their father for the last time, and then quietly buried him next to his beloved wife.

* * *

Six more years came and went, and Saul received word that Daniel and Rebecca had died. He packed a few items for the journey and left Uz to go pay his respects to their family in the western lands.

He and Ariel still lived at their parents' house, tending to the house, the gardens, and the remaining animals still living there. They didn't have the heart to let the property be sold or fall into ruin. There was still plenty of work to do and maintenance projects from the last century, when Jacob and Naomi no longer had the strength to perform them any longer. Perhaps one of their many brothers or sisters or their families would want the property someday. But until then, Saul and Ariel were more than happy to stay there and honor their parents.

The trip to the Sea of Fish took nearly two days, and Saul had no problems finding his old friend's home. Some of Daniel and Rebecca's children were there, already busily dividing up their parents' belongings. Saul sought out the oldest of their children to introduce himself to and to express his condolences. The oldest of their many children was grateful that Saul had come, but he said he was too busy handling the estate to talk long.

Apparently, none of them wanted to stay in their parents' home and keep the property in the family. They would sell it off and divide up the money once their possessions had been cleaned out and distributed. There was a large pile of their belongings in a heap off to the side of the house – evidently the items that no one wanted.

Watching the offspring of his old friend Daniel discouraged him, and he didn't like seeing them squabble over this trinket and that. There were several times when their children were rude to one another and when the younger children among them did not show the proper respect to their parents. At times, their parents grew frustrated and raised their voices, and it wasn't until then that the younger ones would pay attention and listen to them.

That was not a good sign, Daniel thought – when the children stopped listening to their parents and the parents could no longer do much about it. After that would come disobedience and then later rebellion. Once he called one of the ruder children over to him and told him to respect and obey his parents, the child more or less looked at him with a funny face, and then completely ignored what he had said. He saw few of the other parents intervening and taking charge of their children, and that saddened him even more.

When parents stopped consistently training their children and demanding their obedience, the entire society would decline. The parents were the authority of the family, but when they did not assert their authority and left their children to themselves, rebellion and disobedience would quickly take root in a society. Eventually, a young generation would arise and assert their own authority over the society, and the older generation would step aside and let the younger ones do as they wished, doing little other than grumble about it. Within a few generations, the society would be completely undone, and the world would be unrecognizable to those who had lived there only decades before.

He had seen the end result of this long ago in the old world, and knew about how the generation after World War II had led to the decline of every nation where they had exerted their influence. It often happened after long wars had finally ended and the people began to rebuild. Their parents had been tired from the devastating times and had only wanted the best for their children. They had worked hard to provide for them and gave them nearly whatever would make them happy. But they had failed to properly train their children in their values and teach them obedience and respect for authority. Soon afterwards, their children and their grandchildren had cast off all the morals, traditions, and foundations that had made their civilizations prosperous.

Saul remembered what was destined to happen at the end of the age, and that if not corrected in this family very soon, would eventually lead to their judgment and destruction.

Hours later, when they finally stopped scurrying about and had all sat down for the evening meal, Saul stood up and introduced himself to everyone. He told them how he had met their father back in the early days before the Tribulation, and how both their parents had suffered greatly to help others stay alive and find safety during those terrible years. Everyone was very quiet as he spoke – even the young children – and seeing his opportunity, Saul began to speak firmly to the entire group.

He told them about what had happened in the old world, about how only in a matter of years the institutions of their society had been overturned because of parents who had not taken the time to train their children, who later rebelled as a result. The rebels had overtaken the nations, and had caused the deaths of millions of people by their foolishness, selfishness, and lawlessness. Everyone did what was right in their own eyes in their father's generation, which was just as bad as the times of the Judges in the Bible. Everyone only respected their own authority and not that which the Lord had set before them, namely the government, the priests, the elders, and even their own fathers and mothers.

The rebellion and the decline of a society started in the home, with busy, misdirected parents and untrained children. He preached that another time of great rebellion on the earth was coming in only another hundred years, and the rebellious people of the world would try to overthrow those who governed them, and even the King Himself!

Saul then became personal with them and told them how he saw the same problems and roots of rebellion rampant throughout their families and in their children, and admonished them to not chase after prosperity and passing things any longer. They must exert their authority over their children and compel them to obey and respect them. If they did not, their own children and children's children would take part in the rebellion to come, and they would be punished and destroyed.

He told them to remember the King and all the blessings He had bestowed upon them, and this wonderful world He had refashioned for them. They must not take it for granted and they must all walk in His Ways. Saul could see that many of them were thinking about what he was saying, but a few were offended at his words.

He soon finished and thanked them for their hospitality, and then sat back down. The rest of the meal was much quieter after his speech, and the children seemed somewhat calmer and more obedient.

At sundown, he thanked the older of Daniel and Rebecca's children, and then left to stay in one of the local inns for the night. He was saddened by what he had seen at his old friend's home, and considered the few years that were left in the long era of peace the world had known. The small, but widespread problems that had begun in the homes would soon grow to larger upheavals across the world. Lastly, it would culminate in the Last Rebellion after the Adversary was released.

As he set out the next morning for Uz, he considered what the Scriptures said about the future revolt and destruction of the rebels. Over one hundred years remained of the Millennium until Satan would be released. Ariel still lived at the great house with him, and it was his responsibility to protect her in the years ahead, unless she married, of course. His spirits darkened when he thought of the possibility that some of his own relatives might partake in the uprising, but there was little he could do other than minister to them and love them.

Even in the dark days ahead, there was still much good that could be done, and souls to win for the Lord. Daniel's and Rebecca's offspring had been the first he'd had to admonish in centuries. And though it had saddened him earlier, the situation had served to re-awaken a purpose deep within himself he had not nurtured in many years.

He resolved to strengthen the faith of those he knew and anyone he met. He was still in the King's service, after all. And he would continue telling of the Lord's goodness as he had done when he had been called many centuries before.

*　*　*

One thousand years after the Great Judgment – to the very day – Satan was released from his gloomy prison in the Abyss.

Many of his lieutenants and most powerful allies were set

free along with him, and they hearkened to their dark master's call once again. He ordered them to not be overly aggressive in their maneuvers – clever deception was all that would be needed to foster mankind's allegiance with them. Most of the mortals on the earth had never known spiritual warfare and would be easy to manipulate and control.

A shadow of unrest and distrust slowly crept over the earth, and some of the people began to feel worry and discontent for the first time in their lives. Crime and civil disobedience increased dramatically within a very short time, and the elders and the leaders grew concerned.

To those who were spiritually alert, something had perceptibly changed on the earth in the days and months that followed the end of the Thousand Years. From their knowledge of the Bible and the Millennium prophecies, they recognized what was starting: the final rebellion of man. [141]

Satan's first widespread deception after his release was the distortion of the Bible prophecies of what would transpire after the Millennium. He planted his deception in the minds and hearts of the youth, and it quickly spread from there. The Thousand Years of Peace had ended – where was the widespread rebellion that was supposed to occur? Were the Scriptures and the Church in error? The Millennium had come and gone, and nothing had happened afterwards as it had been foretold.

Where was this Great Dragon who was to have been released? The Dragon could be fictitious for all they knew, an invisible fear to keep them obedient and submissive to the authorities. Had anyone ever seen him with their own eyes? Had the Tribulation really happened? Where were all its survivors, and how could they know if they were really telling the truth? Had their parents, elders, and government really been honest with them all those years? Was this so-called Dragon even really evil? Who could they trust to tell the truth?

The unrest and instability steadily increased, and large numbers of the young people, most of whom were under two hundred

---

[141] Revelation 20:3,7-9

years old, began to desire to forever throw off "the Old Ways", and began referring to the Church, the elders, and even the Lord Himself as harsh and oppressive, especially their treatment of those younger than themselves.

Their demonstrations, speeches, and gatherings were peaceful, but rebellion and independence flowed throughout their messages. When confronted about it, they said they only wanted to be free to think and do as they wished, and what was wrong with that as long as no one else was hurt? Some of the leaders were arrested and punished for rebellion, but that only seemed to further fuel their movement and increase their numbers.

Then some of the older people began to join the ranks of the rebels, some of whom were over five hundred years old. Evil spread throughout the earth, in tiny amounts at first, but it was there nevertheless. Immorality and secret sins began to permeate the people, and they soon considered the elders, the Church, Israel, and even the King Himself to be their undeclared enemy.

They would not compromise or cease their disobedience, for soon their numbers would become so great that they would be the democratic majority of the earth. They began to teach that everyone should be able to vote on their leadership rather than have it forced upon them – after all, wasn't that fair and just?

And by their doctrines and calls for independence, millions more who had formerly been loyal to the King were drawn into their ranks and joined them full-heartedly.

* * *

Egypt was the first nation to show outright signs of rebellion, but the seeds had been festering in its heart for decades.

Assyria and Egypt were sister kingdoms of Israel, and multitudes of people flowed through their lands on their annual migrations for the Feast of Tabernacles in Jerusalem: those from the south came through Egypt, and those coming from the east and much of the north through Assyria. Billions of people toured Egypt because of her beautiful lands and great monuments, even though the land of Israel was where the greatest wonders were, along with the Holy City, the many palaces and the great Temple of the King Himself.

At the start of the Millennium, Egypt and Assyria had been restored to their former glory and were both tropical paradises, and both had the great rivers that ran through their land. The Nile River in Egypt had always been its pride and glory, and the never-ending source of silt-filled freshwater once again made it grow proud and prosperous. Assyria was not nearly as prideful as Egypt, since it did not have all the history or the monuments that Egypt had. Also, Egypt produced some of the best fruits and vegetables in all the world, and was renowned for the vast quantities of grain she produced year after year. [142]

Several of Egypt's ancient pyramids were still standing or had been restored over the last few centuries – first and foremost was the Great Pyramid of Giza. After its exterior had been repaired and polished, the King had placed the great capstone on the top, a huge, uncut pyramid of crystal that had His Name written on each of the four sides. When the sun shown on the Great Pyramid, it gleamed for miles, and the capstone radiated colored light like a gigantic prism. The Great Pyramid was a monument to the King, and He had finally explained its shrouded, mysterious history to the entire world upon its dedication. [143]

The first indications of the future rebellion began innocently enough, as most do. The desire of the Egyptians had little to do with outright revolt against the King, but as one source of pride led to another, those feelings and aspirations grew greater and greater. With all the traffic and commerce coming through Egypt, tourism had become a major industry, and some of the businesses had become greedy from all the wealth that they were accumulating. They began raising their prices to just below the level that would be considered "unjust", and then they began creating additional costs for those passing through Egypt, such as toll fees, tourist taxes when staying in a particular city, and using advertising and other means to pressure people into visiting the

---

[142] Isaiah 19:22-25
[143] Isaiah 19:19-21

pyramids and other tourist attractions that would bring in additional wealth.

Some of the younger people began to look forward to visiting the Great Pyramid and its wonders more than Jerusalem, and the excitement and amusement that Egypt had to offer made the annual feasts in Israel seem boring and increasingly tedious to them. Those who had never known the death, hardships, or suffering of the old world often took the perfection of the new world for granted. Instead of seeking after justice, peace and righteousness as their parents and the other original survivors had taught them, they increasingly sought after comfort, entertainment, and pleasure. And in this way, Egypt inadvertently began to lead the people astray.

A few years after the end of the Millennium, Egypt threw a great festival, the Festival of the Pyramids, to celebrate the Great Pyramid (and the King, of course) two weeks before the Feast of Tabernacles in Israel. The festival lasted five days, but as it drew to a close, the festival planners decided to delight the people and extended the festival for another five days. The more prudent of the visitors realized this would be too close to the Feast in Jerusalem and that they would run out of money before they reached the Holy City if they extended their stay in Egypt, and so they left. But many of the others had no such concerns, and stayed as long as possible in Egypt. When the time came for them to continue on their way up to Jerusalem, they realized they were either too tired from their time in Egypt or did not have enough money to complete the pilgrimage. So many went back home without going to Jerusalem that year, and found that they were not overly disappointed they had missed it.

But the businesses and administrators of Egypt had made so much money from the tourism and festival that they decided to not send a delegation up to Jerusalem as the King and the Law required. They too had grown tired of the ritual, and were too busy coming up with new ways to further increase their profits and their greatness. Why couldn't the people worship there at the Great Pyramid instead of having to go all the way up to Jerusalem? After all, the monument had been completed by the King

Himself, and wasn't that just as good for those who didn't have enough money to make the entire trip?

The year after Egypt decided not to send a delegation up to honor the King, no rain came to their entire land from that day onward, until the next year they sent up another delegation. The first year was not as difficult as the administrators had feared, and the businesses still had record profits from the tourists that came through. But by the third year, the water levels of the Nile River began to drop dramatically, and the land began to suffer. The Egyptians constructed intricate canals that extended from the Nile to their orchards and fields, and managed to grow their crops for another two years. But the land was beginning to return to the desert wasteland that it had been for thousands of years, and the farmers, fishermen, and other common people cried out to the Lord against their elders and leaders.

By the sixth year, the pride and stubbornness of Egypt was broken, and the elders sent another delegation up to Jerusalem with many gifts, and rain promptly returned to their land. After that, they never again refused to send another delegation to the King. The people also demanded that the businesses cease their unjust practices and change the Festival of the Pyramids back to only three days, instead of the two weeks it had grown into. The festival planners were afraid of losing their positions and authority, and complied with the peoples' demands. [144]

But the damage from Egypt's rebellion had been done. Other nations began to refuse to send delegations, especially those very far away such as the land of Magog in the far north. But they did not refuse for more than a few years at a time, and soon found themselves sending delegations simply to guarantee that their lands would receive rain during the next year, instead of sending them to genuinely honor the King and worship at the Temple. The annual festivals at Jerusalem had become a burden to the nations, and they began to secretly loathe the King, His land, and His people.

The seedlings of the Final Rebellion were growing quickly.

---

[144] Zechariah 14:16-19

THE TIME OF JACOB'S TROUBLE

* * *

Over the next several years, the world became more and more segregated. The earth that had once been united in peace and harmony under the King, was now fractured and divided from the smallest families all the way up to the largest groups of elders. But it didn't separate because of racial, cultural, lingual, or even traditional differences, but by those who wanted to keep to the "Old Ways" as they were called, and those who wanted to create the "New Ways", in which the people themselves would have a direct voice in their government, instead of just the elders and the administrators.

But those who wanted the New Way were cautious, and they were careful to not break the existing laws outright, lest their movement come to a quick end. They bought large tracts of land near the source of the larger rivers, and then others who held their views would then sell their property and move there. As more and more people came to join with them, they grew too large for their new lands, and they pressured those outside their lands to sell to them at a lower cost, or they would make life difficult for them if they refused. And in this manner, the world began to divide into large regions of those who wanted to keep to the "Old Ways" and those who did not. No action was taken against them, other than grumblings and complaining, and so both their numbers and their pride grew at a steady rate.

Among the regions that wanted democracy, change and the freedom to do as they pleased, they were still careful to keep the law, or at least the letter of it, and even kept the feasts and rituals of the King. The leaders of the movement were biding their time until their numbers were sufficiently large. Many of the leaders searched the Scriptures and the old stories of what the world had been like before the King, and they relished the thought of so much individual freedom and independence, and the right to do what was right in their own eyes. Yet they were not strong enough nor numerous enough yet, nor had any knowledge or experience of warfare in order to gain their independence.

So they would wait and grow their territories and their numbers, and study warfare, so when the time came to rise against the King, they would be ready. Much of their new knowledge of warfare came from the very Scriptures they had grown to loathe, but in their pride and rebelliousness, they relished the notion that they could use those same Scriptures against the King Himself and His saints.

But even as the knowledge of what they were learning and preparing for became known, no punishment came from the King or His Church, and the rebels grew more and more bold and hard-hearted. The Thousand Years of Peace had ended, and the King and His servants no longer ruled them as harshly as before (or so they felt), and the rebels began to press their advantage.

Those espousing the New Way came to think of the King of Kings as the Tyrant of Tyrants, and grew confident that one day they would, without any doubt, succeed against those who had kept them enslaved to the Law. After all, how could their defenseless adversaries stand against them when the chaste knew nothing of war and they did?

The cloud of rebellion that had been only a wisp just decades before began to cover large portions of the earth.

* * *

The leaders of the New Way formed an assembly and gathered openly to discuss their next steps on the road to independence.

They first decided that if the King were overthrown, then His saints, elders, and those loyal to Him would quickly fall and follow Him into exile. They would drive all those loyal to the Lord and His King off the earth, and if that meant that billions would be killed in the process, then that was the cost of freedom. Freedom for the people had become more important than the people themselves. If the earth was this fruitful under His tyranny, how much better would it be under their rule with unbridled freedom?

The New Way groups began to unite and show their strength in huge numbers, and openly defied the King and His servants, who only years before they had willingly obeyed and submitted to. But no longer – peace was taken from the earth, and in some cities and villages, the rebels overthrew the elders and drove them away, declaring their lands "free" and "independent". After all, the people had not chosen their leaders, so why should they obey them? The King sent some of His ambassadors to negotiate with them and admonish them to return, but the rebels killed some of them and sent the rest back humiliated. The rebels expected Him to send His armies against them, but He never did, and they perceived that He had grown weak and would not punish the free people of the new world.

And so they put the next phase of their plans into motion – they would all arm themselves and then march upon the Holy City and the other places where the King's servants ruled, lay siege to them, and forcibly drive them out. They would burn, destroy, and kill until the King and His servants surrendered, and then they would let each city choose their rulers for themselves.

In their eyes, their cause was just and righteous, and they could not cease until the entire world was free. The most opportune time for them to declare their independence was during the Passover, when all those still faithful to the King went up to Jerusalem. They would strike at the heart of the Holy City and bring it to its knees. How could any stand against their might and their terrible numbers now?

On the most solemn day of the Passover, when all the leaders loyal to the King and His servants were gathered in Jerusalem, the rebels arose from their places all over the earth and surrounded the cities and villages that had not joined with them, and began to raid and lay siege to them. An innumerable army of the rebels also rose and surrounded the Holy City, and they began to burn the buildings and homes on the outskirts thereof, and shouted their demands for the King and His servants to leave and go into exile immediately.

Suddenly at the height of the uprising, great torrents of fire blazed from the skies and completely vanquished all the rebels over all the earth, even the ones who were not involved in the sieges. The devouring fire kindled against the rebels instantly consumed billions of people, and all the ground around the Holy City and the other cities were burnt black from the firestorm.

The parents, relatives, and friends of the rebels who had not joined with them and had stayed faithful to the King did not mourn nor weep for them. The rebels had knowingly made their decision to follow Satan and his ways of rebellion rather than follow the King's righteous laws and teachings. [145]

On the same day the rebels had been consumed, Satan and his allies, who had been released from the Abyss only decades before, were captured and brought forward to the Great Throne of the King in Jerusalem. And just like in the days at the end of the Tribulation, a huge pit of burning sulfur was opened once again to the left of His Throne.

In front of the Throne, Satan was chained securely to the ground directly before the King. But he no longer had the form of a beautiful creature of light or mighty angel, or even a terrible great dragon. Now he had the form of a normal man, weak, fleshly, and naked. He struggled and raged at his chains, even though he knew it was hopeless. Everyone around the Throne gazed upon him in astonishment – was this really the one who had deceived multitudes of men and angels, and who had wrought death and destruction upon all Creation for so many centuries? [146]

One by one, Satan's emissaries were condemned and thrown into the pit before him, and he ranted and cursed and struggled, but he could not speak nor rise from his knees. Several times, Satan ceased his struggling, but only to gather his strength for his next tirade. He was bound so tightly that he could scarcely move, but he was too obstinate and proud to give up, even at the very end. He had been warring against God since his first rebellion, and he would continue until his last breath.

Finally, kneeling before the King of Kings, the great adversary of both man and God, who had enslaved all Creation with his deception and deceit, was condemned for all eternity to the

---

[145] Revelation 20:7-9
[146] Ezekiel 28:18-19; Isaiah 14:10-20

Lake of Fire. All the saints and the servants of the King looked upon him as he was brought forward, and watched as he was cast alive into the very center of the molten pit.

Satan would never deceive anyone ever again. Never again would he roam freely about the universe, inflicting his evil and deceptions upon those he met. [147]

*   *   *

Soon after the rebels had been destroyed from the earth, and Satan and his followers had finally been judged, the entire sky changed to night and it seemed as if the earth and the heavens were no longer there. All Creation seemed to have vanished and only black, thick darkness remained. The darkness surrounded everyone and the very Temple they stood before disintegrated in front of them. And as they watched, the great Throne of the King was transformed into a Great White Throne and highly elevated.

Suddenly in front of the King, an infinite line of people stood before Him. Sheoul, the temporary resting place of the dead, had been removed from the center of the old earth and emptied of all its inhabitants. [148] Everyone who had lived or died during the Millennium found themselves standing before the Throne. And with them, every person who had ever lived was resurrected and standing before the Judge according to their date of conception.

The only people not among the multitudes were those who had chosen Jesus (or Yeshua) as their Savior during their days on earth. They were those who had been born twice, and given new life by the Creator Himself.

Billions upon billions of people stood before the Great White Throne, with the vast majority of them trembling and shaking. They were the ones dressed in sackcloth from head to toe and most were wailing terribly and weeping. Others were dressed in white linen and appeared to be quite calm.

---

[147] Revelation 20:10
[148] Revelation 20:13

Many among them had come from the first world that had been destroyed by the Flood, but billions more had come from the millennia that had followed. They had been resurrected to their former bodies, but all their ages had apparently been set to the age in which they had reached maturity. Before the Great White Throne, all the people had finally been equalized in terms of class, age, wealth, health, and vanity. [149]

Most of those in sackcloth instinctively knew why they were there, and that there was no chance of salvation for them any longer. These had trusted in their own good deeds and works of righteousness (or what they had thought that were works of righteousness) for their salvation, and they had come up short. The only requirement for salvation was the new spiritual life that could only be received by accepting Yeshua as their Savior, and that required only the simple belief as that of a child.

Others who had never heard of God, Yeshua, or the Gospel, stood with the multitudes, but most of them did not seem to be as afraid as many of the others. Everyone knew they stood before the God of Justice, and that they would indeed be judged with truth and fairness for what they had believed, thought, and done during their lives on earth. Still others had followed the Lord and been faithful to Him during their lives on the earth, and were there to receive their rewards and commendation, rather than judgment and punishment.

The believers among the resurrected were judged first – all those who had placed their faith in Him from Adam to the last person who had died before Yeshua was resurrected. As the old world believers received their rewards, they took their places with the saints alongside the Great White Throne. Then those who had never heard the Gospel were judged according to their deeds, and according to their own laws and how they had treated those around them. And then lastly, the non-believers arose for judgment.

One by one, their names were called and they approached the Great White Throne and then knelt before Yeshua, the very

---

[149] Revelation 20:11-15

one that many of them had openly refused and scorned. And there they proclaimed that Yeshua was indeed the Almighty God, the King of Kings, and the Lord of Lords.

From the deaf who had never heard a spoken word to the blind who had never seen the light of day, all the way to the staunch atheist who had died peacefully in his sleep – everyone acknowledged that Yeshua was the Lord God who had created the entire universe with His spoken word. The kings of the nations, the rulers and teachers of men, and all the destroyers of faith came and finally knelt before the King, and awaited the sentence of damnation that was surely in store for them.

Each soul who knelt before Him confessed their works and deeds – both good and bad – to the Judge. And then they were given a choice to either accept the Judge's ruling or argue for their own deliverance. Those who wanted to argue would each be granted to present their case, but their peers would also testify for or against them. Knowing their fate, nearly all the condemned sought to argue and appeal their case.

After each made their arguments, great books were handed to Him, and He read to all Creation their deeds they had done during their lives. Every careless word they had ever uttered was judged and brought to account.

Most were filled with shame as all was made public – all their unseen deeds, secret thoughts, and hidden motives were uncovered and made known to all. Then their peers, both the righteous and unrighteous, rose to accuse them for their unbelief and wickedness and testified against them before the Judge. For the Jews, Moses and many of the prophets accused them, along with Abraham and even many of the Gentiles from their time. [150]

Lastly the Book of Life was opened, and if their name was not found within its innumerable pages, they were condemned to the Lake of Fire. For those who had not heard the Gospel, they were judged solely by the deeds they had done in their lives according to the Law of Moses, and according to their own laws, whatever they happened to be. And they were judged ac-

---

[150] Luke 11:31-32

cording to their reverence for the Creator, whoever He had been in their knowledge and culture.

As the dead were judged and condemned, many cursed the King and quickly found themselves silenced, but most openly wailed and wept – and so did many of the Redeemed who looked on. Nearly everyone who had been saved saw people they had known during their first life, and had either not witnessed to them or had been refused. They were their mothers, fathers, sisters, brothers, and other family members, friends, acquaintances, and even strangers they had met only briefly.

Some who had even professed to be saved stood among the condemned, and they knew deep in their hearts that they had never received the new life that the King had offered. They had been offered new Life and a pardon from the eternal death sentence, but they had never accepted it, and so there they stood with those bound for Hell.

But the saved also saw and heard that many of those condemned had refused the Gospel many times over the course of their lives, not just once or twice. Over and over He had spoken to them either by Himself or through others, and yet they had always refused Him.

The ones who were perhaps the most mournful were the preachers, church leaders, missionaries, and others who had served among the believers but had not believed themselves. Along with them were multitudes of those who had regularly attended church services and mass, but nevertheless stood among the unsaved. And both they and those who were saved were shocked at some of those that stood before the Judge.

After each of the faithless were condemned, they were sentenced and thrown into the Lake of Fire where Satan, his angels, David Medine, Franco Pontiffica, and their followers were still burning in eternal torment. Their wailings and shrieks grew louder and louder as more of the damned were added to the pit, and the flames seemed to burn brighter and fiercer.

Finally, the pit was closed and they were heard from no longer. Those trapped in the Lake of Fire would remain there forever – forever burning, forever tormented.

CHAPTER 20
THE NEW CREATION

T he Great King of the universe, the Creator of all that had ever been made – from every galaxy, star, and planet to every grain of sand, and everything in between – stood up from the Great White Throne. All the guilty had been condemned and thrown into the Lake of Fire. All those who had been declared righteous before Him, either by His atonement or His judgment would now receive their new eternal bodies. And the time had finally come for them to receive their everlasting homes.

Many among the saved were still weeping and mourning over those who had been condemned – the squandering of opportunities to present the Gospel during their lives while in the old world, and the refusals by those they had witnessed to. The King knew perfectly well how they felt; many people He had spoken to during His own earthly ministry had rejected Him and all the good He had planned for them. But their grief, sorrow, and pain would be soon forever taken away, along with all the regrets and bad memories from their old lives. Only the good would remain, and all the grief, regret, and sadness in their lives would be burned away once and for all.

As He stood up from His Throne and saw all those who were now part of His family, He raised His nail-scarred hands and the old universe rushed back to reappear before them. But they were no longer standing on the earth, but far outside it.

And then He gave a mighty shout and threw down his arms, completely letting go of His hold on Creation. Every atom in the entire universe suddenly collapsed upon itself and exploded into empty space, and then all matter vanished away with a horrendous roar. Even space and time was taken away, and within mere moments no trace of the former universe remained. [151]

And then Yeshua raised His hands again and gave another mighty shout, one of supreme triumph, authority, and joy. Just as suddenly as the old universe had been torn away, a new one appeared and came to life. But this one was completely new and perfect, one that had never known any death, destruction, fatigue, or evil. If the first heavens and the first earth had been awesome, then the new heavens and the new earth completely overshadowed them in glory and splendor. All the constellations were entirely different, and even the earth itself was wholly new, without blemish, and perfect. [152]

The new earth was much larger than the previous one, and was already covered with lush gardens and parks, rivers and streams, trees, grass, and vegetation that were entirely different from anything that had been seen before. Mansions, buildings, and streets were interspersed all over the earth, and everyone had their own mansions and property. There would be no more construction or building to do though, because the earth had been created with buildings and streets that would never wear out nor decay. The rivers and streams were crystal clear, and a variety of environments were also interspersed over the earth, from deserts to mountains to lakes to plains, and many others no one could have ever imagined. [153]

The heavens were garnished with stars of every size, shape, and color, and many of them had planets that were as diverse as the earth. But there was no sun or moon that gave light to the earth any longer, because the glory and presence of the Lord God Himself surrounded the earth, and it was full of brilliant, beautiful light. The stars in their constellations moved and changed in such a way that they appeared to be frequently changing shapes and signs. But whereas the previous stars had been mainly for

---

[151] 2 Peter 3:9-13
[152] Psalms 102:25-26; Isaiah 65:17-19, 66:22-23; Revelation 21:1
[153] Revelation 21:1-4

observation, these were meant for exploration and discovery.

And instead of the bleak blackness of space surrounding them, waves of brilliant colors shimmered about, much like the aurora borealis that had shown near the poles on the old earth. The heavens, like the earth, were full of the glory of God, and everyone could instantly go to any location in the new universe they wished by simply a thought.

* * *

All the redeemed soon found themselves standing on the new earth on a huge, flat plain before His Throne. They were all startled at first, but only for a brief moment. The people looked up at the King, and then began glancing around at one another. Everyone immediately began smiling and beaming with joy – this was the moment they had been waiting for, many of them their entire lives. This was the moment they had been reborn – the moment they had received their eternal bodies.

Every person standing on the plain was glowing with equal luminescence, and clothed with brilliant white, seamless robes. There were no infants, children, young adults, middle-aged, nor elderly in the entire crowd of billions who stood there. All the people appeared fully-grown, and everyone looked approximately the same age. There were neither males nor females any longer, but each person had retained certain aspects within their new body and character that showed what gender they had been before on the earth.

Everyone was beautiful and glorified, and thrilled with their new eternal nature. No one looked much like they had before when they had been flesh and blood, but they were still recognizable and identifiable. Many cried, but these were now tears of joy – there would neither be mourning in the new universe, nor even any reason to. [154]

Each person was surrounded by the people they had known during their previous life on earth. In fact, everyone had been

---

[154] Revelation 21:4

arranged in a gigantic tree-shaped structure that seemed to stream out from the very Throne of Yeshua Himself. As each person had had a physical, genealogical family tree that had started with the First Adam (and Eve) and eventually spread out to the distant branches, they also had a spiritual family tree, which started with Yeshua, the Last Adam.

And this was that tree – their new family tree: the Tree of Faith. In front of the Throne, Adam and Eve stood next to the Disciples, and a large branch of the Tanakh saints streamed out from them, and another huge branch came out directly from the Disciples that spread off far into the distance.

Everyone stood next to the person that had either introduced them to the Lord or had helped them along on their path into the Kingdom. Some stood with their earthly families, the parents next to their children, and those next their children, showing the heritage of faith that had been passed down from one generation to another. Many stood next to others who were alone, sometimes with just one or two people. Often they were not even from the same family, tribe, nation, or race. But everyone had been brought into the Kingdom because of someone else, who frequently had no idea who they had helped into the Kingdom. [155]

They all seemed somewhat surprised at who they saw around them. Countless people were in the Kingdom who others had not expected, while others they had expected to be in the Kingdom were missing. Many of the religious, the strict, and the chaste were nowhere to be found – those who had trusted in their own righteousness and goodness to enter into Heaven, instead of by His sacrifice and new Life. But in their place, many of the "unrighteous" from every walk of life were there, such as multitudes of murderers, thieves, prostitutes, gamblers, the poor, and the downtrodden. Many of those who had been "first" while on the earth were now "last", and many of the "last" on the earth were now "first".

From Sunday school teachers, preachers, soup kitchen workers, church janitors, office workers, bartenders, farmers,

---

[155] 1 Corinthians 13:9-12

tax collectors, sailors, soldiers, salesmen, and priests, to mothers, children, students, fathers, carpenters, foragers, lawyers, accountants, and salesmen, people from all walks of life were present before the Throne. But no longer did their pasts, professions, or backgrounds matter to anyone. Their former statuses as being single, married, divorced, or widowed were of no more concern either, and their identities as fathers, mothers, sisters, brothers, sons, and daughters had been wiped away as well. All were now members of His Family, and that was all that was important now. It was all that had ever really been important. Everyone there had been born imperfect into Time, but now reborn perfect into Eternity. And all had been remade according to His will and His good pleasure.

As the people began to adjust to their new surroundings and to speak to one another, they discovered that they knew who everyone around them was, from those immediately next to them, all the way to the most remote sections of the vast crowd. They knew their names and their story of faith, and how they all fit into the tree. They knew both their physical and spiritual lineage and the history of the families of the earth from Adam to Noah and his sons, and from Noah's sons to their immediate family. And they would spend the rest of eternity learning more fully about one another and interacting with each other in the new heavens and the new earth. Before they had known in part, but now they knew in full.

Jacob found he was standing next to Naomi, his wife of both the former two ages who had helped lead him to the Lord. Surrounding them were their dozens of children, grandchildren, and the rest who had been born into their family during the Millennium. Next to Naomi stood Saul, and next to Saul was Ruth. But next to Ruth was someone they had not known before, yet they knew how she had come into the Family through him, and even how he had come into the Family. Around him stood a small number of other people, evidently more he had helped along on their journey of faith.

A short distance away from Ruth was a huge crowd of people who had come from all over the world, gathered around a man, an

American Bible teacher who had made his tapes available worldwide on the Internet. He still seemed surprised at the crowd around him, evidently having no idea how many people he had reached through his simple audio ministry. He had brought many into the Kingdom, even though he had only initially intended to make the recordings available to those in his local Bible study.

All of them were now glorified like Ruth had been when she had arrived with the King in the previous age. They all had new, eternal bodies that looked nothing like their former, frail bodies on the first earth. They could still easily recognize one another, and they still looked human, for the most part. All of them shone with an inner light that came from the Life of the King Himself, and they rejoiced at having all been finally remade in His Image and His Likeness. Their new bodies also had many new senses and characteristics and capabilities, and it would take awhile for them to explore what all they could now do, sense, and feel.

*   *   *

Everyone on the new earth all spoke the same language now as well – the language of Heaven, the language of the King. This was the language of the Words He had spoken when He had brought the first heavens and the first earth into existence, and the same language He had spoken to Adam and Eve and their first children with. There were no more divisions or boundaries between any of them – they had been completely united in one great Family, and thus would remain for all eternity.

Someone from the front of the crowd raised their voice for all to hear, and everyone bowed low on the ground to honor their Creator and King, and they gave a great shout of joy that made the One on the Throne smile with delight. The King rose from His Throne, and suddenly a brilliant light began to shine down upon them from the sky. Everyone rose and looked up, and the sight took their breath away.

It was the great city, the New Jerusalem, shaped as a perfect, gigantic cube descending to rest just above the surface of the earth at the northern pole, There were twelve levels (or foundations) to the city, and each foundation was made up of a different type of precious stone. The sides of the walls were made of transparent, thick crystal, and twelve huge gates ran from the bottom level all the way to the top, with three gates on each side of the structure. Brilliant, beautiful light streamed from within the structure of the city itself. At the highest level in the center was the breathtaking Throne of God the Father.

Next to each of the twelve great gates on the four walls, twelve angels stood welcoming every person who would enter and exit, and the gates were never closed. The names of the angels were written on each gate, which were also the names of the twelve tribes of the children of Israel. These were the guardians of the tribes when Israel had been upon the first earth, and they had looked over all the survivors of their tribes and had ministered to the remnant. Every gate was made up of one huge pearl that had been hollowed out and carved into the shape of a gate, and the streets of the city were pure gold, looking as if it were transparent crystal. And each wall was perfectly aligned with the direction it faced: north, south, east, and west. [156]

On each foundation of the shining city, the names of the twelve apostles were written: Simon Peter; Andrew his brother; James and John the sons of Zebedee; Philip; Bartholomew; Thomas; Matthew; James the son of Alphaeus; Lebbaeus; and Mattias. Paul was not listed among the apostles of Israel, because he had been designated an apostle to the Gentiles during his earthly ministry.

The foundations of the Holy City were garnished with all sorts of precious stones. The first foundation was jasper; the second, sapphire; the third, a chalcedony; the fourth, an emerald; The fifth, sardonyx; the sixth, sardius; the seventh, chrysolyte; the eighth, beryl; the ninth, a topaz; the tenth, a chrysoprasus; the eleventh, a jacinth; the twelfth, an amethyst. [157]

The angels who had remained faithful to the Lord during the thousands of years from their creation to the end of the world,

---

[156] Revelation 21:10-13
[157] Revelation 21:14-27

were now the servants who tended the Holy City and those who visited and dwelt therein. During the era of the first earth and the first heavens, they had been His messengers and their guardians, and now for eternity were their faithful, humble servants that ministered to them as well as their Creator. [158]

* * *

The inhabitants of the new earth and the new heavens began to slowly explore the new creation. It was like nothing they had ever seen nor experienced. It was an entirely new creation from the smallest bit of matter to the furthest reaches of space – none of the old materials from the first had even been reused – not even the very atoms and molecules. For the first time, both the angels and the redeemed of man experienced the same awe and wonder at their Master's power and creativity.

The people soon began to spread out to their new homes and experience the new earth, and the differences between their new world and the old one were dramatic. There were no oceans or seas any longer, but the world was filled with lakes, ponds, springs, rivers, and streams of all shapes, sizes, colors, and depths. There were no more wastelands, neither hot nor cold, but there was an incredible variety of environments, and the wonderful creatures that inhabited them. There were many cities with beautiful mansions and buildings of every sort, but all were empty and waiting to be inhabited.

Many of the creatures that the people were familiar with were there, but much more beautiful and elegant. Along with them, there were many other types of creatures that no one had ever seen nor even imagined before. Some of them were of completely different forms, like mixtures between animals and plants, and also birds and fish.

Most of the creatures were also endowed with speech, and could freely interact with the people and the angels. Like the creatures in the Millennium, all of them were vegetarians, peace-

---

[158] Hebrews 1:14

able to one another, and entirely tame. Since sin had no part in the new creation, there was no more death, not even among the tiniest creatures. There was also no more reproduction or mating, since there was no need to ever replenish and fill the earth.

There were no more physical, spatial, or temporal limits on mankind or the angels. People could move through matter and refashion it to suite their desires and purposes with little more than their thoughts. If they wanted to experience life underwater, they could merely think of what they wanted to do and then instantly reduce their body size and shape to that of a fish and swim with them. The same was true for flying with the birds, running with the great horses, and living with the other creatures. There were no limits to the possibilities of how they could experience God's Creation, and even their imaginations had been enhanced to accommodate the new universe.

As for the new heavens, all of the planets, stars, galaxies, and every particle in between could be explored. Those of the former creation had never been explored, at least not by mankind, because of the limitations of time, space, and matter imposed upon him at the Fall. But they had served their purpose, in showing the magnificence and awesomeness of God, and for many generations, telling His Story in the stars and His plan of redemption. The first heavens had been vast but finite, because matter, space, and time were all finite. But in Eternity, the new universe was limitless.

The people could simply look to a star and then instantly appear within its vicinity in the middle of space, without concern for their survival. They could then look to a planet nearby and explore its surface, atmosphere, or even its core without limitation. They could even travel through the stars themselves, or stand on a star's surface. Many of the planets that orbited the stars were home to many other varieties of creatures and plants that were not found on the earth. There was no limit to God's creativity and genius, and He expressed His Greatness to the fullest in the new creation.

Earth was, of course, the most blessed and wonderful of all the planets. It was not the largest, but was by far the most glorified. It was the habitation of both God and man, and therefore there was no other place like it in all the rest of the universe. There was no more sun, since the King Himself provided the light from His Glory. The people went back and forth between the earth and the heavens at will, and they would spend eternity exploring and experiencing His Creation to their hearts' content.

* * *

Far outside the new earth and the new heavens, and in an entirely different dimension altogether, was what He called the Outer Darkness, or Hell.

When He had remade all of Creation, He also set aside an area far below and far outside of it, which no one except Himself could reach. Just as no one in the first creation could ever physically reach Sheoul, though it was in the very center of the earth, no one would ever be able to enter or leave the Outer Darkness other than Himself. And it was there that He had thrown the Lake of Fire and all those who were tormented therein at the start of the new creation, and all those who had been condemned at the Great White Throne Judgment.

The Outer Darkness was as far removed from the rest of creation as it could possibly be. It was like a terribly huge black hole – a never-ending pit – and in the very center of it were the prisoners. No light came in, and no light ever went out from it. The eternal fires in the pit were still burning the multitudes of prisoners, but the flames gave no visible light.

In their dungeons of the Outer Darkness, the prisoners alternated between terrible scorching and freezing, deafening silence, and raging noise. One moment, they were tearing each other apart, and then the next moment they would be in horrible solitary confinement. There was not a single moment of peace or comfort for them, no matter how hard they tried or how loud they cried out and wept. [159]

---

[159] Deuteronomy 32:22; Isaiah 14:9,15-17; Ezekiel 32:21-32; Matthew 13:49-50, 22:13-14; Mark 9:43-44; Luke 16:23-26

THE TIME OF JACOB'S TROUBLE

Whatever comfort they sought after, it was taken to the extreme, and would be changed into a terrible horror to them. When it was searing hot, as soon as they desired coolness, they would find themselves naked and freezing, with bitter icy winds tearing through them. When they then wanted warmth, the fires came back and scorched them. When they wanted water, they found themselves drowning; when they wanted dryness, they found themselves suffering from unquenchable thirst as if in a horrible desert. But they could not die – never – all they could do was experience pain, fear, and suffering – the fruits of their chosen master. This was their new eternity, and forever their existence would be only that.

Some realized that if they focused on the Lord, they could receive some measure of relief from the extremes, but within moments, the feelings of unending hatred and anger they had for Him boiled to the surface and their torture immediately resumed.

There was only one source of Peace: Him. There was only one source of Comfort: Him. And there was only one source of Rest: Him. And as they had rejected and excluded Him and His people from their lives during their time on earth, so He excluded them from His Life in Eternity. Where else could they go other than away from Him if they didn't want to be a part of His Creation? How could they receive everlasting comfort when they had rejected the only source of everlasting comfort?

Just as there were varying degrees of rewards in Heaven, so there were varying degrees of punishment in Hell, six levels to be precise. Many of the people who had tried to lead good, moral lives while on earth, yet knowing about and still rejecting Yeshua the Messiah suffered the least, along with those who had had a limited revelation of God and His Providence for their sins.

The murderers, thieves, and other unrepentant criminals were next, followed by those who had shed the innocent blood of people both born and unborn. The mass-murderers such as Hitler, Mao, Lenin, Stalin, and Nimrod were next, followed by the false prophets, charlatans, false teachers, and those who had taught rebellion, evolution, atheism, idolatry, and so on.

At the bottom-most levels were Satan, the Beast, and the

False Prophet, and all the angels that had followed Satan into rebellion against the Creator and then helped him corrupt mankind.

Part of their eternal torture was also the ability to observe those in Heaven, to see the destinies of those they had scorned, misled, persecuted, and murdered while they had been alive. There could be no greater contrast between the Saved and Unsaved, and thus it would remain forever. The Saved could not see or hear them, but they knew where they were. But thoughts of the unsaved never entered into their minds any longer. No one missed them, no one mourned for them, and no one cared about them any longer. The Lost could see the great gulf between them and the Saved, yet they could also see a very focused, personal view of whoever they thought of, and it made them rage and weep all the more.

Ahban was in the highest level of Hell, but was still suffering horribly. He could see his family on the new earth, and he alternated between fits of rage against them and himself, and times of great sorrow and regret. He had made his choice where to spend eternity and had completely rejected Yeshua. When he had a fleeting moment of clarity, he could acknowledge that even now he didn't really want to be with the King, but only wanted to be relieved of his torment. Sometimes he hated his former family, and other times he longed for them. But there was no peace, no rest, and no comfort – only brief moments of less torment and a slightly reduced amount of suffering.

In every level of the Outer Darkness, Fear, Hate, Sorrow, and Anger reigned, ruled, and raged, and it would continue without end, just as Heaven would continue without end. And in the Outer Darkness, the condemned of the universe were imprisoned forever, and would trouble no one ever again.

* * *

On the new earth, the people soon settled into their eternal homes and residences. Those of the Church resided in New Jerusalem with the King, while all the other believers of the other ages lived on the earth.

THE TIME OF JACOB'S TROUBLE

Everyone had their own land, mansion, and belongings. Whatever one desired, it was granted to them, from furnishings to books to food to other comforts. As the mere thoughts of those in Hell brought them inconceivable torment, rage, and hate, the thoughts of the redeemed brought them unimaginable comfort, rest, and peace. There were no more unmet needs, or any pleasure left unsatisfied, yet they never grew tired of them nor took them for granted.

Many of the people mentioned in the Bible were there of course, and people frequently met with them and introduced themselves, especially those known by everyone from the Bible stories often told to children, such as Adam, Noah, Daniel, Abraham, and David. Many from before the Flood were also there, among them being Seth, Enoch, and Methuselah, and even Cain, who few had expected to be there. But he was, along with many of his descendants. There were many surprises among them, especially for Noah and his immediate family – many people had been saved in the final moments before the Flood had destroyed them, being too late to save themselves and stay alive, but not too late for God to bring them into Eternity to be with Him.

In some of the silent years of the Scriptures, such as from end of the Flood to the covenant with Abraham came Shem, Ham, Japheth, Job, and a great company of their descendants. They had lived during the Ice Age, through the turbulent years when the old earth's climate was transitioning from its pre-Flood, ideal state to the more erratic, extreme climates. Their generations had repopulated the earth and had formed the first of the nations, tribes, and tongues, which had then lasted for thousands of years in one form or another.

Other well-known people from the Bible were there too, such as Abraham and Sarah and their nephew Lot. Along with them were Isaac and Rebecca; Jacob, Rachel, and Leah; Joseph and many Egyptians; Moses, Aaron, Joshua, and a multitude of the children of Israel who had come out of Egypt.

From the times of the Judges and the early Kings came Ruth, Naomi, Samuel, Abigail, David, Jonathan, and Bathsheba. But during and after the period of the Kings of Israel there were few to be found up until the reign of Josiah.

Most of the prophets were there, such as Daniel, Isaiah, Jeremiah, Zechariah, Jonah, and many others never mentioned by name in the Scriptures. From the New Testament were those such as Mary, Mary and Martha, Stephen, Paul, Silas, Barnabas, the Apostles, and many of the people who Yeshua had healed and preached to during His first ministry on the earth. Many others from the Gentile lands of the early Church period showed what an incredible impact the Apostles had had on the Roman Empire as it had declined and later collapsed. Following the collapse of the Roman Empire were the many Catholics, Baptists, Huguenots, and millions of Protestants who had been slaughtered by the Roman church and the European governments of the Middle Ages.

Millions upon millions of others were with them too, from the multitudes of those who had never heard the Gospel, yet knew of God from their traditions about the stars, personal visions from the Lord Himself, and others simply putting their faith in their Maker, though they did not know His Name or His Story. A great company with them were those who had turned to God in the last moments of their lives, from the victims of shipwrecks to those suddenly caught in earthquakes, tsunamis, and other disasters.

From the Tribulation period came other vast numbers of people, from those who had been saved by the witness and preaching of the 144,000 to those who had refused the mark of the beast and turned to Yeshua in the final moments of their lives, just before they were shot, electrocuted, or beheaded. And from the Millennium were billions more, as the earth once again had been replenished by a small remnant of faithful people.

The new earth was filled for the third and final time. No one new would ever be added to their numbers, and no one would ever be taken away from them. These were all the people that God had foreknown from before Time had begun, and these He had given to His Son as His Inheritance. These were everyone who had ever relied upon God and placed their faith, hope, and fate in Him while on the earth, even if only for a brief moment at the end of their lives.

THE TIME OF JACOB'S TROUBLE

* * *

The Great Throne of God had two seats of equal size, stature, and glory: one was for God the Father, and the other on His right was the throne of God the Son: Yeshua, Jesus Christ, the Creator, Redeemer, and Judge of all Creation. And a pure, transparent river of the water of life flowed out from the base of the throne, and became a great river as it flowed through the city of the New Jerusalem. On either side of the river as it flowed next to the main street of the top level, was the Tree of Life, which produced twelve types of fruit. And it yielded its fruit every month, and the leaves of the Tree were for the healing of the nations. [160]

Every person on the earth now had direct access to both God the Father and God the Son, since they were all now one in the Holy Spirit. They saw Him face to face, and could converse directly with Him whenever they wanted. And God had wiped away all tears from their eyes, and there was no more death, neither sorrow, nor crying, nor any more pain, for all the former things had passed away. Those in the Kingdom had memory of their old days and times on the first earth, but there was no more pain or mourning associated with them. All the bad and evil had been forever wiped away, like a bad dream that had long since passed away into the recesses of the night.

And the desire of God's heart was finally met: He was forever their God and they were forever His children, and He and Man now dwelt together in complete unity. [161]

---

[160] Revelation 22:1-5
[161] Isaiah 51:16; Jeremiah 24:7, 30:22; Ezekiel 11:20, 14:11, 37:23,27; Hosea 2:23; Romans 9:25-26

LaVergne, TN USA
28 December 2010
210369LV00001B/170/P